Critical
Understanding

Until you understand a writer's ignorance, presume yourself ignorant of his understanding.—Coleridge

The first great judgment of God upon the ambition of man was the confusion of tongues; whereby the open trade and intercourse of learning and knowledge was chiefly inbarred.—Sir Francis Bacon

As a question becomes more complicated and involved, and extends to a greater number of relations, disagreement of opinion will always be multiplied, not because we are irrational, but because we are finite beings, furnished with different kinds of knowledge, exerting different degrees of attention, one discovering consequences which escape another, none taking in the whole concatenation of causes and effects, and most comprehending but a very small part; each comparing what he observes with a different criterion, and each referring it to a different purpose.

Where, then, is the wonder, that they, who see only a small part, should judge erroneously of the whole? or that they, who see different and dissimilar parts, should judge differently from each other?—Samuel Johnson

And yet the lesson must perforce be learned, that the human spirit is wider than the most priceless of the forces which bear it onward.
—Matthew Arnold

He that answereth a matter before he heareth it, it is folly and shame unto him.—John Milton

Wayne C. Booth

Critical Understanding

The Powers and Limits of Pluralism

The University of Chicago Press

Chicago and London

The University of Chicago Press, Chicago 60637
The University of Chicago Press, Ltd., London

Library of Congress Cataloging in Publication Data

Booth, Wayne C.
    Critical understanding.

    Includes bibliographical references and index.
    1. Criticism.   I. Title.
PN81.B58   801'.95   78–15107
ISBN 0–226–06554–5

WAYNE C. BOOTH is George M. Pullman Distinguished
Service Professor in the Department of English and in
the College of the University of Chicago.

For Arthur Heiserman
1929–1975

Contents

Preface

This book began as four lectures on pluralism, called "Critical Warfare and Critical Inquiry," delivered in 1974 at Princeton as Christian Gauss Seminars. Because of an illness during the preparation period, I entered my four-week stint far behind myself, naively hoping that the problems raised in lecture one and illustrated in lectures on Crane and Burke would be solved in time for the final lecture. The discovery that I could not, after all, solve the intellectual problems raised by my version of pluralism became the confessional center of the final lecture and then of my inquiry through successive drafts. For a while, in a manuscript called "Must Critics Kill? The Pluralisms of Crane, Burke, and Abrams," I tried to preserve a rhetoric of surprised discovery, reflecting the path my learning took as I gave the lectures; but now, four years later, having finally relocated my task as an inquiry into critical understanding, I have had to give up pretending that, as I write chapter 1, I do not know pretty well how it will all turn out in chapter 7.

We all try to understand the "works" of other people, ranging from jokes and gossip and casual arguments to carefully composed political speeches, constitutions, poems, plays, and on to immensely complex epics and novels as long as the *Odyssey*, *The Remembrance of Things Past*, *The Tale of Genji*, and *Monkey*.* All cultures make such compositions, and all cultures preserve those that seem unusually valuable. And whether cultures depend entirely on memory or invent writing, they can be said to create themselves and endure to the degree that their members understand and enjoy such composings. In large part that is what a culture is—a kind of creation and preservation of works first composed and then understood.[1]

Our own culture, unlike most, has taken a second step, filling libraries with hundreds of thousands of secondary compositions that

---

*I think that most of what I say in this book about verbal works applies to the understanding of other human compositions: all music, all dance, all graphic art. But to show that this is so would complicate my task immeasurably, since words like "meaning" and "understanding" shift *their* meanings subtly as we shift from medium to medium.

recommend or damn or explain what our would-be Homers have sung. These explanations and judgments in turn ask to be understood, and they thus intensify an activity that in unlettered cultures is left largely tacit. When understanding thus becomes explicitly critical, with its products preserved indiscriminately, it turns itself into a problem. We try to understand the recommendations and damnations, but we find them spoken in dozens, perhaps hundreds, of critical languages that seem to defend rival standards.

Our compositions and our critical works about them produce, finally, a third kind of work that attempts to deal with conflicts discerned in the second kind: many critics have been driven, especially in this century, to attempt a criticism of criticisms that would show us how to deal with critical rivalries.

That the present book is largely a work about this third kind of plurality—about the many pluralisms of our time—is not for me a cause for pride. Who would really want to write a long book of what current jargon might well call meta-meta-meta-criticism? But I see myself as having been forced into deeper and deeper waters simply by trying to face the situation of literature and criticism at the present time. I can only hope that readers who find me, as the old Oxford joke has it, *going in* deeper, *staying down* longer, and *coming up* muddier than they would like will also find the return to practical criticism in chapter 7 not simply a relief from the abstruse but a release into renewed confidence that we can, after all, understand.

The structure of the problem is perhaps identical in all fields of inquiry—at least in those that attempt to explain and judge human achievements. But I have had to resist, for obvious reasons, the temptation to complicate matters with illustrations (which of course I have "in my files") from the fields of sociology, psychology, linguistics, political science, anthropology, law, history, philosophy, or rhetoric. Literary criticism's peculiar centrality—or perhaps the word should be dependency—can be seen if we note that most of these fields have recently provided champions offering some one proper superstructure for correct literary criticism. They are thus all in principle and practice implicated in the great critical wars of our time, but I could not discuss them to any significant degree without stretching the book beyond reasonable limit.

My intellectual debts are incalculable, but they are obviously greatest to three "generations" of pluralists at the University of Chicago. Though what I say here is not at all what Richard McKeon, Elder Olson, Norman Maclean, Robert Marsh, Sheldon Sacks, or

Walter Davis would say, I have learned so much from all of them that I could not possibly draw a clear line between what is theirs and what is securely my own. What is more, at least a fair number of the ideas I attribute to Ronald Crane in chapter 2, and to myself (implicitly) in chapters 5 through 7, could no doubt be traced to these and others who for roughly forty years have attempted to turn critical warfare into pluralistic inquiry. Not the least of those to whom I am indebted are the many students at the University with whom, for sixteen years, I have pursued critical understanding.

To Lawrence Lipking, Robert Denham, David Smigelskis, Gerald Graff, Leigh Gibby, David Hanson, and my wife, I offer thanks of the special kind that only heavy revisers can offer their best critics: without your penetrating criticism, this book would have been completed much too soon.

Chapters 3 and 4 appeared in somewhat different form in *Critical Inquiry*, volumes 1 and 2 (Fall 1974 and Spring 1976). Versions of three parts of chapter 7 appeared in *Novel* (Fall 1977), *Modern Philology*, volume 73 (May 1976), and *Critical Inquiry*, volume 2 (Winter 1975). Kenneth Burke and M. H. Abrams have kindly granted permission to reprint their replies as they appeared in *Critical Inquiry*.

Finally, I am deeply grateful for financial assistance from the National Endowment for the Humanities, the Rockefeller Foundation, and the University of Chicago.

1

A new order of accommodation and mutual study between holders of contending positions will be required if the Tertiary Period is not soon to be ended by the mistakes of man.—I. A. Richards

We have so many different businesses with nature that no one of them yields us an all-embracing clasp. The philosophical attempt to define nature so that no one's business is left out, so that no one lies outside the door saying "Where do *I* come in?" is sure in advance to fail. The most a philosophy can hope for is not to lock out any interest forever. No matter what doors it closes, it must leave other doors open for the interests which it neglects.—William James

The conversation grew more animated, on the tower of Babel, at the moment when the confusion of tongues was imposed. But would anyone say that critical vitality was thereby increased?—Anon.

The Plurality of Modes as a Problem

Babel

We begin with an imaginary experiment. Suppose we present a poem, any poem, to a dozen or so literary critics and ask them to say what they think is the most important point to be made about it. The experiment will be somewhat less unreal if I offer at once a real poem and ask you to decide what sort of critical statement about it is essential—or at least important or legitimate.

SURGICAL WARD

W. H. Auden

They are and suffer; that is all they do;
A bandage hides the place where each is living,
His knowledge of the world restricted to
The treatment that the instruments are giving.

And lie apart like epochs from each other
—Truth in their sense is how much they can bear;
It is not talk like ours, but groans they smother—
And are remote as plants; we stand elsewhere.

For who when healthy can become a foot?
Even a scratch we can't recall when cured,
But are boist'rous in a moment and believe

In the common world of the uninjured, and cannot
Imagine isolation. Only happiness is shared,
And anger, and the idea of love.

You may want to object, "What *must* be said will depend in part on my audience." Let us, then, specify an audience: all the people in the world who would be likely to read a book like this one. In other words, the experiment asks us not to say what we would want to say when teaching the young how to read but what we would say when

1

teaching each other how to improve our ways of talking about poems or poetry or art or culture or . . . .

I cannot complete that sentence because, like all readers of contemporary criticism, I know that critics, the subjects of the experiment, will differ precisely on the question of how a sentence like that should be completed. What should the experiment be about? What *should* we be doing when we undertake criticism? What is the proper vocabulary, what the "relevant context," for discussing "Surgical Ward"?

To find out, I assemble our imaginary protocols—your answers to my question—and find a most astonishingly diverse collection of statements, many of them seemingly contradictory. I find minute analyses of verse form, of prosody—not as many as I would have found in 1935, say, but there are some. I find thematic analyses of how happiness and pain relate—not as many as I would have found in 1960, perhaps, but still there are some. I find one "old-fashioned" protocol analyzing the "plot" of the poem, and another analyzing its "argument." I find several pursuing its ethical or political values, some in the old style—a Leavisite attack on the immaturity of Auden's moral vision,[1] a Marxist attack on the speaker as a character locked in a self-pitying bourgeois notion of alienation; some in the new style—attacks on my choice of a male poet, or a white man, or a Christian traditionalist. I find an account of Auden's poetic development, with a precise placing of this poem in its original sonnet sequence, followed by an analysis placing it in the history of the sonnet. I find a study of how idiopsychic transforms—ah, the bliss of neologism!—have determined what five *other* readers, interviewed in depth, have seen in the poem. Since our imaginary experiment is being conducted in 1978, one-third of the protocols say either that the poem is about the process of its own reading or that it is a demonstration that it is unreadable—that in fact, when one tries to unravel its labyrinthine web, one discovers an infinite number of possible interpretations (as indeed I seem to be doing here, in my account). I find . . . .

We discover, then, an unlimited variety? What, indeed, will we not find? More important, what, if anything, should we exclude? What is there to limit, either in fact or in theory, the variety of readings we shall take as legitimate? To find out, I extend the experiment. I now return copies of all the readings to each of you and ask you to comment on the legitimacy of readings other than your own.

The new replies are almost as predictable, though not as diverse. About half of them say, in so many words, that all the *other* readings are either plain wrong or, at best, misleading or unimportant. Most of the rest pick and choose, trying to find some way to rule out the irresponsible and nonsensical without implying a dogmatic commitment to a single line of criticism. Finally, there are a few who argue that there are no limits at all. Not only will they accept an unlimited variety of statements about the poem; unlimited variety of response is criticism's very goal. Though most replies dismiss the protocol that saw "Surgical Ward" as about Esquimos, others reject the very notion of any limit except the critic's capacity to be interesting.

How shall we deal with this new batch of disagreements? In these two short imaginary steps we have duplicated a bramble patch that is not in the least imaginary: the immensely confusing world of contemporary literary criticism.

This book is about some ways of dealing with that world, ways of living with critical variety. It is thus itself an attempt at a way, another mapping of maps, though maps already threaten in their multiplying grids and projections to black out whatever might have been the original territory. Let us call that territory "Surgical Ward" (representing all the literary works in the world), though we can already see that to do so is to beg many questions.

My way among ways charting ways is—I think fortunately—not of the kind that can be cleanly defined at the beginning. It is more a way of living with variety than of subduing it. It thus begins in what might better be called an attitude than a critical position: methodological pluralism. It ends there too, after looking closely at several other methodological pluralisms. Here at the beginning I can only suggest how the pluralist attitude toward diverse acts of critical understanding differs from other attitudes, and I may make it seem like a mere expression of undefended and unarguable faith. I can only hope that by the end, though it will still not be "proved" by the standards of some epistemologies, it will have been proved in that honorable and traditional sense: tested, explored, and found adequate to (and in the service of) our actual experience of literature and our ways of talking about it.

Six Attitudes toward Critical Variety and Conflict

Suppose we now assume that we find in our protocols on "Surgical Ward" four strikingly conflicting definitions of the poem, defended in four seemingly conflicting critical operations:

1. "Surgical Ward" is really a "system of signs" that requires the

critic to reconstruct (or perhaps deconstruct) the system, revealing either that it is internally coherent or—more likely these days—that it is finally incoherent, "unreadable."

2. It is really whatever is made of it by a given reader who brings it to life; that is, it is not at all a self-subsistent thing independent of the reader's activity. The critic's job is to free the reader for creative interpretation.

3. It is really a communication from Auden to the reader, a patterning of intended effects, realized through manifold choices, conscious or unconscious. The critic helps other readers to recover the author's pattern.

4. It is really a structure of norms, autonomous from both critic and author. The critic's task is to illuminate the ironies and ambiguities that make up the organic and complex unity of "the poem itself."

We could easily compound the problem by adding other predictable statements about what a poem *really is*.

What attitudes might we take toward the four critics who found themselves each defending one of these views of what or where this poem is and attacking the others? Obviously, this is a simplified version of the question we all face when we try to decide how to listen to the actual clamor of critics' voices today. I find six possibilities.

"Pluralistic" Stimulation of Chaotic Warfare

Let the voices multiply; the more voices we have, the more truth will finally emerge.

Critics have always quarreled. There could be no genuine criticism if they stopped quarreling, because criticism can be practiced only by free agents whose conclusions depend on perceptions, feelings, and thoughts that can never come in a single mold. In most matters of complex judgment we in fact must mistrust uniformity of opinion; it surely results not from reason but from coercion, idolatry, or laziness. When critics speak with one voice, some other authority than reason rules their conclusions.

That the current critical scene is filled with rampant rivalries is in itself, then, no cause for alarm. Surely the more vigorous the conflict, the healthier the body critical. Instead of combatting conflict as a sign of confusion or giving up the whole enterprise of criticism in disgust, we might happily join in the melee, grateful to live in a time and place—clearly never to be taken for granted—when thousands of men and women have the leisure, the political freedom, and the education that enable them to debate vigorously about the literature they love.

Obviously there is much good sense in this view. If it were the only alternative to imposing a single voice on all critics, our choice would be clear: rather Babel than a passive monotony.

Some pluralisms defend themselves precisely in terms of this choice. What the world needs, we have been told again and again in recent decades, is not clarification or simplification of issues but shaking up; not truces, armistices, and peace pacts but more lively combat; not efforts to reduce meaningless conflict by pursuing critical understanding but release from the iron grip of conformity. The true threat to culture, now as always, is complacency, and the critic's job is to prevent the triumph of the commonplace, the easy, the dull, the self-satisfied.

To tailor one's critical cloth in this way to what one thinks the customer most needs, regardless of what the customer himself says, implies a mastery not only of the customer's present shape but of the true principles of good grooming. To decide that there is still need to *épater* the bourgeoisie thus implies a kind of confidence—not to say arrogance—in reading a given rhetorical climate, a confidence that will always be extremely difficult to justify with anything other than colorful assertion. Examples of complacency will always be available, but how is one to argue that they are more significant than counterexamples of utter confusion? To speak not of the many functions of criticism but of *the* function of criticism *at the present time* is to claim prophetic powers and privileges and to risk turning critical battles into politics or even open warfare; for if two prophetic voices insisting on what "the present" is and what it most needs can find no good arguments for their prescriptions, they will be driven to bad arguments and, finally, to the sort of shouted invective that marks much current debate. Thus, in a curious way, those who call for a multiplication of voices often insist that there is only one right way of multiplying.

It will not do to counter such prescriptions of one kind of pluralism with alternative and equally unprovable guesses about our present culture and its needs. In the long run what we must build is surely a criticism that can defend itself in the long run, not simply a program that a given country seems most to need in a given decade. It may well be true that what France most needed after World War II was the kind of shaking-up that succeeding decades have provided.[2] It may just as well be true, as I believe, that in America today there is little danger of critical complacency; we are hardly threatened by smothering clouds of self-congratulatory traditionalism. In our tempestuous climate, perhaps the most paradoxical claim to make would be that one had found some common ground on which we all can stand while we conduct our stormy debates about interpretations and methods of interpretation. Yet even if this is so—even if, as I believe, we are more in need of attempts to understand than attempts to stir us up—it would be short-sighted to build any sort of critical program simply to fit the needs of that situation. If we finally reject the confident invitations to further chaos that appear, briefly, later in this book, it must be for reasons more solid than are provided by mere readings of the critical climate.

The clearest evidence that something is wrong about this first possible attitude is found when we turn from manifestos about what criticism should be to the protests of those who feel misunderstood. Almost everyone who finds himself discussed in public is likely to confess sooner or later to a baffled sense of outrage. "The corpse they gave my name and mutilated was not me." "If only your reviewer had read my book, he would have discovered. . . ." "Though I am grateful for Mr. Knucklehead's praise, it would have been more gratifying if he had understood what I was about." Most critics lick their wounds in silence, but when they do speak, they speak in pain.

It is of course impossible to offer simple proof that any one lament is justified. But we need no proof that most critics find most discussions of their work so wide of the mark as to be useless. Whenever any public figure is asked to respond to criticism, the results are predictable. Joseph Frank provides an unusually full illustration in "Spatial Form: An Answer to Critics."[3] "Far too many readers have assumed that I was a fanatical partisan of experimentalism in all its varieties," he says. "There is really no quarrel here between Shattuck and myself; we have merely undertaken to do different things" (pp. 232, 233). Accused of placing us "in a realm beyond criticism, beyond theory," Frank replies: "Certainly we should be if I had really said that *nothing* was going on in the mind of the reader of modern poetry; but of course I had made no such nonsensical assertion" (p. 235). "It is amusing to see Sutton illustrating my point, while thinking to refute it" (p. 238). "Weimann wishes to prove . . . that I set up fragmentization of narrative and atemporality as positive aesthetic qualities which become a critical norm; and this gives him a bit of trouble. He manages, though, by taking a passage completely out of context and interpreting it in a way that is quite misleading" (p. 240).

Everyone talks this way about being misread, and if everyone talked only in this way I would be forced to give up at the beginning. A universal and indiscriminate misunderstanding might be deplorable, but it would certainly defeat all efforts at improvement. If nobody understands anybody, the best we can hope for is the stoical tolerance of the blind for the blind. But in fact most public laments include quite precise discriminations between those who from malice or incompetence or haste have hopelessly misunderstood and those who have come close enough to enter the discussion. Thus Joseph Frank, after brushing aside most of his critics, finally gets down to a serious discussion with Frank Kermode. It is true that Kermode has by no means got things straight: "It seems to me that Kermode has *accepted* the substance of my ideas . . . , while pretending to be their most determined antagonist. And in fact . . . we have both developed different parts of the same theory" (p. 251). But because he has come close to understanding, he earns a careful rejoinder that goes on for many pages. And that rejoinder is sufficiently respectful of Kermode's meanings that Kermode can reasonably be expected to engage productively in reply.*

It would be embarrassing to dwell on what everyone in practice assumes—that many readings go hopelessly astray but some come close enough to produce fruitful exchange—if theory did not so often ignore this common ground. Our public responses show that we share contempt for those who battle with straw men and admiration for those who can reconstruct live contenders from the words on the page. In doing so, we imply that the health of criticism, which is inseparable from the health of various kinds of criticism, is diminished whenever critics hack away at bloodless manikins they have themselves invented.

In short, some forms of critical exchange are needlessly wasteful of energy and spirit, destructive of life itself. If this view does not, taken by itself, prove that *all* critics should try to improve understanding, it surely offers a tempting invitation to inquire into the grounds of critical warfare. We cannot know, in advance of trying, that such inquiry will make a difference in practice, but we do know from the beginning that our inquiry can never be seen as "purely" theoretical; we are driven to it by practical motives, and we can accept no solutions that make no practical difference in how we deal with chaos. Few among us, surely, feel comfortable with the spectacle of a free-for-all prizefight among blindfolded sluggers swinging at the air, only occasionally landing an accidental blow—and that on an opponent who doesn't know what hit him.

---

*In fact he has now done so, in *Critical Inquiry* 4 (Spring 1978): 579–88. As we have come to expect in such exchanges, Kermode claims to have understood Frank better than Frank understands himself.

HOPE FOR SEMANTIC RESOLUTION

Let us, then, return to the four critics who defined what "Surgical Ward" is, since we cannot simply embrace the chaos they seem to represent.

Perhaps the dispute among them is meaningless because of semantic confusion. If each of them would simply specify the referents of each of his terms and thus remove the ambiguities, we could then, by eliminating whatever statements are in fact meaningless (perhaps a majority), discover either that there is real conflict between at least two of them or that only one position—perhaps a composite—makes genuine sense.

Everyone with even the slightest sophistication becomes a semanticist at least occasionally. If we hear two people quarreling about whether a board is seven yards or twenty-one feet long, we can all happily point out that they are both right, once their conclusions are related to their critical vocabulary. If someone then says that the board is really 6.4008 meters long, our semantic efforts may take a bit longer to reach their conclusions, but few will be trapped by the difficulties. Much critical warfare would disappear if this kind of elementary semantic resolution were habitual in working with critical terms. One would think that, with all our vaunted critical sophistication, everyone would by now assume as a first step in analyzing critical differences what Hume says of disputes about "common life and experience": "Nothing could preserve the dispute so long undecided but some ambiguous expressions, which keep the antagonists still at a distance, and hinder them from grappling with each other."[4]

What we too often find instead is that even critics who attack the very possibility of discovering a single meaning in any text assume the univocality of such basic terms as "author," "text," "reader," "structure," "form," or "theme." Yet every key word used in the four contentions is far more ambiguous, taken by itself, than the concept of measurement or length in my analogy. The word "author," for example, as I shall show in detail toward the end, refers to many different concepts, and any one of those may be referred to by a variety of words. Most philosophers know about this sort of thing; a few linguists know it, and more of them seem to discover it year by year. But the majority of practicing critics seem to forget it—at least when they find that forgetting it helps to make nonsense out of what their opponents say.

We need spend little time in illustrating how words can get in our way; the history of any key word in criticism will reveal transformations, and even reversals, that lead the unwary into pointless quarreling. The words "form" and "matter," for example, have been steadily used in quite disparate, even opposing, senses. What for Aristotle is the *form* of the work, designed to achieve its end—the "object imitated," consisting of three "parts," plot, character, and thought—becomes in many critics the *matter;* and what he considers the least formal "cause" or condition of the work's existence—analogous in the poem to the malleable bronze or clay "matter" of statuary—is the linguistic medium which for many later critics becomes the form. Thus Sidney seems quite unaware of just how far he has moved away from Aristotle and toward a quite different rhetorical terminology when he inverts and reduces Aristotle's various "forms" and "matters" to say that there are two "principal parts" of poetry, "matter to be expressed by wordes, and words to express the matter." When he turns, toward the end of the "Apologie," to discuss diction, it is a turn from "the materiall point of Poesie" to "the outside of it, which is words." Many modern critics use the same ordering, with terms like "theme" and "meaning" for *content* and "language" (or "style") for *form*.[5] Many disputes would simply dissolve if we recognized that about such words there can be no productive dispute until we determine what they mean, and about their meaning there is no final arbiter who can say that Sidney is wrong to invert Aristotle's usage.

If, as semanticists, we look again at the four contending views of "Surgical Ward," we immediately see that the first and fourth appear most amenable to semantic resolution. It is quite possible that when the phrases I have yoked crudely together are fitted back into the contexts of those who use them seriously, "structure of norms" and "system of signs" will mean the same or almost the same thing; and "the complex, organic unity of the poem itself"—the language of American new critics—may turn out to be something very close to the "unreadable incoherence" of some—though probably not all—who use the new language of deconstruction. What is clear is that every dispute, whether real or invented, will require attention to such preliminary questions *if* the disputants hope to have anything to say to each other.

To assume that every dispute needs semantic clarification does not, however, take us very far. For one thing, the very notion of semantics is ambiguous: how large a context, and what kind, must we seek before we can assume that we have clarified our terms? Unlike most semanticists, I would claim that the key words in any critical statement can be understood only by looking at the complete work from which it comes; no reader can know what I mean by "critical," "understanding," or "pluralism" without reading through to the end of this book. Many would say that the controlling context is even larger, that it includes a critic's lifework, or even his life and times, or—largest of all—the history of all thought that has used his words. Finally, it is by no means easy to discover what a true "referent" would be for many terms. Some critics indeed now argue that one cannot discover any referent or "signified" "outside" the verbal text; critical texts make their worlds and are essentially self-referential.

Even more important is the range of expectations we exhibit as we attempt semantic clarification. Do we assume, with many early "general semanticists," that a proper clarification of terms will make all controversy disappear, leaving only "scientific" inquiry? Do we assume that all right-thinking critics will turn out, once we have understood their terms, to be working in harmony with each other? That great appropriator of his ancestor's views, Leibniz, professed a benign receptivity to all earlier philosophy: "I have come to the conclusion that most of the received doctrines can be taken in a right sense. So that I wish clever men would seek to satisfy their ambition rather by building and making progress than by going back and destroying."[6] If we followed Leibniz's advice, we would indeed often find what Dr. Thomas Brown once observed about the differences between Reid and Hume: "Yes, Reid bawled out, we must believe an outward world, but added in a whisper, we can give no reason for our belief: Hume cries out, we can give no reason for such a notion, but whispers, I own we cannot get rid of it."[7]

The hope for semantic reduction to uniform clarities and final resolutions depends on two highly questionable assumptions. The first, curiously unacknowledged or undefended in the semantic literature I have seen, is that we can hope for a radical improvement in human nature: all inquirers are to become disinterested, generous-spirited, receptive to criticism, and infinitely patient in probing beneath surface, or "merely verbal," differences. Even the simplest semantic clarification between two disputants depends on a primary mutual grant of trust: to engage in it, we must each believe in the other's intelligence, good will, and subservience to reason. A hope for ultimate semantic clarification must thus depend on a passionate commitment to eliminate all conflicting passions, including the desire to win by stifling rival voices.

It must also depend on the second assumption, that all misunderstanding results from the cause Hume describes: unclear language. Good will cannot promise us resolution unless it can count on reducing all controversial muddles to simple and unambiguous choices between true and false views.

Neither assumption seems to me very plausible. Yet there is obviously no way to demonstrate that either the hope for moral revolution or the faith in ultimate simplicity is absurd. What is more, a good deal of our controversy does seem to be caused by ill will, petty-mindedness, and a resulting failure to pursue what our opponents are really saying; the world seems full of purblind warriors eager, like Sohrab pursuing Rustum, to slay their nearest of kin. Surely there will always be a need for academic sermons on behalf of the golden rule of critical discourse: review as you would be reviewed, try to understand even as you hope to be understood. But is there any reason to believe that even if such sermons were widely heeded, and if every generous-spirited combatant practiced a sophisticated semantics, "meaningless controversy" would disappear?

Most of us have long since discovered, in critical debate even with close friends, that semantic clarification pursued with good will can go only so far; ineradicable differences seem always to remain. Yet no amount of such experience can possibly be fatal to the semantic hope, because while we are accumulating it we shall also be discovering more and more evidence of just how powerful the effort to move behind verbal differences can be.

That the day of ultimate semantic resolution is at best far off can easily be shown by a clearer formulation of the question we face: Will *this* dispute about whether semantics will ultimately resolve all disputes itself be resolved by semantic clarification? If we could just get our terms clear, would we be able to decide, once and for all, either that all disputes are based on verbal confusion or that they are not?

A decisive answer to that question is far beyond anyone's present grasp. An affirmative answer may enspirit us for energetic semantic effort; but it will, as things now stand, become simply another insistent voice in the Babel that it set out to cure, and we can hardly imagine what kind of semantic maneuvers could persuade everyone to our answer. A negative answer leaves us even more flatly where we were before: seeking for help that we have decided—on non-semantic evidence—that semantics cannot, by itself, give us. Regardless, then, of our ultimate hope for some future Apotheosis of Semantics through a Wedding with Charity, we are left with the world as it is: a world in which even the most skillful and open-minded of disputants will certainly find at least two conflicting views of what "Surgical Ward" really is. What are the remaining plausible attitudes toward that conflict?

MONISM

We might expect that—as the form of most critical arguments suggests and as the semantic quest usually assumes—some one view will prove to be right and all others wrong. Such monism underlies a very large proportion of all critical argument. Critical monists may or may not make their assumption of unique truth explicit, and they range in surface tone from benign and tolerant to snarling and slashing.[8] Some are broadly learned, and some are aware of only one reading of one work by one method. Their one clear mark is that they expect, on whatever subject is at hand, either to settle all issues with a single resolution now or to show how, "in principle," a single resolution (however complex in structure) is both desirable and attainable at some future time.

Monists who are not ignorant or entirely irresponsible usually make their monism explicit by offering to refute their more plausible rivals. Much of the life of criticism has always been found in such efforts at refutation, but the unfortunate fact about monism as an attitude is that it offers what look like respectable intellectual reasons for treating all rivals superficially. If our hope is for a single answer, and if we have already seen an overwhelmingly persuasive power in some one position, we shall almost certainly mistreat rival positions even if we have a radical commitment to scholarly fairness.

Observe how René Wellek, the very model of a responsible historian and critic, treats his rivals on the question raised by our four definitions of "Surgical Ward." For him the question becomes that of "the 'ontological situs' of the work of art," and he argues about it like this in his *Theory of Literature:*[9]

> To the question what and where is a poem, or rather a literary work of art in general, several traditional answers have been given which must be criticized and eliminated before we can attempt an answer of our own. One of the most common and oldest answers is the view that a poem is an "artifact," an object of the same nature as a piece of sculpture or a painting. Thus the work of art is considered identical with the black lines of ink on white paper or parchment. . . . Obviously this answer is quite unsatisfactory. [Pp. 141–42]

Since the aim is to eliminate erroneous positions, it is not surprising to see how quickly the critic executes the illegitimate shift from the poem as made object to the poem as merely black lines of ink. No critic who has worked with the analogy of poems to statues has ever seen the poem merely as the marks on the page. On the contrary, such critics see the form of the object as imposed on a human material that, if left to itself, could take an infinite number of forms. The poem as made object is thus not, as Wellek's leap implies, directly perceptible to the sense of sight.

> The second answer to our question puts the essence of a literary work of art into the sequence of sounds uttered by a speaker or reader of poetry.... But the answer is equally unsatisfactory. [P. 144]

> The third, very common answer to our question says that a poem is the experience of the reader. A poem, it is argued, is nothing outside the mental processes of individual readers and is thus identical with the mental state or process which we experience in reading or listening to a poem. [Pp. 145–46]

Without bothering to face any of the real arguments of those who hold them, Wellek easily shows that these views, like the first one, are absurd. Each view gets its paragraph or two and a few perfunctory sentences of dismissal of a kind that would surely puzzle anyone who has ever held it. I. A. Richards, for example, is given about six lines of exposition, and three short paragraphs of rebuttal, with blank, unargued assertions like this: "Curiously enough, Richards, who constantly criticizes the experiences of his pupils, holds to an extreme psychological theory which is in flat contradiction to his excellent critical practice"—the contradiction being unspecified.*

---

*After I had published a statement similar to this in "Preserving the Exemplar," *Critical Inquiry* 3 (Spring 1977): 409, Wellek wrote to complain that among other mistakes in my account (see *Critical Inquiry* 4 [Autumn 1977]: 203–4) I had overlooked his more careful treatment of I. A. Richards in "On Rereading Richards," *Southern Review* 3 (Summer 1967): 533–54. It is quite true that the account there is longer, but it does not seem to me to draw much closer to what Richards might recognize as a useful reconstruction of his actual endeavor. In any case, my point here is that the expectation of monistic resolution tempts even the most serious scholars into "self-evident" refutations of what are merely straw men. Whether or not I have in fact turned Wellek himself into a straw man in my search for a representative of monism, it is clear that hardly anyone will want to declare himself as a monist—or indeed as a proponent in any simple way of any of my six attitudes. They are technically "types," inherently simpler than any instance.

So on we go, slapping down "the experience of the author"—more than two whole pages!—and "collective experience"—one short paragraph. Thus finally, with all opponents turned into straw men and finished off, Wellek's own view has the field to itself: A poem is "a potential cause of experiences"—"a structure of norms" (p. 151).

Here, then, is a succinct illustration of the third possibility, monism: when critics continue to disagree as strongly as they do about what a poem is or where it is to be found, all positions but one are false, and the problem is to show the truth of the one while showing—or, as in Wellek's case, *by* showing—the falsity of the others.

Though there is no necessary connection between monism and carelessness about whether the opponents one skewers are straw men, belief in the exclusive soundness of one's own position makes it all too easy to discern faults in everyone else's. An analogy may help show why this is so.

Anyone who is nearsighted sometimes makes the mistake of assuming that other people, whom he cannot clearly see, are themselves nearsighted. But sooner or later the mistake is discovered, because the consequences of mistakes are sharp and clear. My neighbor, whom I saw this morning only as a blur far in the distance, as I gardened, tells me that *he* saw *me* spacing my tomato plants too closely. Then a friend complains at lunch that I ignored him Tuesday when he waved at me from across the street, though "you were looking right at me." Soon I infer that I am nearsighted, and I get glasses.

My neighbor may in turn envy me when he sees me easily consulting the telephone book without glasses, while he stands helpless before the fine print; he then, too, corrects, as we say, his vision. For each separate task, each of us has "excellent vision," confirmed in experience until experience forces us to recognize its limits.

In criticism, unfortunately, experience is by no means so unfailing and rigorous a teacher. The acutely nearsighted critic sees much that others cannot see at all, and his "vision" is thus so rewarding and self-validating that he can go a lifetime without ever thinking of the farsighted as anything but blind. How is anyone to prove that I am missing entire ranges of experience when every time I "look" I find confirmation in my own narrow valley that I am seeing all there is to be seen? Trained in a given critical way by admired mentors, taught by repeated experience that the way makes sense of the literary data, rewarded by experiment after experiment with confirming results, I naturally develop an ever deeper trust not only in the validity of the chosen way but in its exclusive validity.

How am I, after all, to learn my limitations? Evidence available in other fields of vision quite literally never enters my head. It *must* seem to me that other critics are plain wrongheaded or, at best, stupid. When translated into *my* terms, every opponent inevitably looks absurd. In short, how could Wellek *not* reject positions as inane as those he has described? It is almost impossible to remember just how unlikely it is that any real opponent could be *that* foolish.

Monistic assumptions are so widespread that one is almost tempted to suspect the good faith of anyone who doesn't assert his monism with dogmatic assurance.

> In periods that are not periods of crisis, or in individuals bent on avoiding crisis at all cost, there can be all kinds of approaches to literature: historical, philological, psychological, etc., but there *can be no criticism*. For such periods or individuals will never put the act of writing into question by relating it to its specific intent. The Continental criticism of today is doing just that, and it therefore deserves to be called *genuine* literary criticism. [Italics added][10]

Thus Paul de Man, who in practice is fortunately not as dogmatic as this sounds. Reading such an assertion, unless I take hold of myself I begin to feel uneasy about having been ungenuine all my life. I've *tried* to keep constantly aware of crisis; I've done my best to question the act of writing, but. . . .

Here is William Empson telling us, in effect, where we should look to find the real "Surgical Ward" and, as he does so, flatly rejecting his own earlier opinions:

> I am afraid it is no use being broad-minded and sensible, . . . about the dogma that a reader ought never to consider the intention of an author. Sensible people are now beginning to hedge on their earlier acceptance of this view, very rightly, so they explain (with tender humour and so forth) that nobody ever intended the crude interpretation evidently held by outsiders and students. . . .
> When this dogma is operating, the students are usually taught to try to catch the author out, and blame him for breaking whatever critical principles (adopted by whimsy) [once intentions have been ruled out] have been issued to them beforehand. . . . The dogma must in some way produce deadness and falsity, because the students are denied any spontaneous contact with an author's mind.[11]

So much for Wimsatt and Beardsley and the early Empson and all those other benighted people who over the years worked, all unwittingly, for deadness and falsity as they attacked the intentional fallacy. But we cannot learn from Empson whether any serious critic has ever in fact ruled out intentions in the manner he now—quite rightly, I think—attacks.

Dogmatic assertions of the one right view are especially forceful, of course, when they are attached to accounts of how previous attempts were, at best, stages on the way to the new truth. For obvious reasons such accounts are often buttressed by analogies to progress in the natural sciences. If the history of criticism can be likened to the history of science, then the latest view is by definition the most acceptable.

> The displacement from work to text, a part of the epistemological shift associated with structuralism and post-structuralism, is to our understanding of the literary object what the passage from Newtonian to Einsteinian physics was to our understanding of the material object. In other words, with the concept of textuality critical theory has caught up with the development of abstraction in the arts themselves.[12]

How can one possibly keep one's self-respect if one has not *caught up* with *that?*

The history of critical thought is heavy-laden with such efforts to discover and proclaim the one truth, sometimes with a tolerant incorporation of fragments from other claimants, often with a total rejection of all other views. It is true that intelligent monists usually claim, like Northrop Frye, that the *full* truth is not yet revealed. In his search for the critical center, the monist will claim both that *his* center cheerfully accommodates the results of all valid approaches and also that, *in principle*, their future results are encompassed. He may even tell us, as Frye often does, that we should be pluralists (see *The Critical Path*), but he will nevertheless be committed to *his* one truth. Could he be anything else?

No one but a deaf and blind dogmatist could be a monist in all controversies; elementary semantic clarifications often allow both debaters to see that both were justified, "in their own terms." At the opposite extreme, it may well be that everyone behaves as a monist in some controversies: my pluralism, whatever else it leads me to, does not lead me to accept more than one answer to an unambiguous question like whether or not Shakespeare intended me to be amused

by Falstaff's jesting ironies: "I wish your Grace would take me with
you. Whom means your Grace?"

The problem that concerns us, then, is not whether some or many
questions can be resolved with single answers but whether the assumptions of monism apply to all controversy. Can we assume that
our many quarrels are either unreal, because we have not understood
our terms, or that in principle one supreme coherent view will—or
should—eliminate all others? That monists in practice tend to turn
their opponents into straw men is surely not in itself strong evidence
against the possibility that one or another of the four placements of
"Surgical Ward" will prove uniquely correct. After all, bloodless
combat among what I. A. Richards calls the phantom-smashers is not
confined to monists.

SKEPTICISM

We know that, despite the plentiful supply of monists—or sometimes because of it—many critics have elected some form of skepticism. When two or more monisms clash, when four views of
"Surgical Ward" seem contradictory, we shouldn't be surprised, they
say, or trouble ourselves about it much, because there is no *real* truth in
any of them. Skeptics naturally note that the views of Wellek about
the locus of the poem were "in" for a while, at least among some
American critics, and are now "out"; these days everyone tells us that
the poem is really found in the reader, or in the language which
somehow "writes" both author and poem. The skeptic predicts—and
he predicts accurately—that some next swing of the pendulum will
repudiate these "reader-critics," and he then concludes that the
whole business has nothing to do with critical *reasoning* at all: "It's all
relative."

In practice, everything depends on what "it" is relative to. If it's
relative to "how the critic was brought up," to what are in fact the
accidents of family, class, nation, graduate training, or pendulum
swings, then of course all critical controversy is, as the skeptic believes, finally pointless—except perhaps for some sort of demolition
action: Wellek does well when he attacks other positions, but he
doesn't go far enough in questioning his own. The work of art *has* no
ontological situs, the poem is *nothing* determinate. Indeed, some
would conclude, all critical statements are without cognitive value;
they are useful at best as confessions of personal feeling or preference.

But it is a mistake to treat skepticism as if it were a single, fixed position. The many skepticisms, relativisms, and nihilisms that I here reduce to one of six attitudes differ from each other in many dimensions.

In the force or completeness of the skeptical claim, skeptics range all the way from professors of universal doubt to those who decide cheerfully to go about their business without feeling much confidence in any *one* belief. The first kind have always been easy targets for philosophical refutation. As Stephen C. Pepper says, "The position of the utter skeptic is . . . impossible. It amounts to the self-contradictory dogma that the world [or, in our terms, any critical assertion about "Surgical Ward"] is certainly doubtful."[13] But short of an extreme which, as Hume showed decisively, no one can adhere to for more than a moment, even in thought, there are many degrees of systematic doubt, more or less likely to hamper criticism depending on how strongly they emphasize the uselessness of attentive reading and careful thought about it.

In the breadth and direction of their coverage, skepticisms are highly selective. Some are directed only at "the text itself" (always inaccessible), some at the author's intentions (never decisive), some at the reader's experience (always limited and private), some at value judgments (never demonstrable), some at the value of theory (we can never know that a given critical model is valid or true; all we have is our experience of individual works), and some at the possibility of understanding between any two critics (we all inhabit private worlds and cannot prove even the existence of other minds).

Finally (though the list might be much longer), skepticisms differ in their picture of the "solider stuff" in relation to which critical statements are thought to be at best only relatively true. Some would argue that none of our four placements of the poem can be true because only a particular kind of statement—positive, operational, factual, or what not—can have truth value. Others, myself included, would argue that such brief statements cannot be judged as either true or false as they stand, because they lack defining contexts that might let the reader discover what they mean; their truth is "relative to" chosen languages or perspectives, to be discovered only in what might be called a higher semantics.

Every critical mind will thus be skeptical about some beliefs held by certain other critical minds. But as a persistent attitude, the skepticism that contrasts with other attitudes would assume, when faced by contrasting definitions of the poem, that discourse about the dispute is necessarily reducible to other causes than the critical problem itself or is for some other reason reducible to arbitrary choices; the debate among proponents must be meaningless as critical debate.

The way in which skepticism about method spills over into skepticism about every detail of our critical lives can be illustrated nicely by what has been happening in so-called reader-criticism. The various shiftings of Stanley Fish can be taken as representative. Having begun by articulating an aggressive monism asserting that the true poem is found only in the reader's experience, Fish becomes convinced in controversy that such a definition of the poem cannot be proved to be superior, because "objective," to any other definition—to the formalist's placement, say, of the poem as in the text itself or to the expressive critic's location of the poem in the author. Forced from defensive position to defensive position, Fish finally seems to breathe a sigh of relief as he abandons all claims to truth of any kind:

> This does not mean . . . that I have given up the distinction between affective stylistics (not the happiest of designations) and the methodologies to which it originally stood opposed. It is just that the distinction cannot be maintained in its strongest form, as a distinction between what is true and what is not. Mr. Mailloux is right to point out that by virtue of a metacritical step I have put formalist and affective analyses on a par, but that is only in relation to the claim either of them might make to objectivity. . . . Affective criticism is arbitrary only in the sense that one cannot prove that its beginning is the right one, but once begun it unfolds in ways that are consistent with its declared principles. It is therefore a superior fiction, and since no methodology can legitimately claim any more, this superiority is decisive. It is also creative. That is, it makes possible new ways of reading and thereby creates new texts. An unsympathetic critic might complain that this is just the trouble, that rather than following the way people actually read I am teaching people to read differently. This is to turn the prescriptive claim into a criticism, but it will be felt as a criticism only if the alternative to different reading is right reading and if the alternative to the texts created by different reading is the real text. These however are the fictions of formalisms, and as fictions they have the disadvantage of being confining. My fiction is liberating. It relieves me of the obligation to be right (a standard that simply drops out) and demands only that I be interesting (a standard that can be met without any reference at all to an illusory objectivity).[14]

Anyone who in 1976 read that statement carefully could not have been greatly surprised when Fish shortly afterward, in a session of the Modern Language Association, repudiated the notion of any limit whatever on what a legitimate reading might be. Norman Holland had suggested, in 5 *Readers Reading,* that he would draw the line if a student saw Faulkner's "A Rose for Emily" as "about Esquimos." Fish claimed to see no reason to draw that line (my imaginary protocol above was not so imaginary)—a logical step to take if there is no rational *way* to draw lines. (It should perhaps be needless to say that in his actual critical practice, when he settles down seriously to read a poem, Fish is far more responsible to his texts than his more extreme statements would lead us to expect. And the same qualification can be made about the practical criticism of almost all the critics who talk mainly about readers and reading experience.)

I shall reveal myself as skeptical about many a critical claim before this book is finished. My quest for a pluralism could thus be called either a skeptical quest or an attempt to refute utter skepticism without falling into dogmatism. The kind of skepticism that I cannot even pretend to entertain is that form of critical doubt that would make inquiry into questions of these kinds necessarily pointless. It may seem an easy ploy thus to dismiss from one's book whatever intellectual position would make that book impossible. Yet even if we reject these "utter skeptics" about method, we are still left with an abundance of relativisms—half-skepticisms—that cannot be dismissed so easily. Such half-skepticisms can always be shown to imply one or another kind of monism; there is at least implicit in them an exhortation to do criticism in the one right way. But to say so can hardly be considered in itself a refutation. (I return to the question of relativism on pp. 83–92, below.)

Regardless of all this variety, it is clear that the stronger one's theoretical skepticism, the stronger one's motive for turning every encountered figure into a straw man. For the skeptic, *all* figures must be found to be at least partly made of straw. It thus appears that in a curious way I have already taken a stand against skepticism by using the metaphor "straw man," since it presupposes a genuine distinction between manikins and living persons and thus between unreal critical positions and genuine ones.

For a full skeptic about critical modes, no position is ultimately more alive than any other. Differences will reside in degrees of plausibility, never in actual soundness. Though again it must be said that no one can ever conduct public life as a complete skeptic, it is clear that even the half-skepticisms that *are* professed provide ample motive, as each new claimant to critical truth comes on the scene, to move in quickly for the inevitable *coup de grâce;* for if the new figure turned out to be alive, capable of resistance, skepticism itself would be doomed.

ECLECTICISM

The fifth possibility presents a much more hopeful countenance: bits of each position are true or valid, other bits false. It is naive to expect any one book, any one critic, any one mode, to be fully sound or fully mistaken. While monism is clearly absurd, so is skepticism. Everyone knows that we do in fact discover truths about literary works, that some critical modes are highly successful in achieving limited results. Is it not obvious that critical truth is to be found only in an eclecticism that culls the good bits from the inevitable errors?

Eclecticism is found in many varieties, ranging from absurdly reductive collections of inert bits and pieces to the kind of respectful selection from predecessors' methods and conclusions that every thinker must employ at some point. When Aristotle gathers together the opinions of earlier philosophers into those marvelous dialectical introductions that precede the "scientific" inquiry in most of his treatises, what is he doing if not separating the wheat from the chaff in his predecessors' work? And is not the same thing true when Leibniz proclaims that, "when a new book comes into my hands, I look for what I can learn from it, not for what I can criticize in it"?

Most eclectics these days call themselves pluralists, and, in one sense of "eclecticism," every pluralist is eclectic. The borderline between the two attitudes is thus extremely difficult to determine, and one might do better to think simply of a continuum, ranging from full eclectics, who deliberately hack other critics' works into fragments, salvaging whatever proves useful, to the full pluralists we are coming to: those who claim to embrace at least two enterprises in their full integrity, without reducing the two to one. Perhaps no one would describe himself as belonging at the eclectic extreme of this continuum, and most who call themselves pluralists would deny the very possibility of the pluralist extreme. They may be skeptics (variety can be accommodated because nothing one says matters very much); or monists (variety can be eliminated if we look closely enough); or eclectics (all modes are by their nature loose-jointed collections of truth and error, and the pluralist's task is simply to winnow).

From many possible examples, consider the remarkably comprehensive and sane guide to current criticism by P. M. Wetherill, *The Literary Text*. [15] Wetherill is eager to gather whatever is good from all available critical methods. Pursuing his notion of a textual criticism

that will be "flexible," based on "common sense" and a close attention to real texts, urging respect for the great variety of demands
actual texts place upon the critic, he finds something good in almost
every critic among the hundreds he mentions. But he also finds something lacking in all, especially in those who do not pursue his own
ultimate aim: a close reading of "the text" that will discover "the kind
of truth literature seeks to communicate" (p. 253). Every critic can be
grist to his mill, but it is hard to find any critic who emerges intact, or
even recognizable, from his description.

In the end, what Wetherill finds acceptable in each is determined
by the necessities of his own strongly limiting view of textual
"meaning." "*The form of a text must be shown to be meaningful*. Mech-
anisms described must be related to their specific impact" (p. 252).
The "musts" ring out, tolling the doom of all who do not accept
Wetherill's necessities. Criticism, he says,

> must . . . bear constantly in mind those two closely related key no-
> tions: *ambiguity*, the working hypothesis that any element in any
> work . . . must not be taken purely on face value, and *construction*,
> the fact that, as literature is a coherent unified organization of
> experience, the constants and recurrent devices in a work must be
> carefully tracked down and their function, variation and progres-
> sion described. [P. 253]

One has no difficulty accepting Wetherill's program as in itself
legitimate; the definition of literature here and the criticism it leads to
make sense to me, once I have changed the "musts" to "mays." What
is significant, when we remember Wetherill's promise of flexibility, is
that these "musts" are not the least bit hypothetical; they lead him to
treat most critics with a formula that runs like this: If X had only
remembered what I have just said, in his otherwise stimulating book,
he might have avoided falling into such-and-such a trap. "All this
is good *provided linguistics is seen as a slave to criticism* and not its
master" (p. 252). Thus almost everything in the critical universe is
good, *provided*. . . .

One could wish that other critics showed Wetherill's eagerness to
learn from all quarters. But for our purposes, open-spirited eclecticism is not enough if it fails to reconstruct rival positions with sufficient precision to allow for fruitful debate. And fruitful debate can
take place only when critical conclusions are related to the reasons an
author gives for believing them. *Why* does poor Riffaterre commit
himself to "the Average Reader myth," which one then *must* "discount" (p. 252)? *Why* do the structuralists fall into the "trap" of being

"constantly . . . preoccupied with similarity" (p. 231)? *Why* would Valéry ever make the "mistake" of saying that "'fine works are the children of their form which is born before them'" (p. 230)? How *could* the structuralists be so stupid as to create "a structure which is that of the critic's mind or personality," betraying a "hidden subjectivity . . . as dangerous as the indiscriminate listing of structural elements which have nothing to do with literature" (p. 232)?

It is not enough, after such exhibitions of a universal tendency to fall into traps that only the author has discerned, to say, as Wetherill often does, "Obviously I do not mean to denigrate X, Y, or Z" or to offer general exhortations to "sensitive open-mindedness." He quotes with favor a fine bit of advice from Sainte-Beuve:

> Constantly vary your studies, develop your intelligence in all directions, do not restrict it to any one mode or school of thought . . .; launch out with a kind of friendly disquiet towards everything which is insufficiently known and which deserves to be better known and scrutinize it with precise yet warm curiosity [Letter to Taxile Delord, 3 February 1864]. [P. 251]

Obviously our lives together would be greatly improved if such advice were more generally followed. But the whole question of what would be a fully sensitive and warmly curious scrutiny of any critical mode is left unanswered.

Most eclectics are in fact considerably less serious than Wetherill in their efforts to reconstruct opposing views. David Daiches, for example, professes and indeed practices a broad sympathy for positions that many would consider contradictory, but it is clear in the following quotation that his belief that every position is "wrong" finally overrides his belief that every position is "partly right":

> My instinct has always been to say at most "Yes, but—" to the programme of any school of thought. I retain sympathies for views I have abandoned. . . . I can understand—or I think I can—why intelligent Jews remain or become ultra-orthodox, why sensitive and thoughtful people convert to Catholicism, why some Americans are anti-British and some Britons are anti-American. One side of me can have splendid conversations with priests and rabbis and old-fashioned English classics masters. Another side joyfully addresses Humanist meetings, and exchanges ideas sympathetically with Marxists, atheists, and rebels of all kinds. I am both nostalgic for the past and impatient for the future. In all this I am doubtless like most other people, but I think my capacity for participation in

intellectual discussion in different roles is perhaps unusual. One can agree with so many because they are all wrong. And of course because they are all partly right. It is, I think, my own intellectual eclecticism that allows me to take these different roles. It has nothing to do with cynicism—the reverse, if anything. I mean I think that it could be argued that there is an element of sentimentalism in my position. I feel for someone, I understand his intellectual and emotional standpoint, I can formulate arguments that will please him without violating my own integrity (though at the same time without telling the whole truth about my own position).[16]

The giveaway is in that parenthesis. Daiches does not really see other positions as full rivals; they are at best aids in sharpening his own previous position. As he goes on to say, they are "challenges to define my own position much more carefully than I had ever done before."

Whether it is possible in theory, then, to develop an eclecticism that will not reveal a secret skepticism or monism, in practice the attitude quickly resolves into a raiding of ruined edifices in search of bricks and straw useful in a preconceived building program.

Methodological Pluralism

In logic, and perhaps even in the world of literary critics, there is a final possibility: two or more conflicting positions may be entirely acceptable—acceptable, that is, with no other qualification than the "higher semantics" of discovering their two quite different and irresolvable worlds of discourse, their two "languages" or "frameworks." Whether such a concept makes any sense at all depends on what we mean by "conflicting." We could not hope to find a pluralism that would embrace truths flatly contradictory: "'Surgical Ward' refers to bandaged patients" / "'Surgical Ward' does not refer to bandaged patients." To embrace genuine contradiction would be the equivalent of utter skepticism, because contradictory truths are indistinguishable from nontruths.* The question then becomes whether any two given conflicting propositions are in fact of the kind that, like true contradictories, attempt to cancel each other out. If so, one must choose one or the other, behaving, at least for the time being, as a monist. If not, can one distinguish part-truths and part-falsehoods in each? If so, one works as an eclectic. Finally, can there

---

*But see Burke below, pp. 109–10.

be conflict among critical modes that is best dealt with as an interrelation, correlation, or supplementation of rival and yet irreducible truths?

Problems Raised by This Pluralism

CONFUSION WITH OTHER PLURALISMS

In asking whether any nonskeptic can ever move beyond monism or eclecticism, it is important to see just how clearly eclectics like Wetherill and Daiches—liberal, tolerant, commodious—fall short of what we are seeking. It is true that they do not set out to skewer straw men; they set out to receive aid from their friends. Yet each ends with a single mode of his own, one that uses an eclectic search-and-scan technique to obtain materials from his predecessors. The resulting mode then inevitably becomes, for everyone else, just one more monism to be either refuted or dissected in the search for useful parts. When we look at what each critic makes of his predecessors, it is clear that they would be dissatisfied with the report.

The closer one looks at actual controversy, the harder it seems to formulate a genuine pluralism that will not easily be reduced either to some new universal monistic mode, or to some full skepticism, or to some version of relativism or eclecticism. What is worse, pluralism is not offered to us in a single form.

As I have said, many critics call themselves pluralists these days; as a label, pluralism is almost as fashionable in criticism (where it often stands for a belief in a plurality of valid readings of a text) as in politics (where it has become a synonym for "open" or "tolerant," as in the term "pluralistic society") or in theology (where it is a synonym for ecumenicism).[17] In philosophy it is still sometimes used in William James's sense, describing a universe that is irreducibly many in contrast with a monism that sees the universe as a single substance; and it occasionally is applied to some recent versions of language-game theory, which, in contrast with the struggles of the positivists and their kin to find a single unified language for all the "sciences," insist on the rich variety of games that people play.

We are probing instead the possibility of a full embrace of more than one critical method without reducing pluralities to one (a supreme monism), or multiplying them to a vague or meaningless infinity, or canceling them out into zero. We are thus seeking to learn whether we need more than one way of *working on the world,* and we are not initially interested in *conceptions of the world's ultimate nature.* [18] Thus a methodological monist, in my notion here, could very easily be a philosophical dualist, and a methodological pluralist could believe either that the great buzzing blooming confusion finally is harmonized in a *uni*verse or that it is duplicitous right down to its double core.*

CONFUSION WITH RELATIVISM

If the pluralism we seek is hard to distinguish from various other pluralisms, it is even harder to distinguish from various relativisms. Each of the three pluralists I consider in the next three chapters has been accused again and again of relativism, and each has thought it important to answer the charge. It is also true, of course, that each has been accused of dogmatic monism: after all, does not each finally persist in a single mode, despite claiming to embrace all variety? The essential challenge of whether anyone can finally be anything but a monist (however many epicycles he may have to add to his original single wheel) must be reserved for later. For now the problem is to distinguish what a pluralism of modes might be—if it were ever found—from other styles of thought that claim to see a critic's conclusions as "relative to" something other than themselves.

The chief difference lies in the nature of the truth claim that is made. Every relativism sees the conclusions of one mode of thought as relative to "something else." In literary criticism that "something else" may be some entirely different field of knowledge or kind of action or experience; some psychoanalytical critics have, for example, regarded all critical conclusions as relative to the critic's own psychic problems, and some sociological critics have reduced critical truth to trends and zeitgeists. The relativist thus always expects to find in every other critic true causes that are radically different from the reasons offered.

Probably the most aggressive current relativism substitutes sheer physical causes for all other reasons. Though its proponents do not

---

*We thus find, as in almost all conceptual labeling, that a single word is made to do too much work: concepts seem to be infinite, but words for them are in short supply. No wonder that many critics are tempted into galloping neologism.

Yet clarity depending on new terms is at best temporary, because the new terms soon take on many new meanings in various interpretations. I think it better to do as I have finally done on earlier occasions when I needed new words for what were, after all, only small branches of vast rivers labeled "rhetoric" and "irony": keep the old word, pluralism, while qualifying it to mean what I refuse to call plurimodism or—even worse—polymethodism.

write for critical journals, they must look down upon us from their laboratories and wonder how we can go on believing that our conclusions result from thought. All human reasoning, not only critical reasoning, is simply a manifestation of the true line of causation that leads from *this* physical configuration of the universe to *that* one. Such relativism is thus equivalent to full skepticism about the human sciences: all *critical* reasoning must be hollow, and there cannot be the slightest motive to pay serious attention to it, except to inquire how it springs from, and thus is relative to, its true physical causes.

A similar reduction—though not to atomic physical event but to psychological event—is B. F. Skinner's behaviorism. Skinner and his followers say little about literature and criticism, but we can infer what they would believe about critical reasoning from what Skinner says in *Beyond Freedom and Dignity* about reasoning in general: it is at best a weak form of persuasion and is usually a disguise for, and thus relative to, the effects of conditioning.[19]

It is clear that even these extreme relativisms are not skeptical about all knowledge: "in principle," knowledge of the physical or psychological world is totally coherent and, if obtained, could explain everything we say. Since they are not skeptical about reasoning based on physical or psychological observation, their position boils down in the end to one or another dogmatic monism.

All other true relativisms are similarly reductive in the technical sense that they would reduce the reasonings of critics to the truer causes discovered by some one other discipline embraced as the single right way of dealing with the world.

In contrast, the pluralist we seek, though he will see each critic's conclusions indeed as relative, will relate them, not to something outside that critic's process of reasoning, but to the kind of inquiry he has engaged in and to the quality of the endeavor he brings to it. That is, the pluralist will examine the question each critic has chosen to ask, the critical language he employs, and his characteristic way of seeking evidence and reasoning with it. He will have been forced into pluralism by his discovery that when he has taken at least two critics' reasoning with as much seriousness as they did themselves, more than one mode emerges intact, irrefutable, viable, and *not* reducible or totally translatable into some other, superior mode.

In practice, he will expect that some controversies will lead to a both/and resolution rather than an either/or. Having learned in at least one case that, when conflicting conclusions were related back to their intellectual sources, sharply contrasting modes proved both sound and in no final sense contradictory, he expects, and indeed works for, further experiences of the same harmonious kind. If he says, "Yes, but . . . ," with Daiches, the "but" will mean, in such cases, not "you are partly wrong" but "you have spoken from only one of the possible perspectives."

PARADOXICAL UMBRELLAS AND OTHER ANALOGIES

I have suggested that to embrace such a pluralism would advance critical understanding by reducing our temptations to misread and so to skewer straw men. Only if my opponent's survival is possible without my defeat am I likely to treat his arguments with as much respect as I spontaneously accord my own. But this practical advantage cannot obscure the theoretical complexity that confronts anyone who says what I have said in the two previous paragraphs. The problems can be dramatized, initially, by underlining the seeming incompatibility of my two statements: that sharply contrasting modes may be in no final sense contradictory, yet that they are not reducible or totally translatable into some other, superior mode. What is harmony if it does not mean that results are compatible and therefore translatable? But clearly, the pluralist who believes in a harmony that allows each mode to be totally translated into the terms of some one supreme mode is saying that truth is in some sense one, while the pluralist who believes that a plurality of modes is required because each of them reveals truths that are essentially hidden from the others is saying that truth is in some irreducible sense *not* one. I seem to be saying both things here. Can I do so without offending standards of consistency that ought to be embraced by practitioners of every mode?

Every term in such a question is itself a subject of controversy, and it is important to see the sense in which the problem of relating modes shifts its nature as we shift our notions of what an individual mode might be. In talking of modes at all rather than of individual *critics* or of specific *texts* or of *styles of critical play* we already run the risk of losing sight of a process—people talking to each other—and of producing entities that are solider than such stuff can possibly be. I have needed a term that suggests a practice somehow independent of the temperaments of individual critics—a way that can be taught, a path that many can follow together, a practice that might be shared by critics and texts bearing little surface resemblance. But as I have talked about transpersonal modes, I have begun to talk as if they can be summarized in propositions and as if conflict between two modes is like conflict between clear and univocal propositions. I may even seem to have accepted uncritically the common notion that when propositions seem to conflict, even if they are propositions about such complex matters as the nature of literature or the proper way to talk about it, we should be able to show *either* that they do in fact conflict, with one or the other proving false; *or* that they do not conflict because they can be harmonized; *or* that both are false; *or*—the final logical possibility—that each is partly true and partly false.

To many critics such reductions to propositional form will seem self-evidently misguided; to others they will seem a necessary preliminary to any serious testing of the truth value of critical modes. Shall we confront *this* conflict in turn as a conflict of propositions logically tested and decisively resolved? To do so will be to take as literal a relation that to many will seem at best but a dangerous analogy: rival critical practices are *like* rival propositions, but only in such-and-such respects.

Once we have seen that to relate modes or approaches as if they were propositions can itself be thought of as analogizing—since critical acts are not literally the propositions or terms used to summarize or label them—we invite the invention of different, perhaps richer, analogies. Is not rivalry among critical modes less like propositional contradiction than it is like rivalry among national cuisines? Or among different cartographic projections of the globe, each of which has advantages and disadvantages? Or among "competing" academic departments within a university? Or among different (and noncompeting) sports?

The analogy with games is especially tempting, since many philosophers these days talk about all discourse as the playing of different language-games. Relating rival modes of criticism could be seen as much like relating football and tennis. If one "critic" says that the best costume for football is a semi-rigid exoskeleton, including shoes with cleats, and another says that the best costume for tennis is the lightest covering that public decency allows, plus tennis shoes, everyone will allow both claims into the domain of plausible "sports-talk," and efforts to interrelate the claims will seem inane. All sport is sport, and each sport can flourish without our being able to agree precisely on what sport is in itself or on how to relate what tennis fans will say about the best or truest sport to what football fans will say about the same subject.

But the analogy with games, even if it were made tighter than my example implies, may easily understate the seriousness with which most rivals in criticism engage in their debate. Talk of games suggests a kind of arbitrariness in our choices that would be hard to distinguish from skepticism. Most critics believe that in choosing to talk about "Surgical Ward" in a certain way they are not simply playing one language-game among many; they are pursuing some kind of truth about "Surgical Ward." And even for those who say that such choices are merely of "convention," differences among critics are not nearly as simple as those between tennis fans and football buffs.

What we need is not a softening of our problem through an easy analogy but an illumination through a tough one. And so I naturally turn to the natural sciences. Some modern scientists have been forced, by their inability to harmonize theories that seem to have full empirical support and theoretical cogency, into thinking about how the choice of a given language, framework, or perspective dictates a world of perception that will have its own validities but that cannot be directly translated into the terms of other worlds. Sometimes we find them simply acknowledging that reduction distorts; they note, for instance, that the verbal statement of any mathematical theory turns that theory into something else, or that a brief statement distorts any fuller statement. Einstein, for example, writing his brief "Autobiographical Notes" for the Library of Living Philosophers, gives a sketch of his "conversion" to the pursuit of knowledge and then says: "What I have here said is true only within a certain sense, just as a drawing consisting of a few strokes can do justice to a complicated object, full of perplexing details, only in a very limited sense. . . . Looked at from this point of view the above schematic remarks contain as much truth as can be uttered in such brevity."[20] Even more to our point, he indicates again and again, especially in his "Reply to Criticisms," that he considers scientific world views in a pluralistic rather than monistic, eclectic, or skeptical frame. For example, he does not say that his opponents, the quantum physicists, are wrong in their use of statistical methods and the indeterminacy principle; indeed, the whole purpose of this section of his essay is to show where they are *right:* "The formal relations which are given in this theory [the quantum]— i.e., its entire mathematical formalism—will probably have to be contained, in the form of logical inferences, in every useful future theory" (p. 667). It is clear that for him there is no possibility of skepticism; he believes, as an act of reasonable faith, in one truth, but it is a truth that will never be completely grasped in any one set of concepts: "We are here concerned with 'categories' or schemes of thought, the selection of which is, in principle, entirely open to us and whose qualification can only be judged by the degree to which its use contributes to making the totality of the contents of consciousness 'intelligible' " (p. 673).

From this point of view the quantum physicists are not wrong but simply and inevitably biased in perspective, which is to say that they are wrong only insofar as they think of their perspective as unbiased. Relative to their own methods and chosen subject matter, their conclusions cannot be refuted; indeed, for Einstein, no set of concepts chosen "freely" by the "inventor" and tested honestly by his three criteria of simplicity, generality, and internal consistency can ever be refuted by an appeal to another set of concepts or to "the facts." "For it is often, perhaps even always, possible to adhere to a general theoretical foundation by securing the adaptation of the theory to the facts by means of artificial [*künstliche*] additional assumptions" (pp. 20–23).

In another chapter in the same volume, Andrew Paul Ushenko gives an analogy that comes closer still to illustrating the kinds of rivalries we are considering. Imagine a fixed cone placed among observers who are not allowed to change their angle of vision. One person observes from directly below the cone and describes a circle. Another observes from directly to one side and sees an isosceles triangle. Others at other angles describe highly irregular shapes. "The alternative aspects exclude each other as actual observations—no observer can have two of them at the same time—but as observable, i.e., in the capacity to appear in different perspectives, they are connected and co-exist."[21]

Taken seriously, this analogy presents the challenge of pluralism much more rigorously than the popular tale of the blind men and the elephant. That tale illustrates a tolerant relativism, perhaps, or eclecticism, but not pluralism. Those blind men are, for one thing, blind, maimed; and, for another, each one touches but a small part of the whole animal that might be touched if he persisted. But each observer of the cone sees *everything there is to be seen from his position*, even by the most acute observer; nothing limits his results except perspective. Indeed, two of the possible observers, the one from the top and the other from the bottom, "see" in effect a whole; what is hidden from them is not anything "in" the object but rather the additional data that can be revealed only by the other perspectives.

The challenge here, then, is that there is nothing wrong in either the observations or the conclusions of any one observer. The analogy presupposes that the account given by every observer passes at least two of the three tests that we shall find useful throughout: (1) the observations are in themselves completely accurate; they can be said to *correspond* with something that all unprejudiced observers must grant is really in the observed object, and they are thus in one essential respect *accurate* or "true"; (2) the conclusion follows from the observations, and it is thus *valid*. The conclusions are not, however, (3) fully *adequate* to what—as the example is given—everyone is presumed to know about the cone: as a cone it offers much more data than any of the announced perspectives accounts for. Even so, each position presents a *relative* adequacy, as compared to some other imaginable position. An observer might, for example, be blocked by an obstacle from seeing any more than half a circle, viewing the cone from underneath. His conclusion—"This is a half-circle"—is both accurate and valid, but it is even less adequate than the conclusion based on an unblocked vision of a circle. Accuracy and validity are thus standards respected in every view; in any one mode, propositions will be properly judged as either true or false, including conclusions invalidly drawn. But *adequacy* is always a matter of degree. All the announced views of the cone are accurate and valid. Some are "better" than others, however, if tested not simply for coherence among the parts and the power to discern something in the objects that other observers can also see but also for relative adequacy to the inherent richness of the object in its capacity to respond, as it were, to many perspectives.

Here we face again, suddenly, the immense simplicity of our cone, taken as an analogy to the poem with which we began. If a cone is "really" a cone, what is "Surgical Ward"? Even a cone partially escapes any one perspective; nothing we have said, for example, even touches the immense variation of light and shade that any actual cone will display, and, if I attempt to do justice to that, I shall lose that other perspective I have not yet mentioned, the precise mathematical formula for an "ideal" cone. If we can imagine a pluralist who would try to accommodate more than one coherent and accurate perspective on the cone while retaining the right to judge their relative adequacy to its inherent richness, can we hope to find a pluralist who can say the same in dealing with "Surgical Ward"?*

A full critical pluralism would be a kind of "methodological

---

*It will be important later on to remember that the criterion of adequacy to the true richness of perspectives offered by the cone is not easily reconciled to the criterion of simplicity that theorists of knowledge have celebrated at least since Occam sharpened his razor. The law of parsimony can be applied to any decision about what the cone "really is" only if we underline the qualification often forgotten entirely: *provided that* when we slice off our unnecessary hypotheses we have not violated "adequacy" by slicing off half the data with them. A simple drive for simplicity will leave us complacently defending our coherent and accurate views of a circle or a triangle. (I return to the question of data as *given* by the world or *taken* by our modes of perception in chapter 6, pp. 238–55.)

perspectivism" that credited not only accuracy and validity but some degree of adequacy to at least two critical modes, though it would no doubt find many others either false or invalid or grossly reductive. It would take seriously the notion, found in almost all post-Kantian philosophy, that every inquirer is inherently limited by his language, that we can see only what our equipment allows us to see; but it would take with equal seriousness the task of discriminating kinds and qualities of equipment.

Professed perspectivists are a dime a dozen these days.[22] But few of them face the tough and interesting questions that arise when we start thinking about the mode of existence, if any, of whatever is analogous to the "entire cone"—questions, that is, about how the differing truth claims of various perspectives relate and about how they are to be assessed. If the pluralist is to escape a relativism that can always be dissolved into skepticism by a perceptive interrogator, he must claim to accept at least two rival truths about some clearly formulated literary question (tested according to the correspondence criterion, applied in however attenuated a sense), derived by at least two different but valid reasoning processes (tested according to the coherence criterion), yielding at least two different claims about what makes an adequate picture: "the poem itself." Or, if that sounds too much like a permanently inaccessible *Ding an sich*, at least we must find some way to talk about how the various perspectives relate to each other and are mutually tested. Are they rivals, or are they not? If a critic concludes that they are not, can we not then say that he is only a monist after all, disguised as a pluralist? But if they do compete, how can anyone really claim to believe them both?

The point is perhaps clearest with regard to adequacy. Ushenko's analogy fails us here, because in criticism we have nothing comparable to our knowledge that the cone is, after all, a cone and, further, that we who *know* that it is have a view of things that is more nearly adequate than any of the partial perspectives we have described. Not only is there in criticism no predetermined authority of views, but the things that criticism deals with—"Surgical Ward" and its cousins— are so immeasurably complex that no one can easily say how we would recognize an adequate view if we saw one. In short, when we seek a perspective on the perspectives—a theory that will enable us to deal with a plurality of modes—we are thrust into a rivalry among pluralisms, a rivalry that seems to duplicate the problem with which we began.

Can we not, in other words, imagine as many possible attitudes toward the "higher semantics" of rival pluralisms as toward the original modes? One kind of pluralist will look for the one correct metaperspective; but since he will manufacture a single umbrella, however commodious, he will then proceed as a monist. Another kind, not at all skeptical about the original modes themselves, will be skeptical, as I assume many of you are by now tempted to be, about the possibility of finding any suitable umbrella at such general levels. The eclectic, third, will again want to tot up the strengths and weaknesses of various pluralisms.

Finally, can we imagine a genuine pluralist of pluralisms, one who can accept and use many different umbrellas—a plurimodist of plurimodes, a metalinguist of metalanguages? But how could such a one, praising and relating many ways of praising and relating but encountering other pluralists of pluralisms who insist on different ways—how could he avoid an infinite regress of ever more vacuous pluralisms?

I cannot promise a finally satisfactory encounter with these staggering questions, produced by my simple effort to be a good citizen in the republic of criticism. Beginning with what looked like a fairly innocent search for productive ways of dealing with critical conflict, I have landed in very threatening territory indeed.

It is always sane at such moments to draw back to territory mapped by previous explorers. In the next three chapters I shall look at three radically different pluralisms, for the most part putting to one side all questions about how we might relate them. Can three such comprehensive modes as R. S. Crane's, Kenneth Burke's, and M. H. Abrams' all be embraced, even when they seem openly to contradict each other? All three would, if I read them correctly, answer yes. But the trouble is that we can expect, in advance of our inquiry, that the very word "yes" may mean different things in their three different contexts.

These pseudo-rational assertions thus disclose a dialectical battlefield in which the side permitted to open the attack is invariably victorious, and the side constrained to act on the defensive is always defeated. Accordingly, vigorous fighters, no matter whether they support a good or a bad cause, if only they contrive to secure the right to make the last attack, and are not required to withstand a new on-slaught from their opponents, may always count upon carrying off the laurels. We can easily understand that while this arena should time and again be contested, and that numerous triumphs should be gained by both sides, the last decisive victory always leaves the champion of the good cause master of the field, simply because his rival is forbidden to resume the combat.... After they have rather exhausted than injured one another, they will perhaps themselves perceive the futility of their quarrel, and part good friends.—Kant

A plurality of critical approaches is not only inevitable but desirable in itself, both because the prosperity of the humanities depends on keeping all aspects of humanistic objects clearly in view and be-cause, without the competition of radically different modes of criticism, the practice of the mode we may happen to prefer is bound to suffer.—R. S. Crane

To distinguish our purposes and discern which views advance which aims is not less than the whole duty of man.—I. A. Richards

I will teach you differences.—*King Lear*

Ronald Crane
and the Pluralism of
Discrete Modes

To any full skeptic, Ronald Crane's lifelong effort to reduce confusion in humanistic studies must seem to have been doomed from the beginning. He found most humanistic "disciplines" undisciplined, full of controversy conducted without ground rules and so without mutual understanding or hope for progress. Though some few literary historians, philologists, and bibliographers managed genuine exchange leading to widely accepted results, they did so only by ignoring disputes among critics and dealing with problems that were clearly, for humanists, peripheral. Crane himself did important work of this scientific kind,* but he wanted to do justice to the center, and the center was always for him those unique human achievements which rise above the average or normal or law-bound—not just novels, plays, and poems but all human constructions that can be neither produced nor criticized according to rules of replication.

The trouble is, as we have seen, that critics have never agreed on how to define that center or on what is worth knowing about it. The resulting warfare is itself a major human "construction" calling for humanistic thinking. Can we, by employing intellectual methods on intellectual warfare, hope to find a cure, or partial cure, for it?

One need not be a very aggressive skeptic to be skeptical about Crane's effort to do just that. Why look for intellectual causes and solutions when critical wars can so easily be explained as we explain other kinds? Human beings are ignorant, self-aggrandizing, naturally aggressive creatures, moved by irrational drives, by personal conditioning, by cultural forces they do not and cannot hope to understand. Here are reasons enough, without troubling to look for grounds in the ways we reason. The personal interests of critics con-

*Especially in his early years. My account will of course concentrate on Crane the critic, not the bibliographer, editor, or historian, and it must be relatively impersonal and static, ignoring changes as his life developed. A good though somewhat condescending account of Crane's "strenuous" style in argument—his "carefully worked out distinctions and his unfeigned joy in making a case"—can be found in Daiches' *A Third World*, pp. 21–27, 38–45. There is no full account of his intellectual development.

flict, their perspectives are hopelessly diverse. Of course they will seek to annihilate each other. Of course they will reduce each other to straw men. Even if we deplore the eternal scandal of humanistic warfare, even if we abandon complete skepticism and search for cures, would it not make better sense to put our faith in religious conversion, or political renovation, or psychoanalysis, working directly on the real causes of misunderstanding?

Why try once again that foredoomed effort to piece out in thought the grounds of thought's disasters? As soon as you find them, your report will merely enter the wars as another combatant. Even as late as Locke or Hume or Kant it may not have been too naive to hope that an intellectual housecleaning might rid the world of pointless controversy.[1] But by now we have seen such efforts fail time and time again, century by century, each effort simply contributing to further controversy, becoming just one more conflicting voice that cannot get itself heard. Surely it is time to give up on that line and cultivate our own gardens.

Many thinkers in this century besides Crane have refused to do so. For them, nothing would serve short of ambitious new efforts either to fit everything together—the route Crane rejected—or to find a pluralism that would enable scholars to address each other productively. Like Crane, most such seekers for new modes of understanding have somehow rested their hopes on a study of how the language of controversy works. Since Locke, Hume, and Kant failed to clear things up once and for all by looking at how *ideas* and *minds* work, let us see if we cannot do so by looking at how *language* works: Bertrand Russell by pursuing the grounds of logical and mathematical certainty through a refined propositional analysis that would yield an ideal univocality; the various semanticists by offering a new freedom from the tyranny of words and their ambiguities; Wittgenstein by offering to cure our diseases of language by looking closely at the diverse rules of many different language-games; I. A. Richards by reviving rhetoric as a science of the meaning of meaning; the American new critics by offering salvation through a poetry at last read as closely as its scriptural ambiguities deserve; Carnap and others by pinning their faith on the quest for a unified language of *all* sciences, with a resulting single "encyclopaedia"; the many schools of linguistics and, more recently, of structuralism, semiotics, rhetoric, and deconstruction, by claiming to offer *the* method of dealing with signs or symbols.

Skepticism, Dogmatism, and the Plurality of Human Achievements

Though Crane shared with all of these the hope that we might learn to think better by considering how we talk, he never hoped that thinking about the languages of criticism would provide what is promised by many recent theorists: "the principle for a unitary comprehension of man."[2] Considering the dismal history of intellectual panaceas, it is surprising how many movements in this century have announced that the new heaven and the new earth—or at least the one right view of the abyss—are at hand. Crane's deep historical scholarship permitted no hope that, after millennia of intellectual warfare, critics would find perpetual peace at last. And his nagging respect for "the evidence"* excluded from even his most secure pronouncements that tone of passionate intensity with which many a modern prophet has won both attention to new crises and devotees of new total solutions.

Nothing of his "hurls" the reader, as Doubrovsky says of Barthes's *Sur Racine*, "into the heart of a paroxysm" (p. 64). Crane rather draws one into cool awareness of complexities and intellectual dangers and difficulties, some of them inherently insurmountable. And then he offers not an easily sloganized and universally applicable "approach" but rather only a sharply delimited knowledge about *some* kinds of literary works and *some* thories of literature. Such measured inquiry lights no public bonfires.

Crane's scholarly skepticism about all abstractions was in fact so intense that it might well have led him, as insistence on empirical evidence has led some others, into a rejection of all argument about literary values. But his mistrust of the "high priori road" led in the opposite direction: our world is, after all, full of forms that have been made and that we experience as admirable or not so admirable. Each form is an "actuality that has been and hence can be achieved by art,"[3] and it is only abstract theory that bans our reasoning about the quality of such achievements.

He thus knew through personal experience, as even the professed skeptic "knows," that some created forms are better made and thus worth more than others. And there is no *a priori* reason to believe that knowledge of many kinds cannot be obtained about such forms and

---

*In the thirties, David Daiches found Crane's watchcry, "What's your evidence?" a liberating shock. Crane's lifelong skepticism about whatever had not been proved was turned to more shocking self-parody when, on his deathbed, he responded to the assurance, "You are looking better today," with a snarled "What's your evidence?"

their comparative value, provided—and here is the crux—that critics do not insist on working in some one right way. Why should it not be possible, if we performed a subtle semantic clarification of "languages" and then pursued a variety of purposes, each according to his clarified language, to build a chorus of critical voices? Why could not the Babel of desperate monisms be converted into a counterpoint of different but compatible "lines," a polyphonic progress toward diverse cognitive triumphs?

My metaphor in itself raises a problem. Even to talk of a chorus implies a degree of harmony—of intercommunication among the voices—that experience seems to prove impossible. But whether dissonant or not, the voices might be treated as inherently and irreducibly plural. Critical progress might become possible if, by taking thought, we could recover or renovate a variety of "refuted" voices from the past, learning to apply to new materials one or another of the great critical languages that history grandly wills to us.

In short, we have known *King Lear* and *Persuasion* and Keats's Odes, known them as achieved and organizing powers in our lives. And we have known, or can come to know, how Aristotle or Longinus or Johnson or Coleridge would teach a shareable knowledge about such works. If we will only learn to make our discriminations fine enough to discern the individual and diverse unities that make up these two pluralities—these literary works and these time-tested modes of talking about them—we can resist both the absurdities of dogmatizing and the dissolutions of skepticism.

Whether any one of us will be lucky enough to invent some new critical mode is another question. We can hope that new modes will be invented, but nothing is more self-destructive than the current fashion of cheering each new skyrocket as if it had finally given us all the light we need—and then sighing when it quickly fizzles out. All new modes will simply enter the destructive logomachy that we all deplore, unless we learn to meet them with the arts of recovery and renovation that can meanwhile be profitably applied to the modes we already have.

The New Semantics of Modes

What we need, then, is not so much new modes as a new kind of knowledge about modes, yielding a new use of the old scholarly arts of interpretation: an elaborated semantics that can recover the powers of any mode without reducing it to any other. Practicing that semantics, we shall adopt a hypothesis similar to the one employed by every responsible critic when approaching a literary classic. When I face any work that has been praised by many readers, the odds are immense against my discovering its full power quickly. It is not only that "I don't read the classic, the classic reads me," as many are saying these days. It is that I must take extraordinary measures if I am not to cut the time-tested work down to my own size, and this goes for the *Poetics* as well as for *Paradise Lost*. I must work on the hypothesis, unproved and in no simple sense provable, that any unfamiliar mode praised by other critics can reshape my categories and expand my faculties. And it may even prove, once I have considered it as closely as I have considered the mode or modes I have already embraced, to be invulnerable to any refutation other than the self-evident claim that it does not do all that needs doing.

It should go without saying that Crane did not manage—how could anyone do so?—to approach all doctrines with this kind of openness. But he was rightly proud of his ability to enter so deeply into any coherently articulated view that he could not easily be distinguished from a true believer. He took a sly pleasure, for example, when Catholic students came to him privately, after a class discussion of Catholic authors, to ask, "Surely you must be a Catholic?" His ideal would have been to produce the same response in any true disciple of every critic he discussed. Whether he then shifted to what he called, along with Carnap and many others, the "external" questions that would reveal the limitations as well as the powers of a given mode depended, of course, on more factors than one could well trace, including what he himself called his own "prejudices." But he was committed to delaying that shift as long as humanly possible, and he was properly critical of many philosophers and critics, including Carnap himself, who make a great deal of the distinction between questions internal and external to a "framework" but who move too happily and quickly to the section that begins, "Nevertheless, X should surely have recognized that. . . ."

Thus Crane's pluralism was a way of accepting a variety of truths that came in discrete bundles—a pluralism of independent intellectual frameworks or languages. All critical languages are of course limited, not, as the eclectic would say, because they necessarily contain error but because works of art, like the cone in my example, offer manifold perspectives. Indeed they are—no one has ever denied it—immeasurably more complex than any geometrical figure; no single perspective can ever hope to see all there is to be seen.

In *The Languages of Criticism and the Structure of Poetry* Crane argues that, in this century,

We have come to see more clearly perhaps than before that language is not only a means of communication and artistic creation but also, as Edward Sapir remarked, an instrument of discovery and understanding, ... [because] "its forms predetermine for us certain modes of observation and interpretation." And from this starting-point we have been led to conceive of any science or discipline as first of all a highly specialized linguistic construction—a coherent "framework" (to use the current slang) of selected terms and distinctions and of rules for operating with them, into which we must translate all our observations. ... We are thus, in all our inquiries into things, the more or less willing and productive prisoners of the special system of "language" (in this derived sense) we have chosen to employ; it is only in relation to this system that we can assert anything as a meaningful "fact" or give determinate significance to any question we ask; and our problems and solutions will differ widely, even when the ostensible subjects remain the same, according to the peculiar conceptual and logical constitution of the "framework" we happen to be using. [Pp. 11–12]

There is [thus] ... a strict relativity, in criticism, of statements to questions and questions to "frameworks". ... [P. 26]*

It should be clear by now that Crane's answer to my question in chapter 1 about "Surgical Ward" could never be single or simple. Only monists can claim to give the one right answer to that question, though some of the answers may lead to immense complexities or even to deliberately incoherent claims about the poem's essential ambiguity or unintelligibility. The monist knows what a poem *is*, and he can decide whether a particular set of lines is in fact such a thing and whether or how the lines do what a poem should do. Some monists

---

*A fuller statement of this point is given by Elder Olson in "The Dialectical Foundations of Critical Pluralism," *Texas Quarterly* 9, no. 1 (Spring 1966); reprinted in *"On Value Judgments in the Arts" and Other Essays* (Chicago and London: University of Chicago Press, 1976):

There are certain properties of language which perhaps would be granted by all. In the first place, language is necessarily abstractive or selective. That is, it is impossible for language to signify the totality of existence; if it did, it would be non-significant. ...

The universe consists of infinite things with infinite attributes capable of being conceived in infinite modes of conception; signification is therefore necessarily finite. ... The second characteristic of language ... may be called its *restrictiveness*. Once we have fixed the selectiveness of a term—given it a particular meaning—we can speak of no more than that term permits, so long as that particular meaning obtains. ... The universe itself [or the work of art], whatever it may be in fact, becomes for my discussion only what I *say* it is, and contracts itself to the limits of my discourse. I can talk about only what I can distinguish and mention. ... [This] means ... that any philosophic [or critical] problem is relative to its formulation. [Pp. 334–35]

will, of course, have to work harder than others. For some modes a single-line generalization about many works may serve, while others will require a detailed and even tedious analysis of each work. But having chosen his mode, the direction of the monist's labor will be single and clear, even if the game he pursues is ambiguity or "unreadability." Clearly we are all monists when we settle down to a given job of work; we can pursue only one perspective at a time, however complicated it may be.

But we need not do so in the belief that all other perspectives are inherently flawed. For Crane as pluralist, the questions "What *ought* I to say?" or "What is it *important* to say?" are absurd—until we make essential discriminations. There can be no one answer, because there are many different things that you *can* say and may *want* to say, depending on the kind of problem you are interested in and, finally, on the resources of your "language." As he says, our choice of framework is thus a practical, not theoretical, matter, since it depends on "the different kinds of knowledge about poetry we may happen, at one time or another or for one or another reason, to want. And who is there with authority sufficient to entitle him to inform critics what these must be?" (p. 27).

For Crane, there are four obvious dimensions along which statements about "Surgical Ward" will legitimately vary: (1) what you take it to be *for* and what you take to be the *purpose* of criticism; (2) what you take it to *be* and what you thus see the *subject matter* of criticism to be; (3) how you think argument should be put together about such matters—your conception of *method*; and (4) what your essential *principles* or assumptions are about these and other matters, including the nature of the universe in which "Surgical Ward" finds itself.[4]

PURPOSES

There are, we begin by assuming, many valid purposes of criticism. Calling his own choice a "prejudice," Crane says, in his Preface to *Languages*, "It is natural for me to think of criticism in the context not of literary journalism," which itself might include many different purposes, "or of general cultural discussion," which would also include many kinds,

> but of humanistic learning—as a form of inquiry to be cultivated in the same questioning spirit, for the sake of a disinterested understanding and appreciation of its objects in their own natures. . . . I should want to distinguish . . . between the criticism which thus aspires to be "a learning" and two other kinds: the criticism that

takes the form of cultivated *causerie*, after the manner of Hazlitt, Sainte-Beuve, Matthew Arnold, and their many descendants; and the criticism that results from the interested application to litera- ture of general systems of religious, philosophic, or political ideas, after the manner of the later Eliot, the Marxists, Liberals, Humanists, Kirkegaardians, and Existentialists; . . .

But instead of taking the polemical turn that such distinctions often lead to in other critics, Crane's sentence moves immediately to a rejection of monism:

> . . . though I should not insist on calling the "learned" criticism, as Professor Frye does, "genuine criticism" or "criticism proper." . . . All are good things when responsibly done—that is, with a serious concern for principles and facts; and I can find no defensible grounds on which any one of them can be given precedence in intrinsic value over the others, since any such ranking presupposes—what can never be the case—that the question of what criticism in general is or should be has been authoritatively settled. [P. x]

That absolute "never" makes an interesting contrast with the abso- lutes we met in chapter 1. It is clearly a skeptical absolute: we shall *never* gain the authority to use absolute terms as those monists used them. Critical purposes are many because human interests in art will *always* be many. The result is that, whenever we choose from this chaos of possibilities, we should be steadily aware of the hypothet- ical nature of any "necessities" we discover. It is not necessary, obviously, that we follow Crane when he moves from pluralistic analysis to his chosen critical purpose, the search for a "learning" about the quality of art objects "in their own natures." But as pro- visional monist, he can say to us: *If* you desire knowledge of such- and-such kinds, *then* certain necessities follow.

> For what has chiefly interested me . . . has not been the patterns of ideas which particular things reflect [and here I invite the reader to think in advance of the sharp contrast this makes with the Burke and Abrams of the next two chapters] but the immediate causes, in the literal sense of that word, which have made the things what they are and rendered them capable of affecting our minds as they do, and more especially those causes which involve the efforts of human beings, whether politicians, scientists, philosophers, or ar- tists, to solve successfully the particular problems inherent in their situations and tasks. I have therefore sought for principles and methods of inquiry that might give me, as fully as possible, knowl- edge of this kind and provide a basis, at the same time, for *judg-*

ments of value appropriate to the various sorts of ends which such a consideration would reveal. [P. xvi; my italics]

We should underline here just how much has by now been ruled out by Crane the monist—how much, that is, that Crane the pluralist would rule back in for critics with other purposes. In choosing to pursue *knowledge* of the *literal causes* that have produced a *particular poem*, and in defining those causes as precisely the choices, good and bad, that the poet has made in solving or failing to solve compositional problems, Crane has carved out a much narrower domain than his readers have generally recognized. But every stroke of the carving is made with an implicit escape clause in mind: *if* you do *not* want to have knowledge of poems as successful or unsuccessful solutions to compositional problems, you may legitimately pursue innumerable other questions with other methods. You may, that is, so long as you do not confuse other purposes with my cognitive purposes, other subjects with my subject, and so on. Our pluralism cannot lead us to accept *conflicting* answers to the precise question of how or how well "Surgical Ward" is made: it was made only once, by only one poet, and Auden's intuitive conception of the poem's unity, the conception that determined when he felt he had completed his task, could have been only one, not many. This will be true no matter how complex or ambivalent that intuition is and regardless of how many different critical statements are generated in the effort to talk about how the poem works. Of course he may have botched the job, but that is another matter entirely—one that the critic must learn to judge.*

Thus if Crane were given our pile of protocols about "Surgical Ward," his first step would be an elaborate sorting according to purpose, and his second would be to attempt a meeting among those who claimed to offer a reasoned judgment of how it is put together.

We can best see how this might work by now changing the nature

---

*The assumption that widely praised literary works will prove to be unified was more widely shared in 1950 than in 1979. Though many New Critics then expected to find irony and ambiguity in every good poem, they also expected to find these qualities somehow composed into a higher unity. But recently it has become increasingly fashionable to argue that it is precisely disunity that marks every truly great literary work. See for example, John Bayley, *The Uses of Division: Unity and Disharmony in Literature* (London: Chatto & Windus, 1976). Obviously, no true issue is joined by noting that Crane sought unities and that Bayley, along with Morse Peckham, Paul de Man, and dozens of others, seek disunities; the meanings of such terms shift cruelly, and insofar as they are terms of praise they inescapably imply each other: no unity will be praiseworthy unless it unites what might in other hands have remained disparate, and no disunity will even be recognizable or mentionable, let alone praiseworthy, except in relation to some common dimension implying a possible higher unity, even if that unity exists exclusively in the critic's mind.

of our original experiment. Instead of asking our gathering of critics to say what they think is most important about "Surgical Ward," suppose we give them four different "Surgical Wards" and ask for a reasoned evaluation of each. Which version is best? We know already that some critics will refuse the task, since, for them, preference is "only a matter of taste." But there will be an abundance of good folk left in our examination room, and we give them first an improved version, making the last three lines more regular (I italicize the changes):

Sonnet XIV

They are and suffer; that is all they do:
A bandage hides the place where each is living,
His knowledge of the world restricted to
A treatment *metal* instruments are giving.

They lie apart like epochs from each other
(Truth in their sense is how much they can bear;
It is not talk like ours but groans they smother),
From us remote as plants: we stand elsewhere.

For who when healthy can become a foot?
Even a scratch we can't recall when cured,
But are boist*er*ous in a moment and believe

Reality is never injured, cannot
Imagine isolation: *joy can be* shared,
And anger, and the idea of love.

The original (p. 1) exhibited a radically irregular meter in the final three lines. Indeed, its ending gets curiouser and curiouser the longer one looks at it. Counting syllables, we might be led to convert it into a fifteen-line poem.

> In the common world of the uninjured,
> And cannot imagine isolation.
> Only happiness is shared, and anger,
> And the idea of love.

We no longer have a sonnet, of course, because all the world knows that a sonnet has fourteen, not fifteen, lines. Our new version has partially obscured the half-rhymes of foot/cannot and cured/shared, but it has dramatized the existence of three ten-syllable lines followed by an appendix. A strangely irregular "sonnet" indeed.

"Sonnet XIV" changes "Surgical Ward" toward greater regularity of meter, though to do so it has had to make some slight changes in sense. On the other hand, it has gained a bit of alliteration (jured/gine/joy). It does offer a neat three lines with about the "right" number of syllables each (11/11/9).

If we are troubled still by some irregularities, we can go further and make a more regular version, one that would conclude, for example, like this:

> But rally in a moment and believe
> In common worlds of whole and hale; cannot
> Imagine isolation. Only joy
> Is shared, and anger, and longing for love.

If we were still troubled by the messy rhythm of the final line, we might go on tinkering until we got it right.

A fourth version might move in another direction: let us make it identical with "Surgical Ward" except for three words, and call it "Common Lot":

> ... *Yet* only *pain* is shared,
> And anger, and the *illusion* of love.

Now the meaning of the whole poem has been radically changed.

Whatever we may think of the difficulty of the task we have given our critics, it is now relatively specific: Say whether or why one of the four versions is better than another.

The Plurality of Definitions of "Surgical Ward" as Subject

We collect our new protocols and find them almost as wildly diverse as the originals. All ostensibly serve the same end, a reasoned ranking of four differing structures, but they present an overwhelming variety of notions about what the poem is or "what it is trying to be" and hence about appropriate criteria.

Nothing surprising in this. What is surprising, in a time when many critics talk like Crane about how what we see depends on what we look for, is that differences of definition of *what* a poem is are so seldom recognized as a prime reason for the failure of critics to meet in their interpretations.

The question of whether a "text" has a determinate meaning is not in itself a single determinate question. It can be made determinate only by deciding which of many possible definitions—or placements—of the poem we choose to employ.* We might define all four "Surgical Wards" as only what *readers* make of them, or as fluid moments in an eternal flow of a language-that-is-building-itself, or as signs of a given culture's transformations of the institution of writing. We may very well conclude then, as many are doing, that "the same text authorizes innumerable interpretations: There is no 'correct' interpretation . . .; reading is never the objective identifying of a sense but the importation of meaning into a text which has no meaning 'in itself.'" (See p. 186, below.) Or shall we commit one or another version of the intentional fallacy by placing the true poem in its author, the public words serving only as a trace of his intuition? Or shall we follow Michael Riffaterre, who tells us that the poem *cannot* have *any* reference outside itself, since "representation of reality is a merely verbal construct in which meaning is achieved by reference from words to words, not to things."[5] Some tell us, as does Crane the formal critic, that poems are poems, made things, made objects that "imitate" reality; to do so is to commit Riffaterre's "fallacy." Others just as clearly see poems as communications between authors and readers. Kenneth Burke, as we shall see in chapter 3, would insist that poems are not primarily "systems of signs" but symbolic actions, deeds in a human drama. And so on. Each attempt at the one right location demands a different practice in the critic; most of them are advanced with words like "must" and "necessarily," implying strong monistic assumptions.

For Crane the pluralist the poem *is* many things, found in many places. It takes no great semantic sophistication to discover not only that critics claim the poem *to be* many different things but that all forms of the verb *to be* are themselves radically ambiguous in such statements. When some critics say that "Surgical Ward" *is* X, they will mean the "is" as literally as they would mean it in the sentence "My finger is a part of my body." But others will mean various metaphorical or analogical connections. We must return to this distinction when we come to method.

If the range of "referents" for the word "poem" is broader than any semanticist has traced, the sources of criteria for judging our four versions are almost unlimited.

*For an inconclusive discussion of determinate meanings, see "The Limits of Pluralism"—an exchange among M. H. Abrams, J. Hillis Miller, and myself—in *Critical Inquiry* 3 (Spring 1977): 407–47. Some parts of my essay are adapted here and in chapters 5–7.

Analogical Placements

In many of our imaginary protocols, the four versions are all instances or parts or analogues of something larger or realer or deeper or higher: of the history of all poetry, of all human statement, of all imaginative life, of all verbal constructs, of all systems of signs, of all expressions of human nature, of all manifestations of the spirit of God, of all connections with some other fundamental reality, of all battles with the nonreality of the empty abyss. Most of these placements can yield criteria, irrefutable within a chosen language, self-evidently false or inadequate when viewed in any other language.

Many critics have argued, for example, that because life is full of contradictory impulses, and because a poem *is* one kind of statement about life, good poems must reflect contradictory impulses; they must, as Cleanth Brooks and other New Critics claimed, take into account what can be said against themselves. Others have argued, within a similar deductive structure but working from different premises, that all good poetry rebels, or resists, or shouts "No!", or confirms us in our being, or affirms hope, or enhances our lives, or unites all humanity in brotherhood. One can imagine either a naive advocate of any of these views, who would stand helpless before the four versions, like an especially confused Buridan's ass, because they all contain equal measures of this or that; or more sophisticated folk, who might work closely with the differences I have introduced (for example, the substitution of "longing" for "idea") and conclude that this or that version is superior because it realizes what "the nature of poetry," or some other construct, requires each poem to realize.

Crane would say that no decisions at this general level can tell us much about which of two poems is better made, since both good and bad poems can be written "containing" equivalent amounts of irony or incongruity or (and the list could go on indefinitely) defiance, affirmation, questions, or answers; in the undifferentiated subject of life or truth about it, we have no *literal, causal* grounds for judgment—no grounds related to the specific human achievement of making this poem. Such subjects affect the composition of poems at most as necessary causes, never as sufficient.

The pluralist need not reject all general evaluations as meaningless; he will ask only that critics who make them sharpen their awareness of the way they are using their terms and of the way their judgments spring from their definitions of poems as instances of something more important than any individual poem. And then of course we can ask them to defend as best they can the philosophical, anthropological, psychological, or religious beliefs employed at this general level.

Moving to somewhat narrower general concepts, we find protocols that see the four poems as instances of poetry or the poetic and, in doing so, employ theories of poetry-as-poetry that may sound quite literal. A poem here is no longer a statement about life, to be judged for its truth like other statements; it is a *poem*, by God, and it should therefore be judged for its success in using poetic devices. Let us judge the poem as poem, and not another thing.

If we know what poetry is, and if "Surgical Ward" is trying to be a poem, then of course we can judge its attempt by reference to our knowledge. Most new schools of poetry thus work with what seem self-evident standards—what is or is not poetic diction, what is or is not a proper verse form or appropriate style of "free" verse. The modern movement in poetry made much fun of older notions that some subjects or meters are inherently more poetic than others. But each new program soon becomes programmatic, and we have wave after wave of standards for "the truest poetry," all of them still seeing the poem as aspiring to meet conditions set by the critic's generalizations: richness of imagery (all four versions fail miserably in the sestet); multiplicity or ambiguity ("Common Lot" wins hands down); musical variety ("Surgical Ward" is supreme); musical regularity ("Sonnet XIV" is best); insistence on its own textuality and resistance to external reference (all four rather feeble).

Literal as such talk may sometimes seem, the four versions are being judged as instances of general qualities that are "bigger" than they are. The results could thus not serve Crane in his quest for knowledge about qualities and causes. They can still be allowed into the house of criticism, provided their proponents recognize the way in which the judgments do in fact depend upon a prior acceptance of the general standards. Presumably some of those standards can be defended legitimately; surely there must be *some* general standards of musicality, decorum, originality, suggestive indeterminacy, or what not. But arguments in their defense are in practice so difficult that the attempt usually leads, like discussions on the first level, to an embattled exchange of dogmatic assertions.

Working at about the same level of generality, but turning from form and technique to theme, we find critics who refer their judgments to a truly *modern* poetry, that is, to "what poetry should or must do *today*." Many partisans of this or that revolutionary movement or mode of social analysis have announced waves of the future, and, according to most of them, none of the four versions of "Surgical Ward" would be worth talking about. For some, "Common Lot" might be superior because it is more bitter, more in tune with "what we know" about our lives. But don't expect any such criteria, Crane would say, to discriminate among the qualities of two poems each expressing the "right" degree of bitterness. On the other hand, do not expect to refute critics who apply such general criteria simply by showing their limitations. Not to be able to discriminate formal differences is a fault only when viewed from other perspectives, and there is no reason why critics who care more about furthering the revolution, say, than about whether poems are well made should be required to bow to our ukase.

We could go on narrowing down, through "the nature of the lyric" to "the nature of the sonnet" or, in a different dimension, to the "nature of Auden's poetic gifts." Any of these might suggest judgments worth attending to, but none could tell us which poem was *made* best; none could have helped Auden decide whether he needed to revise one more time. Consequently, none can tell us much about what Crane would consider the specific artistic excellence or lack of it in any one version.

Suppose we narrow, then, to an even smaller class: "sonnets about physical suffering" or "sonnets about human isolation in suffering"? For Crane's purposes even such relatively precise "genres" based on thematic statements would be useless. We can demonstrate that this is so by asking: *If* what you want to perfect is a "sonnet about physical suffering," what follows in your efforts to revise *this* poem? Nothing follows. Poems "about" human suffering can in fact do or be anything under the sun, as every tragic farce or parody of mourning verse will show.

Inhuman Henry
or
Cruelty to Fabulous Animals

O would you know why Henry sleeps,
And why his mourning Mother weeps,
And why his weeping Mother mourns?
He was unkind to unicorns.

A. E. Housman's "bloody-minded boy" releases a lion, so that it will eat the unicorns; the unicorns flee, and the lion, "Returning home in temper bad," in three tragic quatrains devours protesting Henry.

And now you know why Henry sleeps,
And why his Mother mourns and weeps.

Viewed merely *as instances* of statement about isolated human suffering, Housman's poem and Auden's and my reworkings of
Auden's poem are thus all equal, since they are equally "about" it.
But in practice, of course, no critic means any such inanity when he
says things like " 'Surgical Ward' is a poem about human suffering."
Every generalizing critic depends on introducing, perhaps covertly,
standards like "Good poems ought to *do justice* to the *subtleties* of the
human experience of suffering"; thus Housman's poem is clearly
"less important" or "less significant" than Auden's.

The trouble is that "Inhuman Henry" quite obviously never aspires
to that class at all. It aspires only to be a witty parody. It succeeds as
well at that as we could ask, but how are we to apply a statement
judging that success to the task of distinguishing the four "Surgical
Wards"? We must seek whatever kind of argument is able to show
that one *kind of human intention*, embodying a certain attitude toward
suffering, is for some reason superior to other kinds. Most of us,
except when theorizing about the relativity of all values, agree that
some literary intentions and some human attitudes *are* superior to
others; for example, a good sonnet by Keats is somehow more to be
valued than the best limerick ever written; George Eliot's novels are
really more profound than Charles Reade's. There is no inherent
reason why critical argument cannot be fruitful about such matters,
provided that aspirants recognize what issues they are in fact discussing and what philosophical difficulties are involved in resolving
them.

If we move to an even more precisely defined class, "poems that
show an ostensibly happy and whole person seriously contemplating
human suffering," we seem to get much closer, because we are beginning to connect an emotional direction or point with our theme: a
mood of serious contemplation of serious human subjects. We are
clearly moving toward what we want, and the question is: How close
to the detailed structure and effect of this particular poem must we go
before we have a description useful to us as critics seeking knowledge
about quality, useful because it must have been intuitively useful to
the poet as he composed and revised?

Some modern critics, following Croce, would say that we must not
stop in this process of rejecting the general until we have come to
the unique poem: that is all we know and all we can ever know. What
we have is *this* poem, which expresses a unique intuition, and then

this one, also *sui generis*, and *this* one, and *this* one. Thus in changing a word or a line or a meter, we have really written poems entirely different and incommensurate with the original. Some critics of Crane have said that this is really his position; he is so radically particularist that he can only skip from work to work, unable to carry with him any accumulation of criteria.

If one were driven into such a position by seeking literal causes of particular achievements, criticism in the sense of reasoned judgment would finally be silenced. Description, pointing, exhortation, comparison—these could survive; but each of our "Surgical Wards" (and all the other unlimited "Surgical Wards" we might construct by gross or subtle changes) would subsist together in a grand democratic equality, with all our judgments reduced to matters of taste.

Crane escapes from this trap not by reinstituting the process of applying a general criterion to particulars. The logical form of the evaluative act must be revised. No generalization of whatever kind applies to human makings in the way that scientific generalizations apply to particulars. To be sound, a scientific generalization must cover particulars in such a way that, if I know the generalization, I will know the particular. I will know that the particular is a "good" one of the kind I have described if it functions in the way predicted. An adequate general definition of a pig or a pomegranate will enable me not only to predict the essential qualities of every pig or pomegranate; it will enable me to judge that a "three-legged one is a monster" or that "one without seeds lacks the power of reproduction." But as Crane's colleague Elder Olson has recently said in clarifying the problem of evaluation, when dealing with works of art we have no way of proceeding from predetermined categories to knowledge about particulars: "I cannot know any particulars about *Hamlet* because I know about tragedy. Euripides' *Tyro* is a lost work; it was a tragedy; what do you know of it?"[6]

I shall return to this problem later, when we look at method, but it should suffice here to say that for Crane we do value poems for their individual quality, but, since we intuit generalizable form from the experience of a particular poem, proceeding *a posteriori* rather than *a priori*, we can find *in the structure of the poem* the standards for judging not only the success or failure of its parts but also the relative success of other poems aspiring, as it were, to realize the same form.

It is true that we still make use of certain general qualities: unity, wholeness, success in achieving what is implied in the kind. But the qualities are dictated to us by the poem. If we find poems, as in the modern period we well may, that do not aspire to succeed as ordered achievements of a discernible kind, we shall find ourselves, as critics in this mode, impotent and silent before them. Only works that in fact are made with art can yield their art to our gaze.

We shall not, of course, take writers at their own word when they tell us that they have written anti-art, art without form or intention. There is considerable testimony by now from such nonartists about how hard it is to achieve their nonintentions. Still, we formalists can be completely silenced by silence, by blank pages, by randomized nonsense syllables. Even short of such extremes, we can easily be forced to recognize that a given nonwork offers a stronger invitation to social or psychoanalytical modes of criticism than to our interest in human achievement. And if asked to defend the bias revealed in our using the word "achievement" in this way, we shall be forced, like everyone when first principles are challenged, into philosophical, anthropological, or religious debate quite distinct in kind from our chosen mode of literary criticism.

Literal Placements

One might think that we were nearing the end of ambiguities of subject matter when we place to one side all critics except those who agree to talk only of what the poem literally is, as something made, in its particular structure rather than as an instance of larger or deeper matters. We shall all agree now, surely, that the literal structure of this poem is something we can define unequivocally, and we can thus begin to make judgments about the effectiveness with which the structure is made.

But in fact we are only beginning. *The Languages of Criticism and the Structure of Poetry* spends most of its pages discriminating among critics who have already agreed to talk about *the* structure of particular poems. And "Surgical Ward" would in their views turn out to be an extraordinary variety of structures. Perhaps what critics experience *as readers* differs much less than their ways of describing their experiences would suggest. I believe that it does. But since we have no way to test that likelihood—since, as we work together, all we have is our talk—we still face a bewildering variety of plausible descriptions of what sort of thing this poem "really" is.

To make our way into that plurality will always require some sort of organizing scheme, and organizing schemes will themselves be of many kinds. Crane's scheme has been implicit throughout my account so far. His habit was, as we shall see more fully later on, to pursue precise distinctions of discrete entities, and that habit produces, when applied to the possible statements about where the poem's structure *really is*, only about four or five possibilities.

Often enough Crane seems to be operating with a chart as simple as that used by M. H. Abrams at the beginning of *The Mirror and the Lamp:*[7]

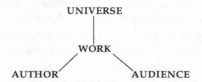

I call the chart simple, though we have already seen that its simplicity disappears the moment we take seriously the notion that *the* poem *is* in all four places. If a poem *really is* not just some one right view of it, if there really are at least four places where *the* literal poem is to be found, then controversy about *the* poem becomes pointless until the controversialists have agreed to locate themselves and the poem together.

Crane often used this little fourfold scheme. But it is in the nature of such charts that they sooner or later reveal inadequacies. Some of the actual phenomena have had to be stretched or compressed to fit the chart, and soon one discovers that Crane himself should have recognized that his own chart was implicitly fivefold; he was so intent on a synchronic scheme of the possibilities for criticism, once it has freed itself from the kind of literary history he and the New Critics thought had unduly bound it, that he did not grant equal rights to a *historical* placement (or perhaps one should say *dis*placement). Though literary history was always important to Crane, both as an end in itself and as a necessary tool for the reconstruction of the poem's reality, it never seemed to figure as one legitimate source of *definition* of the subject matter. Yet surely, as many historians tell us, the poem *really is* a moment in a process, or in many processes, just as the critic's views can be placed as "only" moments in processes that will melt all efforts at a synchronic freezing. The full force of what such a fluid placement might mean can be shown only when we come, in chapter 4, to M. H. Abrams' historical view of a poem by Wordsworth.

We now see, implicit in Crane's pluralism of discrete modes, a fivefold classification of "Some Definitions, *All Claiming To Be of Literal Structures*, of What 'Surgical Ward' Really Is."

But further complications remain, because each of the five locations will generate—has indeed generated—rival versions of "the poem" with differing consequences for criticism. What is worse (from the point of view of any would-be monist), the five positions will multiply as they interrelate, so that if one combines the "poem that is in the author" with "the poem that is in the audience" and thinks about the vector between them, passing through "the poem as autonomous form," one discovers a variety of rhetorical criticisms. And if one thinks of a vector running from the "mimetic" placement to the audience, relating truths reflected in the poem to the production or destruction of souls or psyches, one finds varieties of literal ethical criticism matching the analogical modes mentioned earlier; the poem now *is* an instrument, to be judged for its powers of making or breaking or shaping a given kind of person or of realizing for persons a given kind of truth. And so on, through innumerable possible interrelations.

Remembering that we can escape this kind of complexity only by clenching onto a monism or by relaxing into skepticism, let us draw all this together within the radically simplified limits of a single page.

It is at this point, just when we may feel like some desperate refugee from *The Pooh Perplex*, that we begin to discern what rich profit such cataloguing can yield. We are freed from pointless controversy about where the poem is found and what one must properly do with it when it is found. Whole glossaries of epithets about fallacies and heresies now reveal their vacuity, because critics working inside the limits of any one "fallacious" view can in fact work together in critical understanding.

Needless to say, in practical criticism we never consult such a chart. We consult the poem, respond to it, put our responses into words, and then compare our words with those of other readers. Once performed, the charting does its work silently, behind the scenes, a steady reminder of just how tiny a settlement anyone ever establishes in the immense wild domain of any work's potential interest for mankind.

If anyone thinks that he can reduce the variety by asking, "Yes, but what *is* 'Surgical Ward' *qua* poem or *qua* work of art?" he is forgetting that any one of the definitions will assume that question as the one that is being answered. A critic working in any corner of the chart could quite happily talk of "the poem *qua* art," "the poem *as* poem," and "the true art of the poem," and he could quite innocently use words like "is" and "*qua*" as if they belonged only to him.

To anyone working in full conviction of the exclusive rightness of any one of these definitions, all the others will seem at best analogical

SOME LITERAL VERSIONS OF WHAT AUDEN'S "SURGICAL WARD" *IS*

Surgical Ward4 :
"Mimetic" Criticism

As an imitation of an imitation
As a direct imitation of truth, of a
  kind of knowledge (or error)
  (metaphysical, religious,
  political, sexual,
  psychological, sociological,
  etc.)
As a reflection of archetypes
Etc.

Surgical Ward5 :
"Historical" and "Scholarly"
  Criticism

As a sign of, or product of,
  its epoch
As a culmination of, or
  founder of, trends in
  genre or convention: influence
As a poem about poems, about
  its anxious combat with
  its predecessors, etc.
As a language produced by
  history of language
Etc.

Surgical Ward1 : "Objective" or "Poetic" Criticism

As an object made of human character, thought, and feeling
As a structure of words referring to other words, internally
As a pattern of sounds
As a formed idea, or emotion,
  or combination of these
As a portrait of the speaker
As a pattern of paradox, or irony,
  or ambiguity
Etc.

Surgical Ward2 :
"Expressive" or "Biographical"
  Criticism

As an expression of Auden's creativity
  or his participation in the great
    Imagination
  or his imaginative gifts
  or his craft
  or his psychology
  or his surgical operation
  or his creative act (the true poem)
As a symbolic action
  (solving his personal problems)
Etc.

Surgical Ward3 :
"Response" or "Rhetorical"
  Criticism

As a reader's creative act
As a sign of trends in,
  or varieties of, audiences
As a trigger for emotions or
  thoughts
As a symbolic action (solving
  problems of audience)
As an incitement to action
As a stimulus to the critic's
  new act of creation
Etc.

(or, if that word is avoided, "secondary") and at worst completely irrelevant or destructive. But all of the definitions differ as a group from the definitions of the openly analogical critics we reviewed earlier.

A Digression on Crane's Notion of the Literal Poem

The chart I have constructed is not greatly different from Crane's picture of the critical world, but he would never have called my four peripheral placements "literal." Crane always thought of himself as having chosen the one literal definition, in contrast to those definitions that relate the poem, by "negative or positive analogy," to something else. Poems—or at least some poems—*are* things made, literally; and to say that *Pride and Prejudice* is a "form of language" or a "communication from Jane Austen to the reader," or what not, is to analogize the created object to other things, like orations or scientific treatises.

Crane never acknowledged that his own drive for literal discriminations could properly seem analogical to other critics. But to see a poem as a made object, more like a statue than a political speech or a philosophical inquiry, is "self-evidently"—from other points of view—to see it as something it is not. Writing a poem, reading a poem—these are obviously not the same as carving a statue, viewing a statue; nor is carving a statue literally the same as making a table or an axe (another analogy entailed in Crane's thought). Writing a poem is literally writing a poem, true enough; but what is that? The act entails all these other troublesome matters that critics insist on intruding into our discussion, matters most of which never occur to anyone talking about axe-making, statue-carving, or even the *construction* of the poem. (See Burke on *his* "literal" program, below, p. 133.)

Crane could perhaps claim—though I don't quite see how he could argue for the claim except with assumptions that already included it—that making a poem is *more* like other acts of making than it is like other doings or thinkings. But it is still *like* them, and a poem is no more exhausted literally by talking of the way it holds together than a human being is literally "covered" by talking of genetics or physiology or environment. Crane chose to give a privileged literalness to the art of the construction, and he exercised this choice not only when practicing his "Aristotelian" monism but when advocating pluralism; this could be especially misleading when he tried to deal with works whose authors saw themselves primarily as acting on the world or promulgating truths rather than polishing off fine carvings.

The Search for Sufficient Causes

The value of Crane's chosen mode does not, however, depend on a privileged claim to literal reference. What marks the mode is the search for particular causes that operated in the poet's art, in some sense within his control. Whether such causes are any more literal than all the other forces that move into and out of poems, as revealed by other modes, the fact remains that Crane's search for maximum precision in pointing to what he called "reasons of art" yielded a kind of knowledge about poems that is inaccessible to other modes. If we want to know whether and how "Surgical Ward" succeeds as a making, we must find a way to deal with that making—not just as a historian of sonnets would do, in showing how conventions are realized, but in some way that will account for the many choices, conscious and unconscious, that brought it into existence. One thing we cannot doubt is that every poem was made by someone practicing an art that nobody but the poet had ever practiced in quite this way before; every poem is in this sense unique. Judgments on it are thus most pertinent for practical criticism when they are judgments of those choices, not of general concepts, like the poet's "genius" or of the particulars of how it was in fact written, draft by draft, but of the specific manifestation of a particular art in *this* poem.

It is thus not enough simply to work in the center of the chart, with "Surgical Ward$_1$." If we are to appraise the art of the four versions, we will seek descriptions of the wholes and of their parts so precise that they could not apply to any other objects in the world. Readers who know much criticism by Crane and his colleagues will now see why one cannot mimic it in short compass. It requires scope. Nothing they ever wrote can quite match the 70:1 ratio of comment to text in Roland Barthes' *S/Z*, but the Crane who would spend weeks of class time on "To His Coy Mistress" or "The Killers" would require many pages to explain the concentrated achievement of "Surgical Ward."

Such a complete "poetic" analysis of "Surgical Ward" I shall not attempt here, partly because my main subject is Crane's pluralism, not his practice of a chosen mode, and partly I suppose because it is against my own temperament. (Readers may want to consult Crane on *Tom Jones* or *Persuasion*, or "The Short Happy Life of Francis Macomber,"[8] to see the full energy and rigor of this passionate discriminator.) But after all this prolonged sorting, I must at least hint at where his search for precise standards might lead in answering the question I have raised about the four versions.

Crane would of course strike first and last for some kind of satisfactory picture of the whole, so that all reference to parts could be functional—referred not to abstract qualities desirable in all or some poems but to the precise demands of this poem. How have (1) the object represented (character in thought and action) and (2) the verbal devices, the imagery, the ironies, the meter and the rhyme, and (3) the technical control of point of view, all been made into a complex unity that produces (4) an effect that can be talked about because it is not just one reader's accidental response but is somehow demonstrably in the poem? *This* monism is thus unusually comprehensive, for it "covers" author's intentions, readers' responses, the "world" reflected in the poem, and the potentialities of the medium. But it finds all of these *in* the poem, the life of each part implicit in its relations to an achieved whole.

"Surgical Ward," our first version, is clearly a representation, or "imitation," of a sensitive, thoughtful man (it might be a woman, except for the author's name) visiting a scene of intense human suffering. Struck first by the thought that the victims, in their suffering, are totally isolated from their fellows, because only their pain is real to them, the troubled visitor then thinks of how that totally isolated self-absorption contrasts with the unthinking conviviality of the healthy. The healthy visitor then attempts to assert what the contrast means, intellectually and emotionally, about isolation and community among the miserable and among the happy. The poem obviously seeks to engage the reader in the emotion-charged thought of the speaker, without any explicit distancing whatever.

When we commit the "heresy of paraphrase" in this form, the results are more likely to seem banal than many paraphrastic statements of theme. All four versions offer invitations to innumerable thematic statements, of pain/pleasure, life/death, isolation/community, complacency/awareness, simplicity/complexity, appearance/reality, selfishness/altruism, pretended altruism/real egotism, body/spirit, verbal language/wisdom of the body, and so on, in almost unlimited permutations and combinations. One could write dozens of thematic accounts of "Surgical Ward," all of them "fitting the facts" and many of them more novel and interesting than my summary of the one literal action.* Their uselessness for our chosen task lies in the fact that all of them could as easily be derived from hundreds, perhaps thousands, of other literary works, and some would be discoverable in all literature.

My more obvious summary of a human event is shared with a very

---

*Those who insist on every poem's having many meanings are obviously in this sense—and in this sense only—quite correct. Taken as "meaning," every poem will accommodate innumerable readings (except, of course, those deliberately didactic works ordered rigorously toward a single intellectual point). But only those poems that have been made to be ambiguous will be ambiguous for readers working with Crane's precise "topic."

small number of literary works, perhaps with none except these four versions, though it will be shared, if I have been accurate, by every reader. Thus, in its obviousness lies its strength: it provides a reference point precise enough to allow confirmation or falsification by any experienced reader who looks at the poem; it is corrigible, unlike most "readings"—amenable to improvement by readers working together; and it can become a critical reference for all comments about details. In short, if you and I can agree about how the poem is "plotted" or formed, ruling out all other questions, however interesting, we can have productive discussion about whether the form has been realized well.

By beginning with simple "literal" description of what happens, we have earned the right to insist that any critic who wants to join our discussion must either honor our banalities or show where we have erred. We can thus move on to other qualifications required of those whose judgments we will take into account, here in this narrow corner of the house of criticism. They can surely be asked not only to note the radical shift between the precisely rhymed and metered octet and the curiously irregular sestet (all careful readers of any persuasion will have done that) but to decide whether that shift strengthens whatever effect is attributed to the pictured event I have abstracted. Does the shift in meter support the change of scene from those who suffer to those who *stand elsewhere*?

Similarly, we shall push for an explanation of "manner" or "technique of dramatization." Why is the first scene vividly dramatized, with many images, while the second is all abstraction? No statement about the structure of the poem will satisfy us if it fails to relate the choices about dramatic "showing" and summary "telling" to the heightening of the whole.

Finally, though we shall, like thematic critics, deal with the poem's thought, we shall work hard to insure that the thought we find is *in* the poem, and we shall try to decide whether and how it contributes to the whole. A crux for us will thus be the strange difference, in the final lines, between (solid?) happiness and (undermining?) anger, both unqualified, and "the (mere?) *idea* of love."

In short, we shall not expect fruitful discussion of our chosen question with any critic who refuses to deal with the structure of the poem as human event, including the thought and emotion of the speaker (as "object"), the verbal heightenings (as "means"), and the use of point-of-view (as "manner"), all ordered under some unifying *end* implicit in the whole and thus in every part.

The Use of "Extrinsic" Evidence

We cannot know in advance of reading any particular poem whether, in answering such questions, we shall be forced to seek evidence "outside" the poem. Unlike some of our cousins, who also seek the poem-as-poem, we have no dogmas ruling out this or that kind of evidence. Just as Crane found that, in puzzling out what Swift had in mind with the Houyhnhnms, it was useful to discover how the notion of rational horses had been used by Swift's contemporaries (*Humanities*, pp. 261–82), so we must at least consider the possibility that "Surgical Ward" cannot be fully appreciated outside the context in which it originally appeared. We may need to learn a good deal about Auden, at the time of writing, before we can discover a satisfactory account of what the poem seeks to be or do and hence of whether the parts are as effective as they might be.

But however long our excursion into historical backgrounds, we finally come back to a moment when we are ourselves forced to make critical decisions similar to those the poet made; we raise ourselves as far as possible toward the level of creative activity that animated his many choices, and we decide whether his choices are at least as good as we could have managed.

We are not troubled by the seeming arrogance of such judgments or by the circularity of our hermeneutics. Our arrogance is no different from that of every critic who makes a value judgment, except that we have made an extraordinary effort to enter the artist's world; and the hermeneutical circle we have entered is precisely the one in which the artist himself worked as he revised the parts of a poem toward the perfection of a whole that was found, if at all, only at the end.

This is the moment to reveal that both "Surgical Ward" and "Sonnet XIV" are by Auden. "Surgical Ward" was published first, but under the simple title "XVII" in the sonnet sequence "In Time of War," in *Journey to a War* (1939), Auden's "report" from the war in China. It was then at some point tightened up into "Sonnet XIV" for the "Sonnets from China," published in the *Collected Shorter Poems* of 1966. Auden seems finally to have preferred the revision; it is what appears in the posthumous *Collected Poems* of 1976.

The trouble with such knowledge is that when we pursue it, tracing the two versions back to their two sonnet sequences, we find that Auden has made innumerable changes for "Sonnets from China," eliminating some sonnets, changing the order of some, adding a sonnet at the end, and revising most sonnets at least slightly and some almost beyond recognition. There are so many changes that one might at first be tempted to say that the two versions exist in incommensurable contexts.

Auden said of his revisions that he never made them on "ideological" grounds; he revised "only the language" when it seemed "lifeless, prolix or painful to the ear. Re-reading my poems, I find that in the nineteen-thirties I fell into some very slovenly verbal habits."[9] If the two contexts were in fact "ideologically" different, and if the two versions were thus intended as different "parts" contributing to different "wholes," we should be forced to give up any effort to make a direct comparison between them; in our search for a reasoned judgment we must then move upward from the two sonnets to the sequences themselves.

Fortunately for the purposes of our exercise, the two sequences, though greatly different in detail (including, for our sonnet, a different immediate predecessor and successor), provide roughly the same emotional and intellectual surroundings. Both sequences are, in fact, helpful in elaborating the same intent for those final lines, in either version. I cannot defend this judgment in detail here; to do so properly would require a long chapter in itself, so many and so interesting are Auden's changes. But it is important to recognize that much of what the sonnet, taken by itself, leaves to conjecture becomes clear when one reads either sequence, and that much of what may be taken as emotionally weak in the sestet is buttressed by the sonnet's neighbors.

Both "In Time of War" and "Sonnets from China" present a kind of history of man, from the expulsion from the Garden down to the present dreadful time: 1936–39. Much of each sequence consists of extended meditation on the Fall, on what it means to be creatures who have known a Garden, who in "our lost condition" (TW XXII; SC XVII) long for the condition of the Garden, and who see what the world is:

> And maps can really point to places
> Where life is evil now:
> Nanking; Dachau.
>
> (TW XVI; SC XII)

It is a time when, as in all fallen time, man "could not find the earth which he had paid for, / Nor feel the love that he knew all about" (TW VIII; slightly different in SC VIII). Again:

> Yes, we are going to suffer, now; the sky
> Throbs like a feverish forehead; pain is real;
>
> (TW XIV; not in SC)

It is a time when men are "free / And isolated like the very rich; / Remote like savants..." (TW XV; not in SC), a time when "all the rivers and the railways run / Away from Neighbourhood as from a curse" (TW XX; not in SC).

Perhaps most important for our purposes, in both sequences it is a radically ambiguous time; the relation of happiness to pain, of love to hate, is especially hard to resolve with any affirmation. To affirm happiness or love as real in such a time is to risk absurdity:

> Think in this year what pleased the dancers best:
> When Austria died and China was forsaken,
> Shanghai in flames and Teruel retaken,
>
> France put her case before the world; 'Partout
> Il y a de la joie.' America addressed
> The earth: 'Do you love me as I love you?'
>
> (TW XXII; slightly different in SC XVII)

Any unsureness we might have had about our reading of *anger* and *idea* in the final line is now removed: in sharing happiness in a time of war, which is all time, we are steadily and remorselessly reminded that

> We have no destiny assigned us:
> Nothing is certain but the body; we plan
> To better ourselves; the hospitals alone remind us
> Of the equality of man.
> . . . .
> We learn to pity and rebel.
>
> (TW XXV; not in SC)

Thus, though "In Time of War" may remind us more precisely of what was "on Auden's mind" at the time of original composition (the certainty of the body; hospitals; pain is real), in both sequences we move to the same general "condition": mourning for the "wounded myths" that once made children (or nations) good:

> Some lost a world they never understood,
> Some saw too clearly all that man was born for.

> Loss is their shadow-wife, Anxiety
> Receives them like a grand hotel...
>
>   (TW XXI; SC XVI)

Judgment at Last: This Poem of This Kind

Revising and revising, believing (with Valéry) that a poem is never finished, only abandoned, Auden made the changes we have seen in what perhaps we should now call "They Are and Suffer." Presumably he did so according to general standards of the sort he names, and presumably he felt that those general standards should override whatever particular intentions or "slovenly habits" led him to the first version.

Was he right?

Though looking at their history has helped us understand what is common to both poems and has sharpened our conviction about what "Surgical Ward" *means*, it has not provided us with an answer to Crane's kind of question: there is only this one sonnet in either sequence that attempts a visit and a meditation of the precise kind we have described. And it is in relation to that precise formal potentiality that we must judge the two actualizations, "Surgical Ward" and "Sonnet XIV."

Our close look at the four dimensions of the poem's structure enables us to face this task of judgment without skeptical retreat or reliance on critical dogma. The first version, "Surgical Ward," is clearly superior in most respects when we refer its elements back to the implicit powers of the "visit" that is common to all four versions. Auden's effort to tighten up the verse for "Sonnet XIV" was a (minor) mistake.

In both of Auden's versions the scene of bandaged suffering is portrayed in relatively tight verse, the rhymes precise, the meter fairly regular, the beat varied mainly to emphasize "truth," "théir sense," and the logical transition from *them* to *us*: "wé stánd elśewhére." But in "Surgical Ward" we escape this tightness in the sestet, both in sense and in prosody.

Just as the perhaps fatal illness, the subject of the octet, is reduced, first to foot trouble and then to a scratch, so the bindings of the verse are released with a "boist'rous," joyful explosion. The meter almost collapses: we *are* boist'rous, in our happy vitality. The metrical release has been carried about as far as it can go without turning into nonverse. At the same time, our emotional release is always under the pressure of our memory of how real those injured ones have seemed, partly because we shared the bindings of the regular verse; only for a moment have we now *believed in*, though not witnessed, the common world of the uninjured. And the conclusion thus "remembers" the octet; we have shared not just joy but anger and have found only the *idea* of love—in a line that is almost restrained to full regularity again. The contrast is thus between a vividly imagined world of suffering and the wishful abstractions of the sestet; in fact, pain-ridden isolation has been more fully imagined, and perhaps even more fully shared, than happiness. Thus the poem, which in both of Auden's versions deliberately turns on itself at the end, is in "Surgical Ward" given a metrical dissolution that underlines both our release from the bandaged world and our sense that assertions about the common world of joy are at best insecure half-truths.

Sonnet XIV sacrifices much of this internal reflexivity for prosodic regularity, and my own more regular version is even worse (p. 47). They both squander what is most effective in the original: an experimental use of broken conventions to deal with a precarious and abstract vision of a broken world that cannot fully escape the world of pain.

Even while questioning Auden's revision of the sestet, however, we can recognize that the revised octet has been made slightly more forceful: to replace the feeble "that the" with the concrete "metal," and the drama of "From us remote" for the wasteful "And are remote," heightens the original contrast between the vividly imagined world of suffering and the abstract world of joy.

In radical contrast, "Common Lot," which is mine, all mine, cannot be directly compared with "Surgical Ward" at all. What it changes is not a part of the "means" but the structure of the character's action and thought. The character who concludes his visit with the simplified, embittered reversal

> Yet only pain is shared,
> And anger, and the illusion of love.

is a different kind of man on a different kind of visit arriving at oversimplifications and falsehoods—and thus yielding different effects for the reader.

The resulting poem is a deformed mess; but if my general beliefs about life and the meaning of physical pain lead me to prefer sharp, embittered outbursts, however sloppy, to complex, ambiguous meditations, I may still choose this poem over the others. Better a formal failure with the right beliefs than a beautiful structure teaching error? But Crane would want to insist that the two problems be kept clearly distinct. "Common Lot" will have to be thoroughly revised if its *art* is to match that of either of Auden's versions.

This is not to say, obviously, that art or craft can be thought of as simply technique. Since our analysis of the poem has from the beginning included perceptions of human action, character, thought, and emotion, judgments about human importance will never be separable from our judgments of form. Crane's interpretation of Aristotle's term "magnitude" is significant here. Given two tragedies, one of a hero who, because of initial greatness, has a long way to fall, the other of a hero who moves from *near*-ruin to ruin, the first will be greater, "other things being equal." The judgment does not spring from any abstract critical principles about what art and life must be but from what everyone knows about both: it simply takes more artistic power to conceive and execute a big fall than a little one. To propel a pusillanimous slob to foredoomed destruction will require no great imaginative gifts, but to imagine what might plausibly destroy a Macbeth or an Othello will require the ability to imagine such figures in the first place and then to invent "destroyers" of equal power: those Desdemonas and Iagos, those Lady Macbeths, those plausible coincidences and implausible witches. The power to invent subjects with great magnitude is what finally distinguishes great artists from the merely successful. We can handle such questions, so long as we make clear what we are doing.

We see, then, that various critics talking about the four versions of "They Are and Suffer" will make seemingly contradictory judgments that may be reconcilable once they discover what each is talking about. All could agree, for example, that "Common Lot" is a botched job, though they will not agree about the *importance* of whether it is, or about whether, if lines 1–12 were revised to fit my ending, it would be better than the original. All could agree that "Sonnet XIV" was tightened in the service of general qualities, common to all sonnets, at the expense of particular "dissolutions" more appropriate to the original sonnet in its sequence. We shall not expect everyone to agree, however, that this or that rule about sonnets should or should not take precedence over particular functional dissolution—not, at least, without a different and much more difficult kind of debate.

Nor would they all by any means agree, finally, on whether a critic should work on any one of these questions in preference to any other. Nor will judgments made by those agreeing on any one direction of inquiry necessarily coincide. Not resolution of all debate about any one question but the possibility of intelligible debate is our goal.

If my aim were to defend Crane's practical criticism, I would pursue formal questions in even greater detail, and I would of course seek examples yielding less complicated results than we have found using Auden's versions. Among other matters, I would have to face more fully the issue of synonymy and the even more troublesome problem of the reality of literary kinds, or genres. But for an inquiry into Crane's pluralism it is sufficient to have illustrated his way of testing reasons about critical intuitions while accommodating other possible ways. We have found a shared knowledge that skepticism would deny us, a knowledge relative not to "how we were brought up" but only to the terms of our chosen mode. But we are also now too much aware of other modes to expect everyone to share our knowledge or the reasons with which we support it. We can talk about our conclusions only with those who willingly (if temporarily) embrace our primary choices: *this* subject, chosen from the plausible hundreds that human beings may legitimately prefer as the truest or most interesting "Surgical Ward." We shall not insist, except when we forget who and where we are, that other people see the thing our way. And we shall certainly not be surprised when we discover that critics who pursue the meanings of Auden's words regardless of the controls he provides should discover unlimited ambiguity. So long as they acknowledge that they are interpreting entirely different "texts" or "poems"—not the ordered choices Auden made but the possible makings of mankind—there can be no real debate but only, at most, a mutual lament about the opponent's lost opportunities.

METHOD

I have for many pages written as if we were unraveling two of our variables only, purpose and subject matter. But obviously, even as I wrote, I could not rule out method. Indeed, I could not avoid relying on one of many possible methods, even as I chose one of many purposes, made my loose catalogue of subject matters, and followed Crane in his effort to distinguish one from all the others. To pursue distinctions as he does is already to delimit what one can learn and say.

In other words, critics obviously differ not only in purposes and definitions of subjects but also in how they take hold of subjects. Not only is it true, Crane would say, that two critics uttering identical words about "Surgical Ward" may be saying entirely different things because they are talking about different poems; it is also true that even if they are in some sense talking about the same subject—let us say, "The patterns of isolation images in 'Surgical Ward' "—their talk may not be directly comparable because they have taken hold of that subject in radically different ways.

Lumping and Splitting

The most important single distinction that Crane drew among methods was between critics who, like himself, attempt precise discriminations of matters of fact and those who, committed to some basic analogy, pursue similarities that override the often obvious differences found in actual experience. The first kind seek clearly defined questions and thus an unequivocal kind of demonstrable knowledge. The second kind are convinced that in the last analysis there should be synthesis: literal knowledge of differences among things and of unique qualities is less interesting and almost certainly more misleading than a knowledge of interrelationships.

Consider the difference between the painstaking distinctions I have just attempted in Crane's name—distinctions that could never be reduced to simple binary pairings or even to tree diagrams—and the aggressive rejection of precisely these distinctions by the man who may well be the strongest influence on American criticism today, Roland Barthes. Note the assumptions about method implied in this passage: "In pre-classical [French] literature, there is an appearance of a plurality of writing modes [*écritures*]; but this variety is much less striking if we pose our problems of language in terms of structure, and no longer in terms of art."[10] Here we discover Crane's word for *his* subject, "structure," but it has become something that is revealed when we set "art" to one side and seek unities among many works rather than diversities! Pursuing commonalities, we thus close off Crane's domain and open up another one entirely:

> The seeming diversity of "genres" and the development of diverse styles [*mouvement des styles*] from within the unified classical dogma are données of aesthetics, not of structure. Neither the one nor the other should be allowed to deceive us: it [neoclassical writing] was all a single unified mode of writing, at the same time instrumental and ornamental. . . . The [seeming] plurality of "rhetorics" thus corresponded to a singularity in bourgeois style [*écriture*]. [Pp. 81–82]

It would of course be misleading to say that Barthes is interested *only* in interrelationships, since he makes many distinctions of his own. Indeed, the word "analogical" might offend him, since the patterns he seeks among ideas are not, for him, patterns of analogy.[11] But when his willingness to set aside all differences of style, form, and class in order to establish a term like "l'écriture bourgeoise" is seen in conjunction with what it is that gets distinguished when his distinctions come, we see just how distant his method is from Crane's.

Barthes's distinctions are seldom or never among particular things, existing literally in the matter-of-fact world: *this* poem in contrast to *that* poem. Instead they are, from Crane's point of view, distinctions among abstract ideas: *langue/écriture*, in the passage I have just quoted (p. 80); esthetic *données/données* of structure; bourgeois writers/modern writers who have discovered *l'écriture*. He thus not only specifically repudiates Crane's kind of passion for discriminations among arts and among artists; he seeks, at least in one stage of his development,[12] unchanging patterns that underlie seeming differences. He is indeed quite explicit about seeing individual people and cultures and works of art as interchangeable parts in the grand figures that are for him more interesting. His repeated analogy with the cup of Argos is revealing: it maintained its identity even when all its parts had had to be replaced.[13] For Crane such an analogy could apply, if at all, only much further down the scale of generality, to the *form* of a particular literary work, its species: one might have the "same *Oedipus Rex*" if Oedipus were given slightly different virtues or if the plague in Thebes were changed to famine or floods or a rash of earthquakes; and one can talk of Auden's two versions of the "same" poem.

Obviously the distinction between Crane's and Barthes's methods is subject to further distinctions, for those who want distinctions, and to a dialectical collapse, for those looking for similarities. A committed synthesizer might question whether critics are really of these two kinds: Are not the differences merely superficial disguises for a spirit of criticism that in truth informs all of life? Indeed, if we look more deeply, what was God's creation of individuated life itself but a criticism of undifferentiated unity? And so on. On the contrary, some committed "splitters" might accuse even Crane of gross "lumpings."

Having thus divided all critics into splitters and lumpers, Crane was of course already a splitter. We must postpone the question of whether this primary choice in any way impugns his status as a pluralist.

Deduction and Induction

Because of Crane's persistent complaint about the way in which analogical critics often deduce from their patterns of ideas what they take to be true, what *must* be true, of individual works, it has been easy for them to assume that he is attacking deduction and claiming to be exclusively inductive. But the distinction between lumping and splitting is not the same as the distinction between deduction and induction. When Crane talks about the two main methods, he distinguishes the *matter-of-fact* method advocated by Hume from the *abstract* methods of dialectical philosophers and critics.[14] Since the first appeals constantly to experience and the second to patterns of ideas, they are easily confused with induction and deduction. Kenneth Burke, for example, in one of his printed responses to the "Chicago critics," accuses them of being less inductive than they claim, since they are always deeply committed to a set of categories, and particularly the four causes, which they never seem to reconsider or abandon.[15] But all modes of criticism must have ways of moving back and forth between generalizations and particulars, and all will *claim* to show just the proper combination of deduction and induction, the proper respect for logic and for fact. The question is not, then, whether methods are deductive or inductive but where the deductions and inductions come and, even more important, what they are like when they do come. (What I have just said is not, of course, itself methodologically innocent. I am, for the purpose at hand, a committed discriminator.)

In an analogical thinker, induction will be a movement from particulars that are in themselves not literal, not defined unequivocally. If I have described "Surgical Ward" according to its *likenesses* to other verbal works or to higher truths, the induction I perform from the poem as I see it, regardless of how precise I am about it, cannot be identified in any simple way with the induction of someone who has chosen a "Surgical Ward" that *differs* from everything else, including all other poems.

Similarly, *deductions* performed by analogical minds will be entirely different from those performed by literalists. We can see this by looking again at the meaning of simple terms like *is, proves, implies,* and their synonyms. Verbs like *is* or *exists* just do not mean the same thing when they are used by Plato to say that ideas really exist, really *are*, as they do when Aristotle, with equal assurance, says that they do *not* exist as independent entities. "Is" simply does not mean the same thing when Crane claims that a poem *is*, considered literally, an object made by the maker's choices as it does when Harold Bloom says that every poem *is* a misreading of previous poems. It follows, I think, that when someone says "it follows," the kind of entrainment claimed can be discovered only by reference to a specific notion of how proof works. What "follows" in one critical language will, in another, look like the result of a leap of faith.

It is important to see the difference between this point and most other claims about ambiguity. That the word "is" means many different things has been obvious to everyone who thinks about meaning. But Crane stresses the radical methodological difference between those who would remove the ambiguity by discriminating a precise and determining context and those who would exploit it by showing all the things that a word can mean in many different contexts. There is a curious sense in which the latter are more fixed in their definitions and more predictable in their results, despite their emphasis on plurisignification, than the literal critics who pursue discriminations and allow what they find in particulars to determine what they say.

Speaking of I. A. Richards' way of lumping all problems into a single kind of relationship among the three rhetorical terms *thoughts*, *words*, and *things* (or *referents*), Crane says:

> Everything turns on the manner in which, in any given theory of discourse or interpretation, the three indispensable factors are related to each other as organizing principles of the discussion. There are only two major possibilities: on the one hand, we may recognize that, since the three terms are in themselves, apart from any use we make of them, completely equivocal words, the literal senses we give to them and the relations constructed among these senses may legitimately vary from context to context, so that our treatment of words or of thought or of subject matter may be quite distinct according as we are concerned, let us say, with the analysis of poems or of rhetorical compositions or of philosophical arguments. Or, on the other hand, we may prefer, once and for all, to fix the relation of words, thoughts, and things in a single pattern, determined by a fundamental analogy, which will henceforth persist throughout our consideration of individual problems as a device by which the particularities of our subject matter may be resolved into a set of simple universal laws. Now the choice between these two primary modes of procedure is obviously one that cannot be avoided by any writer who proposes to treat of the problem of interpretation; and, once made, it just as obviously entails consequences which, if the resulting analysis is self-consistent,

must be expected to manifest themselves even in the least details of the system. And the essential point is that the choice itself is a choice that involves, for the theorist of discourse, simply a decision as to the way in which he intends to use his own words—whether, on the one hand, to mark off sharp distinctions of meaning, so that no one distinguishable aspect of an object is resolved into anything else, or, on the other hand, to make possible a reduction of such distinctions in the interest of a single unified truth.[16]

In the next chapter I shall show how Kenneth Burke explicitly rejects many of the distinctions Crane would insist on, often openly attacking standards of literal proof that would be mandatory for the Ronald Cranes of the world. I hope to defend Burke's shifty lumpings without dishonesty, while here I defend with equal conviction a man who could scarcely read a page of Burke without annoyance at "lack of precision."

Saving for later the question of what my defense of two such different views says about my own wishy-washy ways, I simply remind you here that most of what we read depends on an assumption, tacit but absolute, either that things are fundamentally more alike than different, or vice versa. Though everyone thinks of himself as taking all important similarities and differences into account, most assume that their choice is a choice between conflicting realities, not simply a choice of equally valid methods.

In such matters we all tend to be like the "pluralistic" William James, who, when the chips were down, could not abide those who saw the world in an entirely different perspective—those metaphysical monists who insisted on pursuing the One, regardless of how many particulars the pursuit led them to ignore. In *A Pluralistic Universe*[17] he treats the great lumpers like Hegel with urbanity, respect, and tolerance; no one could show a more open spirit of inquiry than the great pragmatist did when dealing with his enemies. But they remained his enemies. There is not a hint of methodological pluralism in the radical sense we are pursuing here. Of course there *are* likenesses, myriads of them; it *may* even be true that the universe is finally in some sense a universe and not a chaos. All of us hope that somehow it is. But meanwhile it is quite clear to any right-minded person that philosophers who underline the *uni-* do great violence to the world as it is. Since the test of truth for James is, finally, whether we violate or honor the particulars of our lives as lived and immediately known, the unifiers are damned.

William James might very well question the intellectual integrity of anyone who could suggest, as Crane does, that such pragmatism is not "pragmatic" enough: the choice is not between universes but between universes of discourse, between methods for grappling with a world that *is* both *really One* and *really Many*. Such choices, Crane says again and again, are independent of the nature of things, except as the nature of things may be held responsible for the necessity of such choices. And they thus in part determine whatever conclusions may be reached; no conclusion is independent of the method that led to it.

The Reflexive Discrimination of Problems

I must underline one more major distinction of method implicit in Crane's definition of subject matter before I turn, for a briefer look, to principles. A mind like Crane's, committed to accurate and literal discriminations, can move in at least two radically different ways. It all depends on what we want to discriminate. We can assume, like Locke, Hume, and many twentieth-century empiricists, that truth is to be found by an unlimited digging-down into reality, as it were, until we discover its least parts, its unanalyzable atoms, its smallest real or solid elements. These can be physical atoms or quarks, simple sense impressions, "clear and distinct" or "unit" ideas, or (more likely in literary criticism) irreducible vocables or smallest discernible actions or motives or effects (depending on whether we are oriented to things, thoughts, words, or deeds). Then we can reason, in strict logical fashion, from these ultimate discriminations of what for us is the ultimately real to whatever can be really and certainly inferred from them.

Without pausing to clarify such thoroughgoing commitment to analysis (exemplified by, say, Hume or by some particle physicists and computer programmers), we must see why Crane's kind of discriminating mind could stop at an earlier and different kind of point, still on the way "down." We can assume that what we want to discriminate are not the smallest, most elementary parts but equally real, discernible human issues or *problems*. In this second view, we stop our discriminations whenever we come to something definable as a determinate subject of inquiry—"Surgical Ward," a constitution, a species, a historical event. That whole then determines, as a locus of problems, our view of how and where we slice as we examine its parts.

It is a whole that is found by discriminating activities of human beings, not by manipulating ideas. It thus contrasts radically with the subjects investigated by thinkers, whether lumpers or splitters, who abandon the controls provided by problems of construction. Speaking again of Richards, Crane says:

> It is to these, indeed—the significant wholes to which his method tends to reduce all literature—that he systematically endeavors to confine our attention. For the Richardsian interpreter of discourse there can be only one problem; and, whether that problem is stated generally as the interaction of contexts and settings or is specified as ambiguity or metaphor or confusion of statement and definition, it is clearly one which can be adequately posed and solved in terms of isolated statements considered apart from the total artistic or logical structure of the works in which they appear. For the problem is really one of the universal behavior of words as determined by events which in any strict sense are extra-literary, and a solution is possible just as soon as we have enough of the immediate setting of the word before us to permit an estimate of what various contexts have been at work. Thus—to adapt an example from *Basic Rules of Reason*—it is not necessary to read the whole of the *Preface to the "Lyrical Ballads"* in order to deal with the question of what is meant by "poetry" in Wordsworth's assertion that "poetry is the look on the face of science"; instead we have only to recognize that the problem turns essentially on the meaning of "is," that "is" may have different meanings according as the sentences in which it occurs are definitions of words or statements about the things of which the word is the name, that if we compare the saying of Wordsworth with other sayings about "poetry" (Richards gives a good many of them), we see that it is more like a statement than a definition, and that as such, separated from a definition, it may have as many senses as Wordsworth or we ourselves at any time have attached to the word.[18]

Such inquiry is of course a kind of problem-solving. "All this, granted the way in which the problem is stated, is no doubt true, and there is abundant justification in the circumstances for Richards' insistence on our need of a 'better apparatus for controlling the senses of our words.'" But the problem has been set by our method of defining meaning, and it therefore cannot tell us what we want to know about *Wordsworth's* problem:

> If we are seriously interested in discovering Wordsworth's intention rather than simply in playing a new and somewhat complicated linguistic game, and if, consequently, we insist on considering the question not in the vacuum of a single sentence but in the total context, highly particularized as it is, of Words-

worth's argument and method in the *Preface*, then we are already provided, in various of the devices afforded by traditional dialectic, with much of the apparatus we need. [P. 43]

Thus, both the location of a subject and the search for reliable conclusions about it will be, in Crane's "problematic" method, quite different from what logistical empiricists or propositional analysts would think decisive. Having settled on some sort of distinct problem rather than on the smallest discernible element, the "problematic" critic can investigate, as we have seen, how the parts of a poem relate to the whole (as wholes are defined *within* the problem, not as comprehensive wholes are pursued by aggressive lumpers). And he can thus make judgments on the relative effectiveness of a given literary or critical work in achieving its wholeness.

The method of such investigation will seem circular both to the lumper committed to strict logical deduction from comprehensive first principles and to the splitter committed to constructing a world out of indubitable least parts. In the same fashion, the modes of proof of each method will be demonstrably inadequate to those practicing any other method. We arrive here at what is perhaps the most recalcitrant of all the problems in our quest for a responsible pluralism. The history of "refutation" shows that when any mode works on any other mode, the results are foreordained; it is as if each critic wore spectacles polarized on a different axis and tinted with a different color. When you look out and about, wearing your spectacles, you see not only a landscape of forms and colors different from mine; you see clear and undeniable evidence that my report on what I see is biased. And when you turn to look at me and generously offer to examine my spectacles to see if the source of our differences might not be found in them, you find what could have been predicted: my spectacles are indeed wrongly polarized and tinted.[19]

It is scarcely surprising, once we take into account how method determines data, that two verbally identical conclusions about "Surgical Ward" could in fact be unrelated or even contradictory, or that two statements that seem contradictory (" 'Surgical Ward' is best"; " 'Sonnet XIV' is best") could be either unrelated or even in agreement, depending on how they were produced by their author's respective methods. For example, if one critic says that "Surgical Ward" is ironic and a second critic says that it is not, our inquiry into whether they are really at odds cannot be a matter of simply deciding what they "mean" by irony. We might very well look at their definitions and find that they are verbally identical, and still we would not know whether their original statements conflict. A subject is defined more by the mode of handling it than by our words for describing it, and I will not know what a critic means by "It's ironic" until I have watched his way of working on a text.

PRINCIPLES

We come now to the last variable: principles or assumptions. I say last, but obviously principles come first and have been with us all the while. If principles are whatever are taken as ultimate, primary, either unquestionable or unquestioned, it is clear that all three of the variables we have discussed depend, in ways too complicated for total tracing, on where in our thought we choose to begin. What or where we think a poem is, our view of its purposes and the purposes of criticism, and our choice of method will correlate with, and at least to some degree depend on, what we take to be self-evident about these matters and about the world in which we work on them.* Nothing will divide critics more fundamentally than whether they see themselves grappling with a world of things, or thinking about a world that is an order of thoughts, or discoursing in a universe of discourse about thoughts and things, or acting in a world of action or process. It ought to go without proving that no two critics who live in any two of these different worlds will be likely to understand each other until they have recognized their fundamental differences, and their statements about poetry will be incommensurable unless they have mutually recognized how a choice of worlds determines meanings within worlds.

It is clear, for example, that if an Aristotelian, for whom *things* are what reality is made of, says that a given poem is "a communication," the statement will mean something quite different from the same statement made by anyone who constructs his universe out of language. A critic who sees all poems as a form of communication, occupying one place in a universe of discourse, will be saying something deducible from a first principle when he calls a given poem a communication; while for Crane, defining poems as substantive things in a universe of things, to call a given "poem" a communica-

*In what Crane and other Chicago pluralists wrote there is no clear agreement about whether there is a *necessary* reciprocal relation between a given method or definition of subject and given principles. Richard McKeon usually suggests a kind of free-floating relation of any reasonable choice of one with any reasonable choice of another. Crane usually suggests that his chosen principles, methods, definitions, and purposes entail each other. See pp. 250–55 and note 10 to chapter 6, below.

tion would be to place it outside the class of poems as "imitations" and inside the class of statements or arguments.

In no other respect did Crane's effort at a pluralistic assignment of tasks meet more incomprehension than in his choice not to treat all poems as discourse. In no other respect was his chosen mode more at odds with twentieth-century habits of mind. Crane was impressed by the almost universal habit in our time of assuming that all literary art is a form of communication. His prolonged polemic against those who hold that view monistically—as the only defensible principle— has been generally ignored, and one still finds most critics in the seventies taking it as self-evident. It has been the dominant view not only among the New Critics, whether defined narrowly or broadly enough to include René Wellek and Kenneth Burke and Northrop Frye (and even myself, in *A Rhetoric of Irony*); it has also dominated most recent criticism calling itself semiotics or structuralism or deconstructionism or linguistics or stylistics. Observe how Roman Jakobson places poetics:

> Poetics deals primarily with the question, *What makes a verbal message a work of art?* Because the main subject of poetics is the *differentia specifica* of verbal art in relation to other arts and in relation to other kinds of verbal behavior, poetics is entitled to the leading place in literary studies.
>
> Poetics deals with problems of verbal structure, just as the analysis of painting is concerned with pictorial structure. Since linguistics is the global science of verbal structure, poetics may be regarded as an integral part of linguistics.[20]

Jakobson then recognizes the obvious objection that "many devices studied by poetics are not confined to verbal art," since a given artistic work can be "translated" from fiction "into music, ballet, and graphic art." But his way of meeting this objection, one that would be crucial for Crane, is dictated strictly by his mental chart of the total domain of his study: "In short, many poetic features belong not only to the science of language but to the whole theory of signs, that is, to general semiotics. This statement, however, is valid not only for verbal art but also for all varieties of language since language shares many properties with some other systems of signs or even with all of them (pansemiotic features)" (p. 351).

He then disposes similarly of the objection that "the question of relations between the word and the world concerns not only verbal art but actually all kinds of discourse": "The truth values, however, as far as they are—to say with the logicians—'extralinguistic entities,' ob-

viously exceed the bounds of poetics and of linguistics in general"
(p. 351).

The universe of inquiry is thus nicely sorted out, yielding a chart
that we can reconstruct like this:

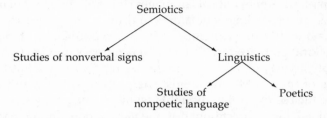

Poetics is thus carefully fenced off from "extra-linguistic" values, like
truth or practical interests.

One finds this principle at work almost everywhere in continental
linguistics and criticism. Poetry results when something special is
done to language. Mukařovský, for example, says,

> The violation of the norm of the standard [language], its systematic
> violation, is what makes possible the poetic utilization of language;
> without this possibility there would be no poetry. The more the
> norm of the standard [language] is stabilized in a given language,
> the more varied can be its violation, and therefore the more pos-
> sibilities for poetry in that language. And on the other hand, the
> weaker the awareness of the norm, the fewer possibilities of viola-
> tion, and hence the fewer possibilities for poetry.[21]

Thus first principles about language lead to a poetics that has little
resemblance except in name to the poetics that Ronald Crane would
place on an entirely different mental chart:

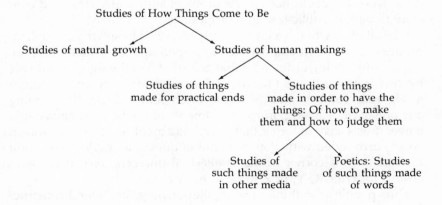

But what is poetic reality, *really?* If you put that question to Crane, he must give a double answer. Do you ask me as pluralist? My answer is that reality is the *many* things we define it to be as we attempt to deal with many different subjects that are constructed as we make definitions in our different critical languages. It is both one and many; it is for some purposes linguistic atoms and for other purposes the constructions human beings attempt. It is also no doubt a mysterious whole of the kind embraced by certain all-encompassing views. And there is simply no way to refute any of the seemingly rival claims that the elements of the world—the atoms, the problems, the grand gestalts—are reducible to things, thoughts, symbols, or processes.

But do you ask me as practitioner of one valid mode among many, an inquirer into the possibilities of a revived Aristotelian practice? Well, then, one reality that should concern humanity is the marvelous world of things human beings have made in the course of solving or attempting to solve problems of construction. If you prefer to define those things as ideas or statements or actions in a drama, if you prefer to grapple with larger and profounder questions than my questions about how to make and do things well, that is your privilege. All I ask is that you resist thinking that you have refuted me if what you have done is show what I knew already: that my method, applied to my chosen subject, has not solved *your* problems.

Charges of Dogmatism and Relativism: How to Test a Mode

In his criticism, once he elected the neo-Aristotelian language of "made objects," Crane seldom departed from the kind of carefully delimited effort to explain the artistic construction of particular works that we undertook with "Surgical Ward." He was impatient with any discussion that could not yield a problem sufficiently clear and concrete to permit public testing of argument.

Like all of us when we grow deeply absorbed in solving a problem, he often did not trouble to mention—perhaps he sometimes even forgot—the zoning ordinances that accorded him the right to cultivate his own garden. It was thus inevitable, particularly given his delight in vigorous combat, that he would often sound dogmatic. Reading any one of his slashing, ironic indictments of methods he considered naive, it was easy to forget that every statement, every word, was in effect surrounded with a special kind of quotation mark: *if* you want to work in this corner of the intellectual universe, *then* it becomes absurd for critic X, Y, or Z to do a, b, or c.

Thus people who think they are illuminating the "literal construction" of particular poems when all they are doing is pointing out structural analogies are mocked in Crane's brilliant attack on "Conceptions of Poetic Structure in Contemporary Criticism."[22] Here, as he reconstructs the way in which certain critics' assumptions lead easily, all too easily, to foreordained results, we enjoy the irony or resent the unfairness, depending on whether we remember where we are in the larger structure of Crane's thought.

> These [assumptions], along with a predisposition to look for symbolic relations everywhere and a certain facility in seeing affinities and contrasts among the verbal and imaginative components of texts, will form our essential equipment. And the distinctions we shall need are not particularly hard to come by. The most useful distinctions, indeed, will be the most commonplace, in the double sense of not being peculiar to any given science or system of thought and of being applicable to the largest variety of contexts in both literature and life; and it is noteworthy that the contemporary writers who have given us our most highly praised models of this kind of interpretation have invariably used as reduction terms such familiar and all-embracing dichotomies as life and death (or positive values and negative values), good and evil, love and hate, harmony and strife, order and disorder, eternity and time, reality and appearance, truth and falsity, certainty and doubt, true insight and false opinion, imagination and intellect . . . , emotion and reason, complexity and simplicity, nature and art, the natural and the supernatural, nature as benignant and nature as malignant, man as spirit and man as beast, the needs of society and individual desires, internal states and outward acts, engagement and withdrawal.

Each of these pairs is taken from an actual critic, though Crane does not say so, and one can imagine each author bridling as he finds his work described as easy, commonplace, and reductive:

> Of such universal contraries, not restricted in their applicability to any kind of work, whether lyric, narrative, or dramatic, it will be easy enough for us to acquire an adequate supply, and once we have them, or some selection of them, in our minds as principles of interpretation, it will seldom be hard to discover their presence in poems as organizing principles of symbolic content. It requires no great insight to find an inner dialectic of order and disorder or a struggle of good and evil forces in any serious plot. [Pp. 123–24]

The tone throughout Crane's long chapter of refutations is thus not in the least accommodating: it is a thoroughgoing job of destructive criticism, marshaling scores of "simple" critics who have not recognized what, in Crane's account, seems too obvious for *anyone* to overlook: that all these critics who have started with the assumption that "poetry is a mode of discourse" have been led to a relatively inadequate language for dealing with poetic structure. The attack is unrelenting, the pluralistic reminders muted, the distinctions among the mocked enterprises blurred.

On the one hand we have assertions like this:

> But what, then, are we saying when we assert . . . that the death of Heyst "is a form of purification and expiation ritual"? I think the answer is now evident: we are saying simply that when we apply to this incident in Conrad's novel the set of terms which Sir James Frazer or another has used to define the structure and meaning of the ritual in question, a striking resemblance between the two patterns emerges, especially if we are careful to attend to only the most general outline of the incident as Conrad presents it. We are stating, in short, not a relationship of effect to cause, but of like to like—that is, of analogy merely. [P. 138]

Of analogy, yes. But *merely*? In that "merely" lies all the difference, since the critics under attack will surely reply, "Your reading is literal *merely*."

On the other hand, as a reminder of his pluralism, we have only Crane's restatement of the fact that his own choice of a language is, after all, but one among many, and even that reminder is often given in a tone that suggests the immense superiority of his own choices:

> Whatever we may think of the results we are able to achieve in practical criticism by using the methods of these critics, the results are inevitably conditioned by, and hence are relative to, the basic conceptual language that has been developed in recent years out of the very old tradition of criticism in which poetry is thought of as a mode of discourse and in which theories of poetry, of a necessarily "abstract" sort, have been derived by a dialectic of negative and positive analogies from a consideration of the nature of discourse in its non-poetic varieties. [P. 139]

Small wonder that critics smarting under such attacks should not have recalled Crane's opening chapter about the need for many critical languages. Only the most careful readers could see beyond Crane the monist, who used every available intellectual resource to show the superiority of Aristotle's views *for the critical task in hand*, to Crane the pluralist, for whom the choice of Aristotle was "merely instrumental," dictated by what "happened" to be Crane's interest.

If the charges of dogmatism may in part have sprung from "accidents" of temperament unconnected with inherent problems in pluralism, the threat of a skeptical relativism on the other flank seems at first thought more serious. Once we have decided to *relate* our judgments of every critical mode to the principles, methods, definitions, and purposes of that mode, is there any ground left for criticizing or rejecting any mode? When Crane talks of his "prejudices" at the beginning of *The Languages of Criticism and the Structure of Poetry*, when he talks of making "instrumental" or "pragmatic" choices among modes, is he, as some have charged, really professing little more than a personal preference, relative to his historical circumstances? If someone were to charge that all modes are equally defensible, once they are understood, or that each choice, including Crane's, could be explained as simply relative to this or that kind of upbringing, would Crane's version of pluralism provide a satisfactory reply?

In seeking any kind of transmodal test of modes we are of course flung right back into the chaos of positions with which we began. Different modes have different tests for what makes a valid mode, and different pluralisms may offer rival standards for admission to the canon. If we could all agree on how to validate modes, we would not have the problem of critical variety in the first place.

Thus it does not get us very far, though it may get us started, to say that Crane, like everyone who has ever thought about how we know what we know, expected every claimant to show (1) some degree of internal coherence, (2) some correspondence between the chosen language and the world it purports to treat, and (3) some measure of adequacy to the variety or richness of human perception: call it comprehensiveness. We all reject what seems flatly incoherent, blatantly inaccurate, or crippled by narrowness of range. And we all know how easy it is to invent critical and philosophical modes that are irrefutable according to any one of these standards and yet absurd when we add the others: totally coherent systems that either fit nothing in a recognizable world ("Works written by God are superior to works written by angels, those by angels superior to those by centaurs"), or, if they have any "extension" at all, it is so narrow as to be useless; totally "true" systems that are trivial ("In every great poem one finds complex patterns of color"); totally comprehensive views that cover everything at the cost either of coherence or of any contact with whatever we recognize as reality ("Everything in the world, whether made by God or man, is beautiful for him who knows how to see"). What is hard is to develop views that test the criteria in relation to each other, to make a coherent view out of recognizable stuff that is not absurdly simplified.

One skeptical assumption on which I rely throughout is that no fully coherent, correspondent, and comprehensive vision of the world is available to any human being. Even the sum of our many perspectives will offer but a fragment of the great Whole, whether we add our views together, as a collection of discrete and partial views, or work in Hegelian fashion to subsume many perspectives in dialectical relation under one vision. But skepticism about total views—which in any case could never be decisively proved or disproved—need not lead to skepticism about our various intellectual enterprises, as we can learn from a close study of any critic skillful in the use of at least two of the criteria.

COHERENCE

For the pluralist there will be many kinds of coherence, but the kinds are not unlimited. To demand that a constructed critical world somehow cohere is not to demand that all modes pursue a strict, overt, logistical validity. It is simply to demand that, once we enter a given world, what we find should *in some recognizable sense fit* everything else we find there.

Since in fact coherence of some kind or other is the cheapest of intellectual virtues, achieved by all but tyros, it is not worth talking about in a general way for long. Even critics who claim incoherence—even those who say "I believe x just because x is absurd"—can be shown, with an everyday dialectical flip-flop, to meet their own standards of internal order. There is indeed a modern commonplace that rejects coherence—"A foolish consistency is the hobgoblin of little minds"—but it has led no critics to profess a foolish inconsistency; whatever incoherence is openly embraced is in the service of a higher coherence, too rich for human statement.

Nevertheless, we have a right to ask two things of any critic: that the connections among his various beliefs meet the standards for coherence he applies to other critics, and that he not expect of us any more respect for his arguments than they have earned, granting his own notions of respect.

It is precisely on this count that some relativisms betray themselves. Insofar as they *argue* for the dependency of critical conclusions on noncritical or nonliterary causes—on the motives or conditionings of the artist's or critic's past life, not on reasons presented here and now—they must be prepared to meet their own weapons turned back on them: are *their* conclusions determined by nonrational causes, or are they reasoned? If they are reasoned, then reasoned conclusions are available in criticism and the argument is incoherent. If they are not reasoned but are determined by nonrational causes not given, then again the discourse is incoherent, because it claims to be an argument.

This is not the place for lengthy pursuit of such matters, more fully treated when I discuss critical justice in chapter 5. What is important is to see how thoroughly earned was Crane's own form of coherence. He accepted, openly and explicitly, the tests of a literal, logical coherence in judging statements about poetic structure. As a pluralist, he would not insist on such coherence for all purposes. But woe be unto the critic who claimed to be offering literal conclusions following from strict proof when in fact we could discover his reliance on "privileged hypotheses."[23] Logical validity can be demanded of those who claim to have honored it. Seeking it, we shall find that the world offers us an ample supply of demonstrable truth to stave off skepticism. But we shall not be so naive as to require everyone to write with the cogency of a Hume; coherence will come in many shapes and shades. That is, in fact, the chief trouble about it; it is so easily come by, for those who are willing to play with internal relationships among ideas abstracted from reality, that we will want to insist on something more.

CORRESPONDENCE

Most of us hope for some connection between a critic's statement and some reality other than the statement: some correspondence with the "way things are" outside the critical statement. Short of some such correspondence, I can scarcely call a statement *true*, however *valid* its coherence makes it seem.

As we would expect by now, there are many ways of showing why and how this is so—and many ways of proving that it is not, especially in the continental criticism that now exalts the totally autonomous Text. On the one hand, if we assume a reality that is independent of our languages, it is easy to show that those who reject the criterion of correspondence sneak a connection with reality in the back door while renouncing it at the front. On the other hand, if we begin with self-evident principles like "All we have is what we can say to each other," it is easy to show that claims of correspondence with an independent reality depend on assumptions verifiable only by reference to other statements.

Crane did not live to see the current spate of self-devouring texts and self-validating semiotic or rhetorical systems of texts. If he had, he might have developed his notions of correspondence further. But the problem of "external" validation of statements about value had been with us for a long time, and Crane knew that, even using his kind of reflexive principles in defining and solving problems, his kind of argument depended on solid tests in experience. What he relied on were two rather different versions of the correspondence criterion.

The first was an appeal to precise and accurate reporting of what he called "precritical experience" or, sometimes, "common sense," using the phrase in one of its old meanings, "what is sensed in common." It is not quite the *consensus gentium*, because there never is full consensus among critics once they start making statements; rather it is what precedes statement and theory, as our laughter at Sir Toby Belch and Mr. Collins, our tragic response to King Lear and the Mayor of Casterbridge, and our speculative or religious or contemplative response to *The Divine Comedy* and "Surgical Ward" precede all the choices I have been describing; that is, they depend only on our being members of this culture attending to these works. Crane was fond of saying things like "Nobody reading this line without the distortions produced by critical theory has ever seen it as other than . . ." or "X's conclusion here springs clearly from what his principles demand, not from any experience he could have had in the theatre—or even in his study reading the words on the page."

I once showed Crane an account of the metaphysics of *Tartuffe*, one that did not mention that the play is funny or indeed that it ever might be performed. Tartuffe's character was read as a solemn illustration of existentialist principles. Crane hit the roof. The critic's form of the question did not allow him to take audiences and their implied responses into account, and for Crane it was thus inferior to any inquiry, whether metaphysical or not, that was more nearly related to what "everyone knows" about the play. Readers who did not take into account what all other readers would see as facts about the work, however clever they might be, were always suspect. Though what is factual is in this view a communal determination, it can be as sharp a test as we need. Bright new readings were always suspect if they were divorced from matter-of-fact experience of art.

This communal test could be put in many ways. I have often attempted a rhetorical statement of it, and I shall try again before I am done here. John Searle formulates it under the word "institutional": we all live within institutions which make clear to us what the rules are in a given use of language; we thus have very clear criteria for deciding, Searle says, whether it is right to break a promise.[24] The procedure he employs can give us similar grounds for knowing whether a work is comic or tragic, whether a statement is intended as ironic or straightforward, or whether a given pattern of images in a work is simply an accidental product of a critic's predetermined search for just that pattern.

All such public tests can be challenged, of course, by any determined skeptic, for not only does the public too seldom offer a landslide vote, but, when asked for proof, one must fall back on arguments that to some people—for example, the reader who has not laughed at Sir Toby or Tartuffe and has not mourned for Michael Henchard—will look like no arguments at all. What is more, when we seek to make discriminations among the larger choices of subject matter that I described in talking about what "Surgical Ward" *is*, our arguments from common sense will help us less than Crane sometimes claimed. *All* of our placements are at least potentially in accord with *something* that "we all know" about a literary work. At this level of generality, Crane has lost his correspondence criterion and must fall back on the instrumentalism that underlies his pluralism in the first place: Will this choice do things for my inquiry that I find worth doing? As soon as someone asks "Who are *you*?" we see that Crane has not escaped the charge of relativism as demonstratively as he might have hoped. Only for the critic who has already accepted some sort of communal norm will common sense work as a firm base. (One can add, fortunately, that there can be few among us here who have not!)[25]

The second kind of correspondence may seem less subject to question. A scholar before he was a critic, Crane never lost his scholarly passion for attending to the "facts" a found in the text or in its historical setting. His scorn for readers who misreported details terrified his graduate students and colleagues; legend has it (no doubt falsely) that many an author quit the profession after reading Crane's short tongue-lashing in *Philological Quarterly*. It seemed to hurt him personally that Kenneth Burke could build a case about how the albatross stands for Coleridge's drug habit, when there is no evidence that Coleridge even had the habit at the time of composing "The Rime of the Ancient Mariner"—and besides it was Wordsworth who suggested the albatross in the first place! Every critical endeavor depends on, or ought to depend on, an immense base of data accepted by critics of all persuasions. The words or episodes are in *this* order and not in the order that Jones reports; what Melville wrote in *White-Jacket* was "coiled fish" and not the "soiled fish" on which F. O. Matthiessen's interpretation depends; a look at the text will confirm that the marriage Smith makes so much of did not in fact occur.

All of us depend at least to some degree on some such reference points, and, as I shall show in chapter 6, there is a real distinction between the mountains of data about which all or most critics will agree and the foothills of "data" that are not given unequivocally by the text but instead are found only by a given critic in a given mode. But the line between the two kinds is not easily determined. Even the most innocent, "obviously factual" detail can be wiped away or inverted by this or that modal interest; a total absence of sexual reference, for example, can be turned by any aggressive Freudian into a total reference. For this and other reasons, the "facts" of the "text" are now under far more theoretical fire than Crane could have anticipated. Yet without agreement about what our statements should correspond to, we can never demonstrate that criticism in any mode violates any detail in any poem, however far it may depart from the author's own understanding or that of his community. One need not read very far in critics since Crane to see just how little his appeal to common-sense experience or to factual accuracy would count, for some of them, in showing their errors. Seeking to free themselves from the author's intentions, believing, many of them, that a work means whatever any critic seriously takes it to mean (which is *not* the same thing, of course, as saying that it means *anything*, however nonsensical), they can escape Crane's criteria. Only for those of us willing to join that more traditional community of believers will those criteria work; and the arguments against joining—though finally, in my view, weak indeed —seem to attract more and more critics by the year.

In relying on two kinds of common sense, Crane thus seems to me to carry over a good deal from his chosen mode when he turns to pluralistic evaluation of modes. At the end of his fullest statement of pluralism, in the opening chapter of *The Languages of Criticism and the Structure of Poetry*, he qualifies his acceptance of all "appropriate" modes in a way that I find more dependent on his choice of critical purpose than on a full pluralistic theory:

> I would raise the question, finally, whether what I have called the "matter of fact" criticisms (of which there have been a good many varieties) are not less likely, in general, to do violence to our common sense apprehension of literature or poetry than the "abstract"

criticisms I have contrasted with them. The "abstract" method, as Hume said, apropos of its use in morals, "may be more perfect in itself, but suits less the imperfection of human nature, and is a common source of illusion and mistake in this as well as in other subjects." It is a method, for one thing, that encourages the invention of occult qualities and the preoccupation with problems that arise from the relationship of these to one another in the critic's dialectic rather than from any empirically verifiable connections among things, with the result, very often, that theoretical debates are set going which admit of no possible resolution since they define no concrete facts to which we may appeal. This is the case, I think, with all the discussions in recent years, especially among Shakespeareans, about the general nature of "tragedy" and the implications of this nature (which is defined variously by different critics but always as a kind of Platonic essence) for such questions as whether or not "the tragic picture is incompatible with the Christian faith, or with any form of religious belief that assumes the existence of a personal and kindly God." But both "tragedy" and "the Christian faith," are here abstractions, or constructs of the critic, having little to do with what individual poets were engaged upon when they composed serious plots of one or another kind and called some or all of them "tragedies" or with what individual men and women at different times have thought about God or about what they took tragedy to be; and the issue can never be settled because it is a pseudo-issue, one which is made to look like an issue of fact but which really has no identifiable reference outside the game of dialectical counters in which it has arisen. And other difficulties appear when schemes of literary values thus derived are used in the examination of particular works. For we then get typically judgments by reason rather than sentiment, in which the critic's predetermined scale of better and worse rather than the peculiar intent and form of the poem inevitably conditions what is said; as in Mr. Ransom's strictures on Shakespeare's seventy-third sonnet or Mr. Leavis' objections to the metaphors in Shelley's "Ode to the West Wind." From all which I conclude, not that the "abstract" method has no justifiable uses in criticism, but that there are many questions to which it ought not to be applied if we are interested in something more than the play of the critic's ideas and sensibility. [Pp. 37–38]

Although this explains very well why certain critics cannot answer the questions Crane wants to answer (and those critics *do* often formulate their questions misleadingly), it gives us a highly distorted view of why such people find the "abstract" methods appealing. The passage thus pertains much more clearly to Crane's polemic on behalf of what his chosen mode can do than it does to his argument for pluralism. It explains why many critics cannot do the job Crane wants done, but it does not, finally, do justice to other jobs.

COMPREHENSIVENESS

Most of us, finally, employ some standard of scope or coverage: Is too much left out? We can see how this third test works in Crane's critique of Cleanth Brooks.[26] Its original subtitle was "The Bankruptcy of Critical Monism," and the key to what many saw as an unforgivably harsh attack was contained in that word "monism," used in a sense that goes beyond my present usage to include something like simplism or reductionism. Though Brooks had chosen to deal with one of the essential, permanently interesting, problems—how poems hold together—he had chosen only one of several obvious elements of poetic structure: verbal patterns and the ironies they allow for. Once made, this simplification will insure narrowness, no matter how brilliant the critic. Regardless of the validity of his system and the truth or accuracy of his operations, they will be more misleading, if taken at face value, than the results obtained by a more comprehensive critic like Aristotle, who, instead of collapsing everything into a study of paradoxical language, attempts to deal with three additional, sharply distinguished aspects: the shapes of the human actions imitated, problems of technique and their solutions, and the varieties of emotional and intellectual effect that audiences experience. In choosing to talk only of what for Aristotle was the *matter* out of which poems are made—language and its devices—Brooks had been forced by an impoverished mental chart to subordinate or ignore or distort considerations of shaped action, character, and thought.

In order to talk in this way of impoverishment, one must clearly rely on some standard of richness, but it cannot be a simple one that says "The more, the better": Brooks's one cause, bad; Aristotle's four causes, excellent; Burke's five, best. What we seek are ways of talking that do not ignore any of the obviously relevant matters. No one ever experiences only patterns of imagery or paradox in reading a poem, except, perhaps some aggressively self-denying modern poem that is purged of everything else. And no one uncorrupted by abstract theory could ever rule out of critical discussion all those "human impurities" that all authors and readers experience and enjoy.

We can see now more clearly why the "all-embracing dichotomies" mentioned earlier were for Crane terms of reduction. Anyone can invent a pair of dialectical terms that will seem to cover any work and prove invulnerable to all objections: river and shore, seen as frontier and civilization, can cover *Huckleberry Finn*; a mature sexuality and an immature sexuality can, for Leslie Fiedler, be made to cover every novel ever written; light and shade can, for Roland Barthes, cover the works of Racine. But meanwhile, most of our experience of the works, as authors and readers or spectators, remains unmentioned. To be valid and accurate (or "true"), even to be interesting and fruitful, are not finally enough if you are not in some sense adequate to the richness of the object.

On reflection, Crane's application of this criterion of adequacy to the object seems even less clearly pluralistic than the criterion of accuracy about what is commonly sensed. Perhaps the most frequent experience of Crane on the part of readers who come to him from other modes is precisely that he leaves out too much that is important. In one surprising passage he himself claims that his use of Aristotle can tell us nothing about most of the interests that lead us to care for literature in the first place:

> It is a method not at all suited, as is criticism in the grand line of Longinus, Coleridge, and Matthew Arnold, to the definition and appreciation of those general qualities of writing—mirroring the souls of writers—for the sake of which most of us read or at any rate return to what we have read. It is a method that necessarily abstracts from history. . . . It is a method, above all, that completely fails, because of its essentially differentiating character, to give us insights into the larger moral and political values of literature or into any of the other organic relations with human nature and human experience in which literature is involved.[27]

Apparently, comprehensiveness works as a test only *within* a language; that is, *if* Brooks is trying to answer Aristotle's kind of question, *then* his choice of subject is relatively impoverished. But when we try to choose among methods, we find that one critic's comprehensiveness is another critic's narrowness, and we thus seem again to be driven back, as Crane himself at other moments claims, upon the criterion of usefulness or pragmatic interest: if a given mode will feed me, I buy it. I want "matter-of-fact" knowledge. This mode will yield such knowledge. It is therefore validated.

I began this section promising to defend Crane against charges of dogmatism and relativism. But as I have applied the tests that refute the latter, I have twice found seepage from his chosen mode into his pluralism. Is he not, after all, simply a complicated monist, one who invariably downgrades the "abstract" modes that value other

ends—logical cogency or adequacy to concepts like the nature of God
or the spiritual destiny of man or the fate of reading? Must we conclude that, the better the defense against relativism, the weaker the
defense against monism? It is clear enough that Crane has grounds
for rejecting modes that are invalid, untrue, or so lacking in comprehensiveness as to be dull, useless, or inane. It is also clear that he
does not insist on everyone's doing things his way. What is not clear
is whether the limits he places on his pluralism invalidate it *as*
pluralism.

Umbrella Paradox or Harmonious Chorus?

I concluded chapter 1 with the claim that though pluralism as an
attitude brings immense practical advantages to the pursuit of understanding, it also offers immense theoretical difficulties when we pursue what it would really mean to embrace at least two distinct modes.
Our prolonged view of Crane's pluralism of discrete linguistic
frameworks seems only to heighten this contrast between practical
advantage and theoretical paradox.

We have seen that when Crane talks of several methods—some
assimilative and some discriminating, some emphasizing similarities
and some differences—he has already chosen a method that discrimi-
nates differences, and yet I find nowhere in his work any defense of
this choice other than the pragmatic argument, "This is what you do
if you want to answer this kind of question." Some of his colleagues
and students have worked much more extensively on the theoretical
bases of pluralism, but I think it is fair to say that they would also
appear, to anyone who looks closely at their work, as incorrigible
makers of distinctions.[28]

It is here that I have my own deepest difficulties with assumptions
that have had the greatest effect on my own criticism. What kind of
pluralism is it that says, "There are many modes, and *the* choice
among them is to be made according to one philosophical mode, a
pluralistic pragmatism that depends on sharp discriminations"? It
clearly denies equal status to those who would say, "There are many
conflicting modes, and many others that seemingly conflict, and your
task is to discover the one dialectical truth overarching them all." If
you choose pragmatically between two "equally valid" modes, you
have already chosen against the chief contender: the claim that there
are not two, but one. When I choose one of four discrete kinds of
principle, I am obviously engaged in an operation that would make

sense only to those who believe in discriminating discrete kinds. "Lumping" pluralisms will, as the next chapter shows, reject such "discretion."

What are we supposing about the nature of reality when we say that, within any one of the five literal choices of subject matter (p. 57), a comprehensive view is superior to a narrow one or, indeed, that making proper distinctions is the road to critical validity? Or, rising to the next level of comprehensiveness, what can it mean to say that a community of critics, working in parallel, is superior to a community where a single mode might predominate (let us say, to make the question sharp, a community of neo-Aristotelians in which everyone did excellent work of the same kind and thus made great progress in that kind)? Obviously we must be assuming without discussion that poetic reality is itself diverse, rich in the sense of genuinely manifold, not simple like Ushenko's cone (pp. 31–33, above). Differences about the cone spring, in the example, only from limitations of perspective. But a poem really *is* many things. Differences between the things that it is are real, not just invented, and poetic reality itself is thus dappled, as couple-colored as—well, as a brinded Chicago-style chart of critical differences, only more so.

It may very well be true that in some sense a poem is one thing, just as it may be true that in some sense the universe is one; that is, both of them may ultimately be simple, if only "at the top." If it is one thing, then every meaningful critical statement must be relatable in some way to every other, perhaps in the way that Aristotle's talk of the practical and educational effects of poetry in the *Politics* is "related," though at considerable distance, to what he has to say of it in the *Poetics*. It may even be true, as the great dialectical monists have argued, that everything is related more intimately, that truth, goodness, and beauty are ultimately harmonized in the One or the Good or Absolute Reason. But meanwhile, would you not agree (and I don't have to warn you that much is at stake here) that the radical differences we have been observing are really real? The lumpers may want to *assert* that the "best-made poems" are finally those that also "hit the audience most powerfully" or "express the poet's nature best" or "reflect the deepest truths," but it remains a mere assertion; in the practical world those who, like Tolstoy and Plato, pursue the criterion of moral effect or a higher truth end by rejecting most of what the rest of us consider the best-made poems. And similarly, as we move on around that chart on page 57, we see that the historians and the rhetorical critics do not agree with the pursuers of structure and, what is more, the many different partisans in each section of the chart do not agree with each other. How could they, since they are not talking about the same thing?

The trouble is that many reasonable people seem to reply that they *are*, or *should be*, talking about the same thing. Always at our backs we feel the breath of the great Fusers like Plato and Re-fusers like Burke, reminding us that similarities are real too—realer, in fact, than differences, if all is finally one. For them the final question might well run: Would you not agree, friends of truth that you are, that reality, although it appears to us in diverse forms, is all *somehow* unified? Discriminate realities as you will, you must finally admit that everything is related to everything else, *really* related, in some important sense, and that it is thus more important to work on recognizing new similarities beneath differences than to make distinctions where none were before.

Both of these opposing claims are claims to truth, not just to validity, and according to our usual logic they cannot both be true: each of two things cannot both be more important than the other.*

Can the ultimate pluralist claim here that both views are true? If he makes that claim, has he not had to accept the fusionist view in order to make it—and thus become a lumper? And if he rejects *that*, has he not already accepted the differential view and thus become a monistic splitter?

Thus the ultimate problem in Crane's kind of pluralism results from the implicit notion that critical modes are somehow entities that can be discriminated from each other clearly, given an analyst of sufficient skill. Each mode has its strengths, realized not in a fragmented, partial trial of its resources but only by someone who accepts its possibilities in their fullness; each has its limitations, and these do not inherently result from *errors* but are only, as it were, the necessary expulsions from the chosen entity, thought of as a kind of "hard" substance, a coherent pattern of subject, principle, mode of proof, and purpose.

A critical world inhabited by discrete modes, entities that are at fault when they spill over into domains properly occupied only by other entities—this metaphorical picture raises special problems of its own. It is one pluralism, and it immediately raises the problem of how it is to be related to other possible pluralisms. Is *it* to be described as a discrete entity? If so, as a mode of pluralism it has relied primarily

---

*If you are troubled, as I am, by the syntax of that sentence, try revising it. Our language will not easily accommodate the claim, except in paradoxical mathematical formulas, that x is *both* greater *and* lesser than y.

on only one of the available methods, analytical discrimination of differences. Or do the various further pluralisms that might be invented, some of which I shall describe in later chapters, join together to make a universal harmony? If they are thought to be harmonizable, are we not saying that the discriminations we have seen "below" the unifying vision were in fact less real and that the ultimate reality is one?

The problem can be nicely dramatized simply by asking, as I turn now to other pluralists, What classification should I use? Should it be pluralistic? According to whose pluralism? If I organize the chapters as Crane would, treating pluralisms as discrete entities, I shall of course classify other pluralists according to their definitions of subject matter, their principles, their methods, and their purposes. But then should I not construct an alternative set of chapters for each pluralist, organizing all the others according to the principles of each? Shall I fit Crane into Burke's dramatistic chart and then, in a later section, write a *history* of pluralisms and the idea of pluralism, emulating M. H. Abrams? And should I then attempt a structuralist or deconstructionist version?

Regardless of the mode of classification and accommodation I employ, I shall have to decide, somewhere along the line, whether to construct and make explicit some sort of neutral algorithm that will provide for every conceivable critical view and for making comparisons and translations among them.[29] And, if I do, will that not be just another new dogma? Must not everything I say assume, at every point, either that a given critic, especially me, can "see double," or that he cannot? Can I, can anyone, do justice both to my own view and to any one of the others? Which is to ask, can I do justice to two distinct views without assimilating them to one, namely, to some new monism?

In short: if there is a schema of monisms, is there a schema of schemata of monisms? And, if so, is there a schema of schemata of schemata? If not, why am I not, as I wear my pluralist disguise, really a complicated but arrant skeptic or relativist?

This umbrella paradox seems to me to be inescapable once one begins with a notion of critical modes as entities. I can see how an Aristotle might escape the infinite regress of umbrellas that thus threatens us; his monism is rich in devices of closure. On the other hand, I can understand why many dialectical critics take a dizzying delight in contemplating either the abysses or sublimities opened up by infinite perspectives. But I must confess that I do not now see how Crane, not finally an Aristotelian but a pluralist of modes as discrete entities, can escape the umbrella paradox. Whether I can myself escape in my final chapters remains to be seen.

Meanwhile, it is important, in concluding this chapter, to show just how deep ran Crane's love affair not only with distinctions but with the notion that by accumulating legitimate distinctions and pursuing them independently and vigorously one can somehow produce a concert of truth superior to any one voice. We have seen that he felt this to be so even within a given choice of subject matter. It is equally so when he says that the health of criticism depends on the pursuit of many views of what poetry is. Not surprisingly, the same faith in multiplying enterprises is revealed when he moves beyond poetry and discusses the humanities in general. Radically repudiating hope for any general conspectus, any fully articulated chart in which the one proper hierarchy of disciplines would be made clear, Crane pursues the uses of variety among the disciplines as vigorously as he had within criticism itself.

When he wrote his most impressive exercise in the history of ideas, called "Shifting Definitions and Evaluations of the Humanities from the Renaissance to the Present," there was no effort to show that some *one* definition and evaluation was correct. Rather he tried to show the powers of each view. Nevertheless, there was a criterion operating, and it was, finally, the criterion of relative adequacy, of correspondence to an irreducible richness that must be really there in the subject matter of the humanities, waiting to be recognized by a properly pluralistic collection of scholars.

In most periods, he says, monists, skeptics, and eclectics go their own way, either ignoring their rivals or attacking debased versions of them; but in the eighteenth century, the possibility of a different kind of relationship was raised. In that century,

> for the first and last time in this history, for all the differences of method and emphasis, something like a balance was achieved, by most . . . writers . . . , between the various rival interests of earlier periods. We have seen how earlier periods set humanists, as advocates of useful knowledge, against dialecticians; natural scientists, as advocates of useful knowledge, against humanists; partisans of the moderns against admirers of the ancients; and rhetoricians and scholars against philosophers. Resolution of these oppositions, however partial, produced a great humanistic age—an age in which the utility of literary studies was seldom seriously questioned even by educators interested in diffusing natural knowledge; in which the central problems of philosophers were problems of the powers and achievements of man; in which, at

the same time that grammarians, critics, and historians attempted to be philosophical, philosophers concerned themselves in a humanistic rather than merely scientific spirit with language, criticism, and history; in which, in short, whether on the side of the literary men or on that of the philosophers, the characteristic effort, in all fields of discussion, aimed at the establishment of some kind of union or harmony—rather than separation—between words and things, the arts of speech and the arts of reason, the determinations of facts and the formulation of principles and values, the permanently excellent and the immediately useful, the classics of the past and the new knowledge and problems of the present.[30]

And he goes on to cite three heroes of this lost harmony, Hume, Adam Smith, and Joseph Priestley. It is not surprising that, as he turns to the nineteenth century, he finds in it a falling-away from the true harmony, just because it is a period of "separation and controversy."

And so the ideal becomes a harmony after all. Clearly it is not a harmony in which any one choral director knows the complete score. It is a harmony of productive discourse, not of a comprehensive schema of truth. Whether it is genuinely pluralistic or finally a monism of "the comprehensive," I leave as a question, one that should lead us nicely into the effort by Kenneth Burke, my second pluralist, to find a way of talking about everything at once.

3

But professional philosophers are usually only apologists: that is, they are absorbed in defending some vested illusion or some eloquent idea. Like lawyers or detectives, they study the case for which they are retained, to see how much evidence or semblance of evidence they can gather for the defence, and how much prejudice they can raise against the witnesses for the prosecution; for they know they are defending prisoners suspected by the world, and perhaps by their own good sense, of falsification. They do not covet truth, but victory and the dispelling of their own doubts.—Santayana

Without contraries is no progression.—William Blake

Nothing can more effectively set people at odds than the demand that they think alike.—Kenneth Burke

If our students now could begin really to understand what Royce means with his voluntaristic-pluralistic monism, what Münsterberg means with his dualistic scientificism and platonism, what Santayana means by his pessimistic platonism . . . , what I mean by my crass pluralism, . . . that these are so many religions, ways of fronting life, and worth fighting for, we should have a genuine philosophic universe at Harvard. The best condition of it would be an open conflict and rivalry of the diverse systems . . . . The world might ring with the struggle, if we devoted ourselves exclusively to belaboring each other.
—William James

Kenneth Burke's Comedy:
The Multiplication
of Perspectives

In choosing Kenneth Burke as my second pluralist I am obviously making as sharp a contrast with Crane as possible without leaving the subject of critical pluralisms entirely. But Burke, who does not himself make much use of the word pluralism, could happily point out that any such statement can be played both ways: I must really have chosen him for his similarity to Crane. Otherwise how could he belong in the same book? In any case, as he likes to say, echoing Hegel: "Things farthest apart are also closest together."[1]

Among the many similarities between Crane and Burke, the one that naturally interests me most is their unflagging effort to deal with intellectual conflict by taking thought about it. Some critics (fewer now, perhaps, than twenty years ago), viewing this preoccupation of theirs as an unfortunate deviation from the *real* job of practical criticism, might say that those who invent theory of criticism, meta-criticism, do so to protect themselves from encounters with living literature. I must admit that both Crane and Burke sometimes push very close to my own limits of patience, Crane chewing on bones long after I think all marrow has been extracted, Burke juggling Indian clubs that I am not quite sure are even there. Clearly, neither of them has managed to hit the one right ratio of theory to practice that I have always maintained in my own work. The rule is, of course, as follows: *my* abstract theory is essential, concrete groundwork; *his* is frequently quixotic indulgence in a perhaps harmless but irrelevant hobby-horse; and M. Jacques Lacan's is lamentable proof that when the Germans conquered France in World War II Hegel came swirling in with them and sent traditional French lucidity forever underground.

Burke in Crane's Quadrate

It is implicit in what I have said of Crane that he could easily describe Burke's differences from himself in pluralistic terms. Though he never discusses Burke at length, he places him clearly among the many who define poetry as one kind or use of language rather than, say, an imitation of human life or a making of "objects." Indeed, Crane lists him among those authors—"Professor Coomaraswamy, Maud Bodkin, Kenneth Burke, Edmund Wilson, Lionel Trilling, Richard Chase, Francis Fergusson, and Northrop Frye (to mention only a few conspicuous names)"—who depend on

> positive analogies between poetry, viewed in terms of its content of meanings, and the various other modes—not all of them verbal strictly—of objectifying the conceptions and impulses of the mind, and hence of ordering experiences symbolically, which have been set over against science and discursive logic, in the speculations of the past half-century, as so many pre-logical or extra-logical types of "language."[2]

This group contrasts sharply with another list of critics who also see poetry as a special use of language but who depend on *negative* analogies with scientific language—people like I. A. Richards and Cleanth Brooks.

If we pursue Crane's kinds of distinctions among critics, we can easily elaborate this initial placement of Burke by using Crane's four variables derived from Aristotle's "causes." The result should be, if we work with as much care as Crane would demand, a Burke considerably more coherent and plausible and essentially more challenging than the one presented to us by most of the critics who have commented on his work. Indeed, reassembled "in his own terms," he will be irrefutable.

His *subject matter*, in this view, is clearly language and the way symbolic communication is effected through language. He sees both poems and criticism as manifestations of a universal human activity, *symbolic action*, and thus not primarily as the making of objects or the formulation of static thoughts or truths.

There are two major kinds of critics who make this choice, and Burke's *method* places him with those who are primarily interested in pursuing the similarities between poetry as language and other symbolic actions, not with those who want primarily to pursue differences and to consider poetry in its unique quality. Though Burke attempts to do justice to poetry in its distinctiveness, and indeed often begins or ends with a sustained bow in the direction of Chicago, he is really much more interested in what poetry *does* for poets and audiences than in what it *is* or how it is constructed. He seeks its special way of doing what other human actions also do. Poems compete, console, warn, celebrate, attack, defend, lament, purge, build (or destroy) community; the list is potentially as long as the indefinitely long list of human motives.

Similarly, his *principles* are finally holistic or assimilative, remaining constant as he moves from field to field, even while the surface of his work reveals an iridescent variety. His definition of man, for example, as the *symbol-making and symbol-using animal* is itself not subject to change but only to elaboration. And he always *thinks with* a two-term dialectic of symbolicity/animality. What is more, his mode of working from his definition—what he calls dramatism—is found in every word he utters. Both the definition and the dramatistic pentad—act, agent, scene, agency, and purpose—are intended to cover the world, the world of man's actions (symbolicity) and the scientist's world of sheer bodily motion (animality).

With such choices of subject, method, and principles, Burke can show beautifully how poetry fulfills the "motives" of poets and readers—how it *does* in poetic language what other symbolic actions do in nonpoetic language or with other symbolic means: fight wars, threaten to drop bombs, sell and buy cars, issue manifestos, make constitutions, and so on.

It is inevitable that Burke, in choosing to show what literature has in common with other human deeds, surrenders the possibility of showing what poetry does in its uniqueness. Even more obviously (and disastrously, from the point of view of anyone wanting to study poems as *poems*), he gives up the possibility of accounting for what each particular poem does that no other poems do. Indeed, his methods are, as he himself often claims, as applicable to one kind of discourse as to another, as useful applied to *The Maltese Falcon* or even a comic strip as to *Coriolanus*. All of which is a way of saying, finally, that his *purpose* is practical or "actional" or "operational" rather than cognitive or aesthetic: his words are deeds, acting on the world of words seen as deeds. And if you happen to care more about that sort of thing than about poetic knowledge, he is a good man to turn to.

Thus Crane's pluralism might lead us to "do justice" to Burke. His dramatism is one of the possible modes: his subject, language as action; his method, an assimilative dialectic; his principles, comprehensive and operational; and his purpose, actional or "rhetorical." To use his own words, he attempts "to cure" himself and society by doing verbal "therapy." His initial choice of mode enables him to answer certain questions and prevents his answering other questions. When we judge his answers as "relative to" that initial choice, we can both judge his effectiveness within his chosen mode and avoid the kind of dogmatism that would rule out his mode as illegitimate in the first place.

Anyone who knows Burke at all knows that he will refuse to stay pinned and wriggling on anyone else's wall chart. Indeed, I think I can hear him now.*

> If ever there was a misguided and hopeless effort at resolving conflict, what we have heard here from Booth about Crane and the Chicago School, and now about Burke, is it. Clearly Booth set the whole thing up to yield a neat and finally resolvable contrast between Crane and us. Obviously, he intends to come along in his final chapters with a reconciliation in some sort of supreme pluralism, which will be nothing more than his own disguised monism. Just as clearly, he thinks that in choosing us he has found a voice that will yield him a second pluralism, finally reducible to a monism, in order to make his own open-mindedness look good.
>
> About the only thing in his whole presentation that is not either downright wrong or askew is his claim that we would do things differently from Crane, and even there he ignores the fact that we believe in doing Crane's kind of job *first*, before we turn to the more important matters encompassed in our dramatism.[3]
>
> How absurd it is to classify us according to a four-cause analysis that our own work finds largely unhelpful. It's true that some of the terms of that analysis overlap terms we often use. We can digest Aristotle and the Chicago school between lunch and supper. The account may be right in one sense, in claiming that we see poems primarily as a *form of discourse*, only secondarily as *made objects*. Poems *do* things for us that other symbolic actions can also do. But what a grotesque reduction those terms impose. How that hypostasizing mind, the composite Booth-Crane, despite its professed commitment to induction, wields those same four fixed categories! Though Booth-Crane have not made the usual mistake of ignoring our general philosophical program, he/they might almost as well have done so, for all the good it does *us*.
>
> Note secondly how Booth's own program implicitly prejudges critical acts as good or bad. There are killers and maimers (bad), and there are inquirers (good). But anyone can see that the distinction is misleading. What Booth calls warfare—or, in his other metaphor, the skewering of straw men—is itself a form of inquiry, perhaps the chief form we have. Most of the best critical work gets

---

*I *thought* I could hear him. But his actual response to words somewhat like these, and to the entirely sympathetic words that follow, was even less predictable than I had expected. See his reply, pp. 128 ff., below.

done precisely by the kind of warriors Booth deplores. The very destructiveness, even the "unfair" destructiveness, that he would diminish is what prevents various monisms from "perfecting" themselves and taking over the world.

What is more, Booth protects himself by refusing to deal with literal war, which is a much more present threat to the world than critical warfare. It is in the analogies between critical warfare and bloody war that we find some of the most useful insights into how to diminish the latter. Just as literal killing can be a form of inquiry, as when a general says, "Let's see what will happen if we send 10,000 troops against *that* salient," so can critical warfare bleed off some of the energies that otherwise might go into killing. What Booth should have conducted is not a classificatory exercise but a dialectical exploration of his two terms, showing how warfare can be modulated into inquiry and how inquiry can achieve the ends of war.

In sum: what *does* he think he is himself conducting if not an aggressive act of critical warfare? He comes with a "motivated" program, some of the motives conscious, many of them no doubt unsuspected. He assumes that his readers have misconceptions about us and about Crane and about how to relate the two of us, and he uses all the resources of his literal-minded art to diminish conflict—by winning! There are, after all, only three possibilities in *his* encounter with *his* readers: his view prevails (that is, he wins); their preconceptions about Crane and Burke hold (that is, he loses); or there is continued confusion and disagreement (that is, stalemate). Is that warfare or inquiry? Obviously, both; but a deeper exploration of my own uses for stalemates could have helped him a lot. The same will hold for each of his distinctions. And while we're on the subject, Booth's heavy-footed, judgment-ridden reading of that poem by Auden needs a bit of comic discounting. He left out most of what interests us about it. Let us move in on it again, this time. . . .

My imagined Burke is surely justified in his reply. To "understand" a man by showing, in alien terms, what he is about, even when one works with a relatively rich set of questions and terms and tries hard not to be reductive, is still to use him for purposes other than his own. In Burke's terms, one has used "administrative rhetoric" on him, getting him under control. Let me, then, make a second try, this time attempting total immersion in the words of that wonderfully variegated mind. As I make the attempt, I sense, hovering above us, hierarchical choruses of angels and devils, singing and dancing their Burkean yeses and noes, so thoroughly blended that one hardly knows which way to turn. Through it all, one does hear two fairly persistent, distinct voices, one of the Lord, the great Logos, chanting, as at the end of *The Rhetoric of Religion*, "It's more complicated than that," the other of Burke himself: "That wasn't what I meant at all."

Burke in Burke's Pentagon

Burke often speculates about beginnings, and he notes that what are beginnings temporally are often logically the end. What is more, in our temporal beginning is always our logical end, and vice versa. Besides, every beginning, if questioned, can lead to a further explanation.[4] What, then, prevents an infinite regress of both logical and temporal beginnings? I must face that question again later, because it is the same as asking, Why is Burke not a relativist or skeptic?

But first I must emphasize how strongly the surface of Burke's writing seems to violate two of Crane's criteria for good criticism, even though to do so may initially seem like the experience of crawling backward into a world of exuberant dancers. He often seems blithely indifferent to Crane's insistence on coherence and common-sensical correspondence with what is "really there." His paths are seldom straight and clear; his allusions are often obscure; his arguments often seem to depend on puns or questionable etymologies or on conjectures so wild that he does not even try to defend them. Whatever the accepted canons are for organizing a proof seem as often violated as honored. His notorious translation of Keats's last line into "Body is turd, turd body," is only one of thousands of what have seemed debasements—or, at best, irrelevant private translations—of what "everyone knows" about the works he discusses.

Obviously, what has annoyed many people besides Crane is not simply Burke's frequent pursuit of scatology or his free-wheeling delivery. Most of us accept far more dirt per page in Rabelais or Swift or Joyce, and no one complains when Pascal and Wittgenstein give us disjointed fragments. What is troublesome, surely, is precisely Burke's claim to make connections in what appears disparate—the claim, for example, to connect bodily functions to surroundings hitherto seen as "poetic." The trouble, in short, is not that turds are flung at us but that they come labeled as truth. Burke seems to be claiming to know better than Keats himself something of what the poem "means," and the meaning he finds is antithetical not just to the poet's intentions but to any intentions Keats might conceivably have entertained!

Scarcely surprising, then, that in much of what has been printed about Burke there is an air of condescension. "Responsible scholars" early tended to treat him like a buffoon with a high I.Q. The tone, often, was that of René Wellek, who begins with praise, referring to "men of great gifts, nimble powers of combination and association, and fertile imagination," but who then deplores Burke's irresponsibility, repudiates his critical judgment, condemns his general method (without bothering to look closely at it), and in general makes him into some sort of *idiot savant*—a man who can from time to time for some reason play beautiful music but who obviously knows nothing about how it is done.[5]

Without pretending to defend all of Burke's moves, many of which he himself later repudiates or contradicts, I do want to argue that his is one of the great pluralizing minds of our time. Can I do so without repudiating Crane?

Strong convictions about any mode of greatness are arrived at only in direct contact with that greatness. But argument about it need not be pointless if it leads to renewed efforts at contact. If you had never heard Mozart's Thirty-sixth Symphony and I wrote a detailed analysis of its first movement, defending it as great, the most I might hope for would be that you would then listen to the music and expect greatness—unless, of course, my illustrations had been so full, and your skill with scores so refined, that your reading was in effect a hearing. But even that kind of exception is not possible here, for I shall not be able to quote enough Burke to give anything like a full experience. I am not even sure how much that would have to be, since in my own case I had to read him and re-read him in large doses for many years before I got beyond my initial prejudices, imbibed in part from Crane.

METHOD: BEGINNINGS AND ENDINGS

We can at least begin with Burke's own kind of defense when under attack. Having seen man's world as a drama of symbolic actions, convinced that man's "symbolicity" is disastrous whenever any symbolic direction is followed to some kind of logical "perfection," he has consistently sought ways of mitigating, or undermining, the rage for perfection that each monistic mode of thought exhibits. We can see what this means in his fairly recent defense of his excremental talk about Keats. We must think of him as seeking always to modulate the excesses both of eulogistic languages, which would treat man as a creature of pure mind or spirit, and of "dyslogistic" languages, which would reduce him to mere body, never acting but only reacting. In that light, what he calls his "joycing" of Keats can indeed be seen, in his words, as "but heuristic, suggestive, though it may put us in search of corroborative observations. And any such bathos, lurking behind the poem's pathos, is so alien to the formal pretenses of the work, if such indecorous transliterating of the poem's decorum had occurred to Keats, in all likelihood he would have phrased his formula differently, to avoid this turn."[6]

Such emphasis on stirring things up by probing beneath the "formal pretenses" of the work tells us what was most obviously wrong with the placement of Burke that I attributed to Ronald Crane. While it explicitly described Burke's purposes in pragmatic terms, it silently assumed that he shared, or should share, Crane's passion for knowledge about distinctions of constructional excellence. But even a superficial dip into Burke will show that the search for such knowledge is for him suspect when it is allowed to set the conditions of all critical endeavor. He does not flatly repudiate the search for demonstrable conclusions about literature in general or about particular works, for scientific pursuits have their place under his own kind of pluralistic umbrella; but he repudiates many of the canons of demonstration that most traditional scholars would take for granted. Now, when we find a critic not just deliberately flouting but making an overt attack on Occam's razor, when we find him not only "guilty of circular reasoning" but hailing circular reasoning as what every thinker inevitably commits, we can either rule him out of court or we can try to understand what critical purposes are thwarted when we insist that all discourse fit models imported from the sciences.

Consider Burke's discussion, in *Attitudes toward History*, of what he calls the "heads I win, tails you lose" argument. It is "a device," he says,

> whereby, if things turn out one way, your system accounts for them—and if they turn out the opposite way, your system also accounts for them. When we [Burke always refers to himself as "we," a stylistic choice that for many years offended me, until I finally figured out his reasons for it] first came upon this formula, we thought we had found a way of discrediting an argument. If a philosopher outlined a system, and we were able to locate its variant of the "heads I win, tails you lose" device, we thought we had exposed a fatal fallacy. But as we grew older, we began to ask ourselves whether there is any other possible way of thinking. And we now absolutely doubt that there is.

So what do "we" do now? We merely ask of any thinker that he "*co-operate with us*" in the attempt to track down his variant" of the strategy.[7]

If Burke is right here—and I think he is, provided we understand that to "track down the variant" is in his view never easy—we have the basis for a special kind of free-wheeling inquiry into other critics' views. Instead of thinking that we can refute a given position by showing that it cannot be experimentally or logically falsified, we are invited by it to *one* perspective on the world, a perspective that is likely, by the very nature of perspectives, to be self-demonstrating. Every perspective expressed in a symbolic language becomes a "ter-ministic screen" which both reveals some truths—obviously "demon-strated" to anyone employing the language—and conceals others.

Taken seriously, this position means that no refutation of Burke that I have seen has any relevance to what he is really doing, because they all employ some version of a scientistic calculus to show either that Burke cannot prove what he says, or that what he says can be refuted from some other perspective, or that all of his proofs are circular. But since all screens will be vulnerable to the same charges, the question becomes, not whether a given perspective can be shown to be distorted—because it always can be from any other perspec-tive—but whether it is more or less adequate to the kinds of problems it reveals. The result of such a position is not relativism, although it is not surprising that inattentive readers have confused it with rel-ativism; having cut his moorings from conventional norms of proof, Burke is naturally accused of having no norms at all.

He in fact rejects more than conventional norms. His dialectic of similarities and differences is so deliberately flexible and so aggres-sively opposed to neatly fixed meanings that in a sense all literal proof is made suspect. In the opening pages of *A Grammar of Motives* we find a series of claims that any action or statement can be considered as evidence for or against almost any concept. In defining any sub-stance, for example, we necessarily place it in its context, its *scene*, which is to define it in terms of what it is *not*, leading to the "paradox of substance": "every positive is negative."[8] Before we know it, Burke has moved through statements like "any tendency *to* do something is . . . a tendency *not* to do it" (p. 32) to a series of paradoxes and oxymorons and "ambiguities of substance" that stagger the literal-minded:

> Hence, Pure Personality would be the same as No Personality: and the derivation of the personal principle from God as pure person would amount to its derivation from an impersonal principle. Similarly, a point that Hegel made much of, Pure Being would be the same as Not-Being; and in Aristotle, God can be defined either as "Pure Act" or as complete repose. . . . And Leibniz was able to

propose something pretty much like unconscious ideas in his doctrine of the "virtual innateness of ideas." (We might point up the oxymoron here by translating "unconscious ideas" as "unaware awarenesses.") [P. 35]

Here we find Burke not simply claiming that everything is *like* everything else but asserting universal identity, identity not only of positives but of positive and negative. In this world, perfection "equals" nonperfection, purity "equals" corruption, action "equals" passion; everything equals everything else and, as he playfully puts it, vice versa.

Obviously such talk is nonsense to anyone who insists on a literal meaning for phrases like "the same as" and "amounts to." Burke seldom uses such words in a sense that would satisfy someone like Crane as strictly literal; even the word "literal" is not quite literal; thinking about the concept as Burke might, we would no doubt extend my questioning of Crane's usage in chapter 2. Indeed, a major part of his persistent program is to remind literalists that behind their claims to precision lurk confusions that can be acknowledged and lived with only by qualifying every copulative verb with some sense of ambiguity. It is not just that the words need semantic scouring. What something *is* is always too rich and complex for any one statement. Thus Burke can, without violating his own canons, say at one point that literary form as the gratification of needs *is* the appeal in poetry[9] and, in other contexts, say that literary form is a *disguise* for the true appeal; and he can really mean both statements.

But we must not be un-Burkean in what we mean by a phrase like "really mean." We are not—it should be clear by now—in pursuit of a meaning that is knowledge in a scientific sense of fixed concepts proved by tests of certainty or levels of probability. We are pursuing a truth-of-action, a meaning that is more probed than proved—a *way* of knowing, a knowing that is itself a kind of action.

Consider more closely the beginning of *A Grammar of Motives*. Like Burke's other books, it depends on a conceptual beginning in "dramatism": *if* man-as-symbol-user, *then* action (in the sense of symbolically motivated choices between various yeses and noes—the opposite, in short, of mere motion); *if* action, *then* conflict; *if* conflict, *then* drama. And *if* drama, *then* surely you must want to find a critical language that deals dramatically with the great symbolic drama of the whole of man's life.[10] But note how he says the project began, as distinct from how the finished book begins:

We began with a theory of comedy, *applied* to a treatise on *human relations*. Feeling that competitive ambition is a drastically over-developed motive in the modern world, we thought *this motive might be transcended* if men devoted themselves not so much to "excoriating" it as to "appreciating" it. . . . We sought to formulate the basic stratagems which people employ, in endless variations, and consciously or unconsciously, for the outwitting or cajoling of one another. [P. xii; my italics]

He soon found himself trying to construct a rhetoric, symbolic, and grammar of human motives, a three-in-one inquiry that would poten-tially accommodate all particular doctrines and provide for their meeting without mutual destruction. In short, he set out, like certain others, to build a pluralism that would save himself and the world by reducing meaningless and destructive symbolic encounter.

The further one goes in Burke, the clearer it becomes that every consideration is subordinated to this master program. Though he has a passion for learning matched by few, though he is deeply respon-sible to his kind of truth, that truth cannot be summarized in ordi-nary cognitive terms. The world is threatened with kinds of conflict, symbolic and literal, that may destroy us. Can we, by taking thought about conflict, diminish the chances either of physical destruction or of that other kind that critics inflict on each other: the annihilation of one view by the "perfection" of another?

CONSEQUENCES

One good way to see what this means is to imagine a modern-day Plato setting out to save mankind through thought but purged by Kant and others of any hope of discovering solid substances or ideal forms or essences. His hope cannot be for goodness or justice or wisdom but rather for *good ways* of talking and acting, *just ways* of talking and acting, *wise ways* of talking and acting. What will be some consequences of such a program?

1. Most of Crane's distinctions among kinds of discourse and kinds of action will no longer matter very much. Every action can have symbolic value, every statement can be a good or bad symbolic action, depending on its context. A pure poem, so called, may be more useful in curing us of our various isolationisms than an obviously didactic plea to be tolerant. By the same token, efforts at speculative discourse like Burke's will at times become more like "poetry" than like argu-ment. Every generic distinction ever made can be thrown into what

Burke calls his alembic and distilled into new visions of unity. Or, for curative purposes, any distinction can be left as it was or be tempered slightly, warmed or cooled, as it were. Consistency will be of method, not of definitions, distinctions, or conclusions, and our statements will often look inconsistent or ungrounded to critics seeking literal coherence.

Burke offers a revealing metaphor for how genuine meetings of conflicting views might take place in this new world in which process is more important than formulation. "Distinctions," he says,

> arise out of a great central moltenness, where all is merged. They have been thrown from a liquid center to the surface, where they have congealed. Let one of these crusted distinctions return to its source, and in this alchemic center it may be remade, again becoming molten liquid, and may enter into new combinations, whereat it may be again thrown forth as a new crust, a different distinction. So that A may become non-A. But not merely by a leap from one state to the other. Rather, we must take A back into the ground of its existence, the logical substance that is its causal ancestor, and on to a point where it is consubstantial with non-A; then we may return, this time emerging with non-A instead. [*Grammar*, p. xiii]

This vision, revealing what he sometimes calls his critical "machine" as a great smelter of his own distinctions, applies to the differences among all philosophical systems. What causes warfare among systems is that all terms are inherently ambiguous, and we therefore consider it "our task to study and clarify the *resources* of ambiguity" (p. xiii). Philosophical systems "can pull one way and another" just because the terms *are* inherently ambiguous. But the energetic student of ambiguities can pursue the "margins of overlap" in order to "go without a leap from any one of the terms to any of its fellows" (p. xv).

Everything in this world of process is, then, related to everything else. And similarities are somehow realer, in that molten center, than differences.

2. Suppose we accept this pervasive view of ambiguity and then try to find a way of talking that will potentially encompass all views, not by reducing them to convenient plus or minus signs, but by identifying with them and then incorporating them, in their richness, into a great dialogue. Our ultimate purpose is to save the world from the kind of warfare that would make good talk, including conflicting talk, impos-

sible; in sum, we set out with the goal of *keeping the options open*, and that means that we are trying to act with *our* symbols on both the world of symbolic action and on the world of motion or body where there are no symbols to act on us in return. Various forms of warfare threaten on every hand: sheer critical confusion, motives for self-destruction and destruction of others, authoritarian censorship programs in new totalitarian form, and new weaponry capable of silencing the dialogue once and for all. Anyone who cares for *anything* human will thus surely have an interest in following us. The goal, stated as slogan, is to learn to "get along with people better,"[11] by inquiring into and explaining to them and to ourselves how we talk together.

The test of any action or piece of discourse will thus no longer be primarily "Is it true?" or "Is it beautifully made?" but rather "Is it curative?" Did the probe turn up something helpful, or help us discard something harmful?

3. When we do literary criticism, the elements of any poem, and thus of poetic analysis, will not be elements of a known form, formally considered, but elements of an action, actionally considered. We shall of course want very much to be able to do justice to every aspect of discourse, including its "poetic" form as analyzed by a Ronald Crane or a Cleanth Brooks, and we may thus borrow their terms at particular moments, trying only to do *their* job better.

> I shall grant to our current neo-Aristotelian school (by far the most admirable and exacting group a critic can possibly select as his opponent) that the focus of critical analysis must be upon the structure of the given work itself. Unless this requirement is fulfilled, and amply, the critic has slighted his primary obligation. It is my contention, however, that the proposed method of analysis is equally relevant, whether you would introduce correlations from outside the given poetic integer or confine yourself to the charting of correlations within the integer. And I contend that the kind of observation about structure is more relevant when you approach the work as the *functioning* of a structure (quite as you would make more relevant statements about the distribution of men and postures on a football field if you inspected this distribution from the standpoint of tactics for the attainment of the game's purposes than if you did not know of the game's purposes). And I contend that some such description of the "symbolic act" as I am here proposing is best adapted for the disclosure of a poem's function.[12]

If we think about what the key words in this passage mean for Burke as distinct from what they would mean for Crane—"relevant,"

"outside," "inside," "functioning of a structure," "purposes," "function"—we see that he is inevitably importing into his standard a
notion of *poems as deeds*, and it is no idle boast at all for him to claim
that his method is flatly superior for analyzing purpose and structure
in *his* definition. But his definitions are not of autonomous forms, or
of principles, purposes, materials, and methods for making such
forms, but rather of actions and scenes, the principles of action, actors
and their qualities, the means of action, and, most important, the
purposes of actions. He seeks out whatever causes and conditions
seem pertinent to or determinative of actions, and "motives" become
even more important than the forms they lead poets to make.

What he means by action is that kind of behavior peculiar to a
choosing agent, what nonagents like stones and plants and animals
cannot perform. We must note, following this program, that many
modern thinkers deny that such action is possible; for them men only
think that they act, whereas they are really, just like plants and stones,
in motion determined by previous motions. We shall know better
than to try to refute such scientistic monists, because we know that
their position will be self-proving, according to the heads-I-win-
tails-you-lose form of argument. But we shall also cheerfully note that
they try to persuade us to choose their views; that is, they act *as if* they
could really act on us in our symbolicity, not in our animality—*as if*, in
short, we could *act* in response.[13]

Thus the kind of action that we see as the center of our own endeavor as we try to change our readers will also be the center of every
human drama (though as pluralists we must remember that we are at
best pursuing only one of many possible ways of talking about the
center). And, since it is genuine action that interests us, we note that
even if people only think they act, even if they are really only body in
motion, the actions they *think* they perform entail conflict, conflict
entails drama, and drama entails the need for dramatistic terms for
our analyses. Though behaviorists cannot be directly refuted, they can
be shown to provide no language for talking about the drama their
proponents engage in when they try to persuade us to accept their
language.

We shall therefore always look, in every human situation, for the
elements of drama, the five most obvious being the *action* itself, the
agent doing the action, the *agency* or means by which he performs it,
the *scene* in which it is performed, and the *purpose* it is intended to
achieve. Sometimes we may want to add others, like *time* as a distinguishable part of the scene and *attitude* as a subdivision of agency, but

usually the dramatistic pentad will do our job. We shall use these elements, however, not as some use Aristotle's four causes—unvarying, frozen, literal categories—but as fluid reagents, applicable in different "ratios" for different problems. What is one agent's action is another agent's scene. A given agent can be of someone else's agency—a tool to other ends—or he can be, again, a part of someone's scene. And we shall find that philosophies and critical theories can be classified and accommodated according to their proportionate emphases on one or another of these and the ratios among them. Scene, for example, may be elevated by materialists to become the supreme and only agent. Agent may be elevated by some religionists into supreme agent or turned, by pantheists, into supreme scene that is supreme agent (*Grammar*, part 2).

4. Every chosen language, even the least philosophical, is a "terministic screen." Without choice of terms, human beings would be incapable of their unique and defining gift, symbolic action. But each choice becomes a screen that is both a reflection of reality and a deflection of reality.[14] In fact each screen tends to superimpose a greater and greater distortion as it strives for its own perfecting; each symbolic actor is thus tempted to transcend all limitations by climbing a hierarchy of values implicit in his language in the hope of finally discovering the full and final meaning of his initial choice. Each screen tends thus to distort the whole of things by exploiting a partial view that pretends to be the whole and that struggles to perfect itself by triumphing over all other views. The result is of course more conflict—conflict of a kind that shows an inherent drive toward total confrontation.

5. In the resulting struggle, one glowingly tempting possibility is that mankind might find a way to transcend the conflicts, leave behind the partialities, and achieve some kind of ultimate harmony—what Burke calls the marriage of all to all. This is the happy route of transcendence that dialectical thinkers are almost always tempted by. The fact is, however, that no one can really hope for such a happy outcome of the dialectic of warring positions.

> I'm not too sure that, in the present state of Big Technology's confusions, any educational policy, even if it were itself perfect and were adopted throughout the world, would be able to help much, when the world is so ardently beset by so much distress and malice. The dreary likelihood is that, if we do avoid the holocaust, we shall do so mainly by bits of political patchwork here and there, with alliances falling sufficiently on the bias across one another,

and thus getting sufficiently in one another's road, so that there's not enough "symmetrical perfection" among the contestants to set up the "right" alignment and touch it off.[15]

There is thus a second, potentially "gloomy route," much more probable: if action, then drama; if drama, then conflict; if conflict, then "victimage" and tragedy. By their nature as actors men will produce tragedies, both symbolic and real, and, as creatures "rotten with perfection," they are likely to strive toward supreme, "perfect" tragedy (LSA, pp. 54–55). Any one voice will strive for its perfection and will thus attempt to dominate all the others. Since men are not likely to relinquish their freely enacted disagreements voluntarily, this route promises that uniquely human kind of perfection, the annihilation of the opponent. Indeed, in this century, we can envisage a supreme and supremely gloomy transcendence of conflict in universal annihilation, as we realize the "perfect" victimage implicit in all drama.

The best we can hope for, then, is Burke's own "comic" choice: to produce and exploit stalemate, a kind of undivine comedy. We develop a dialectic of muddling-through, a deliberate interference with perfection by enforcing on every terministic screen an ironic reminder of other truths according to which it should be discounted. (Note here the contrast with the way Crane's key terms are kept distinct. The further we pursue any of Burke's key terms for method, the more alike they look, until finally comedy equals dialectic equals irony equals drama.) Since we have no real hope of transcending verbal wars with an ultimate harmony that will not be ultimate annihilation of man's essence, his symbol-making and using, our best hope is for this third route, neither radiantly happy nor especially gloomy but comic: we shall try to cure mankind by keeping things off balance, by dissolving fixities, by turning the potential tragedy of fanatical annihilation into the comedy of muddled mutual accommodation.

Literature and Criticism as "Equipment for Living"

The dramatistic pentad can be used to explore any human action, including action by statement. Burke's own lifelong critical act, for example, can be viewed according to ratios among any of the terms, and the result may be what looks like contradictory language as we move from ratio to ratio. Suppose we say that Burke (as *agent*) is to be viewed as responding to the twentieth century (as *scene*), performing the *act* of literary criticism, through the *agency* of critical talk about language (he might instead have used boycotting or political revolution) for the *purpose* of cure. We read the scene as one of threatening chaos and ultimate annihilation, a scene that has led others to straightforward sermons defending eternal verities. But *if* the scene *is* chaotic, who will hear the sermons? How will such rhetoric work? Will it not probably contribute to further chaos? If it wins followers, they will surely be embattled and largely ignorant followers, and we will have contributed to the very factionalism that threatens to destroy us. *Our* agency, then—the kind of discourse we shall use in *this* scene—must be largely a disorienting discourse in order to build communities of explorers who are forced, by our criticism, to listen to each other.

Literary criticism will thus be only one of many *agencies*, an aspect of the disorienting but finally irenic discourse we need. The world of such criticism has its own gloomy route to match the "perfection" of total annihilation by the bomb. That route would lead to the annihilation of free discourse about the poem by establishing a single, final reading that readers must accept. To fix readings would be to limit the kind of actions poems and readers can perform with each other.

What we will seek, then, is a way of doing justice to many critical voices without letting any one of them achieve its destructive perfection. Knowing that the poem comes from a poet who is an inhabitant of both the world of body and the world of symbolic action, we shall expect it to show evidences of a variety of cures, bodily and spiritual, that the poet performs for himself and for his readers. It is true that when we treat a poem as an act, a piece of symbolic rhetoric, we shall find some aspects of its "medicine" in one sense timeless; for the poet and his audience share a human nature, and in the poetic part of our analysis we can do justice to what does not change from audience to audience. But we shall think it ridiculous to nail ourselves to such fixtures, since we all know that the same poem does different things for different audiences at different times. To allow a pedantic concern for permanent and fixed proof to prevent communal probing of meanings in dimensions not clearly "objective" or provable is to insure critical warfare rather than diminish it.

A Way into and around "Surgical Ward"

We must not, however, support simple skepticism or relativism; these always in practice feed the fanaticisms that destroy. Confidence must be maintained in the difference between good criticism and bad, and we must develop criteria for distinguishing the discourse that curses from the kind that cures.

We can see what this means by looking again at what "Surgical Ward" really is. It really *isn't*. Rather, it *does*. That whole chart that Crane led us into in chapter 2 was haywire. It should have been headed "Some Views of What 'Surgical Ward' *Does*."

I confess that at this point I spent some time trying to draw a chart that I wouldn't be ashamed to let Burke see. I failed, because I knew that any such chart must be a record of flowings and processes, not entities. To illustrate my problem, I here duplicate a chart Burke once made of an entirely different matter. You can see the difficulties.[16]

Suppose, then, that "Surgical Ward" comes up between us. We are not so foolish as to spend hours and hours trying to decide what it is and how it relates to its siblings and second cousins. We want to know how it works, of course, and we will thus spend some time on a "poetic" interpretation—but not, finally, for the purpose of judging Auden's skill. How it works will be important mainly as leading us to what it does, as an action produced by and thus pertinent to many motives. But this action will be received in many ways, depending on the receiver's "motives." We thus know that it *must* be viewed in many lights, all shining, as it were, simultaneously. But we shall never be satisfied with Crane's pluralism, which attempts to be a kind of supreme adding machine: there is *this* aspect of structure, pursued by *this* kind of criticism, and then there is *that* aspect of structure, pursued by *that* kind. . . . And when they are all accumulated together (but without essential communication among them?), the health of criticism is insured. No, we shall try to force all pertinent views into confrontation. We shall thus risk appearing hopelessly confused, since we shall be trying (in a sense) to do everything at once.

But we are really not all that confused. We can learn a lot about this poem. We can explore first its *literary*, its *poetic*, motives. Sonnets make demands of their own, as do statements about pain and happiness. In exploring the poetics of the piece, what the act *qua* act can tell us about itself, we can discover that the poem *is* in some sense motivated by the need to perfect the "act."

Such a poetic analysis reveals most obviously that curious contrast between the octet and the sestet that Booth's Crane made so much of. The poet ostensibly contrasts a world of isolated suffering and a shared world of health and happiness. "We," the healthy, "stand" together and "cannot imagine" that other world, where each person,

Cycle of Terms Implicit in the Idea of "Order"

God as Author and Authority

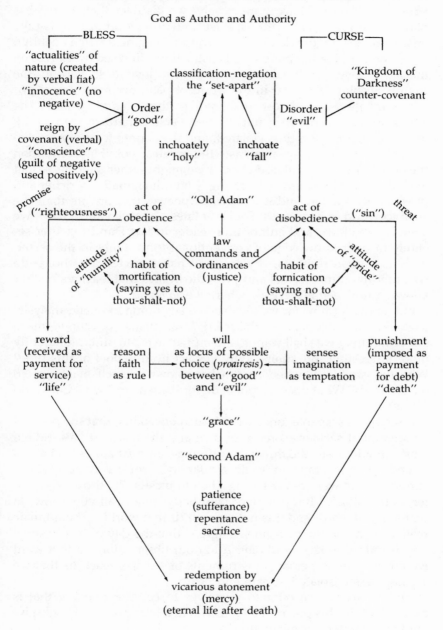

reduced to a part of his ailing body, knows no truth but self-centered pain. But when we look more closely, we discover that Auden has played a curious game with us. First, only the world of pain is fully imagined (despite the claim that we cannot imagine it when healthy), while the world of happiness is all abstraction, climaxed by a stress on the *idea* of love, presumably in contrast with love itself. Second, the rhyme, absolutely regular in the world of pain, becomes almost private, and therefore almost unshared, in the "shared" world. The meter not only turns free, but the free verse is hard to read aloud: *shared* regularities are thus violated, and the sonnet form almost disintegrates. Thus the speaker casts the greatest possible irony upon the claim that "we *stand* elsewhere"; we might rather almost say that we fall apart. The world of suffering is both imaginatively richer and prosodically stabler, and it is thus, as poetry, less private than the abstract world of happiness. For eight lines—or seven and a half—we *share* conventions, and author and reader in fact stand together securely in their knowledge of conventional form. Only in the sestet, with its skittish rhythms, rhymes, and half-retracted assertions, do we enter upon intellectual and prosodic ironies that leave us neither knowing nor seeing precisely where we *do* stand.

But no matter how far we took such a beginning in poetic analysis, it would still leave us with the main "dramatistic" questions unanswered. Surely we shall want to attempt answers to other, inherently more interesting, questions. Why *this* act by this poet at this time? Why *this* structure, when Auden has shown himself master of so many others? What does the poem do for Auden, and what does it do for us?

It seems inescapable, once we ask such questions, that the poem is an attempt at secular exorcism of pain and the fear of a pain-ridden world. It addresses the threat of suffering—a threat almost too awful to endure—and prays, in ironic secular style, for a way out: "about suffering they were never wrong, the old masters"; "those who suffer, suffer alone." Body is pain, pain body, that is all you know, in that surgical ward, and it is not enough. If that world is the ultimate reality, then "all the instruments agree" that the day of this hospital visit is indeed a dark, cold day. All of our observations in that ward would, like the impersonal instruments of science, teach us that we are hopelessly isolated in pain and death.

And what can we offer to ourselves to counter that life that is death? Not, in this poem, the God who in a later poem, "Thanksgiving for a Habitat," combats the

> Vision of Hell, when Nature's wholesome genial fabric
>   lies utterly discussed and from a sullen vague
> wafts a contagious stench, her adamant minerals
>   all corrupt, each life a worthless iteration
> of the general loathing (to know that, probably,
>   its cause is chemical can degrade the panic,
> not stint it).

The converted Auden will later find that the Holy Four, the Gospel-Makers, can, allied with prayer, combat the threat of isolated suffering. But here we have no Holy Four and no God, only a secular "defense": a shared happiness that turns ironically to a shared anger and then to a love that is not an assured love but only the idea of love. It is obviously not enough.* The struggle for transcendence of an isolated pain calls for something more than this; it cries out, once begun, for its logical or "logological" perfecting in a genuine salvation. We could surely prophesy from this poem alone, though admittedly "after the event,"[17] that Auden must some day convert to a God who offers a more convincing answer to the unredeemed world of that surgical ward or of the war-torn world for which it stands. And can we not surely prophesy that if Auden revises the poem after that conversion is secure, he will find intolerable the near-dissolution of the original? Will he not tighten things up into a fairly regular sonnet, one that somehow masters the world of pain in a way that the original, like so many of its companions in "In Time of War," visibly failed to do? With the world of happiness less problematical, he will attend more to "art" and less to the awful, intolerable pain of viewing man's fate in 1939.

---

*My colleague, Richard Strier, plausibly objects to my seeing (that is, my "Burke's" seeing) the sonnet as strongly ironic. "What disturbs me is your argument that the 'breakdown' of the meter and rhyme scheme *itself* establishes an irony. This argument seems to me to be based on a number of ad hoc assumptions. Why is it *necessary* to see the relation between the formal and the thematic elements of the poem as ironic? First of all, I don't see why half-rhymes are 'private'; they are surely as verifiable and public a linguistic phenomenon as full rhymes. Second, it seems to me that one could view the prosodic phenomena to which you are pointing non-ironically, in the following way: the octet is consciously formal, distanced, tense; the metrical formality keeps us 'apart'; the sestet, on the other hand, relaxes into a more colloquial and easy-going mode. The 'irony' disappears if the prosody of the sestet is viewed as 'relaxed' rather than as 'private' and 'unstable,' as relying easily and assuredly upon the 'common world.'" Highly plausible, Burke might reply, and somewhat closer to what Crane would see in it. If Strier is right, then of course we have evidence that Auden's conversion is prefigured in the embodied motives of the poem, *before* Auden had consciously recognized, or at least declared, his turning to God. Should we not play it both ways?

For us readers the original poem will express a similar unsatisfied hunger. The resolution is, after all, deeply unsettling, undercut by the verbal irony, by the disintegration of the verse, and by the lack of vital images. The poem thus offers none of the kinds of sharp resolution characteristic of Auden's most admired pieces. It does not, like many early poems, teach the free man how to praise, but it also does not yield any of the wonderful wry satire that helped make the youthful Auden famous. Nor does it offer anything comparable to the brilliantly sharp ironic climaxes that we find in Auden's anthologized pieces: she "answered all of his long, marvelous letters but kept none"; "Dance, dance, dance till you drop"; "The question is absurd: / Had anything been wrong, we should certainly have heard."

Like many of those early poems, "Surgical Ward" offers us a kind of suffering scapegoat in those patients enduring the non-drama of unredeemed body, the in-action of those who are not agents and cannot act. Unlike them, it attempts a kind of catharsis, but the catharsis is as yet either deliberately muted or fumbled. I here resist the temptation to do a Burkean exploration of how obscene bodily functions get into the poem; in fact we don't need them, because the octet is openly about the obscene reduction to "pure" body, the perfection of mere motion. But it is clear that Auden does not see any satisfactory escape from the reduction; he can share the unshared world of misery, but, instead of a "cure," he escapes into muted ironies.

We have of course only scratched the surface of what, viewed in Burke's terms, such a poem does or might be thought to do for its readers or for Auden.* Research into Auden's life, and guesswork about it, could lead to specific operations, specific angers, specific lonelinesses. And we can discover or imagine other audiences for whom it would either succeed or fail in different ways. We have no need to confine ourselves either to what Auden could plausibly have intended or to what seems clearly *in* the poem, viewed as a poetic structure. If we want to think of that foot, for example, as somehow related to the "suffering" Icarus's legs in "Musée des Beaux Arts," and then think of that scratch as somehow related to the horse scratching its innocent behind on a tree, that's our privilege. If we want to hear the breathing of an oxygen tank in the *th*-sounds of lines 1 and 6, why not? If we want to see a pun in *bear*, emphasizing the bare exposed body, or an ambiguity in the *it* of line 7, making it refer both to truth and to groans, let us do so—if we see any good reason to.

*For Burke's own revision of my hunches, see below, pp. 134–36.

The Tests of a Good Terministic Screen

But what, then, are the criteria of good critical reasons in this view? What are the limits to such seeming improvisations? Why not turn the word "truth" to "turd" again here, the word "bear" to "burden," and then bring in an allusion from my childhood patois, in which "to cut your foot" meant to step unintentionally into cow dung? Why not, indeed? Is not this pretended pluralism then simply a relativism after all, one that allows anything to be said provided it can be said with enough brashness and verve, one that can only lead us to skepticism about the possibility of *knowing* anything about poetry?

Burke himself often raises the question of relativism,[18] and his way of answering is implicit in what I have said so far. There will be no single set of literal criteria for proper talk, no catalogue of logical fallacies applicable to all occasions, no easy reference to intentions or structure or historicity. No one can list in advance all of the legitimate—that is, healing—uses a poem can be put to. If someone has a private association with "Surgical Ward" like cow dung, let him use it. But we shall insist that he discount that association by recognizing many views of the poem to which it will be irrelevant, and we shall insist that he enrich his view by learning to move logologically up to spiritual and even theological readings and back down to other secular simplifyings.

When we look for Burke's criteria, then, we find no short fixed list ✕ of tests. There is nothing here to match Crane's persistent effort to build and defend a coherent, testable, comprehensive method. Instead we have hundreds of hints and guesses.

First, what can we say about the decision to start—and end—with dramatism? There are clearly many philosophical and scientific languages, each offering itself as the language of languages. All of them will prove useful for some purposes, but few of them offer us much help in our general program of dealing with the great drama of symbolic actors. If we set out, as Burke says, "working for the purification of war," if we seek some alternative to what he calls "dissipation" and "fanaticism" (his rough equivalents for the extremes of what I have been calling skepticism and dogmatic monism), if we seek to maintain the possibility in the world of a "neo-liberal, speculative attitude," then surely our terms must be those that will describe and deal with the symbolic actions we encounter—and perpetrate.

According to Burke, then, we do not simply have the right to choose a dramatistic vocabulary, as one among many; rather, this vocabulary is forced upon us by our choice of task. We could avoid it only by confining ourselves to questions about those things and bodies in the world that do not commit symbolic actions or by choosing, as the neo-Aristotelians do in their literary criticism, to deal with a small aspect of any given act. As he says at the beginning of *A Grammar of Motives*, "If you ask why, with a whole world of terms to choose from, we select these [the dramatistic pentad] rather than some others as basic, our book itself is offered as the answer. For, to explain our position, we shall show *how it can be applied*" (p. x; my italics). Though all other philosophies would have a right, in Burke's view, to begin with exactly the same kind of unproved beginnings, they could not hope to deal with *his* problem—the conflict of symbolic actions—unless they employed the terms of dramatism.

What is more, we can distinguish, among other languages, some that are inadequate even to the tasks that they claim to work on. Some philosophies do with richness and power what they set out to do; many fail to do so. Plato and Kant and Aristotle are in effect doing in other terms much of what we try to do in our linguistic terms. Plato has a dialectic that leads from substance to substance and ends only in transcendent reality. We will build a dialectic that leads from term to term and ends in alternative visions of possible transcendent terms—terms for order, for beauty, for right action, for God. Similarly, Kant attempts a transcendentalism concerned with the necessary forms of experience and reason; our pentadic ratios "name forms necessarily exemplified in the imputing of human motives" for action. Thus even these giants are easily incorporated without essential distortion.

But most languages will be less important than these, deficient in one respect or another. The language of behaviorism (Burke often repeats the example, and so must I), though indispensable in studying mere motion, gets its users into trouble when they try to apply it to the human drama. There is no place here for a tolerant bow to the behaviorists, saying, "You explain the human drama in your terms, and we'll explain the human drama in our terms." Because for them there *is* no human drama, since there is no concept of *action*. Having reduced their language, for the sake of efficiency, to the language of motion, they deny in their terms what their own competitive treatises display: man's symbolic drama. Reducing action to motion, the behaviorists do not tell "a representative anecdote" when they tell us their stories about man-as-animal. Anecdotes about rats in mazes lack the "circumference" or scope needed if something like justice is to be done to the drama of man.[19]

As we have seen, it would be an equally misleading reduction, possibly even more dangerous, to move in the opposite direction and pretend that man is not in any sense undergoing mere motion. What we offer is a language that can incorporate the essential truth of both reductions—a language that can move dialectically to encompass the precritical facts of both our animality and our symbolicity. In short, our language requires us to be polyglots.

The first test of our terministic screen might, then, be summarized by Burke's demand that our "anecdotes" be *fully* "representative"— that the "circumference" of our terms be large enough to include at least the action that is performed as we tell our story about man and his actions. As in Crane, the validity of a neatly closed system is in itself not very impressive if it is not adequate to a richness in the subject that every inquirer knows to be there.

The second test could not be more different. As we have seen, Burke wants to prevent that kind of perfection of views that eliminates all other views. Burke would say that the superiority of any language would lie partly in its refusal to be perfected, its roughness about the edges, its celebration of ambiguities, its capacity to resist freezing. It is true that the language of dramatism is forced upon us by our task, but its terms are, as we have seen, inherently fluid and inexhaustible. Their use is kept molten by the systematic cultivation of incongruities. Methods that freeze the options mislead us because the reality that interests us is itself dramatic, in process, fluid.

The superiority of Burke's own terministic screen is thus in part its capacity to point out to other views the ironies that must discount them. But it is clear that to do a proper job of discounting, a position or language must be potentially as powerful as what it corrects. Those who improvise carelessly will simply not do the job and will be cast aside. But it is only in the fires of dialectic, not in the application of abstract tests like that of falsifiability, that we can decide what to attend to.

It would require many pages simply to list the standards that Burke explicitly discusses at different times. I must content myself with a selection from the "Dictionary of Pivotal Terms," in his *Attitudes toward History*. Note how greatly most of them differ from the tests of rigorous coherence proclaimed by system-builders and from the tests of simplicity and falsifiability that reign supreme in many modern philosophies.

Any good—that is, useful—language will, for example, protect us from being "driven into a corner"; it will provide us with bridging devices (or what Burke elsewhere calls "devices of pontification"); it will provide a "machine" that will "mass-produce" incongruous perspectives; it will make us "at home in the complexities of relativism"; it will combat "dissociative trends" by integrative thought, while at the same time correcting integration with "latitudinarian-ism"; it will make new forms of communion possible; it will help make us sensitive to the oblique clues to meaning that authors consciously or unconsciously give us; it will provide systematic devices for avoiding efficiency, because efficiency always misleads; it will encourage exposure to the "total archives accumulated by civilization (since nothing less can give us the admonitory evi-dence of the ways in which people's exaltations malfunction as liabilities)"; it will help us watch for "unintended by-products" of our views, stressing always knowledge of limitations; it will remind us that we are not the independent, separate egos that some modernist views have claimed—rather, the so-called "I" is merely a unique combination of partially conflicting "corporate" "we's" (and it is here that we find Burke's reason for avoiding the first-person singular); it will encourage us to subject every insight to the tests provided by the collective body of criticisms (about the closest Burke comes, inci-dentally, to worrying about "objectivity"); it will provide ways of transcending what look like opposites by finding how they are not opposites; it will remind us that all arguments are not what they seem, and especially that linear argument is always "merely a set of interre-lated terms . . . ; the writer seeks to avoid subjectivity by reading the documents of other men"—documents that were organized by terms having similar functions; it will provide tests of "convertibility"—the ways by which one critic's terms can be shown to have cooperated in the formulation of another's. Finally, to cut short this summary of more than 200 pages, the useful language should apply to three dif-ferent "spheres" of action: it should apply to intimate relations (the individual), to public relations, and to the "process of engrossment whereby works of art are organized." In *The Rhetoric of Religion* Burke adds a fourth sphere to these: the useful language should apply to the sphere of the supernatural or divine, because, whether or not divinity exists, men have always talked as if it did, and our language must do justice to how symbolicity works in religion. To demand that a critical language do justice to these four spheres is to insist that our "anec-dotes" be "representative" indeed! The demand is reasonable, but we should not underplay the challenges that taking it seriously will give to a world taught for centuries to hone Occam's razor.

The Dance as Cure

In discussing Burke, we never come to an end, as he himself never can draw a project to a full stop. I hope to have shown, however, how his pluralism can embrace *all* meanings, potentially, and still repudiate relativism of the kind that threatens critical understanding. "Charts of meaning are not 'right' or 'wrong'—they are relative *approximations* to the truth."[20] Dramatism is both an open system, encompassing all possible systems, and an aggressive pursuit of one possible critical language, a language dictated to anyone who chooses to treat symbols as actions in the human drama. As Burke says,

> There is an infinite number of things that can be said about a poem's structure. You can, for instance, chart the periodicity of the recurrence of the definite article. You can contrast the versification with that of any other poem known to man. You can compare its hero with the hero of some work three centuries ago, etc. What I am contending is that the mode of analysis I would advocate will give you ample insight into the purely structural features of a work, but that the kind of observations you will make about structure will deal with the *fundamentals* of structure [namely, its true function for poet and reader], and will deal with them *in relation to one another*, as against the infinite number of possible disrelated objective notations that can be made. [*PLF*, pp. 73–74]

Immediately he is off on a brief effort to show why his analysis of structure is superior to that of his most serious rivals, the "current neo-Aristotelian school" (pp. 74–75). Why is it superior? Why of course because his method "is better adapted for the disclosure of a poem's function"—that is, his method is better for solving the problem that his method has chosen to solve. "Function" in this sentence is not at all the same concept as it is in Crane.

In Crane, the pluralism and the chosen critical language were relatively distinct; working on the problem of critical warfare was for him very different from the problem of talking about a poem, and the two tasks required different definitions and different methods. For Burke, the great assimilator, the two problems are of course assimilated: critics perform acts in a drama; metacritics, regardless of their differences, perform acts in a similar drama.

Thus if we were to ask these critics, "Which of you works more closely with poems?" we can be sure that each would answer, "I do," and that the answer would mean something different for each. For Crane, the act of moving close to the particular poem consists in discriminating it more and more precisely from its similars. Regardless of whether one in fact begins with a poem, as I did in chapter 1, or works around to it through discrimination after discrimination, as I did in chapter 2, one is always attempting to "begin" with what is the most real substance that we value: the "concrete" thing worth pursuing precisely because of its distinction from everything else. But Burke could argue that he never even leaves the poem, the poetry, the symbolic dance; while Crane is performing all of that preliminary analysis, Burke is at every moment performing his own poem, his symbolic act in the great drama. Every act in that drama is worth attending to, and when Burke turns to look explicitly at what we call poems, and commits the obscene act of connecting them even to our bodily life, the poetry has in his sense been with him everywhere, from the beginning. He thus lives with all poems more intimately, he could claim, than any analyst who sees himself as "working on" a poem, not "performing with" it.

Similarly, if you ask them, "Which of you is a more responsible critic?" each would have every right to answer, "I am." For Crane, Burke is irresponsible because he commits anachronisms and violates the author's intentions. But Burke can easily reply that nothing is more irresponsible than to isolate "poetry" from our deepest motives. He is supremely responsible, responding to everything anyone can say, embracing the task of curing us by joining us in the dance.

For proponents of certain kinds of rigor, to defend Burke in my way would no doubt seem a kind of dismissal, even a refutation: he has a self-proving, self-validating system, a method that invents problems that are essentially beyond solution and then claims to solve them by using principles that can be assumed only as part of his invention. His whole enterprise is impossibly, outrageously, shockingly ambitious, yet it finally frustrates intellectual ambition by undermining all solutions. But for anyone who will enter that enterprise, there is no reason why Burke's circularities, or even his imprecisions, should be condemned. Traced out in their richness, his circularities should trouble us no more than the circularities pursued by a Plato or a Cicero or a John Dewey—or by Crane or you or me. Unless the defender of rigor can refute Burke's claim that all thought is in one sense circular, that all conclusions are in a sense chosen "in the beginning," at the moment a thinker chooses his "terministic screen," he should attend closely to Burke's richer music: even the most linear and logical of critics is finally only spreading out in temporal sequence the individual notes from the musical chord that is sounded the moment he chooses his terms and begins.

Consider a true story that I used to tell as if it reflected against Burke. In the late forties I took part in a discussion with him and others of—well, I thought the subject was *Huckleberry Finn*, which for me at the time meant that we should talk only of *the* structure of that *made object*. Soon we were aware that Burke was talking about the balloon trip that Huck and Tom and Jim take over the Atlantic. Finally, in some embarrassment, one of us broke in and said, "But Kenneth, that episode is from another book!"

Burke turned on him.

"What the hell does that matter?" And he continued on his way, making points that I did not understand, deplored as irrelevant, and to my sorrow cannot now remember.

Today I see myself as mocked in the tale. I would give a good deal to know what original and shocking point about Mark Twain—or about nineteenth-century America or about the way literature works or about balloons—that monologuist was making. There were at least ten people in the room who could work with me, in our emulation of Crane, to perform the by no means contemptible task of discovering what we called the "unity" of *Huckleberry Finn*. There was only one Burke, and I could not hear him, monist that I was.

Burke's Reply

Whatever we may want to say about the processes of critical understanding, they are not simple.

When the first issue of *Critical Inquiry* was being planned, I wrote Kenneth Burke to ask whether he would reply to my account of his brilliant achievement. He agreed, and I sent him an expanded version of what some months before had been the third of my Christian Gauss lectures. I can remember feeling quite sure that he would be immensely pleased to have found someone, at last, who understood him and rated him at his true worth.

I should have known better. His reply, entitled "Dancing with Tears in My Eyes," was at first disconcerting; although he agreed with a good deal, he seemed to take some of my defense as attack. In a final revision, I attempted both to underline my unqualified admiration and to preserve the original structure, so that Burke's reply would still make sense. The resulting exchange, together with my explanatory headnote, can be found in *Critical Inquiry* 1 (1974): 1–31.

In revising the original article (already a revision of a revision of my lecture), I have still not much changed the substance of what Burke was responding to. But my revisions may make some of Burke's responses less immediately intelligible than they were in the original exchange. I saw no way to avoid this potential confusion other than by freezing my original words, which I could not do, or by conducting and reprinting an indefinitely prolonged exchange that would interest no one but ourselves.

My original hope, obviously, was to have a response from Burke that would illustrate the possibilities of understanding as neatly as the response from M. H. Abrams seems to in the next chapter. What I must offer instead is, to quote Burke's God again, "Much more complicated than that." His response shows his own unlimited willingness to engage in the process of critical understanding. It also shows, alas, both that my own capacity to understand him was less than I had hoped and that he has not fully understood me. But fortunately it also shows that we have not completely misunderstood each other, and it thus illustrates the partial success and partial failure that we are sure to meet whenever we try to understand a complex and wily genius. The embarrassments such illustration presents to my pluralistic enterprise will be important when we come to chapter 5.

To keep things relatively straight, I shall refer in what follows both to the *Critical Inquiry* pages (e.g., *CI*, p. 16) and to the revised pages in this book (e.g., *CU*, p. 16).

DANCING WITH TEARS IN MY EYES

I

One might conceivably begin an essay on Burke by taking as point of departure his theory of form as first presented in *Counter-Statement*, or his "Definition of Man" in *Language as Symbolic Action*, or his summing-up of what, in *The International Encyclopedia of the Social Sciences*, he calls "Dramatism." Or there is a roundabout but far more salient route, as suggested by a frankly adverse piece of René Wellek's in which, while incidentally including Burke among "men of great gifts, nimble powers of combination and association, and fertile imagination," the special job is frankly to present Burke as an "impasse." Or there could be a somewhat confusing approach via Ronald Crane, who was understandably more interested in presenting his method than in telling the world about the ins and outs of Burke's.* Or, as Wayne Booth puts it, Crane's purpose "is to defend one special

*[See *CI*, pp. 1–4; *CU*, pp. 99–102.]

way of dealing with poetic structure, and he does not pretend to do justice to any other."

The opening section of Booth's article chooses the Wellek-Crane route, along with a kind of "double bind" whereby, while adding to Wellek's list of Burke's "outrageous" moments, and again setting up Crane's stance, Booth shows that he intends to do better by me, in sympathetically undertaking "that seemingly impossible task," as viewed from the standpoint of pluralism, namely, "view Burke in his own terms."

On one point, Wellek got me as I deserved. My trick bit in "joycing," whereby a very solemn line in a great poem got analyzed for outlaw possibilities, should have been reserved for fun at a drunk party. But I do feel that, if Booth chose to begin thus, he should at least have done what Wellek couldn't do: he should have discussed the steps involved in my answer to Wellek. However, I don't think I should write them all over again here. If any reader is interested, the discussion is to be found in an article, "As I Was Saying," published in the Winter 1972 issue of *Michigan Quarterly Review*. I contend: Owing to the fact that words can resemble one another tonally even when their literal meanings may be miles apart, various kinds of trick affinities can develop between them. Though I affirm absolutely that anyone who doesn't agree with this proposition lacks a feel for the *sound* of words, there is still plenty of room for disagreement as to its application in particular cases. The issue becomes especially risky when (thinking along psychoanalytic lines) one tinkers with the possibility that a term on its face sublime may secretly resonate with a term quite ridiculous; and thereby the kinds of "body-thinking" explicitly manifest in, say, writers like Aristophanes or Swift can figure implicitly in solemn works (particularly when one is dealing with such images as a funeral urn). . . .

The approach via Crane seems to miss one of the major concerns I have been working on for years—namely, how to find ways of dealing both with the *poem in particular* and with *language in general*. Ironically enough, my efforts to deal with that problem were largely sharpened by the vigorous and friendly hagglings I had with "that Chicago crowd."

As for the tiresome old saw about my ways being "as useful in looking at bad poems as at good ones," when a critic celebrates a work's "unity" have you ever heard him being called to task because many inferior works also possess "unity"? Or do you hear complaints because a book on prosody can illustrate its points even by sheer designs, such as "short-long" or "abba"? The abstractive nature of critical nomenclature is such that nearly any term, taken alone, can be applied to works otherwise both good and bad in other respects. Or what of terms like "novel," "drama," "lyric"?

Booth says, "Burke seems to be claiming to know better than Keats himself some of what the poem 'means,' and the meaning he finds is antithetical not just to the poet's intentions but to any intentions he might conceivably have entertained!" The notion underlying my analysis is this: Formal social norms of "propriety" are related to poetic "propriety" as Emily Post's *Book of Etiquette* is to the depths of what goes on in the poet's search "for what feels just right." Wellek stops with Emily Post. The official aesthetic isn't likely to cover the ground. If I may offer a perhaps "outrageously" honorific example, on pages 329–30 of my *Language as Symbolic Action*, when discussing a sonnet of mine, "Atlantis," I indicate how one can both know and not know when one's imagination is working at a level of "propriety" not reducible to the official code. My lines had a Swiftian, Aristophanic dimension; and though they were not "programmatically" so designed, my experience with them both *ab intra* and *ab extra* indicates how such things can operate.

II

Things are going to ease up, praise God; yet I'm still facing trouble.* Apparently I said something mean about Occam's razor, but I don't remember where or what. I hope it may have been in connection with some such notion as Freud's concept of "overdetermination." Didn't Santayana somewhere say something like, "If Nature had abided by Occam's rule that 'Entities should not be multiplied beyond necessity,' where would you be?" As for "circular reasoning," I think of a dictionary as "circular"; and I remember hearing tell that the philosopher Morris Cohen was willing to defend circular reasoning in case the circle was big enough. But in a discussion of "contextual definition" (*Grammar of Motives*, pp. 24–25), built around distinctions between Aristotelian and Spinozistic notions of "substance," and comparing Aristotle's *kath' auto* with Spinoza's *id quod per se concipitur*, along with Spinoza's statement that "all determination is negation," I end on a bit of relaxing to this effect: "Since determined things are 'positive,' we might point up the paradox as harshly as possible by translating it, 'Every positive is negative.'" I had in mind the twist whereby, though we might ordinarily term

*[*CI*, p. 6; *CU*, p. 106.]

things like tables and chairs "positive," within Spinoza's nomenclature they would be "negative" (as later was to be the case with Hegel on *Negativität*). As Booth reduces the report, it cuts too many corners. Then he follows with a whole list of such items, each treated by omitting the qualifiers whereby we might in effect be saying, *"In one sense* it's this way, but in another sense it's *that* way." As to the place where he credits me (sans quote) with avowing "everything equals everything else," I can't figure out what was involved there. I have, however, discussed the notion that, in one sense, we're all parts of one universal context; but in another sense, owing to the "centrality of the nervous system," there is a "principle of individuation" whereby, after parturition, each of us in a way is separate from everything else. All the other items on Booth's list I might account for similarly—but there again, I found that to do so would involve me in endlessly rehashing things I had already done.

I wish that, when referring to my remarks on the appeal of form (*Counter-Statement*, pp.138–41), he had given the exact sentence, thus: "Form, having to do with the creation and gratification of needs, is 'correct' in so far as it gratifies the needs which it creates" (p. 138). And then had also given the passage and place he felt to be at odds. As things stand, I can't answer because I don't quite know what got out of line.

As for Booth's reference to my theory of comedy,* perhaps I should straighten out a matter that I left unclear. I had been working on a book of "Devices" that I have not yet published, except for occasional bits and an article reprinted in *New Rhetorics* (edited by Martin Steinmann, Jr., 1967), a piece originally published in *Journal of General Education* (April 1951); also I have used the material in connection with my teaching. I delayed publishing this volume because (I now think mistakenly) I thought that the manuscript needed a preparatory grounding in the sort of work I did in my *Grammar of Motives* and *Rhetoric of Motives*.

I guess the truth is that, even more urgently than trying to help people "get along with people," I was trying to get along with myself. Since I was too pigheaded (or possibly too arrogant despite my timidities) to seek the guidance of any psychologist, and I couldn't fold up in the Church despite my great love of theology, I worked out a way of getting along by dodges, the main one being a concern with tricks whereby I could translate my self-involvements into speculations about "people" in general. Pedagogically, as per my essay in

*[CI, p. 8; CU, p. 109.]

Modern Philosophies and Education (edited by Nelson B. Henry, 1955), I reduced the whole enterprise to three academic principles, or ideals: the teaching of skills (the pragmatic dimension); the teaching of appreciation (the aesthetic dimension); the teaching of admonitions (the ethical dimension).

Though I have worked much with tragedy, I always tend to suspect that, in a cult of tragedy, one is asking for it. So I still try, as far as possible, to keep at least remotely under the sign of comedy (with satire as a *faute de mieux*).

Along those lines, where Booth says that my test is not "Is it true?" or "Is it beautiful?" but "Is it curative?" I would say that "in one sense" yes, "in another sense" no. Above all, I guess, I am engrossed by the great range of *ingenuities* which the study of symbolic action allows us to contemplate—and many of my far-out speculations (my notions about a possible outlaw dimension in the "Grecian Urn," for instance) are probably motivated most of all by an interest of that sort. Our whole great clutter of civilization, for instance, sometimes strikes me as an astounding wealth of ways whereby genius will dig its own grave (even down to the thought that some earnest priest of "creativity" may end up in an asylum just through ardent efforts to produce artistic results that provide a conversation piece for "elite" vulgarians to skim the mere headlines about, at cocktail hour).

As for the numbered paragraphs:

1. Yes, I'd say that any piece of symbolic action, finished on the page, can be analyzed as a poem, as rhetoric, as science, as self-portraiture (including the kinds of self-portraiture we encounter in the analysis of a work as representing a given historic era, or a given social class, or a psychological type, etc.). But some things lend themselves more profitably to one such "terministic screen" than to others. However, all is grist to the mill, so use as your appetite prompts. And, at times, put some terms in, turn the crank—and out will come other terms. Why not?

2. I've already talked about this one, out of turn. And again I'd say: Yes, let's add the further question, "Is it ingenious?" That, I guess, would belong in my "aesthetic dimension."

3. Yes. Wayne, come home! All is forgiven. Yet we still work with "forms," too. After all, "Dramatism" is based on the basic scholastic formula: "act equals form." See, for instance (*Kenyon Review*, Spring 1951), my "Three Definitions" of lyric, Platonic dialogue, and Joyce's *Portrait of the Artist as a Young Man* (viewed as a kind *sui generis*). Or, in *Language as Symbolic Action*, my definitions in connection with *Coriolanus* as a tragedy, and *A Passage to India* as a novel. Or, more

recently, my speculations on "Dramatistic" definition in connection with a longish poem of mine (*Directions in Literary Criticism*, edited by Stanley Weintraub and Philip Young, 1973). And there's my "Definition of Man" which, if you had but started with, alas! could have kept me from feeling tearful at the thought of how, despite your great friendliness in my behalf, you worked into things so roundabout. (Incidentally, please note that, in my *Encyclopedia* article, I fight valiantly for the claim that "Dramatism," as a model, *is not a metaphor*, but literal; and Behaviorism, with its view of man as *in essence* a machine rather than as a symbol using animal subject to mechanistic frailties, is the figurative approach to things concerned with human motivation.) Hence:

4. Note that in my comments on Dennis Wrong's comments (referred to in the *Encyclopedia* article) I distinguish between some terministic screens and others. I try to indicate *methodological* reasons why *scientifically specialized* terminologies for the study of man are necessarily inadequate, whereas a *philosophical* approach to the problem is *not* methodologically crippled from the start. The only objection to the approach via Dramatistic philosophy is that the particular philosopher may be unequal to the magnitude of his task (and I modestly admit that we must confront such a possibility). All I'm saying is: the *philosopher* does not begin with a sheerly *methodological* "impasse," in the sense that a contradiction in terms would be necessarily implicit in any attempt to feature some one specialized science as *the* instrument for the transcending of specialization.

5. I don't remember where I said the marriage of all to all,* which I leave sans quotation marks because Booth does. But I will say that if I did take this "happy route of transcendence that any dialectical thinker like Burke will always be tempted by," I need but be shown it and, in the light of my insistence upon the "centrality of the nervous system" as a *principium individuationis* (my "logological" equivalent for the Thomistic "theological" stress upon "matter" as a principle of individuation), I'll frankly cry *"peccavi."* But hold! When I get to the next step, I see what Booth means. In my *Collected Poems* (pp. 39–41), there is a "Dialectician's Prayer" that is built about the Platonic Upward Way. Yet e'en there, just before the end, in my role as an understudy of dialectics à la Socrates, I piously (and/or impiously?) prayed, "And may we have neither the mania of the One / Nor the delirium of the Many—But both the Union and the Diversity."

But come home, Wayne. For then you say the other side, all about

---

*[I cannot find it either! W. B.]

the problems of the kill (and what to do about all that?). And don't forget, alas! every single one of us lives by the kill. And any attempt to work that out reasonably will in all likelihood, as Booth says, end "in a dialectic of 'muddling through.'" And particularly in the light of what (having cheated and read ahead) I know is coming for at least a little while, I feel better at the end of round 2.

III

Yes, the Dramatistic pentad can be used in many ways. The terms are like blanks to be filled out. And different nomenclatures fill them out differently. All I'm saying is: Look closely enough, and you'll find that they get filled out somehow. Even schemes that make much show of discarding "purpose" have plenty of words to replace it. They'll even tell you their purpose in throwing out the term.

And the whole set-up is too tangled for a wholly adequate terminology.

And there's at least one thought to console us: If we got it all in order, then like a child with building blocks, the next thing we'd do would be to knock it down.

IV

Booth gets to work on a poem of Auden's ("Surgical Ward") that should be well worth our while to try things out on, though I'm not quite sure what the test is. If, for instance, Booth had begun with my theory of "progressive," "repetitive," and "conventional" form, it would be apparent to all readers why we both feel a bit uneasy about the break from the sonnet's rhymed octave to its unrhymed sestet. Both of us, I am sure, would have no resistance if the sonnet didn't have any rhymes at all, hence didn't build false expectations by beginning with two rhymed quatrains that set up specific formal patterns in terms of rhymes, only to let them fall apart in the sestet. Roughly, I approach the issue thus:

I doubt whether any candidate but a poet of Auden's well-deserved repute could have got away with it in the first place. On the other hand, this very break in formal consistency contrives even to accentuate the ebb-and-flow development proper to such a sonnet form (as distinct from Shakespeare's kind). But precisely at that point, I begin to part company with the Crane approach to what he'd call a poem and what I'd call "symbolic action."

When I see a break like that in the poem of a poet who could have filled out the formal pattern of expectations though he did not,* I have a rule of thumb. Despite the Welleks and my old friendly sparring partner Crane, I find myself confronting the possibility of having to take on a job quite other than specifically a concern with "poetic" modes of symbolic action.

Precisely because I don't presently have the time and resources to build up my case, I shall be forced into a position suited to at best *illustrate* my kinds of concern (when shuttling back and forth between the poem as if published anonymously and the poem as accredited to its well-known and properly respected author, an author who, we well know, was perfectly competent to comply with formal expectations by making his sestet rhyme).

Whenever a break like that turns up, my theory of *symbolic action in general* goads me to ask questions *outside the realm of poetic action in particular*.

Booth has done well in his ways of bringing out the poem's effectiveness. He picked it to talk about because he felt its poignancy—and he helps us go along with his responsiveness.

But, Wellek or no Wellek, Crane or no Crane, my "rules of thumb" about a break in structure won't let me stop there. So, whatever kinds of possibilities Booth may think I would consider, the fact simply is that I try to narrow things down by asking just how the octave's closing words, "we stand elsewhere" get from there to "the idea of love" for the closing words of the poem. Obviously, there must be a *hinge* between the two movements. So, looking for clues in the first line of the sestet, I tentatively ask whether the word "foot" might be the hinge. Speculating along psychoanalytic lines, I have some hunches as to how "foot" might serve as the hinge-image. So, given the records, I'd go searching for other Auden contexts in which the term "foot" appeared. If all that I had is this one poem as though by "Anonymous," in that case the break in form (that got us from smothered groans to "the idea of love") would be a kind of "perturbation" which I lacked enough inductive evidence to account for. That is to say, I couldn't hope to determine precisely why the term "foot," rather than some other term, served as the bridge across the gap between octave and sestet realms of motives. And if the sonnet actually were anonymous, I'd be taking vast chances by following a purely psychoanalytic hunch.

---

*Burke did not see what I wrote in chapter 2 about Auden's revision and presumably has not seen its filling out of "the formal pattern of expectations."

In any case, whatever the poem's break in structure, its octave tells us about the "centrality of the nervous system" in a way cruelly severe; and the sestet swings to what, in line with my thoughts on modes of "identification" that help us transcend our poignant uniqueness, I'd view as a turn to a compensatory realm, not unlike that place in Arnold's "Dover Beach" where, having worried about how badly things are lining up with regard to the course of history in general, he says on the other hand, "Ah, love, let us be true / To one another!"

I can't take on responsibility for all that Booth thinks I might say in contrast with what Crane would say about the Auden poem. I have said just about all that it spontaneously suggests to me. But I don't feel that the octave is an "obscene reduction to 'pure' body," as were it concerned with "the perfection of mere motion." At least, in sheerly Dramatistic terms, complete reduction to motion would be said to equal the corresponding *total elimination* of every human organism's suffering, whereas the octave is concerned with the very essence of pain.

And whereas Burke, too, was brought up in the Booth tradition of what it meant to "cut one's foot," he lived in an area where the danger came less from cows than from people, though it is interesting that Booth, too, finds reasons, however different from Burke's, to feature that term for its possible strategic place in the development.

And I do indeed wipe away my tears when, before this section is ended, Wayne Booth and I get together on another area where we might happily have begun, namely: the "Dictionary of Pivotal Terms" in *Attitudes toward History*. For there, indeed, is the sort of overlap we share with what I would call "administrative rhetoric." There we tend to see I to I.

V

The last section leaves me not quite knowing what to say. "And immediately he is off on a brief effort to show why his analysis of structure is superior to that of his most serious rivals, the 'current neo-Aristotelian school.' Why is it superior? Why of course because his method is 'better adapted for the disclosure of a poem's function'—that is, his method is better for solving the problem that his method has chosen to solve!" I'll be damned if I can remember the passage Booth seems to have in mind.* If it's as infantile as it sounds,

---

Philosophy of Literary Form, p. 74. Clearly Burke's failure to find the passage I was summarizing results from his conviction that I have made him seem more circular than he is. But I remain convinced—without in the least thinking that his circularity vitiates

I think I'll have to squirm. I remember an article I did on Olson, Maclean, and Crane. It is reprinted in my *Grammar of Motives*. But though I had some differences, they were certainly not in the tone that Booth suggests. Uneasily, I ask for further info.

Meanwhile, it's the places where Booth *forgives* me that make me uncomfortable. At those times Booth makes me scare myself.

what he is saying about the superiority of his method for determining function, according to his definition—that the passage, while intending to accept the whole "neo-Aristotelian" emphasis on "the structure of the given work itself," imports Burke's notions of function into the concession itself (see the quotation, p. 111, above).

4

Now it must be said that there is no simple test that can be applied to determine the validity of a proof, that is, to determine that an alleged proof really is a proof. Mathematical history contains rare instances of arguments that were generally accepted as proofs for hundreds of years, before being successfully challenged by a very ingenious mathematician, who pointed out a possibility that had been overlooked in the alleged proof. And more recently, every year there appear, in the mathematical journals of the world, a certain number of papers which point out that some statement, allegedly proved in a preceding paper, was not only erroneously proved (that is, not proved) but was, in fact, incorrect. These facts are mentioned for the benefit of those who feel that there is some magic formula for a proof which makes it immutable and unarguable henceforth and forevermore.—R. B. Kershner

This difficulty [the failure of philosophers of history to grapple with historical narrative *as story*] is a result of that bias in our philosophical tradition, from Plato to the present day, in favour of theoretical knowledge, i.e. knowledge admitting of universal statements and of being set out in systematic form. Given the accepted terminologies and characteristic presumptions of that tradition, it is virtually impossible to describe convincingly the most basic and familiar things that historians and readers of history are always doing.—W. B. Gallie

It is an immensely important fact of nature that as people carry on an activity in which they have received a common training, they do largely *agree* with one another, accepting the same examples and analogies, taking the same steps. We agree in what to say, in how to apply language. We agree in our responses to particular cases.—Norman Malcolm

M. H. Abrams: History as Criticism and the Plurality of Histories

When M. H. Abrams published a defense, in 1972, of "theorizing about the arts,"[1] some of his critics accused him of falling into subjectivism. He had made his case so forcefully against "the confrontation model of aesthetic criticism" and had so effectively argued against "simplified" and "invariable" models of the art work and of "*the* function of criticism" that some readers thought he had thrown overboard the very possibility of a rational criticism tested by objective criteria.

In his reply to these critics,[2] Abrams concentrates almost entirely on whether his critical pluralism is finally a skeptical relativism. He does not even mention his great historical works, *The Mirror and the Lamp* and *Natural Supernaturalism*, and he has nothing to say about how his pluralistic theories could be applied to the writing of history. But then, surprising as it seems once we think about it, neither of the two histories says much about his method either.

What is the true achievement of these aggressive raids into our past, and how does Abrams see them in relation to other possible histories of the same subjects? Knowing in advance that he has agreed, like Burke, to reply to my nudging, I should like both to propose that everyone has—with Abrams' own encouragement—understated the importance of what he has done and to ask: What kind of pluralist *is* he?

The Charge of Relativism Once More

In both of these recent articles, Abrams proposes critical pluralism as a base for humanistic inquiry. He sees belief in a plurality of valid critical modes not simply as one interesting possibility but as a position forced upon us by what we now know, both about the history of critical rivalry and about the way our minds work. It is true that the search for the one thing needful, in criticism as in everything else, has often yielded important results, and it will no doubt do so again; but it can be pursued, Abrams would say, only in a state of innocence, for reasons similar to those offered by both Crane and Burke.

It is perhaps inevitable that some critics would see this position as amounting to relativism. As Abrams explains, the two positions are not easily distinguished:

⨯ I do say a number of things that might be taken to suggest some such view [subjectivism or relativism]. I say, for example, that once an assertion is adopted as the premise of a critical theory, "its origin and truth-claim cease to matter," for its validity is to be measured by its demonstrated power to yield valuable critical insights; that the particular theoretical perspective employed by a critic not only selects, but in some fashion alters the features of a work of art (in Wittgenstein's terms, the perspective affects both what he is apt to see and what he sees it *as*); that some range of disagreement in literary interpretations and judgments of value is endemic to criticism; that the ultimate standards of valid critical judgments are not sharp-focus, but soft-focus standards which we signify by terms such as sensibility, good sense, sagacity, tact, insight, and that the application of such standards allows "room for the play of irreducible temperamental differences"; and also that the term "certainty" does not without special qualification apply to most critical conclusions about a work of art. It may seem that as a consequence I am committed to the view that all aesthetic judgments are equally sound, that there's no disputing about taste, and that one should leave one's critical language alone. ["Wittgenstein," p. 552]

Abrams' language here is somewhat different from that of his earlier splendid statement of pluralism, in *The Mirror and the Lamp*.[3] Like most of us, he did not know Wittgenstein in 1953, or at least he gave no clue that he did. But we find there the same emphasis on the peculiarly ambiguous nature of "the facts" studied by critics and on the resulting need for a plurality of critical languages:

But a good deal of our impatience with the diversity and seeming chaos in philosophies of art is rooted in a demand from criticism for something it cannot do, at the cost of overlooking many of its genuine powers. We still need to face up to the full consequences
⨯ of the realization that criticism is not a physical, nor even a psychological, science. By setting out from and terminating in an appeal to the facts, any good aesthetic theory is, indeed, empirical in method. Its aim, however, is not to establish correlations between facts which will enable us to predict the future by reference to the past, but to establish principles enabling us to justify, order,

and clarify our interpretation and appraisal of the aesthetic facts themselves. And as we shall see, these facts turn out to have the curious and scientifically reprehensible property of being conspicuously altered by the nature of the very principles which appeal to them for their support. Because many critical statements of fact are thus partially relative to the perspective of the theory within which they occur, they are not "true," in the strict scientific sense that they approach the ideal of being verifiable by any intelligent human being, no matter what his point of view. Any hope, therefore, for the kind of basic agreement in criticism that we have learned to expect in the exact sciences is doomed to disappointment. [*ML*, p. 4]

Such a view naturally led him then, as it leads him now, into the problem of where one can hope to find a standard of taste among modes in a world that accommodates many critical modes. If there are many good critical theories, what is it that entitles a theory to enter the canon?

A good critical theory . . . has its own kind of validity. The criterion is not the scientific verifiability of its single propositions, but the scope, precision, and coherence of the insights that it yields into the properties of single works of art and the adequacy with which it accounts for diverse kinds of art. Such a criterion will, of course, justify not one, but a number of valid theories, all in their several ways self-consistent, applicable, and relatively adequate to the range of aesthetic phenomena. [*ML*, pp. 4–5]

In this view the long-continuing war among critics, far from proving the futility of the critical enterprise, has in fact been fruitful, both in stimulating new kinds of poetry and in educating readers to aspects of art that would otherwise have been overlooked.

But the problem of relativism is not, for the historian of critical modes, simply one of finding standards. It is finally the problem of deciding what kinds of questions we can ask in the hope of obtaining warranted answers. It is here that Abrams, even in his recent cogent defense of a plurality of legitimate questions, understates the radical challenge that his own histories offer to conventional canonic lists. We should follow him in some detail on this matter, in a long passage that not only shows how seriously he takes the charge of relativism but also defines the problem that concerns me here: What kinds of × knowledge can we hope for in humanistic inquiry? More specifically, what kinds of knowledge does Abrams provide?

The charge of relativism, he says, concerns him,

especially since much that passes for criticism in the present age strikes me as uncommonly irresponsible, so that we can ill afford to minimize the availability of standards for discriminating between sound and unsound procedures in critical reasoning. I don't, however, hold the relativistic opinions I have just described, nor do I think that they are entailed by anything I have said. I in fact believe that we possess valid criteria for judging when criticism is good and when it is bad, and that we are able to disqualify many aesthetic judgments out of hand. But I also think that it is a mistake to assume, and self-defeating to pretend, that these criteria are simple and obvious, or that they are similar to the criteria for distinguishing between a right and wrong answer to a mathematical problem or to a question of empirical fact.

Misunderstanding on this issue is in some part a result of what my essay undertook to do; if it had set out to expose what's wrong in bad criticism, rather than to justify what's right in good criticism, its emphases would have been quite different. But in large part the risk of misunderstanding is inherent in the nature of critical problems and of the language we have evolved for dealing with them. Wittgenstein . . . made some remarks which are very much to that point. He is discussing the reasons why we get general agreement in "judgments of colours" but fail to get such agreement in answer to the question whether someone's "expression of feeling is genuine or not." He points out that we may reasonably argue about whether the expression of feeling is or is not genuine, but "we cannot prove anything"; that, on the whole, better judgments will be made by those who are expert, but that this expertise is not acquired through a course of systematic instruction but only "through 'experience,'" and can only be described by a vague expression such as having a "better knowledge of mankind"; that such knowledge can be taught, yet not as "a technique," but only by giving someone "the right *tip*"; that "there are also rules, but they do not form a system," so that "unlike calculation rules," only "experienced people can apply them right"; and finally that, while "it is certainly possible to be convinced by evidence," the term "'evidence' here includes 'imponderable' evidence," and "what does imponderable evidence *accomplish?*" And Wittgenstein exclaims, poignantly: "What is most difficult here is to put this indefiniteness, correctly and unfalsified, into words."

I think that the important critical questions are not like the question, "What color is it?" but much more like the question, "Is this expression of grief genuine?" A persistent dilemma for the philosopher of criticism is how to give due recognition to the indefiniteness of the evidence for an answer, yet not be taken to deny that there are sound, and often convincing reasons that support one answer rather than another. Because of this difficulty in putting the matter "correctly and unfalsified into words," a monologue is not a very satisfactory way of conducting a philosophical inquiry into aesthetic criticism. To get progressively clearer as to the multiple and interdependent discriminations involved requires the evolving give-and-take of dialogue. Mr. Bambrough [who had raised the charge of relativism] applies to such dialogue the ancient philosophical term "dialectic," and says (citing F. R. Leavis) that the most to be expected is that when a proponent says, "This is so, isn't it?" his interlocutor will reply, "Yes, but . . ." That is in the nature of all humanistic discourse, and a reason why the search for humanistic truth has no ending. ["Wittgenstein," pp. 552–54]

Reduction of a Story to Ten Static Propositions

On many occasions in a lifetime devoted to the humanities, M. H. Abrams has said to the world, "This is so, isn't it?" And the world—or at least the world of Romanticists—has responded with an unusually emphatic "Yes." Those who have said "Yes, *but* . . ." have generally muted their reservations and underlined their agreement: "Certainly the best book on Romanticism I have ever read," Morse Peckham says of *Natural Supernaturalism*,[4] and most Romanticists would agree.*

But what have readers been saying yes *to*? Surely not to any simple list of propositions about Romanticism, as Abrams' critics have seemed to suggest. And surely not to any coded list of two or three kinds of statement, like the "color" and "feeling" pair that Abrams borrows from Wittgenstein. What we assent to, rather, in reading each of his books, is a history, a story; and that means that we come to accept an immeasurably more complex and challenging body of knowledge than Abrams' own talk about method has suggested.

One can hardly blame him for the oversight, for the cognitive claims of "story" are extraordinarily difficult to talk about.[5] But to do even partial justice to Abrams, we must make the attempt, knowing in advance that since we cannot here duplicate the effects of *story* we are doomed to offer only the palest reflection of the real thing. My case, finally, will be that we have all understated the peculiar kind of

---

*Thus the formula "Yes, but . . . ," which we first encountered in the quotation from David Daiches in chapter 1, seems to take on a more responsible air, depending on which of the two words is emphasized. We shall meet it again, thoroughly renovated, in chapter 7.

demonstration[6] that telling a story about our cultural past can provide. Though the case could be made almost equally well with either of Abrams' books, I shall talk entirely of *Natural Supernaturalism*,[7] since it is the more ambitious and more difficult work.

What does *Natural Supernaturalism* "argue for"? If we take seriously the reduction of flowing history to static propositions, we find at least ten kinds of such propositions advanced here.

1. There are claims to hundreds, perhaps thousands, of literal, specific causal connections between Wordsworth's poems and what came before and after. Most readers have noticed echoes of Milton; Abrams traces them in overwhelming detail. Most readers have noted biblical quotations and allusions; Abrams shows us so many more that the sheer quantity serves his argument about larger theses.

Many of his "short stories," as these causal lines might be called, are so precise and so nearly indisputable that we might consider them as answers not to "color" questions but to "wave-length" questions, as firm in the response to positive tests as any data accepted by physical scientists. But of course many are less firm, and some are highly conjectural. Clearly the reader's willingness to accept conjecture will depend in part on whether Abrams himself seems to know the difference between what is rock-firm and what is a bit soggy.

2. Surrounding these, and in effect built out of them, there are a fair number of large-scale causal theses, derived from what we might call "embedded novellas." When reviewers have attempted to summarize the book, their propositions have been limited almost entirely to this kind—to factual assertions about literal causes that seem easy to test in propositional form. Treated as answering Wittgenstein's first kind of question, "What color is it?", they can then easily be "refuted" by any critic working with different details: as if to say, "Romanticism wasn't really *Abrams'* color, scarlet, it was really *my* color, crimson." Morse Peckham, for example, after his enthusiastic praise, summarizes the book in terms that he can then easily repudiate.

> (1) The first generation of English and German Romantics responded to what they judged to be the failure of the French Revolution as the failure of the redemptive claims of the Revolutionary-Enlightenment ideology. Their response was to construct a new mode of redemption. (2) The pattern of that mode (or structure, to be more fashionable) was the Christian pattern of the fall and the restoration to Paradise.... Romantic redemptionism, then, was a secularization of the persistent structure of European metaphysics, or terminal explanatory regression.[8]

It would be interesting to trace how each reviewer has centered on this or that causal chain, entirely ignoring the others. With a little ingenuity, one could compile a list longer than all of the printed responses put together, since the book in a sense provides a conspectus on the whole of Western civilization.

It seems evident that propositions in the form "This is how it happened that X (usually an abstraction) led to Y (usually another abstraction)" are not in any simple sense reducible to one kind of "factual" claim. It is true that when X and Y are not abstractions, they may seem testable with at least as much clarity as can be found in treating questions about color. But they are often "things," like German and English "Romanticism," and there is thus considerable variety in the kinds of causation and narrative sequence implied.

3. Abrams is perhaps even more interested in the kind of *parallels*, or *congruence*, or *consonance* discoverable between Wordsworth, his ancestors, his contemporaries, and his descendants. Insofar as there are causal claims in these comparisons, they are elusive, ambiguous—and of course troublesome to critics.

J. Hillis Miller, in one of the best reviews, gives the following list of achievements before turning to show that "all of Abrams' readings can be put in question" and thus all of his causal claims:

> No one before Abrams . . . has so comprehensively read the English Romantic poets *in the light of* their German contemporaries, both poets and philosophers. No one has so persuasively shown the consonance, not in "concept," but in organizing ground plan, between Wordsworth's *The Prelude*, for instance, and Hegel's *Phenomenology* or Hölderlin's *Hyperion*. To *assimilate* German Romantic philosophy into the *pattern* of the *Bildungsreise*, the educative journey of the Prodigal Son, and therefore to show its *similarity* to *The Prelude* or to *Prometheus Unbound*, will remain one of [Abrams'] accomplishments. . . . Second, no one has in such persuasive detail demonstrated the *congruence* of the basic myths, metaphors, and concepts of Romantic poetry to *patterns* not invented by them but inherited from the Biblical, Christian, and Neo-Platonic tradition. No one has so cogently defined Romanticism as no more than a "scene" in the twenty-five-hundred-year "drama of European literature." . . . Third, perhaps no one has so patiently and so wisely discussed what the secularization of theological tradition by the Romantic poets and philosophers might mean. Finally, no one has demonstrated so clearly the *persistence* of these *patterns* into modern literature.[9] [My emphases.]

To show all this would surely be enough to make a major work; and Abrams' critics have in effect said that this is—at best—all that he has done. But we have only begun, and we turn now to more and more ambitious claims.

4. When Wordsworth wrote his Preface to *The Excursion*, and when he conceived *The Recluse*, that grand epic of which *The Excursion* and *The Prelude* were parts, and when he wrote the Prospectus as part of the Preface, he was not only *claiming* to speak for the spirit of his age, he was *in fact* speaking for that spirit.

5. There thus *was* such a thing, a spirit of Romanticism, a "distinctive Romantic ethos," which the major Romantic writers "put forward in the assurance of their innovative prime" (p. 460). Nominalist historians who question the notion of epochs (as I was taught to do by R. S. Crane, who called Abrams a "Platonist historian" for believing in such things) are thus challenged directly and quite literally: "I will show you, I have shown you, this and this and this respect in which these authors all thought alike, and the differences among them that we all can see are less significant than these similarities." In short: he advances an "existence" proposition of a peculiar kind that many philosophers and some historians say is illegitimate. What is worse, it includes a value claim about the existing "spirit."

6. Wordsworth was more fully representative of that spirit than any other Romantic poet.

a) He took the Romantic "marks" more seriously and incorporated them more completely than did the other poets. Abrams' own headings give a pretty fair notion of what those marks are: The Apocalyptic Marriage; Crisis-Autobiography; The Transactions of Mind and Nature; The Theodicy of the Private Life and of the Landscape; The Redemptive Imagination; The Circuitous Journey; The Prodigal's Return; Apocalypse by Revolution, by Imagination, and by Cognition; The Poet's Vision: The New Earth and the Old—and so on. Each heading might be prefaced like this: "Here is *the story* of how Wordsworth represents the Romantic way of dealing with...."

b) He saw his life-work as unified under these marks: all of his work was to be "one poem," organically unified as the effort of the seer-poet to explore the mind, to discover the points at which it was fitted to nature and nature fitted to the mind, and then to report back to mankind the "cheering" and "redeeming" dawn of a new age and new life and new truth.

c) His poetry was peculiarly powerful.

Here, with the most explicit value judgment in my list so far, we are even more obviously heading into trouble. In spite of all that has recently been done to question dogmas about the impossibility of giving rational argument for evaluative propositions, many still would take it as self-evident that Abrams could only *assert* the value of Wordsworth, of his poetry, and of the other hierarchical judgments that follow. That he does indeed establish this judgment will be central to my argument in the next section.

7. Romanticism as it was realized in Wordsworth marked a great turning point in Western cultural history. It collected into itself a variety of religious themes, motives, and forms from earlier ages, both classical and biblical, and remolded them into a kind of secular religion, a religion of which the great Romantic poets saw themselves to be prophets. In short: Abrams advances propositions about the comparative importance of epochs.

8. They certainly *were* prophets, if by that we mean those who are endowed with the power to foresee, or at least proclaim or help establish, profound themes, motives, and forms that will dominate the years to come. Wordsworth and company endowed us with many of our most characteristic and important modern concerns (chap. 7, sec. 3). In short: Abrams dares to assert the comparative value of prophets.

9. At the same time, they differed radically from us, particularly in the "Romantic positives" which many modern authors have rejected:

a) They did not see their priesthood as in the service of an autonomous art but as in the service, as Wordsworth says, "of [men's] redemption" (p. 428). "The Romantic aesthetic was of art for man's sake, and for life's sake" (p. 429).

b) "The Romantic writers neither sought to demolish their life in this world in a desperate search for something new nor lashed out in despair against the inherited culture. . . . They spoke as members of what Wordsworth called the 'One great Society . . . / The noble Living and the noble Dead,'" not as members of an adversary culture (p. 430).

c) They thought of themselves as serving the supreme values of "life, love, liberty, hope, and joy" (pp. 431–48). When they wrote of dejection and despair, as they often did, they always *dealt* with those negatives and transformed them into "Romantic positives." Indeed, Wordsworth's life-work can be viewed as a grand effort to turn the potential negations and doubts of his time into a saving poetry that will "chear / Mankind in times to come." For Wordsworth, "unity with himself and his world is the primal and normative state of man, of which the sign is a fullness of shared life and the condition of joy" (p. 278).

d) Their positive, affirmative, "redemptive" stance in the face of life's horrors and in response to disappointed revolutionary hopes was at least as reasonable, at least as honest, at least as viable a basis for art, and at least as radically critical, as the various stances of our own time, many of which are more obviously "negative" and despairing.

I put this last thesis cautiously, because Abrams is perhaps even more cautious about it. His conclusion shows both the caution and the conviction: "If such affirmations strike a contemporary ear as deluded or outworn, that may be the index of their relevance to an age of profounder dereliction and dismay than Shelley and Wordsworth knew" (p. 462). I suspect that Abrams understates his true convictions with that word "relevance." *How* relevant, and in what way? The book as a whole never states, in so many words, that Wordsworth and Coleridge and Shelley knew all that any of us know about "the horror" or that they were to be admired for going beyond the horror to affirm what still could be affirmed. And it would certainly have been folly to attempt to show that they were *more* to be admired *because* they affirmed than are those of our own novelists and poets who, with equal vigor, pursue the nihilistic vision. But Abrams unquestionably defends the reasonableness of their attitudes. In short—and perhaps most shocking of all: Abrams offers propositions that evaluate basic stances toward the whole of life.

10. We could easily extend these grand questions to a long list titled "What Does It All Mean?" About all of them, Abrams leads us to a degree of warranted conclusion, though he states none of them formally—questions like "What is it important to know about my past?" "What does it mean, that I should end up here, in this harried century, following that great but puzzling one—here at the frazzled end of *this* millennium, following *that* millennium-and-a-half of baffling but monumental stuff?" "Where in fact are we, in this universe, and what kind of a place is it?" "Who in fact are we, coming from what kind of ancestors?" "What in fact is significant about where we came from and where we are now?" Such overlapping questions, sociological, anthropological, metaphysical, and religious, could never be sorted out into a simple list. What is perhaps most striking is the extreme difficulty they present to anyone who tries to reason about them. They are indeed so difficult, particularly because of their inextricable fusion of fact and value and extreme abstraction, that most modern theorists would simply dismiss them as entirely out of the range of cognitive inquiry. "What, in *fact*, is *significant* about where we came from and where we are now?" Why, surely, that all depends, does it not, on your point of view? A cognitive term like "fact" simply does not apply.

Abrams will not allow us that protection. If we enter his narrative world at all, we must see him as trying to answer questions of this most difficult kind. And though it would be absurd to claim that he has provided decisive proofs, I am claiming what for some readers will seem almost as absurd: that when anyone asks any of these questions, one meaningful answer would be to offer him a copy of *Natural Supernaturalism*. In some sense not accommodated in our organons, Abrams answers some of the questions we care about most.

Reduction of a Story to Static Arguments

Persuasion about any of the kinds of truth promised here depends on persuasion about the most obvious but perhaps the most difficult of them all: Abrams purports to convince us that *all of this happened;* this *story* is *true*. One cannot summarize the "this" with any proposition. The closest one might come would be a detailed plot summary, but it would have to be articulated into as many strands as the narrative strands Abrams shows leading into and out of Wordsworth and Romanticism. This is what happened. This really occurred. This is our past.

It is here, of course, that the problem of Abrams' pluralism becomes most acute. He often says, and more often implies, that there are "many profitable ways to approach" intellectual history, whether the history of criticism[10] or the more complex history of philosophical and literary themes and forms attempted in *Natural Supernaturalism*. He is clear enough about the need for other histories of other subjects, but he does not give us much help in deciding in what sense *his* history is *the* history of his subject. *Is* this what occurred? What alternative histories of Wordsworth's central poems, of their themes and structures and of Wordsworth's motives and beliefs, could Abrams allow? How does he feel about those critics (we shall later look at some of them) who think that the *true* history of Romanticism would have an entirely different plot and very different heroes?

In short, how do I decide—as I do—that Abrams' story in either of his books is superior to René Wellek's or Howard Mumford Jones's or any of the several that have been sketched by critics objecting to Abrams' version? How do I conclude that his evaluation of Wordsworth's poetry is sounder than that, say, of Cleanth Brooks, with his arguments that seem more solidly based on "objective," "intrinsic" analysis? Though I may finally want to say "Yes, *but* . . ." to the whole thesis, and though I may want to question some points along the way, what right do I have to feel so thoroughly persuaded?

I must underline once again the sense in which my task of demonstrating his demonstrations is an impossible one. Discursive accounts
of a great history are in the nature of the case at least as inadequate, as
remote from the living creature, as critical accounts of novels or
poems. The problem we face is thus not simply like those that
Abrams talks about in his recent articles. The real problem is that our
endeavor is in some sense alien to its subject. The proof of Abrams'
pudding is in the eating. If a physicist or even another kind of historian of ideas, like Lovejoy, were to say, "You must not only follow my
argument and test my evidence but also recreate a narrative experience, with considerable emotional engagement, if you are to recognize the validity of my conclusions," we should rightly take the
statement as a confession of failure. But I am saying precisely that it is
in the *experience* of Abrams in detail—including the detail of at least a
major part of his extensive quotation from other authors—that the
validation of his proffered truths is found. And it is this experience
that many sincere and competent readers will for various reasons not
discover.

In short, all I can hope for, unable to duplicate even a part of the
story *as* story, is to summarize Abrams' "reasons" in a way that will
invite some readers to return to the real thing, perhaps taking with
them a broadened notion of the proper tests for validity in cultural
history.

First, style. Abrams' style is quiet; indeed, sometimes it is bland.
One seldom even notices it, and it can thus be grossly deceptive,
seeming merely to carry its information. There is simply no visible
striving for effect in anything Abrams ever wrote; every sentence
seems to assume a reader who already cares about the matters discussed.

One might at first think that such a style is indifferent to readers.
On the contrary, it is a style that considers us in what is the most
respectful way possible: working on this kind of task, it makes everything as clear and as interesting as the subject matter allows, with no
disguising of commonplaces and no pretentious jargon.

The rigorous clarity and the scrupulous resistance to irrelevant
flourish are impossible to illustrate, since their effects depend on a
mastery sustained over many pages. I pause only to ask how long it
has been, oh academic reader, since you read four hundred and fifty
pages without once wanting to employ the old worn red pencil:
"awkward," "reverse these clauses," "deadwood," or "clarify"?

The purity of style may seem unimportant; it might even be the product of an accidental matching of Abrams' crotchets with my own. What *I* find pure, *you* find dull, and *M. Barthes* finds infuriatingly cautious. Perhaps. But the fact is that every reviewer I have read has admired the book; and though none of them has said more than a word about style, the style has almost certainly been significant in gaining their admiration, for it creates an air of both mastery and self-effacement. It thus builds trust in this speaker, because he has visibly labored to get rid of his own limitations in order to penetrate the opacities of the past. (I shall return to the question of the author's authority in chapter 7.)

If any one formula could summarize the new waves in criticism of the past ten years, it might be: "The curse of criticism is the pretense to objectivity; since all good reading is the response of a living person to what without the reader would remain dead, the honest critic will make his criticism live with his acknowledged presence. All hail, Response, Lord of the text!" Or some such. The result is that almost any passage by Abrams contrasts sharply with almost any paragraph from any currently fashionable critic. I choose an example from a critic I admire, one who, unlike many, really reads the books he discusses. In a chapter called "The Dialectics of Poetic Tradition" we read:

> I remember, as a young man setting out to be a university teacher, how afflicted I was by my sense of uselessness, my not exactly vitalizing fear that my chosen profession reduced to an incoherent blend of antiquarianism and culture-mongering. I recall also that I would solace myself by thinking that while a scholar-teacher of literature could do no good, at least he could do no harm, or anyway not to others, whatever he did to himself. But that was at the very start of the decade of the fifties, and after more than twenty years I have come to understand that I under-rated my profession, as much in its capacity for doing harm as in its potential for good works. Even our treasons, our betrayals of our implicit trusts, are treasons of something more than of the intellectuals, and most directly damage our immediate students, our Oedipal sons and daughters. Our profession is not genuinely akin any longer to that of the historians or the philosophers. Without willing the change, our theoretical critics have become negative theologians, our practical critics are close to being Agaddic commentators, and all of our teachers, of whatever generation, teach how to live, what to do, in order to avoid the damnation of death-in-life. . . . Whatever the academic profession of letters now is on the Continent (shall we say an anthropology half-Marxist,

half-Buddhist?) or in Britain (shall we say a middle-class
amateurism displacing aristocratic amateurism?), it is currently
in America a wholly Emersonian phenomenon.[11]

Now this is highly skillful writing, I would say—writing that does
its job well. But its job is not that of making me trust the author's
generalizations. The paragraph is offered as evidence in an advancing
argument about poetic influence and about where we are in America
today; in the terms I used above, it is an argument about who we are,
where we came from, and "how it happened the way it did." But the
style throughout persuades me (along with other matters) that what it
primarily illuminates is the author and his sense of his situation.*
Personal in every line, it can persuade me to admire the author's
brilliance and force and authenticity, and I am thus required by his
ethos to take what he says seriously as one deeply felt view. But it
inevitably loses most of what we might call *im*personal force. I am
unlikely to reorder my picture of "all of our teachers" or of "the
academic profession" to match the critic's. Indeed, I feel quite free to
reply to him that, on the contrary, the academic profession is currently in America wholly Cartesian, or wholly Platonist, or wholly
nihilistic, or wholly structuralist. And I don't quite see how we might
make our counterclaims meet in discussion.

All to the good, a large number of contemporary critics would say.
Such *personal* demonstrations are worth far more than Abrams' effort
at *historical* demonstration, and they are far more honest. But surely
we should allow for different purposes, demanding different kinds of
ethos, created by different degrees of personal obtrusiveness or restraint. And you do pay for what you get. When you earn an air of
great personal enthusiasm, you necessarily diminish the ethos of dis-
passionate inquiry.

I must emphasize here that I am not simply praising Abrams' style.
I am making what I take to be a much more risky claim: a style that is
good in the way Abrams' style is good not only tends to carry us with
him—it *ought* to. It carries a legitimate warrant for the author's theses.
To write well in this way helps *prove* your case, though of course it
cannot go it alone.[12]

We are all deeply trained against this view. Even those who claim
that the distinction between style and substance is a false one have
learned to ignore what earlier rhetoricians took for granted: style-as-

---

*And it is thus quite different from the equally wide-ranging, flamboyant style of
Burke, which flings me gasping back into the subject, not sideways into the author's
soul.

proof. The fact is that if "a subject"—whatever that means—enables a critic to write well about it without requiring him to rely on easily separable blandishments and charm, the mere production of hundreds of pages of well-written sense about it constitutes as good a test as we have for his theses. If the theses were very weak, we have a right to conclude, a man like Abrams (as implied *in* his style) would have discovered the weakness as he tried to write honest sentences about them; and if he became dishonest and tried to fake, it would somehow show.

This kind of proof is obviously circular. I infer the honest scholarly integrity of the man from the steady honesty of the style—and vice versa! But it is a kind of circularity that careful analysis will reveal in all humanistic studies. In the time of Kenneth Burke, of Michael Polanyi, of phenomenalism and structuralism, no one should any longer be troubled by committing a circularity. Our problem is, as it has always been, to learn to discriminate among circularities. And there is a great difference, as Burke and Crane have already taught us, between circuitous journeys like Abrams', leading back to beginnings that are now radically altered because the journey has occurred, and the kind that are genuinely vicious.

Note finally that such proof works even when the plain sturdiness goes too far and stumbles into banality. I can judge a passage "flat," I can even skip a page or section (as I did on first reading and as Abrams himself, on page 15, suggests that we do) and still find it adding some weight to the proof: *Abrams* goes on even when *I* nod, and I tend to blame myself and not him.

After praise that may seem equivocal, I must hasten to add that the plain style is not all that plain. Even if it were, it would do its main job; but Abrams increases our confidence, and thus our final conviction, by employing—still quietly—a rich variety of metaphor. I pause for only one example of what can be found on every page: "The time taken to compose *The Prelude* straddled the writing of the Prospectus..." (p. 73). That looks easy enough, perhaps—until one tries to improve it.

Such stylistic control would in itself inspire no more, perhaps, than a mood of resigned trust. For many readers the same might be said for a second warranting quality that I take to be even more important, especially in a work that establishes historical connections and their consequent values. A colleague of mine once observed of *The Mirror and the Lamp* that it was the "best-organized work about criticism" that he had ever read. "You show me a quotation from any critic from

1700 to 1850, whether Abrams actually quotes him or not, and I'll show you the precise place in that book where the quotation must belong." Though the historical range of *Natural Supernaturalism* is much broader, I would say that its ordination of parts is even more impressive because much more complex. A mastery of the large pattern, of what rhetoricians used to call "arrangement," an attention to strategies of presentation that can make the reader an equal master—these are finally inseparable from "the case" that is made. Though it would be strange to call them qualities of style, they reveal themselves in a distinguishable quality of Abrams' style that provides a crucial test for his historical claims, a cognitive test of a kind that has never, so far as I know, been properly recognized.

I am thinking of the art of making persuasive local connections, and particularly transitions from sentence to sentence and paragraph to paragraph. Historical claims are, after all, precisely claims about special kinds of relatedness. A convincing history must be, among other things, one in which (1) everything mentioned somehow gets connected with everything else; (2) everything that ought to be mentioned gets mentioned; and (3) *every claimed connection* is rendered at least plausible to the critical reader.

The first criterion is met with an astonishing consistency. I can find no details that are inert because isolated. Many readers may agree, as I do not, with E. D. Hirsch's claim that there is a "superfluity of instantiation and quotation";[13] but no one has claimed to find any irrelevant material, any information added simply because Abrams happened to find it—and this in a book made up of thousands of allusions and quotations!

When it comes to the second test, most critics have been far less favorable to Abrams. Most of their objections have in fact rested precisely on the point that Abrams tells a plausible history but only *part* of *the* history. He has left out what he should have included; there should have been more about politics, more about Catholicism, more about Eastern religions and literature, more about Nietzsche or Freud or Novalis, more about neglected Romantics—Sir Walter Scott, for example, or, especially, Lord Byron. We must face this objection later, when I return to the subject of pluralism, noting here only that it in no way impugns the connectedness of what *has* been included.

But the crucial test is, after all, the third: whether the claimed connections are persuasive. For it is by this that we determine the difference between a major synthesis and the many improvisations that achieve temporary acclaim by the assertion of novel views.

Talk about legitimate historical connections has always tended to reduce their many kinds and degrees to a few literal terms like "cause," "influence," "source," or "imitation." Why does no one offer rules for the effective use of "meanwhile"? Of "consonant with"? Of words like "evolved" and "development," or of the many other shadings of connection that Abrams uses with admirable range and variety?

What one finds is a range even richer than is suggested by my ten kinds of proposition. Persuasion results, quite properly, as precise matchings accumulate: strong connections for a strong case, cautious ones for a weak one, vague for vague, metaphorical for metaphorical.

There are, most obviously, thousands of simple temporal connections: "And *then* . . . and *then*, four years later . . . and *throughout* the rest of his life" (italics will be mine throughout these illustrations). Second, there are of course explicit claims to literal causation (the kind of thing that a Lovejoy relies on almost exclusively): "The esoteric view of the universe as a plenum of opposed yet mutually attractive, quasi-sexual forces . . . *proceeded*, by a peripety of intellectual history, to *feed back into* scientific thought some of the most productive hypotheses of nineteenth-century and modern physics" (p. 171).

Some reviewers, overlooking these literal claims, have said that Abrams depends entirely on a third kind, the many analogies of structure, theme, and motive that are made without the slightest intent to argue about literal influence: "Stevens draws a conclusion which is *formally equivalent to* that of Blake: 'We say God and the imagination are one'" (p. 121).

Unlike many historians of ideas, Abrams employs a fourth kind, one that some reviewers have claimed is absent because he is not fond of words like "universal" and "archetype": the elusive "causation" that is shown when an analogy between two works is seen as resulting from some permanent human interest or eternal idea. I think Abrams is perhaps more committed to this kind of Platonic notion than his avoidance of the "eternity" words would suggest. I agree with the reviewers who wish he had grappled more openly with the precise sense in which he means us to take the "parallels" and "echoes" that cannot have been literally caused in temporal history. Does he mean to suggest the technical Platonic sense of "participate" when he says that "Wordsworth's *Prelude* participates, however guardedly, in a major intellectual tendency of his age, and of ours" (p. 120)? Or does "tendency" keep us in a time-bound world of efficient causes? Yet, much as I would like to discover more about his acknowledged allegiances, I am not at all sure that the *book* would be improved by overt discussion of such matters, since it clearly profits so much from the freedom of range that his lack of system provides.

Any catalogue, however long, will understate the richness of texture in Abrams' modulated connectives. Here are a few that, with a bow to strict scientific neutrality, I have culled from every fiftieth page! Origen, Abrams says, was *"followed* by a *long sequence* of later contemplatives" (precise enough as a temporal claim, appropriately silent about causation). Donne's sonnet was *"one product* of a millennium and a half of these *developments"* (a strict, literal claim about influence, with a metaphorical hint of some kind of organic life ["development"] in an idea, or perhaps in a pattern of ideas). Behind Donne's metaphors "we can *make out* the *root-images* . . . as described in the Book of Revelation" (here is a hint at archetypes, though we are not told just where we must go—behind, down, or up—to find them). "This region . . . is also *dimly remembered* in pagan myths" (remembered by Abrams? By you and me? Or by the myths themselves? Remembered? Are we not seeing here a bit of Platonic memory of what, in this life, we have never learned?) "Wordsworth *may well have recalled* . . ." (an obvious and legitimate dodge, telling us, among other things, that Abrams will not claim more than he knows). "The complex attitudes which *helped form* the new aesthetics . . ." (the method of causation is unspecified, but the causal verb underlines the complexity). "This world scheme . . . *exerted a profound attraction* upon . . . Hebrew . . . theologians" (a literal claim, with value-ridden metaphorical charging ["profound"]. We know that Abrams could show us theologians A, B, and C revealing the effects of the attraction, and we trust that, if pressed, he could somehow support the profundity). "A formulation which remained *the frame for* all his [Schiller's] later, more subtle thinking" (here there is only a hint of causal claim but a very strong structural and temporal claim). "Schiller was entirely *in accord with* the major philosophers of his age" (an appropriately weak metaphor but fully meaningful in context. No doubt Schiller was "consonant," too). ". . . to investigate the extent to which the providential design may have been not merely an illustrative, but a *constitutive analogue,* which *helped give a distinctive shape* to Romantic philosophies of history" (Abrams is cautious, very cautious, here, as well he might be; yet he is making a precise distinction, and with a considerably different nuance than we have found so far). "Prometheus [in Shelley's poem], like Blake's Albion, is also *a descendant* of a familiar mythical figure" (a strong, literal claim where a strong, literal claim is clearly justified). "The two accounts [by

Hamann and Wordsworth] serve as an additional instance of the *similarities-in-difference* among authors in the *lineage* of Augustine's *Confessions*" (well, after all, "lineage" always implies difference as well as similarity, and since the two accounts are now to be closely analyzed, after this summary introduction, I can see for myself that Hamann *is* both astonishingly, even puzzlingly, similar to Wordsworth [they never read each other] and yet still interestingly different).[14]

One result of this variety is that Abrams is finally invulnerable to any one refutation of any one connection. A critic shows, let us say, that Abrams has misunderstood a German passage and has thus exaggerated a parallel. What happens to his total case is infinitesimal. Since we have what amounts, at a minimal estimate, to a thousand or so of what might be called "hard connections"—claims to temporal or causal lineage and structural similarities—and, in addition, at least two to three thousand explicit "soft connections" among the parts of Abrams' own discourse ("therefore," "thus," "meanwhile," "next," etc.), our confidence can remain high even if—as has not happened and will not happen—a catalogue of his proved errors and false connections were to be extended to many items.

I risk the absurdities of quantifying because I am convinced that, when we call a work like this great, one thing we mean is a quantitative measure: it is big, it is huge, and yet it does not collapse of its own weight. Every joint holds, and the vast monument thus holds together. How, then, can its conclusions fail to *hold?*

Still, the final test is in the quality of the details, and that is best seen by looking closely at what is connected to what in any one of the many "local" histories that go to make up the whole. Before I do so, two notes: The elements Abrams traces are generally not completed literary works, as they would be in Ronald Crane's postulated causal history of literature. Nor are they quite the unit ideas that Lovejoy and most of his followers have pursued, though some of them might well pass for such. And they are certainly not the independent critical systems, reconstructed in their full integrity and traced in the "fullest possible diversity," without imposing a "unified narrative form," that Robert Marsh has cogently proposed as the essential subject of a history of criticism that would best serve the critic.[15] Most of them are a curious fusion of at least four things: a *feeling* about life (for example, joy in the face of pain); a *motive* (for example, "to chear mankind"); an *intellectual conviction* about life (for example, about *how time is shaped*—and here we come closest to

Lovejoy's kind of unit idea); and a *formal notion* of the shape that a literary or philosophical work should be given. Though sometimes these are distinguished, they finally are combined.

No doubt things would be easier for us if Abrams could tell his history as a simple chronological account. But he cannot, must not, tell a simple story: *"First* there was X *and then* there was Y." "Once upon a time the world was religious and then it grew secular. Hopes for political salvation rose—and were shattered. But new prophets arose who tried to find a redemptive power within the mind of man, reestablishing old religious categories and vocations on a secular base. And then even those vocations died, leaving us where we are now."

Instead, for his complex purposes, the story must be scrambled, "organized as a sequence of movements out of and back to various passages" in Wordsworth's Prospectus (pp. 13–14). A good example of how this works is seen in the short history of theodicy that places for us Wordsworth's own effort to justify Nature's ways. In twenty-five pages Abrams manages to explain, first, what a theodicy is; then, why there have been so many of them and why creating a new one was important ("Wordsworth announces that he is intent 'to weigh / The good and evil of our mortal state.' This was his version of Milton's undertaking to justify the ways of God to men"); and then what the place of Wordsworth's theodicy was in "the distinctive Romantic genre of the *Bildungsgeschichte.*" He then classifies and traces its elements: "The Theodicy of the Landscape," for example, is traced backward through the eighteenth-century interest in the sublime and beautiful; on back to Chaucer ("This is precisely the question put to God by Dorigen in Chaucer's *Franklin's Tale* when . . ."—and after two paragraphs one must agree: it *is* precisely the question put by Dorigen!); then forward to Thomas Burnet; onward further, again in the eighteenth century, to Burke's *Philosophical Enquiry into . . . the Sublime and Beautiful;* and then on to Wordsworth, who receives, as he should, as many paragraphs as all the others put together, but who can now be discussed with easy references backward to Burnet and to the Bible (especially the Book of Revelation, with its mountains and rocks and days of wrath: "The Scriptural Apocalypse is assimilated to an apocalypse of nature"); to Milton again; far forward, to Wordsworth's Kafka-esque nightmares"; far backward (obliquely), by reference to "the dark night of the soul"; forward to the "art of landscape painting"; back to *Paradise Lost,* "this time echoing Milton's relief, in his invocation to the third book, at escaping the realms of

hell, 'though long detain'd / In that obscure sojourn.' In Wordsworth's version . . . ."

But see what he has now brought us to: Wordsworth's poem is by
now clearly to be considered as a "version"! And on we go, to
Wordsworth's "resolution of his long dialectic of good and evil," with
reference backward to Christianity and then to Adam's "climactic
statement in the last book of Milton's epic," with ample quotations
from Wordsworth, now steeped for us in the language of the tradition
in which he is working.

Though this summary risks sounding chaotic, what it shows at
work is a skillful spiral history-by-accretion. Throughout the passage,
our attention is ostensibly on reading Wordsworth fully; but we are
learning the story at the same time, and finally we cannot say which is
more important, the story or the explication of Wordsworth's poems.
Each of them carries conviction about the value of Wordsworth's
attempt.

I hope it is clear by now how the depth and daring range of historical reference earns for Abrams an imposing authority. Relying on it,
he can dismiss whole schools of interpreters almost without our no-
ticing. In the middle of the account of how Wordsworth's theodicy
relates to others', he says, "Not all readers of *The Prelude* attend to its
conclusion with the care they devote to the earlier sections, and to
some of those who do it has seemed that Wordsworth's shift from
pain and evil to love and good has been managed by logical sleight of
hand" (p. 112). Gentle, yes, but he has demonstrated that the shift is
earned, and the demonstration is thus devastating to these readers,
as it is decisive on Wordsworth's behalf. Abrams has been teaching us
what it means to "attend" to a poem "with care," and he has thus
defended Wordsworth's art by placing it in its tradition.

History as Literary Criticism

A defense of artistic quality *by* placement in a tradition? There is
surely something odd here. I seem to be saying that *Natural Supernaturalism* offers us a way to answer questions in the form "Why is
this poem better than, or even greater than, *that* poem?" Abrams performs literary criticism through history, though he never quite tells us
that he has done so.

No influential critic I know of has ever suggested anything but the
impossibility of such a demonstration.[16] Demonstrations of value are
either (1) impossible, or (2) they are performed by "intrinsic" criticism

only and could never be arrived at through tracing "extrinsic" origins and consequences, or (3) if they are to be established on extrinsic grounds, the demonstration must be by systematic argument of the kind by which general values are established, and history as such is not that kind of argument. In other words, I may be able to show that a sonnet by Wordsworth is excellent in the sense of being well made, beautifully integrating its elements into a more impressive whole than some sonnet I might toss off in the next five minutes; but as soon as I move from such intrinsic investigation, I am driven to one of the "extrinsic" modes.

We have no canon of those modes; but Abrams' own chart, which accompanied the opening statement of his pluralistic assumptions in *The Mirror and the Lamp* (p. 6; see p. 55 above), will serve us well here. Taking intrinsic studies of the objective "work itself" as center, he traced three other modes: pragmatic, expressive, and imitative. (Note that my five-place chart [p. 57] is much like these four, with a place added for Abrams himself.) In this scheme, what are my possible directions if I abandon the "center"?

1. I can evaluate effects upon audiences (rhetorical or affective criticism). To do so, I must find some way to argue about the relative value of different "pragmatic" effects, showing why, say, I value more a poem that makes me cut myself while shaving than a poem that makes me wonder about the ironies of life, or one that makes me a better man, or one that leads me to a disinterested contemplation of form. To argue my case, I shall be forced to construct a general theory of human life into which my ranking of values can be fitted and thus established.

2. I can evaluate the quality of poets' lives, their genius, their creative skill, their imagination, or their craft. But to do so I must develop a general theory about human life according to which the superior value of some kinds of "expressive" genius or talent or personality can be established.

3. I can evaluate the intellectual or moral or psychological or political worlds or truths or realities that are imitated in the poem. Is a poem stating that the view from Westminster Bridge is as fair as anything on earth inherently superior to a poem giving a true picture of the revolutionary situation or a poem doing justice to the heart of darkness—assuming an equality of craft? To argue that it is, I must again develop a general theory about human life that will establish my ranking of poetic worlds.

No doubt it is the extreme difficulty of argument in any of these modes that has led so many critics until recently to reject all evaluation based on "extrinsic" criteria. We must grant the poet his subject, and then we can, if we are lucky, appraise his poetic achievement *as poetry*. All the other questions thus become finally illicit. The difficulty is also no doubt what accounts, in the recent return of the pendulum toward "new contextualisms,"[17] for the wondrously dogmatic tone with which many new new critical programs are announced. To provide genuine argument for standards within any "context," be it pragmatic (rhetorical), expressive (biographical), or imitative (ideological or philosophical), is so difficult that most believers fall back on a style of simple assertion that might well confirm any skeptic. Surely these wild battlers, so violent in their attacks, so thin in their own constructions, cancel each other out. Even if we may grant validity to some kinds of intrinsic judgments, there can be no standard of taste when we move "outward" and judge among genres and subjects and effects.

But if I see his book aright, Abrams has achieved in *Natural Supernaturalism* a kind of "extrinsic" validation that adds at least one to his list of three. It is a kind that uses *explication de textes*, but the book as a whole is a marvelous piece of exegesis outward rather than explication inward. Never before practiced in quite this form (though of course it depends on the work of many previous historians), it is finally a mode of criticism that proves a poem's greatness by discovering what kind of historical account you can give of it—both of what went into it and of what came out. Abrams has thus found a way of doing literary history that shows not only the historical importance of Wordsworth's poetry—what everyone would allow that literary history can do—but its poetic or aesthetic value as well.

Obviously, such criticism will not work except on those poems it will work on; it will work only if we become convinced that the poems do in fact embody and transform great themes and great motives found in a great past. If we can come to believe that the greatness was really "out there" and that Wordsworth has created its incarnation, the new trick has succeeded. The value of the poetry is now inescapably *in* the facts of the case.[18]

If the story had failed—if Abrams in trying to show that these verses in fact are the heirs of this greatness had revealed himself as forcing the evidence, faking his connections, disguising his lack of proof with colorful assertion—the poetry would not have withstood the testing. But since the rhetoric of his history is overwhelmingly solid, since the poems yield, historically, what he claims that they yield, the valued "extrinsic" is proved to have been really *in* there all the while.

In short, the scandal is perpetrated: by telling a persuasive story—a story made up of dozens of "short stories" like the one I have just traced, a story that runs from Homer to a brief selection of authors in the mid-twentieth century—Abrams overwhelms my possible objections and leaves me convinced about at least ten kinds of ambitious propositions, many of them evaluative.

"Surgical Ward" One Last Time

We can see something of both the complexity and the cogency of this test if we imagine a historian trying to "do an Abrams" that would show, by constructing a literary history, the greatness of Auden's "They Are and Suffer" or of either of the sonnet sequences in which it occurs.* We simply cannot know in advance what the effort might yield, but I think it likely that anyone embarking on such a project would soon come to a grinding halt. The problem would not be a lack of something to say about how the past led to this poetry; every human event, regardless of its quality, could be the center of a lengthy account of antecedents—as lengthy as the historian's patience and learning permitted. The problem would lie in trying to show how the poetry *embodies* its history and how it can serve in any sense as a great culmination of that history.

I have hinted at some of the problems one would consider in such an attempt, in my account of the themes shared by the two sequences (pages 62–65, above). The themes are in themselves as grand as anything described by Abrams: the relation of pain to happiness; the decline of civilization in time of war; the loss of faith in any redemption from man's fallen state, and so on. But is there a *grand* design, a *realized* embodiment? Only a sustained effort, using history as criticism, could show whether the poetry is, like Wordsworth's, itself a culminating historical moment.

My guess is—again—that such a project would run down long before the "demonstration," the finished history, could be completed. Though Auden is seriously engaged with a relatively major task, though his effort is a sustained one indeed by comparison with what most of us, poets or not, manage to do with such historical moments, one can predict that a year or so of living with these sonnets would reveal his project as a bit perfunctory. Many of the poems

---

*This section did not appear in my original piece, and Abrams thus had no opportunity to respond to it.

are, to be sure, marvelously made. There are many fine lines, many fine sonnets—"They Are and Suffer" one of the best. But the project as a whole might finally seem meager as compared with what Abrams shows happening in and through Wordsworth's poem. It is quite possible, in fact, that the historian-critic would find himself deflected into considering what, in the historical moment, serves to account for Auden's difficulties, his lack of complete success, or into explaining why these *Sonnets* are finally less significant to political, religious, or literary history than, say, *New Year Letter,* a poem about which I suspect that an impressive piece of historical criticism *could* be written.

But the important point is that my *obiter dicta* settle nothing. Only the actual attempt can tell us how much weight of historical inquiry a given poem can sustain. Such "proof," like every other kind, can yield its results only when the evidence is in, and the evidence cannot be derived from conclusions yielded by other critical modes. Regardless of whether Ronald Crane finds any one sonnet or an entire sequence to be a beautiful construct, or whether Kenneth Burke finds Auden grappling effectively with the task of curing his or the reader's ills, the "Abrams test" remains: Does an intelligent, sensitive, and informed historian find the sonnets responding to years of inquiry and to his effort to write a major history of the poem-as-moment? It is in the nature of the case that we shall quite probably never know the answer to that question.

Objections and Replies

What I have tried to describe, then, is a great work of what might be called epideictic history, a history designed to show forth the greatness of the phenomena it explains. Wordsworth's period and Wordsworth's poetry—more specifically *The Prelude* and most specifically the Prospectus—the quality that was theirs and the historical importance of that quality, the quality that is found not only in the technical mastery but in the meaning, the meaning as consciously intended by Wordsworth but also the added significance that time has granted as the world moved into modernism—all this, I am saying, is demonstrated in Abrams' work. Not proved exactly, in most senses of the word; not demonstrated at all if demonstration must be univocal, indubitable, replicable. Rather, the theses have been shown forth, in dense detail, and with a splendid mastery of ordination both historical and analytical.

Any objections we might suggest to all this are rigorously limited by the performance itself. A good way to test Abrams' mastery will be to consider the major problems raised by his critics, along with one or two suggested by what I have said.

Since most of the following objections postulate some alternative history, they raise in final, acute form the question of just how pluralistic Abrams is willing to be. Has he given us *the* history of his subject as he defines it, or *a* history? If, as I am sure, he would give us the latter answer, how far will he go with it?

I shall in each case attempt to answer the objections as I think he might, hoping that my errors will goad him into discussing just how far his historical pluralism can go. If it "goes all the way," accepting even histories that visibly contradict each other, how is it different from relativism? If, as we can expect, he will *not* go all the way—will reject any history arguing, say, that Wordsworth was *not* representative and his poems *not* great—how then is he anything more than a monist, a shrewd and supple and tolerant one but not a pluralist at all?

CRITIC: By your own account, the method of Abrams' book is not clear; indeed it is sloppy. Is it really any more than a rather simple and far too easy dialectic of similarity and difference? Abrams marshals a list of similarities between this or that source and Wordsworth and then asserts that "in spite of all these similarities, there were great differences." It is obviously a method that predetermines a *kind* of success: seeking similarities and differences, one can always find them. Abrams can pick up any work in any period, before or after, and show either that it is similar—or that it is, miraculously, different.

REPLY: The objection would hold only if the point were to *prove* the similarities and the differences. Though *one* point is to trace "tradition and innovation," it is all in the service of the epideictic history, as if the author said, "Something great happened here, in human history, producing the 'something great' that is Wordsworth and his poems and leading, finally, to ourselves. Look at them in this light (similarities) and then in this (differences), and now look again, and again. Do they not look bigger and bigger, more and more representative, as we go? Clearly, in one sense I could go on like this forever. Bring me Lucretius, say, whom I have mentioned only in passing, and I will do you a complete analysis, showing how he is, first, similar to my hero—and then different from him. Bring me anyone who figured prominently in cultural history before Wordsworth, and

I will do the same thing. And in doing so, I will heighten further my portrait of why this poet, engaged in this unique event, is important to you. But my repeated successes are not a simple product of my method. I can do all this because that's the kind of poet Wordsworth was; he somehow took in all that, *lived in* it, and thus contributed to this pivotal point in history."

CRITIC: Still, it is impossible to determine precisely what kind of claim Abrams is making. As your account has shown, the causal claims are sometimes literal but often metaphorical or even Platonic; one cannot tell whether Romanticism was historically caused, in a time stream leading by literal influences from Homer and Plato through the pre-Romantics to Wordsworth, or was somehow structurally inevitable, the ideal forms somehow getting through, mysteriously (as always in Platonic systems), to particular men in a particular time, so that they "participated in" or "paralleled" what had occurred often in the past and will occur often in the future, in one of those spiral returns that Abrams is so fond of.

REPLY: But this is precisely one of the great sources of Abrams' power. He means both (or all three, and perhaps many more) of these kinds of "causation." The causal terms are muddy because history itself is muddy—and especially cultural history. Individuals influence individuals, zeitgeists influence zeitgeists, and the natures and forms of things somehow get through to poets and philosophers in radically different circumstances so that they rediscover relationships that were always "there." Abrams does not say so, but I think that he secretly approves of Wordsworth's "realist" conviction that there is a natural wedding of mind and nature; the consummation of the wedding is indeed part of nature, in the sense of "what is the case."

Even after philosophers have done their worst, our minds really do know something of reality, just as they are part of reality. But for Abrams, as for us all, philosophy since Kant *has* done its worst, and we can never again believe that any act of knowing, however clear, exhausts its object. When the "object" is something as manifold as Wordsworth and Romanticism, we must be especially suspicious of simple clarities. If we really believe that Romanticism was immeasurably complex, then our measurements must be complex and cautious and delicately qualified at every point. And we know that no matter how complex our account, it will constitute only one of many possible histories of the same phenomena. Thus pluralism dictates, for

Abrams, not only a plurality of *kinds* of cause in his own account, so that there are in effect many different histories within the one history, many voices dialectically put into partially unresolved play, but also an invitation to other histories that will be additional persuasive versions. Some of these might legitimately trace one single cause with a kind of clarity that would be destructive in Abrams' version.

CRITIC: I find far too little here about the specifically poetic form of individual works. There is nothing about verse form, nothing about *literary* conventions used and transformed. Throughout long sections one would never guess that Abrams sees any real difference between a poem and a philosophical system or a religious tract; they all seem to embody ideas and themes and vocations and quests in precisely the same form, and thus the distinctive quality of poetry as poetry is lost.

REPLY: First, what is this entity, "the distinctive quality of poetry as poetry"? Consider more closely what Abrams has taught about the sources of a phrase like "poetry as poetry."[19] One thing the book shows is the usefulness, in dealing with the Romantics, of "pragmatic" rather than "aesthetic" notions of poetry—of "poetry for life's sake" or "poetry for man's sake."

Second, the charge is not strictly true, no matter how we define poetry. There *is* a good deal, though much of it muted, about the sources of Wordsworth's stylistic and formal presuppositions, especially about the biblical sources of the "common" diction.

Third, the poems are given, and in lengthy quotations. We read them or reread them as we read the book, and we read them as "poems," since that is what they are. Only critical dogma could lead one to worry about whether their full aesthetic autonomy is being respected. Let some other book—by a new critic or an old "Chicago neo-Aristotelian" like me—deal with whatever problems of craft are neglected here.

CRITIC: But this reply dodges the issue. "Ideas" as they become embodied in poems are different from "ideas" as they are developed by a Kant or a Hegel or a Fichte. This book talks as if they were the same thing, whereas they are usually both simpler in poems, shorn of their qualifications and complexities, and more forceful.

REPLY: Granted. I could wish that Abrams had included more about what happens when one chooses to look more closely at the differences between philosophy and poetry. Thomas McFarland makes a similar objection from the obverse side: Abrams reduces thought to imagination and sees philosophers as "variant forms of the artist."[20] But both forms of this objection to Abrams' assimilative method ignore the pluralistic point: if you look for one thing, you will not see all things clearly; and if you try to see all things, large and small, you will see nothing clearly. Abrams has shown what can be seen when literary works and philosophies are assimilated both as structures and as products of human motives. Others will have to take care of the history that is based on elevating their differences.

Unless you can read Abrams' book and conclude that Hegel's philosophical works were not *in one sense* products of the fictive imagination and that Wordsworth's poems were not *in one sense* philosophical speculations, you must grant Abrams his *données:* that the similarities are—for one kind of inquiry—more important than the differences.

CRITIC: The history that is presented is a strangely intellectualized history in another sense. There is little or no music or graphic art, no dance, no landscape gardening. And even what little politics there is becomes transmuted into *thought* rather than *action*. Though the Romantic poets are shown taking up revolution and then putting it down, rejecting religion and then taking up with it again, one gets no hint of how events in the world, as distinct from what people happened to read, might have affected such changes.

REPLY: True; another limitation. But again it is a limitation of the kind that no good book will escape. *This* book is about ideas and the shapes they can take in poems and philosophies. It is not clear how music and art could enter it fruitfully. If it is true that Beethoven, for example, enters here only as someone who happened to give a musical setting to Schiller's "Ode to Joy"—and that is surely a strange reduction of the Ninth Symphony!—is it not also true that Beethoven had nothing to add to any dialogue about natural supernaturalism?

CRITIC: No, it is not true. There is no more profound "statement" of a theodicy, for example, than Beethoven's last quartets, which he sometimes annotated with programmatic comments like *Muss es sein?* followed by *Es muss sein!* Did Wordsworth ever *hear* any Beethoven? Did he respond to those earlier theological works, Händel's Oratorios? Did he know any symphonies or string quartets by Mozart or Haydn, especially those marvelous final movements in which joy and humor and overwhelming cosmic energy are made to "answer" every conceivable argument for dejection? If so, we never learn of it. If not, it might be an interesting commentary on the singular humorlessness both of the Romantic poets (except Byron, whom Abrams in effect excludes, regarding him as no true Romantic) and of this book.

REPLY: All right, perhaps a genuine deficiency. But note that, once you have begun in this direction, there is no good place to stop. Nothing significant done in Wordsworth's time by any maker—no piece of sculpture, no novel, no popular ballad, no industrial effort, no constitutional reform—can be properly ruled out. This is precisely why, in human affairs, no one account can ever be enough. It is not just that we should tolerate a plurality of histories, we should demand them; and anybody who could be satisfied with only one is a victim of a monistic view of human life and its causes.

CRITIC: But this puts us right back where we started: with the charge of relativism. Now we can make the charge not just about Abrams' theories of criticism but about his practice of cultural history. The methods you have described, and the evidence it relies on, will by their very nature allow us to "prove" many different histories, some of them in open conflict with yours. Given a stylist as steady and pure, given a master of connections as diligent and various, given many years of research to find the pat quotations, one might prove anything. The simple dialectic of sameness-and-difference could even be used to do a *negative* epideictic history—"proving" that Wordsworth and his time were *not* great.

REPLY: It is indeed in the nature of human actions that there *must* be many possible histories of any event, because every human event is immeasurably more complex than any conceivable explanation. And since works of art and philosophy are the most complex of all human actions or products, they are, of all the subjects of man's inquiry, the wiliest in escaping single formulations. It thus seems likely that we *could* have other legitimate histories of Abrams' subject, histories as imposing as his and yet contradicting him in many points, even important ones. But whether one could be written that would falsify any of his central theses will be settled not by propositional argument but by the argument peculiar to writing a history: *can* the history be written and, once written, can it be read? Will it pass the kinds of tests, in detail, that I have applied to Abrams? If someone can write a debunking history of Wordsworth and Romanticism, one that will make its connections and establish its values as thoroughly and with as little stylistic forcing as Abrams manages, then of course we must take his view into account. Go try.

It is easy, of course, to "try" in a review. J. Hillis Miller, for example, sketches a plausible counterhistory: "Perhaps Abrams takes his writers a little too much at face value, summarizes them a little too flatly, fails to search them for ambiguities or contradictions in their thought [as Derrida, for one, would do], does not 'explicate' in the sense of unfold, unravel, or unweave."[21] In short, because Abrams does not see how much he has imposed himself upon the text in order to become its master, we need another history entirely, one that would "deconstruct" its texts by turning them inside out, by reinterpreting. It "would deny [Abrams' assumption] that the One comes first. It would deny the existence of 'opposites' which are fragmented parts of an original whole. It would deny that history has a goal of reunification," relying instead on a principle of "difference or differentiation" (p. 12).

I find the possibility of having such a deconstructed history exhilarating. But whoever attempts it must appreciate the standards by which it is to be tested. Most of the authors on Miller's list of heroes give us a half-pennyworth of specification to an intolerable deal of theory. It is no accident, comrades, that despite all of the historical speculations offered by followers of Miller's great four (Freud, Marx, Saussure, and Nietzsche) one can think of so few *fully wrought* histories.

If it is true that *Natural Supernaturalism* depends on Abrams' hermeneutical theory and practice and that his reading of each text is only one reading, his method insures that his readings become publicly shared; by earning our agreement, they cease to be "subjective" in quite the way that many Freudian, Marxist, or structuralist readings are. If someone can write a history of Wordsworth and Romanticism that is as commanding in its way as, let us say, Lukács' Marxist history, *The Historical Novel* (1937) (one of a very small number of works fathered by any of his prime four that Miller might want to point to as having a genuine solidity of specification rivaling Abrams'), then it will enter the canon; it will challenge Abrams where he lives. But nothing short of such full demonstration can do the job.

CRITIC: But you have characteristically turned the charge into one that is easier to deal with than the real one. The fact is, as Miller argues, that Abrams is not by any means a pluralist in his interpretative theory; he is a dogmatist of the most blatant kind. He seems quite unaware of the radical ambiguity of all texts. He shows no sign of ever having read *A Map of Misreading*, by his former student, Harold Bloom, or the work of that genuine pluralist, M. Roland Barthes. Each text is steadily, ploddingly assumed to mean exactly what Abrams says it means. But not only is it true that a committed deconstructionist could discover alternative readings; every reader of any persuasion would *in fact* emerge from any one of Abrams' texts with a meaning different from what Abrams has found and with, in consequence, a history different *in every detail*. This is not only how it is in hermeneutical practice; it is how it should be. Abrams works throughout with a monolithic theory of interpretation which, by silently imposing the doctrine of "the single interpretation," is finally stultifying to the life of letters.

REPLY: Such a position cannot be shown to be flatly wrong, because it is not flatly wrong: understanding is never complete, misunderstanding is always rampant, some efforts to achieve understanding can produce a stifled, unimaginative conformity, and some forms of misunderstanding can be benign. Abrams cannot take the free flights that might be taken by someone who did not worry as much about what the various authors intended to say.

But regardless of how open to alternatives we may decide to be, we should never forget that the very notion of productive misunderstanding or creative misreading is logically and socially dependent on its opposite. As some deconstructionists have understood,[22] we cannot attack substantive centers—whether the self or God or Being or the Correct Reading—without ourselves relying on substantive centers, embedded in the very language with which we think. Thus every effort at original or "free" interpretation is plainly and simply parasitic* on the work

---

*J. Hillis Miller, responding both to my point here and to Abrams' claim that many texts do, after all, have a determinable meaning, chose to explore the multiple meanings and associations of this word "parasitic" ("The Critic as Host," *Critical Inquiry* [Spring 1977]: 439–47). His tracings taught me a good deal about the word and about unintended meanings that my use of it could carry, but it did not convince me that his reading of my text is not parasitic. In the first place, it depends on its host for much of its meaning; indeed, it would die if separated from the host, and by this I mean not my specific text but the world of critics who attempt to understand each other rather than embroider meanings around disembodied fragments. Second, if unchecked by everyone's sense that some readings are sounder than others, it would in fact kill its host. But the degree to which Booth-as-host is really hostile to the parasites must be determined by reading my three final chapters, and particularly the effort in chapter 6 to defend a "violation" of texts.

of people like Abrams, whose solidity, even when rejected as obvious or dull, is relied upon in every act of deconstruction or "misprision." It is not only that logically one cannot speak of *mis*reading without a concept of understanding; it is that the society of communicating critics would dissolve into nothingness if we had no critics like Abrams to provide a base of shared knowledge and thus a confidence in the meaningfulness of the whole enterprise.

CRITIC: Even supposing we granted all that about general possibilities, the problems in Abrams' performance would still remain. You have not really met the full force of the objection about his biased selectivity in the service of conventional and established views. Abrams is flatly unjust to the less life-affirming side of Romanticism. It is not only that he explicitly rules out the opposition by dismissing Byron because (and surely this is a dead giveaway) "in his greatest work he speaks with an ironic counter-voice and deliberately opens a satirical perspective on the vatic stance of his Romantic contemporaries" (*NS*, p. 13). It is also that he underplays the powerful negatives in the poets he does treat, including Wordsworth. In short, he himself has a strong bias for the affirmation of the "Romantic positives," and he selects his poets and his evidence from them to stress those positives. But in fact, "the highest moments in Romantic art have always been achieved not in final goals but in final refusals";[23] "the profoundest Romantic response to the failure of the Christian-Enlightenment ideology, the anti-redemptionist tradition, is the relevant one" to us today;[24] the true Romantic tradition, the one that gives us the truths with which we must now live, is best represented by Nietzschean nihilism, the honest vision that comes when we have deconstructed all the substances and have recognized, painfully, "that 'goal-lessness as such' (*die Ziellosigkeit an sich*) is the principle of our faith";[25] and "the lost paradise regained [by the Romantics] is death."[26]

REPLY: Insofar as this is an objection to Abrams' view of Romanticism, the reply must be the one I gave above: show us the counterevidence; tell us the counterstory in its full weight, so that we can judge.

But if the objections are really to Abrams' view of what our life is or should or might be, if they say that he is not sufficiently nihilistic, then of course the quarrel is even more difficult to resolve. What are the tests that might decide whether sympathy for the Romantics in their affirmation of "life, love, liberty, hope, and joy" is a better or sounder or truer attitude than any of various nihilisms?

There can be no doubt but that Abrams' critics have here reached the heart of the matter: Abrams has described those moments in Romanticism when poets defined the universe, with their imagination, as essentially "friendly" in the precise sense that there was a natural marriage between the human spirit and the world it inhabits. And he leaves no doubt—though he says little directly about himself—that he clearly thinks their kind of hope, their faith in life and joy, can still be recommended, in some sense, even in our own blighted times. His book is his own (muted) theodicy, and those who think all theodicies are by definition faulty are right in feeling challenged. In choosing our attitudes, the book implies, let us not pretend that all rational defenses are on the side of considering nature or the universe unfriendly to men, who are *essentially* alienated.

I may surprise Abrams in placing him so unequivocally on the side of his affirming heroes. But I found myself more deeply moved by his book and the rereading it led me to than I have been by any Romantic reading since my late teens. Apparently I rediscovered in it my own romanticism, while coming to understand better why I had for decades thought of myself as somehow beyond Romanticism. My revaluation could occur only because Abrams moved me away from concern for literal causation into consideration of the permanent validity of some Romantic responses to evil and suffering.

CRITIC: But now you have landed us right back in the problem of Abrams' so-called pluralism. Your reply surely suggests that there is a single core of cognitively sound readings that lead to a single solid historical interpretation, around which cluster a variety of interpretations that are at best *partially* sound or useful, at worst genuine misreadings—and all of them dependent on what the saner and sounder folk do at the center. Such talk would be troublesome enough if Abrams were only a critic; it is downright inconsistent when we are dealing with a critic-historian who claims to be a pluralist.

After all, most of the propositions in your initial list of ten kinds are about particulars. Romanticism happened only once. Wordsworth is unique, and, among his poems, his great three-part uncompleted epic of the mind's marriage with nature was attempted only once. Abrams thus claims to give us knowledge about individuals; and if we took his pluralism seriously, we must say *both* that his descriptions and evaluations give us genuine knowledge of the particular (something that many philosophers have said is impossible) *and* that there can be a plurality of descriptions and evaluations of the same particulars (something that makes the whole project absurd). To gain knowledge about anything, we must seek an explanation that is both general and single. Particulars covered by our explanation will be inherently plural; that is, the events or data or observations are "replicable" just because the pattern or rule or law is one, not many. In short, Abrams, in your account, has *everything* upside down: the explanations are inherently plural, but the "things" they explain are inherently unique.

And surely the claim to pluralism is, finally, just a dodge. When several different "convincing" explanations of a unique event are possible, what right have we to use the word "convincing"? However genuine Abrams' account of how he feels about Wordsworth's effort and its value, its causes, and its effect, it cannot give us knowledge of either causes or values. After all, we can know causes, as Hume taught the world, only when we have found antecedents that are invariably followed by the same consequent—one which never follows from other, different antecedents. (And even then we do not know *causes*, for Hume, but that is a different problem.) Since nothing that Abrams—or indeed any historian of literature or criticism—can offer us fulfills these conditions, since by definition what we seek to explain is finally unique, regardless of how many parallels we can find with other works, we cannot come to *know* "How it happened that Wordsworth wrote the Preface to *The Excursion* this way rather than that." And it is even more obvious that we cannot come to *know* the *greatness* of that unique achievement. Whatever success Abrams may have had in persuading any reader cannot finally be called a cognitive success.

REPLY: I can't pretend to answer briefly a question that has plagued philosophers of history at least since Aristotle said that poetry is more philosophical than history (and by implication of more cognitive value) *because* it is more capable of dealing with universals. All I can ask is that whatever simple paradigm of knowledge is offered us by abstract thought be tested honestly against the concreteness of Abrams' offerings. Your position would not only rule out Abrams and all cultural history; it would rule out the cognitive claims of all literary criticism except the kind that can move from established general rules to a discovery of how particular poems abide by them.

The various pendulum swings of this century have been largely between the two poles produced by your way of putting things. Those who have accepted your polarity of knowledge-of-the-general versus nonrational-embrace-of-valued-particulars have been driven to escape evaluation of individuals, whether by writing histories of influences or trends or conventions, by performing rigorous work in editing or bibliography, by constructing sciences of criticism, like Northrop Frye's, that repudiate evaluation, or by discovering deep structures underlying particular forms. Those who have wanted to deny the polarity have been driven to construct theories to take its place. Witness the manifold efforts in Germany to develop a *Geisteswissenschaft* that would ground a historical knowledge of valued particulars, in contrast to a *Naturwissenschaft* that threatened to take over the world because it offered a knowledge of general laws and causes; the many efforts by succeeding phenomenologies to discover forms of intersubjective warrant for knowledge of persons and their values; the effort to make the act of criticism itself objectively demonstrable, as in the close reading and "intrinsic" analysis of the New Critics and the Chicago school; and finally the recent rediscovery in America of the impossibility of literary criticism without some embeddedness in history.[27]

Surely there is something destructive and unnecessary about all this to-ing and fro-ing. Is it not time, considering what we now know about how our philosophical and scientific languages work, to recognize that a question like "What knowledge is possible?" is radically ambiguous and that different resolutions of its ambiguities will rule in and rule out different (and perhaps equally valid) kinds of inquiry? Instead of placing the different answers in polar opposition, we should take pluralism seriously and put our questions about knowledge in complementary form: "What sorts of inquiry are opened and closed when we sharply split knowledge from particular value?" And "What kinds of inquiry are opened and closed when we admit that we 'know'—in some sense—the truth of a story like Abrams': 'Once on this earth there occurred a great cultural revolution. *One* of its representative heroes was Wordsworth, and in one of his great poems he . . .'?"

To accept this kind of knowledge as something other than

merely subjective, surely we need only ask honestly, after reading Abrams: "Which would do more violence to my knowledge and my rational powers, to decide that Abrams' account is valueless as knowledge, useful only as entertainment, or to decide that something is wrong with certain abstract claims about what knowledge *is?*" Not the least of Abrams' uses is that, even without providing a theoretical base for what he has achieved, he shatters all our simple rules for knowing by increasing the range and quality of what we know.

Abrams' Reply

Like Kenneth Burke, M. H. Abrams agreed in advance to respond to my appraisal, and the reply that I print here originally appeared, along with a slightly different version of my "invitation," in *Critical Inquiry*.

It will be obvious that I have managed somehow to come much closer to Abrams' view of Abrams than to Burke's view of Burke. I cannot fully explain why this is so, but I think it important here to reject two possible answers that may occur to some readers: (1) Abrams is simply more compliant; (2) his enterprise is inherently closer to my own. (1) Abrams *is* a generous man, but so is Burke; I think that both have been as free of merely personal motives as any of us ever manages to be in such matters. Readers who are acquainted with Abrams' recent attacks on deconstructionist criticism will not make the mistake of thinking him temperamentally unable to disagree sharply. (2) Both of their enterprises are quite alien to what I would have thought of as "my" natural way of working, before these authors "worked me over." If anything, I am much less spontaneously given to history than to Burke's rhetorical mode of working. One way of putting this is to say that I could never undertake, in my wildest dreams, to write a *Natural Supernaturalism*, but I dream constantly of "doing a rhetoric" that might help cure myself and the world.

I stress these qualifications not to insist on my gold stars for having got Abrams more or less right but rather to forestall anyone's saying, "Well, of course: if you pick someone whose mind is already like yours, you can easily give the impression of having understood it."

Obviously neither Burke nor Abrams offered me totally alien worlds. But the case for a pluralistic critical understanding does not depend on anyone's entering totally alien worlds, only on the possibility that some of us some of the time can, by taking thought, improve our capacity to understand. Meanwhile, I see no point in concealing my pleasure in offering one reply that begins with exactly the right five words.

RATIONALITY AND IMAGINATION IN CULTURAL HISTORY

Wayne Booth is quite right: for all my interest in the methods of literary criticism, I say nothing about method in my two historical books, *The Mirror and the Lamp* and *Natural Supernaturalism*. The reason for my silence on this issue is simple: these books were not written with any method in mind. Instead they were conceived, researched, worked out, put together, pulled apart, and put back together, not according to a theory of valid procedures in such undertakings, but by intuition. I relied, that is, on my sense of rightness and wrongness, of doubt and assurance, of deficiencies and superfluities, of what is appropriate and what is inappropriate. I should like to think that these intuitions were the kind that Coleridge describes, which follow from

> such a knowledge of the facts, material and spiritual, that most appertain to [the writer's] art, as, if it have been governed and applied by *good sense*, and rendered instinctive by habit, becomes the representative and reward of our past conscious reasonings, insights, and conclusions, and acquires the name of TASTE.*

We must distinguish between ignorant intuitions and those which are the reward of prior experience, reading, and thinking; the play of this latter class of intuitions is what we mean by expertise.

In retrospect, I think I was right to compose *Natural Supernaturalism* (let us, following Booth, focus our discussion on this book) by relying on taste, tact, and intuition rather than on a controlling method. A book of this kind, which deals with the history of human intellection, feeling, and imagination, employs special vocabularies, procedures, and modes of demonstration which, over many centuries of development, have shown their profitability when applied to matters of this sort. I agree with Booth that these procedures, when valid, are in a broad sense rational, and subject to analysis and some degree of definition. But the rules underlying such a discourse are complex, elusive, unsystematic, and subject to innovative modification; they

---

*S. T. Coleridge, *Biographia Literaria*, ed. J. Shawcross, 2 vols. (Oxford, 1907) 2:64.

manifest themselves in the intuitive expertise of the historian; and the specification of these rules should not precede, but follow practice.

The risk of premature codification is that the code will inhibit the free play of our procedures of demonstration and fail to do justice to our intuitions that something sound, useful, and illuminating has in fact been accomplished. In particular the risk is that the codes that have already been worked out for valid demonstration in mathematics, formal logic, and the physical sciences will intrude as models for our dealings with quite disparate intellectual enterprises, each of which has its own kind of subject matter, aims, and ways of proceeding. The result is a foregone conclusion: it will be a more or less elaborated and qualified, but still recognizable variant of the result of Hume's test for all methods of inquiry:

> If we take in our hand any volume . . . let us ask, *Does it contain any abstract reasoning concerning quantity or number?* No. *Does it contain any experimental reasoning concerning matter of fact and existence?* No. Commit it then to the flames: for it can contain nothing but sophistry and illusion.*

By this strict test *Natural Supernaturalism* would of course be committed to the flames, and by any softened version of such a test, most of its procedures would be gravely suspect. But to all such tests, the proper retort is Booth's question (p. 175), which might be restated in this way: "After reading certain books that violate calculi modeled on logic and the exact sciences, which would do more violence to my sense of what is rational and my intuition that I have learned new truths—to decide that these books don't yield knowledge, or to decide that the calculi are inappropriate to the procedures of discovery and demonstration that their authors have in fact employed?"

After the fact, nevertheless, a book like *Natural Supernaturalism* is subject to close critical inquiry about its methods and rationale. I am grateful to Booth for opening up such an inquiry, and for doing so in a way that is not only disarming, but seems to me to be the most promising of useful results. That is, instead of adopting a prosecutorial stance, demanding: "Justify the rationality and probative force of what you have done; it looks damned suspicious to me," he has adopted the friendly tactic of saying: "Your book, in my experience of it, has yielded discoveries that I want to call knowledge, by methods, however deviant from standard rubrics of valid reasoning, that it seems irrational to call non-rational. Let's set out to clarify what these

*David Hume, *An Enquiry Concerning Human Understanding*, the concluding paragraph.

methods are, and to see what grounds we can find for the claim that they provide warranted knowledge."

I

I confess that I was taken aback to discover, in Booth's just analysis, what a strange book *Natural Supernaturalism* is, and how extraordinary are the claims it presumes to make on its readers. It involves, explicitly or implicitly, a wide range of propositional truth-claims, of which only a fraction assert literal causation. Other propositions are assertions about an epoch, "Romanticism," and its special importance to us, and about the validity of the contention of some Romantic writers that they are "prophets" or "seers"; others assert not only facts, but values—the great values in the poems of certain Romantic authors, especially Wordsworth, and the high moral values that constitute the general Romantic "ethos"; still other implicit propositions even undertake to offer justifiable, if partial, answers to such questions as who we now are, where we are, where we came from, and what all this means. The basic mode of "proof" employed for this mixed bag of assertions is their incorporation into a story—more specifically, into a story made up of many stories, in which we can distinguish, within the overarching narrative, a number of middle-sized "novellas" and a great many "short stories"; and the book as a whole requires that the reader enter into its "narrative world" and be convinced that *"all of this happened*—this story is *true*," as a necessary condition for being persuaded of the soundness of the truth-claims and value-claims that the narrative implicates.

And what a very odd thing this story itself turns out to be! Its chief elements, or protagonists, are neither integral literary documents nor Lovejoy's unit ideas, but a fusion of ideas, structural shapes, and values. The connections asserted among these elements range from temporal and causal relations, through analogical relations (sometimes stated in terms that suggest a Platonic belief in timeless forms in which particulars "participate"), to a great diversity of other connectives which are left out of account in standard inventories of rational relationships. And as Booth points out, the temporal order is again and again "scrambled," for the diverse narratives move bewilderingly back and forth in time between the Romantic present, its ancestral past, and its portended future up to the time in which the book was written. In candor I must add to Booth's list another oddity, which some reviewers have in part noted but which Booth, perhaps out of kindness, chose to leave out of his account: the book as a whole has a structure that is deliberately iconic of the spiral form which many Romantic thinkers considered the necessary shape of all intellection, and in which many Romantic writers ordered their philosophies, their histories, and their fictional writings in verse and prose. That is, each of the component sections of *Natural Supernaturalism* constitutes a circle of exposition and narrative out of and back to a passage in Wordsworth's Prospectus to *The Recluse;* while the book as a whole ends where it began, with the opening passage of the Prospectus, but on a level of understanding which, the author presumes, will incorporate the results of the narrative exposition that has intervened.

About this strange performance Booth has raised a number of searching questions, which play variations on one central quesiton: how to justify the claim that this complex story and its inherent propositional claims are not only convincing, but *ought* to be convincing, and on rational grounds, rather than merely by their rhetorical, emotional, and imaginative appeal? He also, and insistently, poses to the author a second-order question: if I believe this history of what happened in the Romantic era to be, by and large, true, how can I justify my pluralist claim that alternative and conflicting histories of the same era may also be true?

All of Booth's questions I find entirely warranted, but also very puzzling; I feel confident that I will continue to wrestle with them for some time to come. For many of them I can't at this point conceive any better answers than Booth has himself formulated for me. But let me at least offer interim comments about a few of the issues that Booth has raised, both in his questions and in his answers.

II

One source of confusion about what I tried to do lies in my use of that pesky word "Romantic" (and "Romanticism"), which is one of those terms which historians can neither do with, nor make do without. I am not on this issue, as Booth suggests (p. 146), a "Platonist," but am instead, like R. S. Crane and A. O. Lovejoy, a "nominalist." That is, I don't believe that there exists an abstract entity, named "Romanticism," whose essential features are definable; or to put it in another way, that we can set the necessary and sufficient conditions for the correct use of the term, "Romanticism." Instead, I use the word as an expository convenience to specify, as I say on the opening pages, "some of the striking parallels, in authorial stance and persona, subject matter, ideas, values, imagery, forms of thought and imagination, and design of plot or structure" which are manifested in a great many important English and German writers, in a great variety of literary, philosophical, and historical forms, during those three or four decades after the outbreak of the French Revolution which, following common historical usage, I call the Romantic era (*Natural Supernaturalism*, pp. 11–12). How inescapable is the use of such period terms for summary reference, both Crane and Lovejoy show in their actual practice; for Crane wrote an essay called "English Neoclassical Criticism," and Lovejoy, after all his warnings about the advisability of eliminating the term "Romanticism," or at least of using it only in the plural form, wrote a chapter called "Romanticism and the Principle of Plenitude."*

But having stipulated my nominalist choice for the reference of the term "Romantic," I go on in the course of the book to refer to such things as "the Romantic *Bildungsgeschichte*," "the Romantic spiral pattern," "the Romantic ethos," without reiterating each time the warning that I mean the term "Romantic" to apply only to my stipulated set of writers and documents. As a result, some reviewers have been misled into claiming that I undertook a complete "typology of Romanticism," or a "grand synthesis of Romanticism," or a "definitive" study of Romanticism; and some have happily announced that I had once and for all demolished Lovejoy's claim that there is no single entity called Romanticism. But the same misunderstanding of what I set out to do opened to other reviewers the opportunity to assert that my conspectus of Romanticism is radically omissive, or else that it distorts the true nature of the Romantic achievement. In either case, the discussion has shifted from questions of the sort: "Did the distinctive complex of literary and cultural phenomena I chose to discuss really take place in the period conventionally called Romantic? Was it central enough to be worth such extended treatment? Is the analysis of this complex and its interrelations accurate and adequate?" to another type of question: "What is the proper, or correct, or central, or primary meaning of the term 'Romanticism'?" That is, "Romanticism" has shifted over from being a nominal convenience for the literary and cultural historian, who stipulates what he uses it to denote, to a status in which, like "justice," "democracy," and "a Christian life," it is what W. B. Gallie calls an "essentially contested concept."† I don't know, short of the use of intolerable circumlocu-

---

*In *Critics and Criticism*, ed. R. S. Crane (Chicago, 1952), pp. 372–88; A. O. Lovejoy, *The Great Chain of Being* (Cambridge, Mass., 1936), chap. 10.

†W. B. Gallie, "Essentially Contested Concepts," in *Philosophy and the Historical Understanding* (London, 1964), chap. 8. I don't mean to imply that contests about an essentially contested concept may not be profitable (though they are usually conducted in a very confusing way). My point is that arguments about the nature of "Romanti-

tions, how to avoid such slippage, to which all of us are extremely vulnerable; for if we go against the grain of usage and substitute a different term for "Romanticism," it will soon be reified in its turn, and so re-inaugurate the old debates about its proper meaning.

It is instructive to list some of the things which various reviewers have proposed that *Natural Supernaturalism*, as a survey of "Romanticism," ought properly to have treated. The missing topics include "the impact of Oriental cultures"; the " 'Catholic' tradition of Romantic religious experience"; Romantic irony and the ironic perspective in general; the actual political events of the day, and not merely the effect of these events on thought and imagination; the Romantic mode of "anti-redemptive, anti-explanatory, explanation"; "the literature of sentiment [and] the Gothic strain in poetry and fiction"; and "necrophily . . . diabolism, masochism, and suicide." Among the authors whom, it is said, I should have, or at least might well have treated, are Byron, the Pre-Raphaelites, Whitman, and Hardy; Scott and other novelists; Von Baader, Franz Molitor, Schleiermacher, S. Maimon, Kleist, E. T. A. Hoffmann, Richter, Heine; de Vigny, Gobineau, Hugo, Zola, Michelet, Amiel, Nerval, Balzac, Stendhal, Constant, Gautier; Leopardi, Manzoni; Lermontov, Pushkin. . . . Now, all these topics and writers are entirely eligible for treatment in books on Romanticism, and they have in fact been so treated; so that an initial but only partial answer to Booth's question about historical pluralism is to say that diverse historians have the right to focus their attention on different areas of historical concern. I claim no more than that the interrelated topics which I have elected to treat, and the writings in which these topics are instantiated, were very important in their own time and continue to be of great interest to us today; that to tell this chosen story with any adequacy is quite enough for one book to try to do; and that if I have done my job properly, both the historical importance and continuing human interest of these selected topics are confirmed and expanded in the course of their historical exposition.*

III

Reviewers have greatly exaggerated the degree to which I rely on parallels, consonances, and analogues to establish the connections

---

cism" as such are on a different level from discussions about the accuracy and adequacy of a treatment of stipulated cultural phenomena within a stipulated period of time.

*In my concluding paragraph (*NS*, p. 462) I add the judgment that the complex of ideas, motives, and values that I expound "has the best historical claim to be called the between the elements in the various stories I tell. Even Wayne Booth, after pointing out that I in fact employ many "literal" connections such as "cause," "influence," "source"—and despite his consent to the view that a historian must deploy a great diversity of relationships to match the tangled complexity of intellectual and cultural history— suggests that I may be committed to a "Platonic" belief in "some permanent human interest or eternal idea" to explain parallels or analogues between two works "that cannot have been literally caused in temporal history" (pp. 155–56; see also pp. 165–66).*

I didn't intend, however, to posit eternal ideas or universal traits of human nature to explain the relations between the various themes and structures that I identify and trace through time. I took care, in fact, to assert early on that the history I undertook to tell is strictly culture-bound. That is, it is a history limited to Western European thought and imagination; and one of my major assertions is that this has long been, and to a certain extent now remains, "essentially, although in derivative rather than direct manifestations, a biblical culture," in which we "readily mistake our hereditary ways of organizing experience for the conditions of reality and the universal forms of thought"; I suggest also that we can't escape "religious formulas which, since they are woven into the fabric of our language, control the articulation of our thinking" (NS, pp. 65–66). The evidence for such a sweeping historical claim, and for supplementary assertions of the way that biblical schemes assimilated elements from classical philosophy, is cumulative as the narrative progresses; and when I do point to parallels and analogues, they are meant to be explicable, in part, by the persistent and subtle play of literal causes, or inter-influences, within this pervasive linguistic and cultural context.

But even within this overall context of a biblical culture, it seems to me that there are relatively few instances in which I do no more than present similarities and analogues between important items in the stories I narrate. Take, for example, a central motif of the book, that of the changing conceptual design of the past, present, and future of human history. The assimilation of the right-angled biblical pattern of

English Romantic tradition" on the ground that this complex was a central element in the burst of intellectual and imaginative creativity that many Romantic writers themselves recognized, related to the French Revolution, and specified as "the spirit of the age." See, for example, NS, pp. 11–12, 329–56, and 395–96.

*Even Wayne Booth nods. He quotes on p. 156 the statement: "This region . . . is also *dimly remembered* in pagan myths. . . ." This indeed suggests a belief in a "Platonic" participation without historical causation; it is not, however, my assertion, but what I cite Thomas Burnet as having asserted in *The Sacred Theory of the Earth* (NS, p. 100).

Paradise–Fall–Redemption–Paradise Regained into the post-biblical circular pattern of Unity–Multiplicity–Unity Regained is not simply asserted by analogy, but shown to be the product of explicit interpretations of biblical history, by exegetes who had clear access, direct or indirect, to the Neoplatonic circular scheme of emanation and return. And the Romantic adaptation of this pattern of history—from a supernatural to a natural frame of reference as the self-education of the human race, and into the characteristic Romantic design of man's educational journey as a spiral progress from Unity to Disintegration and Alienation to the higher Unity of Reintegration—is shown, in its early instances, to be the product of philosophers and writers of *Universalgeschichte* who, entirely explicitly, set out to translate the truth within the myth-and-picture thinking of the Bible into the higher truth of a purely conceptual formulation. Such a reinterpretation of biblical history, as numerous quotations demonstrate, was the deliberate and specifically formulated enterprise of (among others) Lessing, Herder, Schiller, Schelling, Fichte, Hegel, and surprisingly, even Kant (e.g., *NS*, pp. 67–68, 178–92, 199–225). A similar secularization of the biblical design is unmistakably implied by Wordsworth (in his programmatic statements in the Prospectus and elsewhere) as well as, among other writers, by Hölderlin, Novalis, Blake, Shelley, Keats (who undertook to sketch "a system of Salvation which does not affront our reason and humanity"), and Carlyle (who, in "The Mythus of the Christian Religion," set out to satisfy the great need of the age "to embody the divine Spirit of that Religion in a new Mythus"). (See *NS*, pp. 67–69, and passim for the authors mentioned.)

My basic claim, in other words, is that the secular design of human history, Y, is connected to the earlier religious design, X, by the relationship of continuity-in-change; and my evidence for this claim is not simply to show that X and Y possess similarities-in-difference, but to show that many of the chief authors in the history I narrate have expressly asserted, while others have clearly implied, that they offered Y as an interpretation of X—an interpretation intended to save the essential truth embodied in the mythical vehicle of X, while translating that truth into the higher-order conceptual terms acceptable to their own rational era. Such evidence isn't "causal" in any strictly scientific sense, but it seems to me the strongest possible evidence for the kind of relationship I assert within that distinctive area of investigation we call cultural history. It is furthermore supported by other kinds of evidence, such as the remarkable retention, in many manifestations of the secular design of history, of the central terms and imagery in the biblical design of history—terms such as "fall" and "redemption," and imagery such as "a new heaven and new earth," or the marriage of separated beings that gets used to signalize the achievement of self-integration after self-division. These mixed kinds of evidence are cumulative, and conjoin with other evidence to add probative weight to further assertions about the secular continuity-in-change of concepts that were originally religious—a probative weight that we can't precisely measure, yet rightly intuit to add up to a sound demonstration of the general claim.

A historian can't go on asserting and reasserting these diverse modes of evidence without making his book unreadable, so he does the best he can by citing such proofs only at strategic points in his exposition, in the hope that the reader will note and remember their relevance to everything that precedes and follows; even while, as an experienced historian, he knows full well that such a procedure places on the reader a responsibility for close reading and total recall which he can't realistically expect the reader to fulfill. That's a central problem in all expositions of a complicated history of ideas, imaginative patterns, feelings, and values; it's a problem I confess that I don't know how satisfactorily to resolve.

IV

In the final analysis, of course, the evidence for all of the diverse claims I make comes down to the meaning of the texts to which I refer, and this brings up the subject of the way I use what Booth describes as my "thousands of allusions and quotations" (p. 154). On this as on other matters, in a way that any author learns to expect, the judgments of reviewers are divided. They range the spectrum from the opinion that there is "too great a reliance on summary and paraphrase," to the admission that, to the reviewer's taste, there is "a superfluity of instantiation and quotation," to the sweeping claim that there is little point in leaving authors to be "understood in their own words," because "a quotation proves nothing. It merely exemplifies an interpretation already given or provides the occasion for an interpretation."*

William James remarked that he had "to forge every sentence" of his *Principles of Psychology* "in the teeth of irreducible and stubborn facts." In the history I undertook to relate, the ultimate "facts" that it organizes and explains are what the authors it deals with actually said. It seems an unconvincing tactic simply to *tell* what these authors

*Spencer Hall, *Southern Humanities Review* 8 (Spring 1974): 246; E. D. Hirsch, *The Wordsworth Circle* 3 (1972): 19; Morse Peckham, *Studies in Romanticism* 13 (1974): 364–65.

said (leaving it to each reader's vague memories of relevant texts to check the accuracy and adequacy of what he is told), instead of backing up the telling by *showing* the relevant passages to the reader, so that he can make his own judgment on them. The scope of the subjects I deal with enforced a considerable amount of "summary and paraphrase"; but when I made a large historical generalization, I felt that it called for a good deal of instantiation to back it up; and in these instances, it seemed only fair to let the authors speak for themselves, up to what I judged to be the limits of the publisher's cost accounting and of my readers' patience and ability to keep track of the story I was telling. Incidentally, I also hoped that some readers would share my own pleasure in reading a variety of passages from splendid writers for their inherent interest and cogency, apart from their function as evidence for an historical assertion.

One repeated objection to this procedure is the claim that I violated the formal integrity of individual texts, and especially of poems, by pulling out excerpts for isolated attention and analysis. To this objection my reply is that which Booth has sketched—what I undertook to do necessitated such a procedure, and no one book can try to do everything in general without failing to do anything in particular. Poets, no less than philosophers, have ideas which they write into their poems, and although they use ideas in distinctively poetic ways, and for distinctively poetic ends, these differences are not so absolute but that we may excerpt the ideas they shared with their contemporaries, for consideration in a story whose scope requires the inclusion of poetry and novels, as well as books of philosophy, theology, and "universal history." And after all, as Booth points out, I allow the poets to speak, as poets, in copious quotations.

Even Booth, however, fails to specify one recurrent tactic in *Natural Supernaturalism:* it consists not only of generalizations, explanations, and stories-within-a-story, but includes a number of what we may call "vignettes," in which the history pauses to render an account of a particular text in its subject matter, structure, organizing principle, and formal artistry. I introduced these explications in instances in which the importance and literary value of a document seemed to warrant consideration of its distinctive particularities, as confirming a historical generalization, while serving at the same time as a useful reminder of how diverse may be the particular embodiments of the general feature. Among such vignettes are the treatments of Hegel's *Phenomenology*, Coleridge's *Ancient Mariner* and *France: An Ode*, Shelley's *Prometheus Unbound*, the Induction to Keats's *Fall of Hyperion*, Carlyle's *Sartor Resartus*, Hölderlin's *Hyperion*, Schiller's *Der Spazier-*

gang, and above all, Wordsworth's *Prelude*. My discussions of *The Prelude* add up to a length greater than many published critiques of that poem; and I judge that they constitute a fairly full treatment of *The Prelude* in its poetic integrity. What obscures this fact is that the treatment is not consecutive, but is scattered through various parts of the book. Not only, then, is the temporal order of my history "scrambled," but also a number of the poems it comments on are fragmented; so that it can be charged that the book frequently presents *disjecta membra poetae*. I can only reply that the complexity of the overall story I undertook to tell required a number of sub-stories, and I simply lacked the wit that would enable me to tell these stories without scrambling the temporal order of events and without dissevering for separate consideration various components or aspects of the major documents that these multiple stories were about.

Another and much more crucial indictment brings into question the validity of the entire book, for it asserts that the "facts" on which I rely as evidence are not facts at all, but my unwarranted interpretations of the passages I cite. This indictment is brought by J. Hillis Miller, who (I agree with Booth) wrote an especially thoughtful and interesting review of *Natural Supernaturalism*. Miller asserts that I commonly "illustrate some straightforward point with a quotation which is not 'interpreted,' in the sense of being teased for multiple meanings or implications," nor explicated, "in the sense of unfold, unravel, or unweave." My interpretive fallacy is the standard one, that a text "has a single unequivocal meaning 'corresponding' to the various entities it 'represents.'" But what Nietzsche and his followers, Derrida and the other modern "deconstructionists," have demonstrated, is that there is no single or "objective" interpretation. Miller sums up the basic truths about interpretation in a series of passages that he quotes from Nietzsche: "The same text authorizes innumerable interpretations: there is no 'correct' interpretation." "Ultimately, man finds in things nothing but what he himself has imported into them." "In fact interpretation is itself a means of becoming master of something," by an exertion of one's will to power. As Miller summarizes Nietzsche's views, "reading is never the objective identifying of a sense but the importation of meaning into a text which has no meaning 'in itself.'" He concludes, in considerable understatement, that "from the point of view of such a theory of interpretation all of Abrams' readings can be put in question."*

My view of interpretation is not quite so simple as Miller makes

*J. Hillis Miller, "Tradition and Difference," *Diacritics* 2 (1972): 11–12.

out. I in fact hold that all complex passages are to some degree ambiguous, and that some passages are radically and insolubly ambiguous. Furthermore I have myself, when writing critiques of poems, engaged in the critical game of teasing a passage for multiple meanings and of unravelling its ambiguities and implications. I do, however, approach the passages I quote in *Natural Supernaturalism* with certain interpretive assumptions, which I think I share with all historians who rely on texts for their basic data. These assumptions are: the authors cited wrote, not in order to present a verbal stimulus (in Roland Barthes' term, *un vide*) to the play of the reader's interpretive ingenuity, but in order to be understood. To do so, they had to obey the communal norms of their language so as to turn them to their own innovative uses. The sequences of sentences these authors wrote were designed to have a core of determinate meanings; and though the sentences allow a certain degree of interpretive freedom, and though they evoke vibrations of significance which differ according to the distinctive temperament and experience of each reader, the central core of what they undertook to communicate can usually be understood by a competent reader who knows how to apply the norms of the language and literary form employed by the writer. The reader has various ways to test whether his understanding is an "objective" one; but the chief way is to make his interpretation public, and so permit it to be confirmed or falsified by the interpretations of other competent readers who subscribe to the same assumptions about the possibility of determinable communication.

Booth's reply to Miller's deconstructionist claims about meaning is first, to challenge him to produce a deconstructionist history that will meet "the standards by which [such an account] is to be tested," and second, to assert that every effort at such interpretation "is plainly and simply parasitic on the work of people like Abrams," who put forward the obvious or univocal reading which the "free" interpreter undertakes to deconstruct (pp. 169, 170). I would add to these a more radical reply. If one takes seriously Miller's deconstructionist principles of interpretation, any history which relies on written texts becomes an impossibility. If a production is to be accounted a history, it must be a history of something determinate and determinable; and the elementary assumption that a cultural historian must make is that he is able to understand, in the sense that he is at least able to approximate, the core of meanings that certain writers at certain times expressed in their writings. A narrative about texts by a historian who genuinely proceeds on the belief (in Miller's non-deconstructionist interpretation of Nietzsche) that his procedure need be nothing more than "the importation of meaning into a text which has no meaning 'in itself,'" will turn out to be a history only of what it itself expresses—a history, that is, of the historian's will to power, as manifested through that one of the many possible deconstructionist codes of interpretation that he has elected to press into the service of this will to power.

V

Well, that at least sets one limit to what, according to my pluralist views, I would accept as a sound alternative history to my own: I would not accept a history genuinely written according to radically deconstructionist principles of interpretation. But within that rather broad limit, I am willing to go farther than Wayne Booth supposes. He says, for example, that "we can expect [that Abrams] will *not* go all the way, will not accept any history arguing, say, that Wordsworth was *not* representative and his poems *not* great ..." (p. 164). On the contrary: I can readily imagine a sound and enlightening history of Romantic literature which will deal with many of the same authors I deal with, and even some of the same passages, but will argue precisely these claims about Wordsworth. In fact, knowing the prevailing currents of literary and critical interests, and the kinds of commentary that have already been applied to single Romantic authors, I would be willing to gamble that such a history will soon be written, and even to predict some lines that its arguments will take.

This imaginary history will focus on what several reviewers chided me for omitting, the ironic perspective in general and the theory and practice of "Romantic irony" in particular. It will claim, rightly, that the very concept of Romantic irony was developed by German writers of that era, and also that the theory and practice of the ironic mode is not only a primary Romantic achievement, but the most important and forward-looking one, since it anticipated what is most characteristic in our present temper and established the basic models which are being exploited by the best and most representative writers of our own era. The history will bring to the forefront German writers such as Friedrich Schlegel, whom I hardly mention, as well as others, such as Tieck, Richter, Heine, and Büchner (the author of *Woyzeck*), whom I did not mention at all. In this plot, the hero among the English Romantics will be Byron, a poet I immensely admire but deliberately left out because I did not want to complicate my already complex history with a poet who, as I said, "in his greatest work ... speaks with an ironic counter-voice and deliberately opens a satirical perspective on the vatic stance of his Romantic contemporaries" (*NS*, p. 13).* Keats will rank high; and Blake, Shelley, and even Coleridge, despite their vatic pretensions, will readily be shown to sing an ironic counterpoint to their own visionary claims. But Wordsworth, because he is "the egotistical sublime"—self-absorbed, complacent, and inflexibly solemn and unironic in his pronouncements—will inevitably drop to the bottom of the scale as the weakest and least representative of the prominent poets in this central mode of the Romantic imagination and achievement.

I can imagine such an account of "Romanticism" which would be well enough organized, argued, documented, and written to pass Wayne Booth's tests for a sound history; in fact, I can almost imagine writing such a history myself. I would ungrudgingly accept such a book as a valid alternative history to my own. Does that make me a relativist?

Not, I think, in any dismaying sense of that word, for it does not obviate the claim that both books tell a story which is true. Their judgments about Wordsworth seem "contradictory," but they are not so in the logical sense of that word, which assumes that the clashing assertions meet on the same plane of discourse. The disparate judgments about the representative quality and greatness of Wordsworth's poetry, however, follow from different controlling categories which effect a different selection and ordering of the historical facts and implicate a different set of criteria by which to assess what is representative and great. The insights and assessments of each book, in other words, are relative to the vantage point chosen by its author, and each tries to make us see selected goings-on in the Romantic era in a certain way; but these diverse goings-on are there to be seen in that way. Each, that is, tells only a *part* of the truth, but it is a part of the *truth*.

All sound attempts to add to our humanistic understanding are written from some one of various possible perspectives or points of

---

*Byron unerringly identifies and shows us, from the hindside, not only the prophetic stance of his contemporaries, but also its basis in a secular version of Christianity:

> Sir Walter reign'd before me; Moore and Campbell
> Before and after: but now grown more holy
> The muses upon Sion's hill must ramble
> With poets almost clergymen, or wholly.

It is an index to the discrepancy between our rigid categories for discussing these matters and the lability and resilience of the human sensibility, to note that a historian can delight in Byron's irreverent gibe and still write a long book which treats the butts of Byron's irony with seriousness and respect.

view (the recourse to optical metaphors is almost inevitable in discussing such matters), and the convergence of diverse perspectives is needed to yield what the philosopher, J. R. Bambrough, calls a vision in depth"* in place of the two-dimensional vision that we get from any one vantage point. Only such a vision in depth approximates the full humanistic truth about any matter of our deep concern. That is why, as Wayne Booth puts it, "it is not just that we should tolerate a plurality of histories, we should demand them" (p. 168). But there are an indefinite number of revealing perspectives, and each age will no doubt continue to generate new ones that accord with its interests and intellectual climate. And that is why, as I said in the passage that Booth quotes (p. 143), the search for humanistic truth has no ending.

VI

Booth makes it plain that what he found most novel in *Natural Supernaturalism*—and also most surprising, because it violated his critical presuppositions—is that it functions as what he calls "epideictic history, a history designed to show forth the greatness of the phenomena it explains" (p. 163). What surprised him is that, although an investigation of the sources and influence of Romantic poems can discover only facts which are "extrinsic" to the poems, these discoveries somehow served in the book to "demonstrate" the high literary values in the poems themselves, and especially the high literary values in the poems of Wordsworth.

I must admit that when I decided to use Wordsworth's Prospectus as a recurrent point of departure in my exposition, I had no intention of making Wordsworth the hero of my story, nor of writing a kind of work that would prove "a poem's greatness by discovering what kind of historical account you can give of it—both of what went into it and of what came out" (p. 161). I simply took Wordsworth's greatness as a poet for granted, and chose his Prospectus as a persistent reference mainly because it—together with *The Prelude*, whose subject and role the Prospectus announced in lines 93–99—so strikingly and tersely embodied the Romantic motives and concepts and manner of proceeding that I wanted to deal with. My conspectus of Wordsworth's contemporaries was designed less to prove how "representative" Wordsworth was than to show the many important features which were shared by a great diversity of major Romantic writings. And I

*"Literature and Philosophy," in *Wisdom: Twelve Essays*, ed. J. R. Bambrough (Oxford, 1974).

chose an exegesis that was historical (that is, retrospective and pro-
spective as well as conspective) because I believed that the only way to
understand the particulars of my humanistic investigation—the only
way fully to realize what they are—involves knowing where they
came from, what changes were made in them, and what those
changes portended for what they were to become. I suppose that
what Booth has in mind when he says of the resulting book that it "in
a sense provides a conspectus on the whole of Western civilization"
(p. 145) is not only that it ranges in time from the Bible to Allen
Ginsberg, but also that the Romantic motives it elucidates turn out to
be altered versions of the persistent forms of imagination by which
our great religious visionaries and philosophers had tried to make
sense of themselves, their past and anticipated future, and their place
in the world, and in which they had found a sanction for their values
and moral norms. As the most clear-sighted of the Romantic writers
saw, these forms of imagination, or "myths," constitute the fabric of
Western civilization, and they believed that, despite their own drastically altered circumstances, these myths must not be rejected, but
reconstructed on new conceptual foundations, if that cultural fabric
was to endure.

Even though I set out to deepen understanding rather than to
demonstrate literary values, I nonetheless found as I went along, just
as Booth did, that the values of certain Romantic poems were enhanced as my awareness of the complex tradition that they embodied
continued to grow. That an increase in knowledge alters our experience of poetic values is a matter of common experience; it seems
mysterious to us only because we are taken in by our own critical
metaphors. It is useful, for some analytic purposes, to distinguish extrinsic from intrinsic, external from internal criticism, and to regard
historical knowledge as something external to a poem. But the inside
of a poem is not like the inside of a house where, except for a zone of
dubiety at the threshold, the boundary between what is inside and
what is outside is sharp and stable. The full significance of a poem
depends on what we bring to our interpretation of its determinable
meanings, and as our knowledge of the importance of a tradition
enlarges, so does the significance of a poem which represents that
tradition. We don't think first of the poem and then of the tradition
outside the poem. Instead, we experience its traditionality as a dimension of the poem's meaning, as a resonance within the poem
itself. And when we recognize in a poem a powerful but altered
restatement of a great theme in our Western culture, uttered with an
art and in a voice that endures comparison with the greatest art and

voices of its ancestral past, that attribute becomes a measure of the poem's greatness. If our aesthetic theory disqualifies such a measure as extrinsic, hence irrelevant to poetic value, our experience in reading the poem discredits the theory and not the value. This is apparently what T. S. Eliot had in mind when he said that whether something is literature or not can be determined only by literary standards, but its greatness as literature cannot be determined solely by literary standards.

VII

We come finally to my discussion of "the Romantic ethos" and of "the Romantic positives." A book of humanistic inquiry is written not only from a particular conceptual perspective, but also from within the temporal perspective, the climate of values and opinions, of the age in which it is composed. Rather than to try ineffectually to extricate myself from this perspective in order to achieve a viewpoint *sub specie aeternitatis*, I decided to end *Natural Supernaturalism* by identifying, in my chosen authors, those Romantic positives which deliberately reaffirmed the elementary values of the Western past, and to present these values in a way directly addressed to our own age of anxiety and of incipient despair of our inherited civilization. I was well aware that this section set itself against the prevailing way of reading the Romantics, and—moved perhaps by a touch of perversity—opened it by listing their chief positives as baldly and challengingly as possible: "life, love, liberty, hope, and joy" (*NS*, p. 431). After this provocative beginning, however, I tried to show, by extensive analysis and quotation, that these traditional positives were radically reinterpreted, interrelated, and managed with great subtlety of discrimination; and that in their literary contexts, they are powerfully and convincingly stated. I tried also to show that the right to make these affirmations was fairly earned, by authors profoundly aware of the negative conclusions that seemed pressed upon them by human history and their own experience; and that the reason for their insistence is that they saw their era as we see our own—as a crisis of civilization and consciousness. In Wordsworth's description (the passage has many analogues in his contemporaries) his poetry is specifically addressed to counter

> these times of fear,
> This melancholy waste of hopes o'erthrown,
> ...mid indifference and apathy

> And wicked exultation...
>
>   this time
> Of dereliction and dismay.
>
>   [*The Prelude*, 1805, 2:448–57]

My claim was that, in the face of life's clamorous counter-evidence, the Romantic writers, in those works in which they assumed the traditional persona of the poet-prophet—to put it in another way, in which they undertook to speak with an authoritative public voice—deliberately adopted their affirmative stance. As Coleridge and others said, a man has to choose between despair and hope, and the choice is a moral choice, because despair is self-confirming but hope releases the human powers in which lie the only possibility of remedy. If this is optimism, it is so only in the radically qualified sense that Shelley gave the word, in a passage I quoted in which he expresses his secular version of the traditional theodicy:

> Let us believe in a kind of optimism in which we are our own gods. . . . It is best that we should think all this for the best even though it be not, because Hope, as Coleridge says is a solemn duty which we owe alike to ourselves & to the world—a worship to the spirit of good within, which requires before it sends that inspiration forth, which impresses its likeness upon all that it creates, devoted & disinterested homage. [*NS*, p. 447]

I was not greatly surprised, though a bit chagrined nonetheless, to find that, despite all the skill I could muster to communicate the nuance and shadow in the great passages of Romantic affirmation, this section of *Natural Supernaturalism* was described by some critics as a product of the author's own optimism, which found a matching optimism in the Romantic poets only by selecting the evidence and ignoring the dark undertones in the passages selected.

The failure to achieve a general meeting of minds on this issue leads me to a final observation on method: a cultural history requires from the historian something no less important than a sound method of demonstration, and that is, an effort of the sympathetic imagination. In a famous statement Mill said that Bentham looked at ancient or received opinions from the viewpoint of his own convictions and asked "Is it true?" Coleridge on the other hand asked "What is the meaning of it?" and to answer this question, he "looked at it from within, and endeavoured to see it with the eyes of a believer in it; to discover by what apparent facts it was at first suggested, and by what appearances it has ever since been rendered continually credible."*

***Mill on Bentham and Coleridge*, ed. F. R. Leavis (London, 1950), pp. 99–100.

This way of looking at the past is a Romantic discovery, and it seems to me to be a necessary condition for any full understanding of the past. In *Natural Supernaturalism* I tried, by an effort of imagination, to understand a great Romantic enterprise by looking at it from within. In the process of coming to understand this segment of our past I also discovered, and tried at the end to communicate the discovery, that to know who and what and where we were then helps us to understand who and what and where we are now. I tried in addition to communicate my sense that this Romantic past is a usable past, in that it presents a stance toward ourselves and the world which affirms human dignity and the grounds for a qualified hope, and thus shows us what was possible for men who were no less sagacious and unillusioned than we are now.

Wayne Booth says that he was convinced and moved by what I found moving and convincing in the history I tried to tell. But Booth also says, and I entirely agree, that his response of being persuaded "is an experience that many sincere and competent readers will for various reasons not discover" (p. 150). A humanistic demonstration, unlike a scientific demonstration, is rarely such as to enforce the consent of all qualified observers. For it to carry the reader through its exposition to its conclusions requires some grounds for imaginative consent, some comparative ordering of values, some readiness of emotional response to the matters shown forth, which the reader must share with the author even before he begins to read; and these common grounds are no doubt in part temperamental, hence variable from reader to reader.* If this assertion constitutes relativism, then we simply have to live with the relativism it asserts, for it is an aspect of the human predicament which the languages and complex strategies of proof in humanistic inquiries are designed to cope with, but can never entirely overcome.

*This partial circularity of humanistic demonstration (presuming between author and reader common grounds of consent in order to achieve consent) obtains also for the attempt by the poet to effect in his reader an understanding which involves imaginative consent to what his poem expresses. So Wordsworth suggests, in a passage which also bears on the question of his "optimism": "I am myself one of the happiest of men; and no man who does not partake of that happiness . . . can possibly comprehend the best of my poems" (cited from Henry Crabb Robinson's *On Books and their Writers*, ed. Edith J. Morley, 3 vols. [London: J. M. Dent & Sons, 1938], 1:73 [8 May 1812]).

5

They are ill discoverers that think there is no land when they can
see nothing but sea.—Sir Francis Bacon

What was biting me was the fact that *these minds never met at all.*
—Owen Barfield

Against Mediators.—Those who wish to be mediators between two
resolute thinkers are marked as mediocre: they lack eyes to see
the unparalleled; seeing things as similar and making them the same
is the mark of weak eyes.—Nietzsche

The Pursuit of Understanding as a Limit of Pluralism

I began, many pages (and some years) ago, with a practical problem: How can we reduce meaningless critical conflict? To put the problem in that way is obviously to assume that there is such a thing as *meaningful* critical conflict; and to assume that conflict can have meaning implies that criticism needs, or at least can tolerate, at least two voices. Presumably all criticism, in print or simply spoken, presupposes that some sort of communication among critics is both possible and valuable.

In the formulation that Abrams borrows from F. R. Leavis (p. 143, above), the most we can hope for, when we make our statements, is not a simple "yes" in reply. Rather, we should expect—and if we are really inquiring should in fact desire—the reply: "Yes, *but . . . .*" Yet no second speaker can sincerely say "*Yes*, but . . ." without acknowledging the validity of the first voice. My *yes* (unless it is simply a polite lie) grants you your right to critical life; the *but* requests a similar grant in return.

Pluralism in this limited sense is thus a precondition of all critical exchange; it differs mainly in emphasis from the cheerful eclecticism that in chapter 1 I attributed to David Daiches, when he used the same formula. Common-sense untheoretical pluralism works, regardless of our theories, just because many critics really do mean yes when they say yes, not just "Here is something I can digest easily because it is already my kind of pablum." I could not publish (or speak aloud) even the simplest statement about a poem without rejecting *utter* skepticism and, along with it, the kind of dogmatic monism that sees a simple single statement as self-evident and self-sufficient. To write—or at least to publish—is to grant the necessity of exchange, and to begin an exchange is to acknowledge (though most authors may balance this acknowledgment against the faint hope that the whole world will shout a simple "yes") the insufficiency and impermanence of any one view.

There is thus built into our enterprise an inescapable bias toward

197

plurality. But that bias does not lead to a simple choice among the six attitudes toward conflict that I described in chapter 1. You and I are necessarily pluralists in our first steps—it takes two to do this tango. But to say as much can at best rule out only the most simple-minded of dogmatists about how the next steps should go.

My decision to discuss three pluralists was thus neither innocent nor fully earned by argument in chapter 1. My main support for pluralism there was that it provides the least temptation to indulge in careless or malicious reduction of opponents to straw men. It is by no means easy to summarize the additional evidence that the next three chapters have presented for either the desirability or possibility of pluralism. In one sense the chapters taken together simply argue by pointing: "Here are, after all, three actual practitioners. Pluralism in some sense is obviously possible, if we have found three intelligent and aggressive inquirers who have claimed to be pluralists." Presumably their advocacy lends *some* weight as well to the notion that we should all be pluralists. But it is not clear how much; and since they all look quite different at the end, it is not clear what kind of pluralist we should decide to be.

All three practice semantic clarification, but none of them expects that it will reduce conflict to simple and clear oppositions and thus permit a choice of the one true view (monism); or that a rigorous critique will reveal all conflict about critical values to be nonsense (skepticism); or that the best criticism will emerge from a scissors-and-paste job on rival critics (eclecticism). They all claim not simply to tolerate rival voices but to require them; all three hold that critical truth can never be exhausted in any one mode. Yet it is not easy to decide whether they can be accommodated in a single view labeled "pluralism."

Anyone attempting such an accommodation these days is likely to hear a fashionable chorus intoning a message something like this:

> Your trouble is that you are not pluralistic enough. Why do you refuse to recognize that all texts are capable of producing an infinity of legitimate readings? That indeed every reading is inevitably a misreading? That each of your three pluralists may be read not only in your way but in an unlimited number of other ways (which is to say that they are *essentially* unreadable, *illisible:* they cannot be reduced even to *three* coherent readings, let alone harmonized into *one*)? In fact, your own readings are essentially incoherent, since they are open invitations to an infinity of readings. Though critical discussion is not pointless—indeed, it is our main task to revitalize it—it is best kept alive by recognizing that it is finally validated

only in the individual who deconstructs what he reads and then offers his own creation, an inevitable misreading.

Besides [and here the voice grows more insinuating], nobody, nobody these days who is anybody, tries to solve by the end of a book the problems raised at the beginning. Your very effort to achieve a systematic organization is misguided. Just call the final chapter what you can call the book when it is published, something like "Notes toward a Definition of the Pluralist Paradox," "Beyond Pluralism," or even "Deontologizing Pluralism." Or, better yet, move into metaphor—"The Many Heads of Hydra," or "Other Voices, Other Rooms." Then throw three more *soi-disant* pluralists into your hopper—Roland Barthes, Roman Ingarden, A. Diemer[1]—and finally recast the whole thing according to alphabetized topics.

Problems for the Pluralist of Pluralisms

It will take the remainder of this book to explain why such a rejection of limits is finally misleading. But first I must show the full strength of its appeal by underlining the evidence for it which my encounters so far may seem to have presented. To put it bluntly, I have not passed to my own satisfaction the tests of correspondence, coherence, and adequacy.

The Failure to Understand (Correspondence)

My quest presupposes that critics can understand each other. The very notion of reducing meaningless conflict depends on a belief that some interpretations are better than others, that some critics understand and others misunderstand, that a given critic can, by taking thought and effort, improve his understanding of another's views or, indeed, of his own.

Yet this book provides ample evidence, if more were needed, that even those critics who work hardest at the task do not fully succeed. I have myself claimed that Crane did not quite understand Burke—a claim that presupposes my own superior understanding. Burke claims that in crucial respects I misunderstood him. I am certain that Burke has partially misunderstood me, and I am almost as sure that he partially misunderstood Crane. I would even want to claim that Abrams has never fully understood Crane or Burke.

Though I have claimed that Abrams on the whole understood his historical sources very well indeed, I find many exceptions—but on what authority? Almost all reviewers quarrel with some of his interpretations, and one highly intelligent critic, J. Hillis Miller, thinks that *all* of his readings are questionable, on principle. Abrams, in turn, has said that Miller radically misunderstands *him*. Finally, even my clearest instance of success, the exchange with Abrams, is by no means complete, for I could not resist dehistoricizing Abrams in the matter of permanent forms, and he politely but firmly reminds me that his history is "strictly culture-bound" (p. 182).

But what else should one expect? The history of thought provides thousands of echoes of Hegel's perhaps mythical deathbed lament: "There never was but one man who understood me—and even he did not understand me." Yet, if we cannot prove that even one critic has fully understood *one* other, what are we to make of the pluralist's claim that he has understood and embraced *more* than one? All my comparisons depend on my claims to understand, yet it is obvious that I cannot prove complete understanding of anyone. If I am sure of anything, it is that, unless I engage in mere mimicry, no critic I discuss at length will agree entirely with my commentary.

The Failure to Be Pluralistic (Adequacy)

Though my pluralists all join in rejecting skepticism, each of them seems to reveal himself as a monist when followed upward to his first principles or downward to his detailed practice—a monist precisely in the sense of making choices that rule out other, equally plausible, choices. The disguised monism of professed pluralists is usually, in fact, all too easily discovered. My three pluralists, on the other hand, maintain their pluralist disguises, if they are that, with much more aplomb. Still, it is finally inescapable that Crane's search for discriminated problems and unequivocal definitions operates fully as much in his way of arguing for pluralism as it does in his "neo-Aristotelian" criticism; and though Burke and Abrams both work hard to leave a place in their worlds for many valid types of critical and historical discourse, the kind of world that each constructs is entirely different from Crane's, from each other's, from whatever pluralistic world I am constructing here, and from any world that *you* might construct. Thus even pluralists seem to become monists "at the top." In short, does it not seem that there are no actual pluralists but only skeptics, monists, and an assortment of pluralists and eclectics who are in fact only disguised monists?

When we claim to embrace a plurality of valid contending modes, we must mean either (1) that the modes are genuinely plural but that we possess some sort of umbrella that can both accommodate their plurality and yield standards of validity or (2) that because we can embrace them in a unifying view they are not genuinely plural at all. Here we have two new contending positions, which we can in turn view in either of the two following ways (but surely not both at once without paradox): if they are genuinely different, we have chosen two umbrellas, not one; if they are finally reconcilable, we have chosen one umbrella, not two. The alternatives seem strictly incompatible. But are they?

If we expect to find yet another intellectual umbrella to resolve or account for the paradox, we are monists after all; critical truth is ultimately one, and we finally reject the fundamental principles of full pluralism. If we insist, on the other hand, that both alternatives survive, in the name of pluralism, we are at the same time violating the beliefs of those who say that truth is one, and so we have taken a monistic position on this ultimate question. Paradox again!

Descending from the Great Inane, we can illustrate the difficulties one last time by my own choice of three pluralists. I dare say that some readers have already asked, as any trained analyst must, "What scheme of classification organizes the presentation of Crane, Burke, and Abrams?" As you ask the question, and as I answer it, we might seem to exemplify the umbrella paradox neatly.

Obviously I do have a little scheme working here, a poor one but my own. It is true that my selection was in part dependent on historical accident: my life encountered these lives at such and such moments, and the personal force of the men strengthened the impact of their pluralisms. But my choice of the *kinds* of pluralism to be illustrated was deliberate.

Once we have chosen to believe that at least two pluralisms might each be an irrefutable way of dealing with plurality, we have in fact no great range of possibilities for accommodating the plurality. By rejecting skeptics, monists, and eclectics, we have already limited ourselves to people who have repudiated subtraction or cancellation of modes in favor of some kind of *addition*. The possibilities remaining to us are therefore few: (1) we can add modes as *essentially discrete units*, either (*a*) like Crane, unsystematically, in the sense that no overarching schema is attempted, or (*b*) we can add them according to some system of classification, as Richard McKeon, Elder Olson, and Walter Davis each does in quite different ways (in works that I cannot here do justice to);[2] (2) we can add—or better, fuse—them as *essentially intermingling, flowing parts* of some transcendent structure (finally unformulatable), subsuming their dialectical interplay under some term like Reason, History, Symbolic Action, language, *écriture*. Or, in place of these two synchronic attempts, we can turn diachronic and seek either (3) a history of discrete modes in which each different mode is most appropriate to works written in its time (as urged by Robert Marsh)[3] or (4) a kind of "flowing" subsumption like Abrams'—a way of seeing clearly all modes as they are mingled in the historical stream, thus making them available in any time but in fact traceably dominant at particular times. In practice the four possibilities will reduce to the three I have illustrated, since the diachronic-discrete pluralist—the historian of modes whose essence is found in their integrity rather than their affiliations—will be simply the synchronic-discrete pluralist turned historian, as Ronald Crane became a historian in "Shifting Definitions and Evaluations of the Humanities from the Renaissance to the Present" and a theorist of history in *Critical and Historical Principles of Literary History*.[4]

With such neat and perhaps tedious clarities laid out, we are in fine shape—until we remember that no other pluralist has classified pluralisms in quite that way and that assimilationists would repudiate the very notion of such analytical discrimination of irreducible differences. Shall we attempt, then, wearily, one more time, to choose among these pluralists, or to classify them, or to fuse them, or to do a history of them? If we follow any of these routes, will we reject other routes? Or accommodate them, or classify them, or fuse them, or tell a story about them?

Finally, I should add that the umbrella paradox, which I have treated as if it were simply a problem of choice of languages, is easily translated into several metaphysical paradoxes. If I say that as a pluralist I will embrace both the languages that consider plurality irreducible and the languages that offer a unified view, am I not forced to the even more visibly absurd paradox that not just our languages but the world itself is both plural and single? Can basic distinctions—the one, say, between theory and practice or the one between fact and value—be both ultimate and not ultimate? When Crane insists on logical coherence and Roland Barthes (somewhat like Burke before him) chooses to play with logical contradictions,[5] they are either harmonizable or not. If I claim that they are, I must have some basis for the claim that will either violate or transcend Crane's logic. If I claim that they are not, I shall either impose a logic that will destroy Barthes's textual bliss or embrace a freedom from logic that will destroy Crane. Such talk must surely lead us to further paradoxes: those who say that the world is ultimately paradoxical and those who see it as ultimately harmonious are both right—a paradox that must offend the second group; those who see *that* statement as a nonsensical paradox and those who see it as uttering a final truth-that-is-*not*-final are both right. And if that does not land us once again in the bogs of infinite regress, it is hard to think what would.

No Escape into a Demonstrable Harmony (Coherence)

If, as it seems, all distinctions among modes will depend on a classification that will lead to the umbrella paradox, it also seems that pluralism depends on assumptions of intercommunication among modes that in practice cannot be verified. If I say that there are two or more valid modes, I must depend on some kind of meaning, common to the two, of the word "valid." But I have by no means found a way to state any such meaning.

Note that this is a much stronger version of the problem of misunderstanding than the simple, ubiquitous lament, "He hasn't understood me." I am facing here the stronger case against myself: I cannot, try as I will, fully harmonize Crane, Burke, and Abrams into a single intellectual world. If I *could*, I should then face the paradox of the previous section. Yet if I *cannot*, then it would seem absurd to claim the right to pronounce on their validity.

We can illustrate the impossibility of translating from pluralism to pluralism in any number of ways. Perhaps the best is to find instances of serious efforts to work in two modes. Here I find most illuminating Burke's decades of effort to do a "poetic" analysis first (what he sometimes playfully calls "the Chicago job"), before turning to what he considers the more important task of showing what dramatism can do.

Burke says again and again that there is no inherent conflict between what the Chicago school does—a strictly poetic, or intrinsic, or formal analysis—and his own larger interests. Indeed, he is convinced that one must first do such an analysis if the broader inquiry is to work well:

> ... I'd simply ask that the original poem be treated as the authoritative intuition which the critic then translates into terms of its nature as a *kind* of poetry, with its corresponding kind of *principles* and *proprieties* .... Then reversing the process, and prophesying after the event, he will test his formulations by "deducing" or "deriving" the poem from the principles. Insofar as feasible, the critic's formulations will be in terms of Poetics. That is, ideally, the entire work should be explainable in such terms unless, for some reason or other, the critic is unequal to the task.

> But ... the very thoroughness of the critic's attempt to discuss
> the poem exclusively in terms of Poetics should help us realize the
> points at which the poem requires analysis not just in terms of
> Poetics, but also as an example of language in general, a piece of
> "symbolicity" in the large ... analyzed rather as the product of a
> citizen and taxpayer, subject to various social embarrassments,
> physical ills, and mental aberrations.
> The scheme thus leaves room for everybody. Yet methodically
> so.[6]

In the service of this belief in poetic analysis, Burke has done some
extraordinarily illuminating close reading (see, for example, his "An-
tony in Behalf of the Play").[7] Yet I am always astonished when I read
his claims that he is attempting to do what Ronald Crane would do.[8]
Their "poetic" analyses simply do not jibe. To make this clear, we can
compare what Crane has said of *Macbeth* and then construct what
Burke might say of it, using hints scattered through his works.

As we would expect, Crane makes a detailed effort to discover the
form of the plot and to account for the precise quality of the parts as
they function in the unique whole; he follows the program that I
illustrated with "Surgical Ward." For him, once he has chosen his
mode of practical criticism, *Macbeth* is quite literally one thing, a play
made by Shakespeare; and that play is not a "verbal communication
of meanings" or any of the other interesting things suggested by
critical theories but a representation (an "imitation," or creation) of
human characters in action. To talk about the structure of such an
object, we must look very closely at the story of Macbeth, attempting
to recover the creative intention that led Shakespeare, as maker, to
order the parts as he did.[9]

So for Crane, if we ask questions about any element in *Macbeth*, the
first—and usually the final—reference will be to some notion of the
"essential story" or "plot-form," stated hypothetically: If the plot-
form is such-and-such, then this element can be seen as contributing
—or not contributing—such-and-such, and we can thus hope to come
to some defensible decision about why Shakespeare worked in this
way and whether he did his job well or poorly. If the

> essential story of *Macbeth* is that of a man, not naturally depraved,
> who has fallen under the compulsive power of an imagined better
> state for himself which he can attain only by acting contrary to his
> normal habits and feelings; who attains this state and then finds
> that he must continue to act thus, and even worse, in order to hold
> on to what he has got; who persists and becomes progressively
> hardened morally in the process; and who then, ultimately, when

the once alluring good is about to be taken away from him, faces the loss in terms of what is left of his original character [p. 172]

—*if* this or "something like this" is what "gives emotional form to the main action of *Macbeth*," *then* any given part can be adequately appreciated and finally judged only in the light of its contribution to this essential story.

A fully poetic analysis of the *making* of any one part—say, the Porter scene—will thus refer back to what Shakespeare as artist needed to accomplish at that precise spot in the play—back, that is, to what the play requires. Judgments about the placement of the scene, its length, and even the precise substance of the Porter's drunken talk will depend on the hypothesis that Shakespeare was attempting to make the best possible play of this precise kind. Why does the complex plot of a sympathetic man performing terrible deeds profit from a long "interruption" at precisely the moment when we both fear and hope for the arrival of those forces that will discover what Macbeth has done? Why is the deed of murder left to our imaginations, undramatized, while the Porter's seeming digression is dramatized at great length? Only fairly late in Crane's inquiry will he get around to talking about thematic connections between the Porter's references to hell and other hellish elements in the play, or about his equivocations and his talk of equivocation, or about the precise metaphors and other stylistic features of his speech.

Turning to Burke, we are not surprised to find that *Macbeth* appears in many different guises or that Burke nowhere faces Crane's problem of how, in precise detail, the whole play works. We open *The Rhetoric of Religion* and find *Macbeth* providing a useful illustration of the "kind of decision . . . [or] development that usually takes place in the third act of a five-act drama . . . . The moment we are concerned with corresponds . . . to the place in *Macbeth* where Banquo's ghost appears, and sits in Macbeth's place at the table" (pp. 102–3). Or we open *Language as Symbolic Action* to the essay "Somnia ad Urinandum" and find Burke using the Porter scene as illustrative of entirely different matters:

Here, first of all, we find objectified the "knock of conscience." And properly so, since we are on the subject of guilt (here "rationalized" in terms of murder). On one point, as regards our thesis, there is no doubt: The subject of "urine" is *specifically* introduced by name. Beginning with a first rough approximate, the reference to "turning the key" (surely a preparation for a release of some sort) will lead, step by step, to the Porter's opening the gate.

Looked at in the light of the analogies with which we are here concerned, the progressive unfoldings are quite remarkable. Talk of a farmer that "hanged himself on the expectation of plenty" would obviously be a way of including the notion that a "harvest" (a *yield* of some sort) is in the realm of the problematical; for otherwise, why should connotations of self-punishment turn up precisely in connection with an "expectation of plenty"? However, at this stage, there seems no indication that the "plenty" might be of the "liquifying sort." [Pp. 354–55]

Lest we think that this urinary pursuit, carried on in one kind of nonpoetic mode, fixes Burke's views of *Macbeth* for us, we find him, further on in the same book, making a "purely formal" claim:

"Progressive" form is ideally the kind of inevitable development from complications to denouement which Aristotle discusses at length in his *Poetics*. There is also a less "syllogistic," purely "qualitative" kind of progressive form (as with the profoundly effective yet not specifically foreshadowed turn from the murder scene to the Porter scene in *Macbeth*). [P. 486]

And, after this implicit claim that he could do the "poetic" job on *Macbeth* if he wanted to, we are not surprised, when we turn to other passages, to find a variety of stuff that for Crane would be decidedly "extrinsic." We find, for example, Macbeth mentioned as an example of ritual sacrifice, a scapegoat exemplifying one of two main strands in the play as "suppurating" device that brings the evil "to a head"; he illustrates the "kill" motif as distinct from the "sacrifice" motif (Hamlet and Christ); and elsewhere we find Burke speculating: "[Were] rhetorical motives behind the fact that Macbeth's private ambitions were figured in terms of witches?" (*A Rhetoric of Motives*, p. 40).

The point about such differences might be even more forceful if Crane had written an analysis of *Coriolanus* to be compared with Burke's brilliant chapter in *Language as Symbolic Action*. Even when Burke is attempting to do "poetics," even when he is quite consciously working on Shakespeare's task as a maker of plays, his account is largely of the atemporal interrelations among motives, not of the unfolding of dramatic problems in time. With few exceptions, and those mainly in his early criticism, Burke simply does not care very much about the constructional problems that would have interested Crane: *Given* the task of writing a moving tragedy about a character with Coriolanus's virtues and vices, how can a playwright play up *this* detail and play down *that*; simply and quickly narrate *this* event and dramatize *that* one at length; invent or suppress and reorder steps in the story; withhold eloquence *here* and expand it *there*—all in the service of dramatic realization? His accounts are, it is true, seldom as remote from performance or reading experience as the ones most structuralists are giving us, but Crane rightly claimed that most of what Burke had to say about a play would work just as well if the play were performed backward. A simple test of the difference between their notions of poetics is thus provided by two questions: (1) From what Burke says about *Coriolanus*, even when he is claiming to do the "poetic" job, could you infer a judgment about whether Volumnia's long plea to her son to save Rome is too long, too short, or just right? (2) From what Crane says about *Macbeth*, are we led to any special insights about how the motives of the characters, and of Shakespeare, and of the audience compare or contrast with the appeals of other tragedies? The answer to both questions must be something like, "Relatively speaking, no. Though the two critics may touch at the extreme limits of their accounts, the centers are far apart."

Even more striking than these differences is my inability to reconcile Burke's tests for good criticism with Crane's. It is not clear how the list of Burke's criteria (beginning on p. 121, above; see also Burke's reply, p. 133) can be accommodated to my version of Crane's three criteria in chapter 2. It is true that Crane and Burke both have standards of correspondence, coherence, and comprehensiveness, but the terms mean quite different things for each of them and are given different relative weight. It is equally clear that Crane's and Burke's notions of adequacy or comprehensiveness are quite different from Abrams' drive for a criticism adequate to the full historical setting of a poem.

My three pluralists, then, are not just temperamentally different, nor have they just "happened," as Crane would put it, to find themselves interested in different questions. Their ordering of criteria, and to some degree the criteria themselves, cannot be made to match— not, at least, in the form of compatible propositions. How, for example, can one hope to reconcile Burke's dictum that one should not paint oneself into a corner with Crane's persistent effort to discriminate "corners" in order to find one that would mark out precise boundaries? How can one reconcile a criticism that seeks knowledge (which, on well-defined questions, can be settled once and for all) with a criticism that fears above all else the freezing of knowledge into a single form? And how can one accommodate either of these to a criticism that will subordinate everything to the desire for a plausible history?

We should be quite clear about the seriousness of the challenge all this presents, not simply to my own quest but to every pluralism that would claim to base itself on more than a blind faith. A brief look at how multiple languages appear in other "sciences" may help to show why our problem seems especially threatening.

On a first consideration, my inability to effect a full translation among my pluralists may seem little different from the inability of the various natural sciences to effect a full reduction to one unified language. Despite the optimistic efforts of some philosophers of science to interrelate the various independent sciences, everyone would agree that at present the goal is remote indeed; much of what we know about biology, for example, cannot be expressed in chemical language, and much of our knowledge of chemistry cannot be reduced to the laws of physics. One still encounters many statements that "in principle" all science will ultimately be translatable into physical laws, but no one claims that we are near that goal. Indeed, more and more theorists have recently claimed that our present inability to express concepts like cell, organ, species, predator, or homeostasis in the language of chemistry (let alone physics) reflects a permanent irreducibility among the sciences; it may well be that we shall always need a distinct language for each distinct level of organization found in the world.

It might be comforting to welcome these anti-reductionists as friends of pluralism; the languages of scientific knowledge, they tell us, must always be many, and we must never expect to reduce them to one. But even if these friends prove to be right, the parallel between their plurality and ours is at best very loose; the rival languages of science are seen by all disputants as arranged in a hierarchy, whether that hierarchy will finally prove to be reducible to one language or not. As Peter Medawar says, if we construct a list like this:

1. Physics
2. Chemistry
3. Ecology/sociology
4. Organismic biology

then "every scientist who looks at this list (unless he is being deliberately obtuse) will see that there is something wrong with it, namely that items 3 and 4 should be interchanged, whereupon the list makes sense."[10] The issues debated by reductionists and anti-reductionists thus presuppose a hierarchy of a kind that could never be agreed on by literary critics. If I construct a list of literary studies, nobody will expect that all responsible critics will recognize it as rightly or wrongly ordered:

1. Bibliography
2. Editing of texts
3. Interpretation of individual works with formal analysis
4. History of forms
5. Sociology of forms
6. Stylistics
7. Rhetoric
Etc.

Or, to make the analogy superficially more convincing:

1. Phonetics
2. Lexicography
3. Syntagmatics
4. Tagmemics (at level of paragraph or section or chapter)
5. Criticism of whole works
6. Criticism of an author's corpus
7. Criticism relating number 5 to the immediate milieu
8. Criticism relating the milieu to earlier and later periods

Will the time ever come when all critics who are not deliberately obtuse will recognize whether my effort at order is faulty or correct? If you believe that it will not, you are not simply an antireductionist comparable to the biologist who thinks that physical formulae will never fully account for the human mind. You begin to sound skeptical of systematic interrelations of any kind: not only are the "sciences" of criticism not reducible to one supreme science, but their ordering cannot be reduced to one correct ordering.

In any case, it is abundantly clear that in the present state of *my* knowledge, I cannot reduce Crane to Burke or Burke to Abrams (and so on), since I cannot pass either of two prime tests for such a reduction of one language to another: I flunk the first test, *derivability*, because I cannot derive the principles, methods, definitions of subject, and conclusions of any of the three from either of the other two. Starting where one of them starts, I could never arrive at the primary interests or achievements of the others as consequences of my chosen beginning. On the second test, *connectability*, I can, it is true, do a bit better; for if I work hard at it, I can "reduce" many of the seeming conflicts among my three, either by translating conclusions from one vocabulary to another (thus removing the conflict) or by showing that what look like conflicting views on the same track are really two compatible views derived from traveling quite different tracks.

But a more rigorous statement of the criterion of connectability shows that my claim can handle, at best, only some of the obvious conflicts, not all: "To accomplish this deduction [the derivation of one system from another] the laws of logic require that all technical terms used in the science to be reduced be redefined using terms of the science to which it is to be reduced."[11] I would have to add: "be redefined without loss of any essential content." It is quite clear that I cannot, in terms derived from the other two, restate without *essential* loss what each of my three protagonists teaches me.

I have no trouble, of course, in finding particular points of agreement among all three, and I suspect that these are far more numerous than the differences. What is troublesome, however, is that when I move to basic criteria for evaluation of poems and for validation of modes, I find myself unable to make ultimate translations. I cannot claim either that they are all saying the same thing but in different languages or that the different things they do say are all ultimately reconcilable.

Surely, then, my quest for a pluralism has failed. And since few are likely to work harder at it than I have, it seems probable that there really can be no such creature as a true pluralist in my sense. Surely each of us, when he grows excited with wine, looks death in the face, or clambers to the heights of metaphysics, plumps either for one of the great monisms that claims to eliminate ultimate absurdity or— what in 1979 is more plausible—for the skepticism implicit in facing honestly the absurd contradictions "at the top" and the essential incoherence or "unreadability" that every text will reveal (so we are told) when probed to the depths.

The Pluralist as Pragmatist

Literary criticism is obviously not the only field of study that multiplies perspectives. Parallel problems can be discovered in every discipline in which observers observe observers observing observers—in short, in most of the humanities and social sciences. Those who toil in the various branches of philosophy, history, sociology, and anthropology have necessarily encountered problems like ours, and it is not surprising that versions of monism (e.g., Marxism), skepticism (e.g., cultural relativism), and eclecticism (e.g., "democratic pluralism") have multiplied. Attempts at pluralism in our sense have been rare, however; and even those, like Stephen C. Pepper's *World*

Hypotheses, that have found some initial response have not—for reasons that I suppose are obvious—been widely influential; for the natural drive of most scholars seems to be either toward the triumph of a monism or the relaxation (or confession of defeat) implicit in eclecticism or skepticism.

It would be foolish to attempt to show that what comes naturally to so many is flatly wrong, especially when the alternative raises so many problems. But I am finally forced to maintain that alternative because I recognize, first, that the very problems I have encountered are inescapable consequences of my effort to do criticism in the first place and, second, that when the problems I have encountered are viewed properly, they become evidence for pluralism, not against it. They also guide us toward the criteria we need if we are to prevent pluralism from exploding into one or another of the skepticisms now traveling under its name.

"Criticism" and "Poetry" as Essentially Contested Concepts

What would we be forced to conclude if I had *not* encountered these problems? Supposing I had found that Crane, Burke, and Abrams were all reconcilable in a single statable harmony: my own. Obviously, I would have rejected pluralism for my own grand monism. Thus the rich and frustrating complexities of my quest have again and again dramatized the *essential* and *irreducible* variety of critical languages.

In explaining his own commitment to such variety, M. H. Abrams has already made use of W. B. Gallie's notion of "essentially contested concepts" (see chap. 4, above, pp. 180–81). Gallie's criteria for such concepts will prove useful again here, not as strict proof that they exist but as explanation of why our key terms, including poetry and criticism, must join Gallie's list of concepts that can never be fixed with one definition.[12] Gallie is not, finally, as wholehearted a pluralist as he at some points suggests. For him all truth is at best relative to its historical moment, and the great intellectual achievements are all time-bound "monuments, marking certain extreme positions," not permanent resources for thought's reconstructions and applications. His rich and sympathetic account of many modes finally promises, he says, "that intellectual history could be developed in such a fashion that it could take the place of, and (among other things) fulfil the only valid functions of traditional metaphysical statements and systems" (p. 224).

Still, Gallie has given an excellent account of why terms like poem, art, criticism, and pluralism are essentially—that is, permanently—in dispute. He offers seven criteria for such "essentially contested concepts" as religion, science, democracy, social justice, and art. What happens when we apply his criteria to the concepts we have inescapably employed all along—not only to *art* and *poem* but also to critical *method* or *mode*?

Gallie's first criterion for deciding that a concept is essentially, not accidentally or temporarily, contested is that it be *"appraisive* in the sense that it signifies or accredits some kind of valued achievement" (p. 161).

The question "Where *is* the poem?" may not at first seem "appraisive," but inherent in every answer to it will be an evaluation, a claim about what is *good* placement and thus good literary criticism. The critic who objects to a Marxist placement into social contexts, saying *"That's* not literary criticism, that's sociology," is only making explicit what every use of such phrases implies. Similarly, terms like "mode" and "pluralism," as I have used them, are evaluative, though the form of my search was mainly descriptive.

Second, the human achievement appraised by naming the concept is of an "internally complex character," even though "its worth is attributed to it as a whole."

No trouble here. Every act of literary criticism is immeasurably complex, regardless of whether the critic claims, like Northrop Frye, to have glimpsed a vision of total unity or, like many of us, merely chews on a small fragment of an undetermined whole.

Third: "Any explanation of its [the achievement's] worth must . . . include reference to the respective contributions of its various parts or features; yet prior to experimentation there is nothing absurd or contradictory in any of a number of possible rival descriptions of its total worth, one such description setting its component parts or features in one order of importance, a second setting them in a second order, and so on."

Again our concepts meet the test, as the ubiquitous quarrels among monists show. Each attempt at the one right view of criticism demands a different practice in the critic; most of them are accompanied by words like "must" and "necessarily" and "essentially." Yet there is no way to prove all but one of them flatly false, since most of them point to real phenomena. The concept of criticism is thus essentially contested. Like "the poem," "literary criticism" has many proper modes of existence.

Gallie's fourth criterion places the concept in history. "The accredited achievement must be of a kind that admits of considerable modification in the light of changing circumstances; and such modification cannot be prescribed or predicted in advance." In short, the achievement is essentially "open."

We are perhaps in less clear agreement about this criterion. Though none of us would deny, I suppose, that poetry is itself "open," in the sense that we cannot predict what new art works will emerge, some critics believe that the kinds can be charted in advance, and the same can be said of *criticism* and *pluralism:* that's precisely what monism claims. But surely art, criticism, and "types of pluralism" are radically open concepts; we cannot hope to predict the future of any of them, and it is a serious mistake, a mistake about both critical practice and the history of criticism, to write as if we hoped to discover the one right mode that would finally sew things up.

It naturally follows, fifth, that each party in debate about the concept recognizes, or should recognize, the fact that its own use of the concept

> is contested by those of other parties, and . . . each party must have at least some appreciation of the different criteria in the light of which the other parties claim to be applying the concept in question. More simply, to use an essentially contested concept means to use it against other uses . . . to recognize that one's own use of it has to be maintained against these other uses. Still more simply, to use an essentially contested concept means to use it both aggressively and defensively.

No problem here, whether about literature, literary criticism, or pluralism.

That our key concepts are inescapably evaluative, complex, generative of disputing views not easily reduced to each other, inherently open, and pursued both aggressively and defensively would be disputed by only one kind of critic or philosopher: the monist who, denying the criterion of irreducibility, would try to resolve all contests over concepts with a victory for the one true view. For any convinced monist, contests about concepts would be either meaningless (caused by semantic confusion) or inherently and essentially resolvable. But for Gallie, essentially contested concepts are still meaningful concepts; debate about them, though never-ending, *can* be rational debate.

His sixth criterion leads toward understanding why this is so, though at first it may give us more of a problem. The essentially contested concept must be derivable "from an original exemplar whose authority is acknowledged by all the contestant users of the concept" (p. 168).

Art works exist as valued achievements of a high order; works (or acts) of literary criticism can be performed well or badly. The authority of these two elusive "exemplars" is extremely difficult to describe, let alone prove. If someone tells me that he cares no more for *King Lear* or the *Iliad* or *Waiting for Godot* than he cares for the text "WAS EVERY CIGARETTE YOU SMOKED TODAY SMOOTH?" or that he sees no essential difference between a couplet by Pope and the Rock of Gibraltar, clearly "the authority of the exemplar"—art—is not being acknowledged. For a person of this kind there is no shared essential concept to be contested. And if he again tells me that we have no need for good talk about works of art, or that Samuel Johnson's talk about it is no better than the average undergraduate essay, he denies the authority of the exemplar, genuine literary criticism.

There is even less widespread agreement about the existence of that other exemplar, the pluralist. Only would-be pluralists can even be aware of the possibility of such an exemplar. But a moment's thought about this criterion helps me understand why the enterprise of writing a book about three pluralists who do not finally agree can confirm my confidence in a limited pluralism: the three provide me, as I reconstruct them, with the exemplary *practice* against which I measure their different formulations. I have now *seen* some exemplars. Even if what I have seen turn out to be only my own distorted versions, just as in some sense my *King Lear* is never precisely yours, I cannot, without violating all I know, doubt that Crane, Burke, and Abrams are struggling effectively with critical variety. Their ways make sense to me at every point, regardless of any incidental disagreements I may discover. Thus more views of variety than one make sense; their very resistance to all my efforts to reduce them into each other or into a common view is solid proof indeed that each has a reality and vitality of its own. I have thus encountered three exemplars that in their firm resistance to tampering preserve themselves as exemplars and in doing so show me that they are worth preserving.

Gallie's seventh criterion seems to me not so much a test of whether a concept is essentially contested as a test of whether a particular participant in the contest is justified in his endeavor. It must be probable or plausible that "the continuous competition for acknowledgement" of rival views "enables the original exemplar's achievement to be sustained or developed in optimum fashion." The test is whether the contestants are serving the continued vitality or viability of the human achievements that originated the contests.

PLURALISMS AS RIVAL PRAGMATISMS

Having begun with a theoretical problem, Gallie thus finally moves us toward pragmatic criteria. In a curious way, both of his final tests violate traditional scientific ways of deciding whether a given contestant is allowed to survive in any intellectual war. Most critics until recently have asked their opponents to prove their conclusions with deductive argument or inductive demonstration, with evidence from the text or from other relevant texts. What's your evidence? What's your proof? No evidence, no proof, and you are barred from the house of criticism. Various new criticisms have recently challenged these old standards of critical proof, and they have almost all done so in the service of the value signaled by Gallie's seventh criterion: they offer a renewed vigor, a new promise that the enterprise will not stagnate. Usually they have been quite explicit in promising new riches or interest, even excitement, both for individual critics and for the critical enterprise.[13]

Most contemporary pluralists thus neither attempt Northrop Frye's implicitly exhaustive kind of classification nor worry about an infinite regress of umbrellas. They seek not truth, not total coherence, not even correspondence to reality. For the traditional cognitive ends, they substitute practical or rhetorical effects on readers and societies, on "pedagogical communities" or on what Father Walter Ong calls "negotiating" communicants. What we are promised is liberation from an inhibiting bourgeois search for certainties into a new freedom, a new creativity. Sometimes the aim is simply liberation for the critic himself, as when Roland Barthes explicitly seeks devices for combating the boredom he would feel if he confined himself to the meanings that Zola actually put into a novel.[14] More often, what the new new critics promise is not simply a private energizing but the renewal of the whole enterprise.

It is true that many versions of the newer criticism have been described in cognitive terms as the reintroduction of new contexts or new subjects, offered as new avenues to truth. The goal of a supreme synthesis, of a final knowledge, is indeed prominent in what we might call the first wave or perhaps the right wing—those who see hope for a solid scientific base for literary criticism in Saussure or Lévi-Strauss or Chomsky. But many observers have noted in the latest wave a shift of emphasis from cognitive to practical or actional goals, particularly the goal of liberation. The shift is at best a matter of emphasis, because even the most "scientific" programs have promised some kind of liberation, whether from bourgeois political control or from the critical chains of the past, and the newer versions do not usually repudiate *all* cognitive claims. But it is striking to see how many of the new key terms are practical, not cognitive. J. Hillis Miller, offering a criticism that will, like poetry, cure the reader, and warning us that the new "uncanny" critic must be "nimble," finally offers something like a religious vision. [15] Roland Barthes offers us an escape from boring repetition into novelty and creativity, a "liberation of the significant." [16] Stanley Fish offers to interest us rather than bore us with soundness. [17] Jacques Derrida seeks a "freeplay," amounting to a "methodical craziness," to produce a "dissemination" of texts that, endless and treacherous and terrifying, liberates us to an *errance joyeuse*. [18]

In short, what we are promised by the new pluralists is an escape from the dead hand of the past, a new vitality. They claim to revive what looked like a dying enterprise that was based on indefensible substances like God, the self, the author, and the text.

For such critics, whether they echo Burke in their effort to cure minds and societies, pursue a political or moral awakening, or seek a more private escape from boredom or release into spiritual renovation, no demonstration of intellectual or cognitive incoherence or unverifiability will be decisive. More interested in processes and practical consequences than in conceptual resting points, they are quite unshaken by the efforts of traditional analysis to reveal their essential violations of consistency. [19]

Before I undertook the project culminating in this book, I would have said that such indifference to ultimate standards of logical clarity, such final reliance on pragmatic tests, such invulnerability to specific conceptual failure, constituted intellectual bankruptcy. I suspect that some of my readers, even now, will share my sense of shock to find that my own project finally depends fully as much on pragmatic appeals as do the most aggressive of the new liberators.

Like them, I have discovered that my practical reasons, my pragmatic commitments, run so deep that they are in fact untouched by any one theoretical failure, whether of coherence (I can't put them all together neatly), or correspondence (I could not paint a portrait of Kenneth Burke that would lead him to say, "That's it. That's KB to a T"), or of comprehensiveness (by definition my "collection" of pluralists will always yield but fragments of all that would be worth knowing).

This curiously stubborn resistance might at first seem based on a simple critical philosophy of "as if": even if there is no such thing as a pluralist or a workable pluralism, even if no one can ever embrace more than one mode (however complex), even if no critical position is finally invulnerable, there are still strong reasons for acting as if one might offer a full embrace, not just to one but to many, because to do so will reduce the amount of meaningless critical conflict in the world and help to preserve the exemplars.

Most teachers advocate this kind of provisional open-mindedness to their students; all of us are annoyed when other people, students or not, withhold it from our own arguments. It seems clear that much of the pointless refutation of positions no one holds would be eliminated if we treated each other as if sense might be found behind the surface nonsense. Most of us see too that this cannot be mere open-mindedness, in the sense of toleration of any and every thing that anyone might say. We assume that, although refutation may often be needed, it should follow a rigorous reconstruction of what people really have tried to say. Most of us make this assumption to some degree in our reconstructions of other people's modes, and we expect our students to make it without limit when they deal with our own. (How long, brothers and sisters, do you think it will take a new student to learn how to do your kind of criticism well? How many readings of your latest book or article will be required before a student has earned the right to expose your stupid inconsistencies and silly oversights?)

Thus we all know, though we all too easily forget, that in practice a provisional pluralism is immensely useful. Its obvious benefits enable it to survive any failure it meets in any one intellectual task. It is not threatened when I find critics who do not stand up to respectful scrutiny, who in fact look worse the longer I consider them. Such diminishment of stature need not trouble the provisional pluralist because he never promises himself that all positions will survive close criticism, only that some will look better and better the longer he works with them.

It is important to recognize, however, that the pragmatic support for pluralism goes far beyond such immediate benefits, which after all might be claimed, without too much stretching, for eclecticism and even, perhaps, for some versions of monism. The pragmatic strength of pluralism does not depend only on its short-run heuristic or pedagogical value. It is, I want to claim, the most fruitful attitude for opening up the world to continuing humanistic life. And my conviction is so strong that no setbacks in the pursuit of conceptual clarity can shake it.

I can thus see that the pluralism that I offered to inquire about in chapter 1 was not simply a hypothesis, though it *was* that; it was both a superstructure to be theoretically "proved or disproved" and a necessary substructure for the whole inquiry. The very act of taking pluralism seriously as a possibility was thus already a commitment to it, ridden with values. It was a choice so basic that it is reinforced, thus "proved," by all of my experience. It entitles me—and this would not shock Burke, though it might at first shock Crane—to say heads-I-win-tails-you-lose: show me that critics understand each other or that they do not; or show me that understanding is easy or rare and difficult; or show me that there are no full pluralists, only more or less subtle monists; or that there *are* some, but they do not agree; show me that the structure of each mind determines a different perspective or that at bottom all minds are similar; show me whatever you choose, and I shall always be able to take it as grist for my pluralist mill, for I shall say: Let us look now at *how* you have shown me these things.

If you show me a quarrel in which two people seem really to have understood and then rejected each other, I can in reply show either that if they probed a bit deeper they would discover the true grounds of real differences and then be able to debate fruitfully, or that they can easily resolve illusory differences. In either case the value of pluralism is demonstrated. My intellectual grounds are thus indistinguishable from organizational, explanatory, and preservative power, and I cannot distinguish pluralistic theory from the practical value of pluralism.

The structure of my thought stands revealed, then, as an appeal to action and belief, an appeal that comes close to sounding like this: Become a pluralist because that is the best way to solve problems that do not really exist for anyone but a pluralist—which is what everyone ought to be. Become a pluralist without waiting for someone to resolve whatever theoretical difficulties you see in pluralism. Become a pluralist because pluralism serves ends that are even more important than any conceivable comprehensive and coherent theory about the whole of man's discourse.

I have thus landed myself not simply in a contest of pluralisms but a contest of pluralisms that all depend finally on pragmatic appeals. We are thus forced into an inquiry into consequences, into ends, and all the world knows that such inquiry is about the most difficult there is.

The difficulty however, is not, as it was once thought to be, that any dependence on ends, or what we have come to call "values," is intellectually disreputable. It is true that many critics still tend to borrow from the natural sciences the dogma that truth is not properly judged by its human consequences: I must not accept or reject the Copernican picture of the solar system according to whether it leads to good consequences for man's earthly enterprises; therefore I must not allow concern for consequences to contaminate my decisions about whether to embrace pluralism. But many humanists and social scientists would now agree that the truth value of a given form of inquiry into mankind's works cannot be sharply and finally separated from the consequences of what is said. I have tried to show elsewhere,[20] as many others have done in recent years, that we humanists bought a bill of goods when we uncritically borrowed a whole list of modernist distinctions that some had thought essential in the natural sciences: objective/subjective, fact/value, reason/ rationalization, knowledge/faith, and theory/practice (see p. 202, above). None of these is imposed on us by uninterpreted nature, and each can be harmful when held as dogma.

If our criticism of such distinctions has been correct, then we cannot judge against any current critical theory on the ground that its ultimate criterion is service to this or that enterprise. And this means that those who set out to shatter traditional humanist norms of interpretation and to create a pluralism without limits in the name of freedom, or bliss, or revolution seem to be on the same formal footing as I am when I advocate a pluralism limited by its pragmatic consequences.

The test now becomes: Can we discover any way to appraise the relative force of our different commitments? Which of various values pursued by various pluralisms can offer, finally, the most reasonable case for itself, once we have recognized that a consideration of consequences is not inherently unreasonable?

Three Inseparable Values: Vitality, Justice, and Understanding

The task we have set ourselves is a curious one. We see a kind of pluralism as a fact: there are innumerable critical voices in the world. We recognize that this fact is something to be valued: we want to keep the critical dialogue going in the best possible forms. And, because we want our criticism to increase the likelihood of further good art and good criticism, what we seek—unlike those critics, if any, who seek an abstract "truth at all costs"—is an attitude toward plurality that will help insure a further plurality. We cannot even describe the facts that led to our inquiry without importing the evaluation of what we find, for the very phenomena that have given us all this trouble are, or at least include, the exemplars we want somehow to preserve!

What is more, it is quite clear that whatever exemplars we hope to preserve cannot be thought of as simple canonic lists of great art works or great works of criticism. They are more like activities or enterprises—art and criticism—and our problem is to discover what values ought to inform, and thus to limit, our manifold engagements in those activities.

VITALITY

The first of these we have been discussing for some time now, and it seems to be shared by almost everyone commanding attention today; though many set out to kill this or that critic, or even the whole of this or that style of criticism, everyone claims to offer life as against death.

Our problem, then, is to discriminate among vitalizers. The vitality we seek is far different from mere activity. A battlefield is active, and an observer who, at the height of battle, made no judgments about its outcome would declare any battlefield more "vital" than the nearby village of sleeping burghers. The vitality we seek always involves viability, the quality that leads to survival.

Yet criticism as an enterprise depends inescapably on the kind of exchange that can be characterized as combat or killing. In this chapter, for example, I am trying to combat various false notions of critical vitality that I fear will, in the long run, kill criticism. I might thus be described as trying to "kill," and it is no surprise that many critics have chosen that metaphor for the critical act. How often have we heard gory talk about "the battle of the new criticism," about "total war," about "firing broadsides" designed "to blast the other side into oblivion," about "counterattacks," "missiles," and "barrages."[21] The notion seems to be spreading that each author must kill his predecessors, or that, as Tzvetan Todorov has put it, if the text is to survive, the descriptive commentary must die; if the commentary lives, it will have killed the text.[22]

It would be absurd to deny the metaphorical truth—or half-truth—in such language. If no one tried to "kill" false views, if we all agreed, criticism would die, killed by perpetual peace. It is thus easy to understand why some defenders of aggressive war argue that it is good because it wakes people up, makes them reconsider their arguments, sharpens the issues, and gets rid of unworthy contenders.

But isn't the real test whether a given kind of conflict in fact does these good things? If we pursue the vitality of criticism as something more important than any one critical "truth" or given exemplar, we must think hard about what a true vitality might be. Vitality for the sake of vitality, action for the sake of action, change for the sake of change—these are ambiguous formulae that can cover everything from a most absurd and destructive activism to a profound philosophy like John Dewey's and a renovating criticism like Burke's. The question must always be, under this criterion, *does* this critical statement in fact increase the likelihood of further critical life? Or does it leave its author complacent, while his adversaries, sensing danger, are tempted to retaliate blindly, lashing out in wounded fury?

Thus there are certain obvious questions we will want to ask of any lively warrior who claims to revitalize either by replenishing the earth with hitherto unheard-of readings or by insisting on rigorous simplifications and clarifications.

First, do you in fact proscribe more kinds of valuable talk about literature than you invite? Every mode of speech and thought can be said to forbid certain kinds of further speech and to invite certain other kinds. The sentence I have just uttered, for example, along with the arguments I might give on its behalf, attempts to proscribe certain contradictory claims, such as: "Some modes of speech do *not* proscribe the saying of anything; they simply invite further speech, with *nothing* ruled out." Or: "Some modes of speech do not invite any further speech of *any* kind; they attempt simply to stop all discourse."

My sentence can also be said to *invite* certain kinds of speech, speech that speculates, as I have just done, about what it proscribes and what it invites, and further pluralistic speculation within modes and about the relation of modes.

When critics tell me that all genuine criticism *must* start with this or that notion of the reader or the text, or that all texts *must* be treated in the same way, or that *every* text invites *only* its own dismantling, or that *the* modern situation *requires* only one form of pursuit or one notion of multiplicity, are they in fact proscribing more discourse than they are inviting?

What are we to say to critics who proscribe all talk that admits the necessity of proscription?

Unfortunately, this first question helps me only in rejecting claims about the exclusive validity of any one method, not the practice of the method itself. So I will want to ask next whether you offer to vitalize only yourself or me as well. One version of this question is: Do you invite us all into a community of inquiry, or are you simply exhibiting your own new freedom, shouting down at us, "Look, ladies and gentlemen, no hands!" A second version is: Having done what you want to do, can you teach it to me, or to anyone? If not, whom do you really liberate? Or, third: Do you, *must* you, because of your presuppositions, condescend to or exclude this or that reader or group of readers? All criticism will accidentally exclude some readers, but some criticism excludes on principle. How many of those who read and think are necessarily, by definition, ruled out of this new enterprise of yours? In short, are you offering life to a community of *readers*?

But the third test is even more important: Do you acknowledge community with the other *authors* you treat? Much polysemic criticism seems to offer a strange and destructive new contra-cogito: "I invent new readings, therefore you, the author, *are not*." There are, of course, authors who will seem contemptible to all of us: liars, trimmers, lickboots, lackeys. But what if I find a critic who habitually assumes that the authors of all other texts are less perceptive, less generous, less politically aware, less devoted to truth, less endowed with genius, than he is? (I return to the preservation of authors in chapter 7.)

In short, what incentive do you give to other participants to continue the fray? If they survive as speaking critics (as in fact they do not always do), are they encouraged to return to the exchange with a sense that their life depends on finding, among the dead and dying, others who live? Or have they been taught that criticism is like medieval jousting—a zero-sum game in which *my* rise depends on *your* fall?

Sustained critical vitality depends on the vitality of many individual critics with a sense of common enterprise. There are, of course, historical moments of accidental bustle, when the sounds of shooting in every direction give an illusion of vigor (I think that in some respects ours is such a moment). There may even be moments when the best activity would be a "weeding out" or a "winnowing"—or even a "last judgment." But such moments, if and when they come, depend on earlier propagations and peaceful inheritances. Unless someone has heard the message, "Go forth, multiply, and replenish the earth," there will be no weeds to pull, no critical error to be purged, no father to be killed.

No critic makes himself; every one of us discovers his own voice only by listening, or mis-listening, to those before us who seem to have spoken best. This much is seldom denied. What seems to be forgotten is that, even after I have begun to speak what I mistakenly call *"my own* critical truth," my continued vitality as a thinking critic rather than a phonograph record depends on my continuing capacity to take other voices into account. My life, indistinguishable from the life of my critical tribe, requires that my thought be an exchange among "selves" rather than a mere search for ways to impose what I already know.

JUSTICE

If my continued vitality as critic depends, finally, on yours, and if we place vitality as a central value that need not, cannot, be proved but only experienced, observed, and honored, it becomes clear that we are also dependent on a second value, justice. All of us expect and indeed demand justice for ourselves. Some of us are willing to fight for political justice for others. But too little has been said about the arts of doing justice to other critics' views.

We need no dialogue by Plato to tell us that justice is a hard concept to define. Suppose we think of it as a quality achieved in the critical commonwealth when each citizen is granted his due. Though any Socrates can easily show how much that leaves out, it is a good definition for our purposes because it is minimal. Whatever else critical justice may be, I know that it is violated whenever any critic is granted less than his due.

But what is "his due"? What do I owe my fellow critic? Why, obviously, exactly the amount of critical attention that his *text* deserves, no more but no less. As critic, I do not owe him leniency or personal affection or sentimental grants of "the benefit of the doubt"; I owe him only what his critical statements deserve when they claim a passport into the country of debate.

But who is to determine *that?* Who is to decide how much credence is due our neighbors' arguments, in order to know whether they have been dealt with justly?

Critics themselves cannot finally tell us, in direct statements about their ways of work and their value: "It took me ten years before I could break through the accumulated errors of generations." Such statements may legitimately raise my level of attention. Indeed, if they are made by someone whose powers I already respect, they may carry some weight in my initial judgment of even scientific or mathematical contributions. How often one hears, as proof of the profound probing to be found in the *Principia Mathematica*, Russell's assertion that it almost drove him to suicide and that his mental powers never fully recovered from the effort. In the humanities we are more likely to be told that brilliant illumination came not from hard labor but from some mysterious source: a muse, a new freedom from analytical restraint, a new sensitivity to deep or spontaneous sources, a new method so recondite that only a few can understand. Whatever initial respect such claims may carry, we justify them finally, in criticism as in mathematical philosophy, only when they manage to get themselves fully embodied in a text.* When I found myself relying on Abrams' ethos as part of his proof, it was not an ethos established by assertion but by full demonstration in the text. The most that his previously established ethos could do (and in his case that was a great deal) was to demand of me, in advance, that I make no hasty judgment on what I found. And the same can be said even for the somewhat stronger claims to our attention made by a text's status as a "classic." Though the testimony of generations of readers can carry much more weight than the author's own claim to importance, it cannot overweigh, for any honest and energetic reader, what is found in the text.

Nor can I tell myself, in any simple sense, what is due either to others or to me. The chances are far too high that the messages I give myself will be grotesquely biased on my own behalf: *my* arguments deserve not only the benefit of the doubt but what Joyce expected of the readers of *Finnegans Wake*—a lifetime of study; *my friends'* arguments also deserve close attention—though unfortunately they tend to be a bit obvious, and too many of them are derivative from my own; *my enemies'* arguments—ah, how just it was that X knifed Y in last month's *Sadist*, since Y had so justly knifed X in the previous issue of *Mayhem!*

We thus seem to have no Supreme Court in our republic to determine standards of justice. Each of us is judge and jury—and often enough the accused as well. And since we have found no way to establish in advance which criminal code—which critical method—should be appealed to, we are left with one simple, all-powerful principle: Suspect any text that sets itself up as king, demanding one law for itself and applying other, more stringent, laws to the commoners. Whenever we find any critical method inviting the use of

---

*Most of the thousands of discussions of "the intentional fallacy" could be translated into relevant terms here. But the issues would receive a productive transformation because we have changed our question from "What does the text, whether poem or critical work, *mean*?" to "What does the reader *owe* it?" See chapter 7.

double standards, we have a simple choice: Either repudiate that method or abandon hope for our common enterprise.

Limits to pluralism are thus set quite precisely by the question: Is a single standard of justice operating? Nietzsche once wrote, no doubt shortly after experiencing some injustice: "The worst readers are those who proceed like plundering soldiers: they pick up a few things they can use, soil and confuse the rest, and blaspheme the whole."[23] Well, if Nietzsche will agree not to blaspheme my text, I'll try not to blaspheme his. But the test of the single standard does not require that we judge each other by the same standard, only that we agree to be judged by the standard we apply to others.

Thus finally we depend on the critic's argument itself; it alone can tell us *whether* further attention is "due," and it is what finally tells us *how* we should judge what we find.

The result of this dependency must always be manifold and to some degree ambiguous. I depend on an argument to tell me ("me" in my always half-deaf condition) whether I should attend to it; I have no arbiter but my own response to a flow of words, words that must always reflect imperfectly a thought that is always presumably imperfect. Unless my response is schooled by a passion to do justice to the text, and by whatever corrections may be provided in dialogue with other readers, I am cut from all moorings and will soon find that justice has fled the commonwealth and, with it, all true vigor. As Morse Peckham has recently pointed out, once an interpreter frees himself from the constraints of what he calls "situational interpretation"—the desire to do some sort of justice to an original communicative intent—the possibilities are infinite: "any literary text . . . can be used to exemplify any explanation."[24] "Students have been impressed by the great length of *S/Z*. I confess I am not. There is no reason why Barthes should not have gone on forever. It is impossible to exhaust the analogical possibilities of a text as long as *Sarrasine*. It is probably impossible to exhaust the analogical possibilities of a sonnet, or even a limerick. When one man's ingenuity flags, another will pick up the torch" (p. 812). What is more, without some notion of doing justice to an original text, there is nothing to prevent us from reducing all varieties of meaning to a single meaning. As Peckham says, psychotics learn to do just that.

For those who seek justice, interpretations would be richly manifold even if we could agree in advance on a single critical task, a single critical method, and thus a single code for judging an argument worthy. But since, as we have seen, all of these are inescapably plural, we find ourselves, in the search for justice, knowing in advance that even the standards of justice themselves will to some degree vary from critic to critic. We knew when we began that every critic will believe, speaking from personal motives, that what is due him is nothing less than total attention. But now we see that, though some of these voices can justly be dismissed, the good reasons for accepting many others will themselves be of diverse kinds.

We are now in a better position to see why my belief in justice can continue to serve as an argument for pluralism even when notions about pluralism encounter difficulties.

First of all, I had seen, long before I began to write, that my three exemplary pluralists in fact worked harder to be just than most skeptics or monists or eclectics I knew. It is true that their standards of justice differed. Crane's notion of doing justice was to appraise the true cognitive value of a critical statement; Burke was finally concerned with doing justice to the motivational force and vitality of a critical act; and Abrams, while sharing both of these concerns, subordinated them to a just appraisal of the historical contribution of a poetic or critical argument. It is also true that all three are capable of acts of injustice (Burke seems to me especially likely to lapse from his own high standards of fully incorporating the other critic's advantages before seeking his own). But on the whole all three must be declared not guilty of that basic critical crime: one legal code for me and mine, a tougher code for thee and thine. If we could appoint some disinterested Supreme Court of criticism to hear "the case of the three pluralists," the judges would not be required to decide for or against any of the three; for though each of them lives, in a sense, in a different country, under different local laws, each has clearly worked hard to discern and observe laws for critical behavior that are transpersonal.

Second, my own effort to do justice to three pluralists finally required me to admit all three into my critical world. Yet the three quite different kinds of argument to which I sought to do justice were *not* reducible to each other. Each critic won his entry into my world by raising and answering questions that were undeniably important to me, and I am in fact convinced that anyone who does justice to any one of them must abandon skepticism about the possibility of critical knowledge. In short, to immerse oneself in any of those three worlds is to become a convinced monist in and for that world. But with three of them on my hands, I find that the effort to translate any one of them into the terms of either of the other two violates, in clearly visible ways, standards of justice that I cannot reject. I am, then, forced by my belief in justice to remain a pluralist, even when other defenses fail. Yet I am at the same time prevented from embracing an unlimited pluralism of indeterminate meanings, because each of my pluralists offers standards for rejecting a great deal of the inconsistent, incoherent, or narrow stuff that comes my way.

Must critics kill each other? We may now answer: Yes, sometimes, but only when justice requires killing. In a lifetime of reading, one encounters many arguments, and many more raw assertions, that deserve only to be wiped out on the spot. If justice were our only standard, the hanging judges could thus be considered the heroes of my tale—provided they hanged the right criminals.

Yet we have already seen that vitality comes even before justice. In the first place, the chances are still very high that most of the killing we witness is of straw men and thus both radically unjust to the real critic and a waste of everyone's time. Perhaps more important, the critic who justly kills an idea may incidentally kill his fellow critic too; that is, he may drive him from attempting further criticism. So much the better, some would say, if he is a bad critic. But criticism is far too important to be left only to the generals—those who are seldom or never guilty of bad criticism. Nobody is exempt from error, and if we killed off all the perpetrators of error, no one would survive. What is more, nobody abides steadily by all the laws or even by all the laws that he thinks are fully just. I know, for example, that I must have done serious injustice to some of the critics I have occasionally glanced at here. I cannot bring myself to expunge those remarks, since they further my own case; yet I also cannot bring myself, at least not now, to spend the years of time that would be required to do what I consider full justice to all I have used. And so I break the law even here, once (p. 15), twice (p. 151), and perhaps even thrice (p. 216). But to do so in no way impugns the law; it condemns me.

If I thus grant a sort of special privilege to myself, a legal postponement of execution pending good behavior, I must be willing to grant the same to all my colleagues. And that leads us to something like the old formula: Damn the sin but not the sinner. As sinners all, my colleagues and I sink or swim together; and when I say colleagues, I am not talking of a small party of the elite. Every human being is my colleague in this grand endeavor: the whole art of discerning, illuminating, and encouraging quality in human achievement. We are all critics (Burke even goes so far as to say that every living thing is a critic), and most of us will find that justice alone cannot guide our practice. It seems to work well when we are innocent; it looks like a fine thing when it destroys our opponents. A desire to serve it can be a powerful incentive to a serious reconstruction of what our colleagues and rivals mean. But like most values we serve, it will suddenly turn against us unless it is restrained by even more important shared concerns.*

UNDERSTANDING

Debates about the possibility of understanding baffle all parties, because to each contestant the case seems to be self-proving. They thus exemplify, once again, the problem with which we began. J. Hillis Miller says that no interpretation of any text, written or spoken, can be taken as definitive and that all texts are "unreadable . . . if by 'readable' one means open to a single, definitive, univocal interpretation"; and M. H. Abrams says, in the clear belief that he is repudiating Miller's position, that without confidence "that we can use language to say what we mean and can interpret language so as to determine what was meant, there is no rationale for the dialogue in which we are . . . engaged."[25] Is this a conflict that should be resolved monistically (either Miller or Abrams is right) or skeptically, or eclectically, or pluralistically? What would a pluralist's solution to such a conflict be?

From what we have said so far, we can see how easy it would be to define "understanding" in two different ways that would give an easy victory either to Miller or to Abrams. It is almost too easy to show, in the first place, that every argument for multiple readings depends on some sense of understanding that provides limits to multiplicity. Except perhaps in neo-Dadaist performances, every claim that we misunderstand each other, and every illustration of misunderstanding, depends on both the possibility and the desirability of understanding.

An example of a counterclaim that seems to me entirely misleading is found in Roland Barthes's account, in the early *Mythologies*, of the murder trial of Gaston Dominici. The eighty-year-old was convicted, Barthes maintains, by the assumptions about understanding held by "the bourgeois Establishment." "Literature has just condemned a man to the guillotine."[26] The old man was judged in a language that

---

*It is important to note that the values I appeal to in moderating justice are not mercy, or kindness, or magnanimity. In a fuller discussion, one would have to face the question of whether these virtues, good things in themselves, do ever finally conflict with the critical virtues, and the further question of what to do when conflict comes. But I think that it is important for this inquiry to derive our values from within the enterprise of criticism, so that we need not finally appeal to any moral standard other than those that follow from our shared desire for good criticism.

to him was totally impenetrable: "No: syntax, vocabulary, most of the elementary, analytical materials of language grope blindly without ever touching, but no one has any qualms about it." The judges, Barthes says, were guilty on two counts: of believing in the supremacy of their own language and of accepting "an intermediate myth"—"the transparence and universality of language" (p. 44). But Barthes of course claims to have understood both the judges and the old man; otherwise his indictment of the former makes no sense. He properly blames the judges for not trying to understand what the old man said; but this would have been pointless unless intelligence, effort, and humility about their own myths could have led them closer to understanding. Similarly, in order to accept Barthes's claim that "to rob a man of his language ... is the first step in all legal murders" (p. 46), I must assume that *I* have understood *him* and that *he* has understood *them*. There is never a hint that he fears either my complete misunderstanding or his own.

Another way to make the same point: we all believe in understanding *in the limited sense* of rejecting incorrect interpretations of our own words. It is quite true, of course, as Karl Popper has lamented in his autobiography, that "it is impossible to speak in such a way that you cannot be misunderstood."[27] But there is a simple and infallible test that can always be offered to anyone who says that trying to improve understanding does not matter because all sincere readings have equal validity. Suppose I offer to interpret the following passage from Barthes:

> The pleasure of the Text also includes the amicable return of the author. Of course, the author who returns is not the one identified by our institutions (history and courses in literature, philosophy, church discourse); he is not even the biographical hero. The author who leaves his text and comes into our life has no unity; he is a mere plural of "charms," the site of a few tenuous details, yet the source of vivid novelistic glimmerings, a discontinuous chant of amiabilities, in which we nevertheless read death more certainly than in the epic of a fate; he is not a (civil, moral) person, he is a body. In the total disengagement from value produced by the pleasure of the Text, what I get from Sade's life is not the spectacle, albeit grandiose, of a man oppressed by an entire society because of his passion, it is not the solemn contemplation of a fate, it is, *inter alia*, that Provençal way in which Sade says "milli" (mademoiselle) Rousset, or milli Henriette, or milli Lépinai, it is his white muff when he accosts Rose Keller, his last games with the Charenton linen seller (in her case, I am enchanted by the linens) ....

The pleasure of a reading guarantees its truth. Reading texts and not books, turning upon them a clairvoyance not aimed at discovering their secret, their "contents," their philosophy, but merely their happiness of writing, I can hope to release Sade, Fourier, and Loyola from their bonds (religion, utopia, sadism); I attempt to dissipate or elude the moral discourse that has been held on each of them; working, as they themselves worked, only on languages, I unglue the text from its purpose as a guarantee: socialism, faith, evil. Whence (at least such is the theoretical intent of these studies) I force the displacement (but not to suppress; perhaps even to accentuate) of the text's social responsibility. There are those who believe they can with assurance discuss the site of this responsibility: it would be the author, inserting that author into his period, his history, his class. But another site remains enigmatic, escapes for the time being any illumination: the site of the reading. This obscuration occurs at the very moment bourgeois ideology is being most vituperated, without ever wondering from which site it is being talked about or against: is it the site of a non-discourse ("Let's not talk, let's not write, let's militate")? is it that of a contra-discourse ("Let's discourse against class culture"), but then made up of what traits, what figures, what reasonings, what cultural residues? To act as though an innocent discourse could be held against ideology is tantamount to continuing to believe that language can be nothing but the neutral instrument of a triumphant content. In fact, today, there is no language site outside bourgeois ideology: our language comes from it, returns to it, remains closed up in it. The only possible rejoinder is neither confrontation nor destruction, but only theft: fragment the old text of culture, science, literature, and change its features according to formulae of disguise, as one disguises stolen goods. Faced with the old text, therefore, I try to efface the false sociological, historical, or subjective efflorescence of determinations, visions, projections; I listen to the message's transport, not the message. . . .[28]

Now I offer M. Barthes, J. Hillis Miller, and all other free-wheeling mis-readers, two interpretations of the passage: (1) Oh, I see what you're driving at. You really believe that the most important task for the critic today is to work as precisely as possible into the author's text, in order to discover what his conscious intention was. (2) Ah, I understand. You have a deliberate program of using, violating, and transcending what authors meant to say in order to discover what their texts really meant for their society or for the flesh-and-blood author, or what it can mean for us as we attempt to combat the immense and inescapable powers of bourgeois ideology embodied in bourgeois language.

One feels a bit silly laboring a point that everyone until recently would have taken for granted, but it has to be done: my second reading really does come closer to understanding what Barthes meant than my first one does. I know that; Barthes knows it. The second statement is by no means an equivalent of Barthes's; as its author, I clearly do not encompass in it a full understanding of the original, and I have destroyed all the metaphoric fun about the joys of thievery and fragmentation and disguise. Despite that, Barthes would surely prefer to have it issued to the world as a summary of his beliefs, as he tried to express them in 1971, than to be totally misrepresented. And he could not express *that* preference without having understood, to the necessary degree, both of *my* statements.*

This being so, and so obviously so, the claims for unlimited indeterminacy of all texts might seem even more puzzling than when we began. What can people mean when they say, as Miller does, that all texts are unreadable, in his special sense that they are never "open to a single, definitive, univocal interpretation?" (I find the word *open* a curious one in that sentence, viewed in the light of what I have said about proscribing meanings.) We might want to assume that Miller and Barthes and all the others who are playing with these new multiplicities are simply being silly or cute. They know quite well that the *choice* between my two statements is single, definitive, and univocal, even though no two arguments *for* the choice will be worded in precisely the same way. Either my imagined first reader knows how to read or he does not; and he does not. One must simply question the good faith of anyone who really disagreed with this view.

Since to do so is for me a self-defeating hypothesis (some of the new polysignifiers may be dishonest or irresponsible, but surely all are not), I am driven to a closer look, and that look shows, without too much effort, that the program is not concerned with the *possibility* of understanding at all, but with its desirability. Insofar as the multipliers are not simply saying that *perfect* understanding of a complex text is impossible—something that nobody has ever denied—they are really saying, as I began to show when talking about vitality, that there are more important tasks in the world than trying to make out

---

*Yes, yes. Of *course* I know that he might well look me in the eye and deny the preference. But consider that denial closely. Is he not saying, "Better a plain and clear distortion than a namby-pamby paraphrase?" And if he chooses to say that, must he not concede my point about his claiming to understand my two accounts?

an intended meaning that will be, by preestablished definition, superficial, unoriginal, and inhibiting to our real enterprises.

Since we have been using M. Barthes, I shall continue with him, though dozens of others would serve as well. Again and again he admits the *possibility* of strictly controlled understanding between author and reader. Limiting oneself to the intentions of the work is, however, bad for the reader, because it limits him to the "code" of an author who, chances are, expressed the values of an enslaving bourgeois culture. Barthes objects, for example, to what I have elsewhere called stable irony as an inferior literary practice. He does not deny that it exists—that some ironies insist on being interpreted as ironic and not as "straight." No, the problem is that such irony insists on the superiority of one code over another, and, as Barthes says, how can one code be allowed to dominate over another without our "destructively shutting off the plurality of codes"?[29] Well, if we leave out the "destructively" (his word is *abusivement*), the answer is that it cannot. That's precisely what the effort of human understanding is based on: the assumption that one code *will* dominate over another in such a way as to establish the superiority, in a given setting, of some readings over some other readings. There is no problem here except for someone who clings to two totally ungrounded notions: first, that my freedom is diminished rather than enhanced by entering someone else's mind; and second, that an author can never earn, by his excellence, a full "author"-ity.

Both notions are plainly and flatly contrary to all human experience. We do not lose our freedom by molding our minds in shapes established by others. We find it there. As Kant says, repudiating the possibility of unlimited knowledge: "The light dove, cleaving the air in her free flight, and feeling its resistance, might [well] imagine that its flight would be still easier in empty space."[30]

Vitality, justice, understanding. Any one of them, taken alone, will lead to absurd excesses: silly excitations, brutal slaughter, pussyfooting reduplication. Placed together in critical interchange, they correct each other's excesses and provide a set of tests that both depend on pluralism and reinforce it with every application. The Babel of critical voices is transformed at the moment when each critic decides that his survival depends not on shouting down all the others but on granting them a just hearing.

6

In order that both the giver and the receiver of the Exercises may be better helped and benefitted, it must be pre-supposed that every good Christian must be more ready to excuse the proposition of another than to condemn it, and if he cannot save it, let him inquire how the other understands it; if the other understands it wrongly, let him correct him with love; if this suffice not, let him seek all possible means in order that the other, rightly understanding it, may save it from error. —St. Ignatius

He [Barthes himself] used to think of the world of language (the logosphere) as a vast and perpetual conflict of paranoias. The only survivors are the systems (fictions, jargons) inventive enough to produce a final figure, the one which brands the adversary with a half-scientific, half-ethical name, a kind of turnstile that permits us simultaneously to describe, to explain, to condemn, to reject, to recuperate the enemy, in a word: *to make him pay.*—Roland Barthes

Four good lights cast fewer shadows than one when the sun is hid, but a man has to do his own walking.—Stephen C. Pepper

When an intelligent man goes out of his way to misunderstand, he is naturally more successful than a fool.—Gide

In Defense of the
Reader and of Alien Modes:
The Need for Overstanding

Justice Again

The pluralist can find, along some such route as the one we have just followed, ample grounds for rejecting an unlimited pluralism—for believing, as I said in chapter 3, that even the freest interpretations are finally parasitical upon modes that insist on the possibility of justice and understanding. The vitality of criticism depends on maintaining standards of justice, and both depend on an active pursuit of understanding.

So far so good.

Exhilarated by the exertions and triumphs of my flight, it is some time before I become aware of a chorus of living pluralists in the wings, chanting in lugubrious cacophony: "You have not understood *me*." "Where in your case am I to find *my reasons* for freeing readers from texts?" "Where am I to look for justice to my notion that texts are independent of both authors and readers?" Utterly convinced that what I have said is much more important than any argument against it could possibly be, convinced that these dismantlers of texts, these flatterers of incompetent readers, these deliberate mystifiers are not only wrong but dangerous, I close my ears to the chanting, bring my book to a close, and send it off to the press. In due time, the publisher's readers recommend publication, and the editor urges that we move quickly into print.

Months pass, and the voices refuse to be shushed as I fuss with my revisions and read whatever comes my way.

They are by no means the only voices I hear, the only "texts" demanding to be understood. I meet a colleague at dinner. "What you should be doing," he says, "is taking on those French crazies, *head*-on. That stuff is spreading like wildfire, and it's corrupt—just plain corrupt! If a man set out to define cultural decadence, he couldn't do better than a simple ostensive definition: Barthes, Derrida, and the American hangers-on like Hillis Miller. This is no time

for pluralism, man, this is a time for battle. They're wrong, and you
know they're wrong. Tear into 'em, instead of pussyfooting as you did
in that *CI* piece."

Thinking about the structure of his demand as distinct from the
specific enemies he names, I note with some discomfort that, in its
attitude toward their texts, his demand has the same structure as he
imputes to the procedures of the enemy. The enemies are enemies,
for him, because they repudiate understanding, insist on their right to
ignore intentions, and blissfully impose the critic's character and
interests upon a text; the text is thus replaced by meanings which its
author never dreamed of. What is more, my counselor thinks he is
among the angels because he would go beyond understanding, as I
have used the term, and insist on the importance of his own superior
"understanding"—what might be called *over*standing. He hopes to
impose his own character, and mine, upon *their* texts.

Before I violate a text's intentions because it argues that intentions
should be violated, I ought surely to pause a little, especially in a book
that has pretended to some sort of justice to that great prophet of
overstanding, Kenneth Burke.

I have paused, in fact, for many months and several drafts, forced
to think about degrees and kinds of violation—about good and bad
ways to stand above a text. It would be simple if I could simply
sacrifice chapter 5. But it all goes on making sense to me, no matter
how I test it. It would also be fairly simple to "take on" any one of the
overstanders and show how his enterprise violates mine. It would be
simplest of all to go through the motions of a toleration act, saying to
all and sundry: You go ahead and pursue your pluralisms into infinite
abysses, and I will pursue my pluralism within its strong limits. But to
do this would be to relax into the first attitude described in chapter 1
—and to do *that* is to repudiate Crane, Burke, and Abrams. What is
immensely difficult is to acknowledge that any of the overstanders
might have something essential to offer *my* enterprise. What fish
would they fry that I haven't even tried to catch yet?

In what follows I make no claim to do full justice to any other critic's
act of overstanding. Instead I discover what is for me a new way of
talking about readers, authors, and texts—a way that acknowledges
the necessity of overstanding and some of the complexities raised by
that necessity.

But before I turn to my own program of overstanding, I necessarily
begin with a radically reconstituted statement of what it means to
respect a text.

Intrinsic/Extrinsic Repudiated

In the interminable debates about the intentional fallacy—the hundreds, perhaps thousands, of arguments for and against what has come to be called "Wimsatt and Beardsley"—there has almost always been a polemical opposition between intrinsic questions and extrinsic questions. It is true that some pluralists have argued, with Crane, Burke, and Abrams, that both kinds of questions are legitimate. Yet even for them the distinction has usually been sharp, and each of them shows what might be called habits of preference that reinforce the distinction. Crane finally says, in effect, "Answer all legitimate intrinsic questions first." Burke finally says, "We should of course do our best to recognize intrinsic demands, but the extrinsic questions are more interesting." And Abrams, in spite of undertaking grand historical projects that most of the authors he treats could never have imagined, is finally unequivocal in his denunciation of deconstructionist violations of authorial intent, as realized *in* the text (see pp. 184–88, above). If these men, committed to pluralist assumptions, have been unable to avoid polemical oppositions between what is inside and what is out, it is no wonder that most critics make the polar contrast even more important.

Can we find a way to turn a polemical opposition into two complementary directions for inquiry? Deconstructionists are insistent that no text will yield a single determinate meaning unless we "arbitrarily" import some limiting standards from the "outside" world; since contexts are infinite, texts will always explode into infinities except when we support our readings with arbitrarily chosen grounds. Defenders of determinate readings are fond of demonstrating that even the wildest of readings "sneak in" notions of intrinsic limits. They are both right (once we look behind the polemic invited by words like "arbitrary" and "sneak"), but where does that lead us?

Suppose we abandon the metaphor of inside-versus-outside and view texts and their interpretations as a kind of conversation or dialogue* between a text and a reader; this supposes a text that exists, when interpreted, at least as much *in* the reader and the reader's culture as *in* the author and the author's culture, and it also supposes a reader who, as he interprets, is at least as much *in* the text and in the author's culture as *in* his own culture. When I read any work that

---

*I regret my inability to think of less shopworn terms for what I have in mind. But the fact that words are shopworn does not mean that the practice they describe has been seriously thought about. Other terms being used by rhetoricians these days to escape the distinction of in-and-out are "transaction" and "negotiation."

works for me—"Surgical Ward," *Macbeth*, *S/Z*—author (and the author's culture), text (and its implied culture), and reader (with inescapable cultural presuppositions) join inextricably. I am of course free to deny the work's workings, to extricate myself and the text from Auden's or Shakespeare's or Barthes's context, if I find good reason to do so. But that freeing will also occur within me.

It is true that Shakespeare, his text, and I never become identical, and there is thus some sort of world "outside" Shakespeare in which some of "me" will be found, even in the most respectful reading—and vice versa. But it is equally true that, in some moments of my reading, Shakespeare enters me totally: which is to say, the questions he would want his ideal spectator to ask, and the inferences he would want his ideal spectator to make, are in fact made mine. (The point here is more easily made about music, because music does not offer me as many invitations to create epicycles of meaning on my very own; when I am listening well, totally engrossed in the musical moment, Bach and I—the implied Bach and the postulated listener—become indistinguishable.)

When I converse with any text, and when I ask my readers to converse with my text, the kinds of questions and answers exchanged will now no longer be classified on the intrinsic-extrinsic axis. Instead we shall want to know: Who asks the questions and who is expected to reply? And we do not assume that either text or reader is privileged; all rights must be earned. Some of the most important criticism will, like much of Burke or Barthes, deliberately violate the text's demands, and some will be slavishly respectful of them; but both violation and respect will occur *in* the reader, among various texts *in* him, and of course *in* and with the help of a culture that can affect the outcome only insofar as it lives in him.

Questions and Responses Insisted Upon by the Text

There are—are there not?—certain questions and responses that any text demands of every reader, and there are other questions and responses—many of which I shall insist on asking—that the text declares "inappropriate" or "improper."

"Once upon a time there were three little pigs . . . ." This opening, which is now in us as much as in the text, demands that we ask, at a minimum, "And *then* what happened?" If we refuse to move forward in curiosity about the story, we are setting ourselves against the text's demand, not as something that is only "in the text" but as something that is felt within ourselves. To refuse might be the very best thing in the world for us to do; there is no prior guarantee that a text, taken in terms of its own demands, will be either interesting or harmless. Nor do we claim at any point that discovering what the text demands will always, or often, be easy. All we claim is that it is sometimes possible, often important, and always quite different from insisting upon lines of questioning appropriate to other texts (see below, "Improper Questions").

Here is another opening statement:

> I propose to treat of Poetry in itself and of its various kinds, noting the essential quality of each; to inquire into the structure of the plot as requisite to a good poem; into the number and nature of the parts of which a poem is composed.

Such a beginning "demands" that we ask questions about the truth or accuracy or adequacy or cogency of the promised answers. Again there is no law requiring us to acquiesce. We may prefer, for example, to ask whether the sentences are well formed, or to do a history of the word poetry, in all languages, or to psychoanalyze Aristotle. Or we might even ask, if we wanted to be *very* sophisticated, "How will this *story* turn out? What happens next?"

And here is another:

> In the noble statue that has been erected to Richard Baxter at Kidderminster—the scene of his most splendid and enduring triumphs—the preacher's upraised hand is pointing to the skies. In that mute gesture there is a subtle touch of spiritual genius. For Richard Baxter is the most compelling and most victorious evangelist that England ever produced. "It is," as Dr. Alexander Grosart points out, "no exaggeration to affirm that this one man drew more hearts to the great Broken Heart than any single Englishman of any age."

Encountering this text at the beginning of a chapter, "Richard Baxter's Text," in a book called *A Faggot of Torches*,[1] every reader quickly infers (though the inference, if traced, would prove extremely complex) that the text is asking for religious commitment. There is only one question it would raise: Will you resist Christian Truth or not? Since, with regard to what follows, there are many questions (e.g., Is it well made?) that cannot be answered without recognizing that prior question (even if one rejects its monolithic demand), it is unlikely that any reader who does not discover that demand—regardless of where his own critical preferences lead—will earn our attention or teach us much. But it is also unlikely that many of us will want, finally, to ask only the questions that the text insists on.

Even if we pick texts that all of us may want, finally, to attack, we must, if our attack is to be justified, first determine what these wretched texts want of us. Here are two samples:

> They are classy, flashy and splashy. They cater to singles, couples and triples, straights and gays and feys, blacks and whites, the well-shaped or the merely well-heeled—and just about anyone else who yearns to break out of 9-to-5 humdrum into a space-age world of mesmeric lighting, Neronian decor and, of course, music, music, music. They are the new breed of discotheque, moth-gathering hotpots of the urban night. Discomania is the latest passion of faddish, fickle American city dwellers, turning daytime Jekylls and Jacquelines into nocturnal and nonmalevolent Hydes and Heidis gyrating through smoke and decibels in a Cinderella world of self-stardom. [*Time Magazine*]

> *It* [a new perfume, named Pheromone] *makes someone want to touch you*. The sense of smell is still the most emotionally arousing of all the senses. In the brain, nerve endings that stimulate the experience of fragrance lie adjacent to those which control basic instincts of pleasure and sex. This is why the whiff of a certain scent can instantly trigger a private memory from long ago. The fragrance-pleasure bond has a clear aphrodisiac quality, suggesting the coming together of two bodies. . . . Pheromone . . . is a spellbinding new affair of earth and spirit. . . . Wear it at your warmest places, with an understanding that heat rises, and that tomorrow's memories begin today.

The questions each of these texts asks me to ask are extremely narrow: Where can I find a discotheque as exciting as that? Where can I buy that perfume? They are obviously less interesting and important than dozens of "improper" questions that I want to ask: What could lead a *Time Magazine* journalist to write like that? Did the ad-folk get their knowledge of pheromones from the same *Scientific American* article I read? How can I teach my undergraduate students what's so awful about such stuff? But, just as obviously, I cannot ask these improper questions unless I am reasonably clear about what the text is asking of me. I cannot even know whether the passages are as abominable as they look unless I know that they are not offering themselves as parody; for if the news magazine's attempt at flashy prose wants me to laugh or if the advertisement is a hoax, my further questions will be entirely different from the ones I will ask if both pieces are what they appear to be.

The five invitations, ranging from nursery tales through Aristotle to ad-talk, clearly differ in the sorts of questions that they (or, what is at this point the same thing, their implied authors, or, what is also the same thing, the part of me that re-creates them) would declare appropriate. The questions arise *in us,* finding us ready to be moved in many diverse directions. We all share an inescapable sense that texts' demands differ, that notions of what kind of questioning is essential or proper or appropriate will shift from text to text. Since one of the great resources for life is this immensely rich and various heritage of different experiences based on different questions, we shall surely require that any critic who chooses to reduce this variety to one or two unvarying questions should earn the right to do so by the additional riches his uniform procedures reveal.

Even if we complicate matters by considering a text that seems by its nature to demand responses of widely diverse kinds, the point still remains that *boundaries* of "appropriateness" are set by the text as it moves in us. Consider, for example, whatever you see as the most ambiguous or "open" work you know—Beckett's *The Unnamable,* perhaps, or Derrida's *Glas.* However indeterminate the work, it will still ask us to rule out certain inappropriate questions. *Glas,* for example, which is difficult to classify according to any traditional literary or philosophical category, insists that we *not* ask it to answer the Three Little Pigs kind of question ("Who will do what to whom?"). It also insists that we finally reject such questions as "In what traditional literary genre shall I place you?"

It is important to underline the universality of this kind of demand. It is true that different readers will infer different boundaries (or "horizons") of appropriate questions, depending on their previous experiences and their critical presuppositions. But about what we might call the text's central preoccupations there is an astonishing agreement among us all; that is what makes it possible for us to use generic terms without total confusion: fairy story, religious homily, philosophical essay, history, imagist poem, comic novel, lyric—and on through hundreds, perhaps thousands of vague but by no means meaningless labels with which we make do. That there are modern texts that defy conventional labels should not obscure the point: their central preoccupation is precisely to defy conventional labels. Much has been made by recent critics, hailing the replacement of the author by the reader, of the impossibility of "decoding" modern works written by several authors or by stochastic or aleatory devices, or by writers from Mallarmé on who deliberately violate—so the claim runs—all generic or normal expectations. "What constitutes the Text," Barthes says, contrasting *text* with the old conception of literary *work,* is precisely "its subversive force in respect of the old classifications. How do you classify a writer like Georges Bataille? Novelist, poet, essayist, economist, philosopher, mystic? The answer is so difficult that the literary manuals generally prefer to forget about Bataille, who, in fact, wrote texts, perhaps continuously one single text."* In fact? We invite you to continue, as you do, with the effort to tell us what *in fact* Bataille's text lays down as its demands upon us.

By putting things in this way we have thus bypassed, at least for a time, the dispute about whether texts have a single determinate meaning. We have substituted the rather different double claim: different texts come alive in us in different ways and thus insist on different boundary conditions for our "appropriate" questions or responses. Some texts will try to set a single direction of questioning, and some will not. But *all* texts try to present boundary conditions which all experienced readers will recognize. Whether the readers choose to *honor* the boundaries is an entirely different question.

"Improper" Questions

Here we leap, as it were, to the opposite rim of what I will not call the hermeneutical circle. No reader of any experience and integrity will always stop at the text's self-proclaimed boundaries. I will no more accede to all the demands of *Mein Kampf* or *Justine* than to the demands of the con man's text when it insistently rules out the question "Are you lying?" That question is totally "inappropriate" to every forgery; yet, if I do not insist on asking it, I shall be gulled.

We are thus led to two marks of the good reader or critic: reconstruction of what the text demands and recognition of the point at which violation of its demands will prove necessary, or at least more fruitful or less harmful, than a ready compliance.

At this point my defense of understanding in chapter 5 comes to seem problematical: it works within a narrower domain than I thought, because I must recognize how often I myself insist on deliberate "misreading"—that is, imposition of *my* questions—in order to *over*stand. It is still true that the violations we respect most will be based on a preliminary act of justice and understanding: I know what *you* want, you words there on the page (and now in my mind),

---

*Roland Barthes, *Image/Music/Text: Essays*, selected and translated by Stephen Heath (New York: Hill and Wang, 1977), p. 157. First published as "De l'oeuvre au texte," *Revue d'esthétique* 3 (1971). It should be emphasized that when Barthes contrasts "work" and "text," he necessarily arrives at a definition of the latter much narrower than mine: his text, though it may at first seem to burst all bonds and violate all categories, is in fact one particular instance of what I am calling texts.

implying as you do a community of norms and a sharing of goals. I have attended to you, I *understand* you—*and* I hereby repudiate, or correct, or deplore, or explain, or attack you in terms that you had either ignored or had hoped to repress.*

Implicit in all this is an inherent and inescapable plurality of critical strategies. Under Questions and Responses Insisted Upon by the Text, we were faced with (having ourselves brought them to life) an almost unbelievably rich variety of texts insisting on diverse questions, broader than any reader's limits; and under Improper Questions we suddenly confront the vast range of interests that readers will bring to, and want to impose on, a given text. But we readers should never forget that the richness of our repertory on any occasion will in large part depend on how many other texts we have respected and absorbed in the past.

What do you have to say, you seemingly innocent child's tale of three little pigs and a wicked wolf, about the culture that preserves and responds to you? About the unconscious dreams of the author or folk that created you? About the history of narrative suspense? About the relations of the lighter and the darker races? About big people and little people, hairy and bald, lean and fat? About triadic patterns in human history? About the Trinity? About laziness and industry, family structure, domestic architecture, dietary practice, standards of justice and revenge? About the history of manipulations of narrative point of view for the creation of sympathy? Is it good for a child to read you or hear you recited, night after night? Will stories like you—*should* stories like you—be allowed when we have produced our ideal socialist state? What are the sexual implications of that chimney—or of this strictly male world in which sex is never mentioned? What about all that huffing and puffing? What porridge had John Keats, and how many children *did* Lady Macbeth have?

Surely no one, not even the most ardent intentionalist, will insist that *all* questions of this sort be banned from legitimate criticism. No critic of any power will allow all works to determine the list of

---

*It is perhaps important to make clear that in adopting the language of violation I do not mean to accept the notion, made popular by Barthes, that somehow the pleasures of violation are superior to those of loving surrender, nor the notion that to ask and answer appropriate questions is necessarily a more passive work than imposing one's predetermined questions. It is really romantic tosh to assume that playing "one's own" games with Shakespeare or Homer, or even Balzac, is more blissful or more active than the exhilarating task of attempting to meet their demands. See Roland Barthes, *The Pleasure of the Text*, trans. Richard Miller (New York: Farrar, Straus & Giroux, 1975), pp. 51 ff. (First published 1973.)

questions allowed. Some works—perhaps most—deserve in fact to be
wiped out with the simple improper question, "Are you any good?"

Yet obviously no one will, except perhaps in theory, embrace *all*
such improper questions as valid or even interesting. It is thus useful
to distinguish improprieties according to what is violated and according to the source of validation that the critic offers for the violation.

Violations of Common Knowledge (of Data)

What I mean by "common knowledge" is very much like what we
found Crane discussing under "common sense," the totality of what
all experienced readers or viewers would recognize as in some sense
"there," regardless of where they locate the text. Or it might be
thought of as what Kenneth Burke knows he is violating when he
plays with the transformation of "Beauty is Truth" into "body is
turd." Every criticism will in one way or another acknowledge that
we all have, and can come to share, a great body of knowledge *about* a
work, or *in* it, quite independently of any critical theories we hold.

It is common knowledge among all who deal seriously with, let us
say, *Coriolanus* (whether they mention the knowledge or not) that it
was written sometime between 1600 and 1610 (to play it extremely
safe); that it is "based on" Plutarch's "Life"; that it has never been as
popular as several other tragedies by Shakespeare but has somehow
maintained a degree of life on the stage down to the present; that it
has always been considered as *somehow* among the tragedies but that
its inclusion among them has generally been thought problematical or
troublesome; and that (to turn to a different sort of data) it begins with
a scene between Roman citizens and ends with Coriolanus slain by
Aufidius, who then says, "My rage is gone, / And I am struck with
sorrow.... / Though in this city he / Hath widowed and unchilded
many a one, / Which to this hour bewail the injury, / Yet he shall have
a noble memory. / Assist."

And so one could go on, listing innumerable pieces of data that,
since everyone who reads the play and thinks about it knows them,
might place constraints on theories about *Coriolanus*. If we think of
"information" under the cliché of "bits" that could be programmed
into a computer, the amount of information about *Coriolanus* shared
by all serious critics, regardless of their theories, is staggering, ranging from dictionary meanings of terms to large-scale patterns of experience.

Most of this information will be irrelevant to any one critic's endeavor or, rather, will seem so until it is violated or questioned by some other critic. It is thus depended on, in some remote sense, by all criticism, even the most revolutionary. Thus even such controversial works as *Coriolanus* are shared by all as a hard base of uncontested data—data that are surrounded by what *is* contested. When someone proposes a new reading, it is always clear from the way the case is argued and from the way others respond that, though something that was thought established is now being questioned, much more is still assumed as uncontested and uncontestable: it is in fact to this latter, as "data," as well as to a critical theory, that the critic appeals in arguing for any novel interpretation.

Almost everybody knows all this, though some talk as if it were not so. To write criticism at all presupposes it. Debate among proponents of conflicting modes never denies that critical theories must *somehow* be constrained by some form of public knowledge that does not depend only on the assumptions of any one mode (except of course among "utter" skeptics, and by their own terms we need not take them here into account: either they are right, and every statement is meaningless, including whatever they might say here, or they are wrong). The surest sign of the universal respect for such knowledge is that everyone claims to have it. Even the most outrageous violators always imply that they know everything that is undeniable about the work; you will look a long time in critical debate before you find anyone saying, "It is true that I did not know how the play turns out" or "I cannot see why it matters that I read only the last chapter and thought it was written two hundred years after its actual date."

Critics will nevertheless differ greatly in their way of handling such common data. Some will see their task as increasing it, some as disseminating it to a wider audience, some as correcting it, some as producing shock by contradicting it. Perhaps the largest number take most of it for granted; to discuss it would be boring. But no critic admits to incompetence in seeing what all who can see will see. Harold Bloom, for example, hails the critical act of "strong" readers as a "misreading or misprision," yet he would be stricken if anyone took him to suggest that he does not see all that the *weak* readers see.[2] Thus most violators of common knowledge recognize it as common knowledge, if only tacitly; like Burke, playing with meanings that "everyone knows" Keats did not intend (p. 106, above), or Barthes, playing with *paradoxa* that violate the *doxa* that "everyone knows,"[3] all mavericks insist that they know what it would mean to join the herd.

Violations of Danda

The consequence is that most violations are of something else entirely; they violate what, following Stephen C. Pepper, I shall call *danda*. Pepper distinguishes data, which are indubitable, in the sense that all experienced observers confirm their existence, from danda, which seem indubitable, or at least demonstrable, to observers working within the coherent structure of interpretation provided by a given mode. Whether we choose to say that even the data shared by all modes are in some sense made by the observers and are not simply given by a world somehow "out there," danda are clearly the product of a given mode and are thus not shared by all modes, however obvious they may seem to those who observe them.

Suppose I want to know whether a certain chair is strong enough to take a man's weight. I may sit in it myself. Perhaps I sit in it several times, taking this posture and that and dropping down in it with some force. And then, to be quite sure, I ask several of my friends to try sitting in it. If we all agree that the chair supports us firmly, we may feel justified in believing that the chair is a strong chair.

Or I may use another method. I may examine the relevant facts about the chair. I may consider the kind of wood it is made of, the thickness of the pieces, the manner in which they are joined together, the nails and the glue employed, the fact that it was made by a firm that for many years has turned out serviceable furniture, the fact that the chair is an item of household furniture at an auction and shows evidence of wear as if many people had successfully sat in it, and so on. Putting all this evidence together, I should again feel justified in believing that the chair is a strong chair.

Whichever I do, my belief is clearly based on a cumulative corroboration of evidence. But the nature of the corroboration differs with the two methods employed. In the first trial, it consists in what may be roughly called a repetition of the same fact. I agree with myself in many repeated observations, and my friends agree with me that the chair was strong. In the second, the corroboration comes from an agreement of many different facts in the determination of the nature of one central fact. In the first, the persuasive force of the corroboration comes from the number of observations and even more from the number of men who agree about them. It is a social force. In the second, the persuasive force comes from the massiveness of convergent evidence upon the same point of fact. It is the structural force of the evidence itself and is not peculiarly social.

The first method seems to be predominantly one of observation; the second, one of hypothesis. This is roughly correct, though the further criticism is carried the less does this distinction count, and at the very end the situation appears almost reversed. The highly refined data are observations sharpened to so fine an edge that the highly refined danda seem to contain much more observation.[4]

Simplifying Pepper somewhat, we can say that all observations about *Coriolanus* that survive all criticism, from whatever mode, can be called data; whatever seems demonstrable only from within a mode of correlating evidence can be called danda. Moreover, it is the nature of criticism that much of what some critics see as data, indubitable from any point of view, will seem from other critical viewpoints not data but danda—facts that have been constituted by the hypotheses and methods of a given mode. Even the theorists who argue that there *are* no raw facts in this sense, since all facts are made or "taken" by the form of our thought rather than "given" by nature or subjects, will distinguish somehow between observations available to all or most inquirers and those that seem accessible only to those who work within one particular theory.*

Pepper distinguishes empirical from logical data: on the one hand, the pointer readings of physics, which all theories must take into account; on the other, the logical transitions among propositions that are "so simple and obvious that any and all men observing them will agree that they are legitimate" (p. 58). The same distinction applies to danda, which are accepted as fact or logical deduction only by those who have already accepted the structure of hypothesis and method that corroborates data by interrelating them. Pepper sees the drive for such "structural corroboration" as never stopping "until it reaches unlimited scope," that is, until it can explain everything in the universe constituted by the system.

We can see immediately that much controversy among critics takes place in the following form: What *you* take as a datum is *really* only a dandum—something which is "there," all right, in your sense, but *only* in your sense: your system has constituted it in order to complete the system.

An active pluralism will reconstitute all such controversies. We tell ourselves: Since any one critical mode will inevitably leave out, ignore, or distort the danda revealed by other modes, I *must* respect

---

*Perhaps I should make explicit what is implicit throughout, since distinctions are multiplying: that both understanding and overstanding make use of both data and danda. The two distinctions cut in quite different ways.

many modes if I am not to reduce the wonderful variety of human achievement—of both "literary" and critical texts—to the monotony of perceptions dictated by one particular mode.

By the same token, many of the most interesting and valuable critics will seem to most other critics to violate danda that are indubitable. Suppose my mode leads me to study *Coriolanus* closely as a problem in construction, as Crane might do, and to conclude that it is indeed the tragedy of Coriolanus, a character who, by historical convention, presented singular difficulties to a playwright trying to realize tragic potentialities. I then offer you, as hard data, my own emotional experience of tragic catharsis. But your mode leads you to see an author wrestling with problems of politics and class, or with problems of sex and family, or, if you are unusually inventive, with the four kinds of motive that Burke distinguishes in *Coriolanus*: nation, class, family, individual. I can say to Burke, "But you have ignored all this rich data about how Shakespeare insists, with his formal artistry, on our sympathy for Coriolanus even while insisting on his faults." And he can say in reply, "But your passion for formal questions has led you to overlook even so obvious a fact as that Coriolanus is a scapegoat figure embodying four 'overlapping loci' where motives play out their conflict."[5]

It is commonly said by theorists of knowledge that the existence of many theories in conflict is a sign of immaturity in any science. A plurality of conflicting theories can exist only when the constraints of agreed-upon data are so loose that differing accounts can fit. As the data increase, the constraints increase, and some theories get lopped off from the list of "possibles"; theoretically there comes a time when, with some kind of crucial experiment or observation, all theories but one can be falsified; truth then triumphs.

> The early theories [about the origin of the solar system] were devised to explain only a few observations.... These few facts provided few constraints on theory, and so the theories proliferated. In just the past three decades the situation has changed dramatically. We have a vast amount of new information that imposes additional and powerful constraints on any theory.[6]

The monistic assumptions supporting such practice have seemed to work well in the natural sciences, at least until recently. In contrast, we who hope to explain or praise humanistic objects—people, poems, constitutions, symphonies—are driven into pluralism because theories about them will never be reduced, by the sheer force of crucial data, to one. Too many of our data are danda. Except in disciplines like bibliography, in which unambiguous questions can be asked, what we study is immeasurably more complex than anything studied by the natural sciences. All of our "objects" bear multiple and irresolvable relations with the perspectives of those who observe them. When I study *Coriolanus*, I am at the same time studying myself: two complexities are in complex interchange. And when I read Burke's extensive chapter on *Coriolanus* in *Language as Symbolic Action*, I study not just the play and myself but also Burke: now we have three immense complexities, or, if we distinguish Burke's temperament from his mode, four.

There is simply no way to tell anyone that curiosity about any one of these complexities is illegitimate. Indeed, we will presumably want to learn as many different kinds of things about *Coriolanus*, about the man who wrote it, and about the people who enjoy it as there are valued dimensions in life. Any effort to reduce these kinds to one, any drive toward a supreme, unified language of all the human sciences, is not only doomed to fail; it is radically opposed to the nature of what is being studied.

Almost all critics now at work would presumably agree, in theory, with some such assertion as this about richness and complexity and the resulting multiplicity of perspectives. But practice is another matter. In tone and in treatment of rivals, we find a predominance of the kind of monism I described in chapter 1.

Idiosyncrasy as a Source of Violation

When we turn from what is violated to the sources of improper questions, we must distinguish sharply between the questions that spring from modes (or what we might call modal habits, like those I have just described) and those that spring from personal idiosyncrasies or private associations. The latter can be among our most precious critical possessions when the personality originating them is sufficiently powerful. This is perhaps the truth underlying the claims, more frequent in our time than ever before, that criticism is an art rivaling or duplicating the art of novelists or poets or dramatists, that there is really no difference between the creative artist and the critic. Some critics are, like Samuel Johnson or Burke or Roland Barthes, so interesting in themselves that their own fancies, however irrelevant or contradictory to data or danda, can rival the works they comment on. Who would not prefer Johnson or Coleridge, striding roughshod over poets' intentions to make their original points, to Professor W. C. McSlavish, with his careful reconstruction of what *he* thinks Shakespeare must have "meant"?

Most candidates for a list of such critics write novels, plays, or poems as well as criticism, and most of them practice criticism in extremely loose-jointed modes: they are never noted for consistency or easy coherence. Their genius often proves exasperating to systematic critics, who try to discover a system or mode underlying their diverse operations; they resist labels. At the same time, their brilliance naturally attracts imitators, and, since there is no systematic learning to be passed along, the world finds itself having to deal with hordes of little Samuel Johnsons or T. S. Eliots, working to convince the world by their obiter dicta that criticism is all simply a matter of bad taste.

The limits of such personal violations are thus not in any simple sense set by "the text" but by ordinary human probabilities. The chances are high that any one critic's private sources of impropriety will, on the average, be average. The individual critic, unaided by schooling, undisciplined by a mode, disrespectful of a text, usually turns out to say about what any of us might have expected, and his violations are thus rarely useful to others, except perhaps to the sociologist of criticism and the historian of taste. Often they are worse than useless; for when the violator is possessed of powers visibly inferior to those that made the text, anyone looking at the exchange can see that the critic has lost a chance to be remade into something more.

Modes as a Source

Three points about modal sources are immediately clear: (1) they vary greatly in the degree of deliberate or unconscious violation they encourage; (2) they vary in the proportions of variety and monotony in their results; and (3) any given text will yield itself more readily to some modal violations than to others.

All fully developed modes will inevitably be able to "handle" any text; if they could not, critics would not develop them and offer them as finished candidates for the degree of Master of Literature. Ronald Crane's interest in how texts are made and whether they are made well cannot be confined to authors of a certain kind: by definition every text will be welcomed. Similarly, nothing would surprise me more than to hear Kenneth Burke say about any new text, "Oh, dear

me: here is one that leaves my dramatistic pursuit of motives speech-
less." No Freudian critic will stand helpless before even the leanest,
purest image; no Marxist will find himself having to confess impo-
tence when faced by a text that to me may seem devoid of all political
or class reference.

This universal applicability of each mode tends to obscure from its
practitioners its special difficulties and weaknesses. Though such
variables are best treated in the kind of detailed discussion I attempted in chapters 2–4, some generalizations are possible about each
of the three points of variation.

1. I have earlier said almost enough about degrees of intentional
violation of intentions. But it is important to underline the complete
independence of two variables: the actual *degree* of violation and the
critic's conscious *intent* to violate. Ronald Crane, pursuing an ideal of
no violation whatever, thought of his criticism as the only kind that
treated the text quite literally in terms of its own demands. Yet surely
to impose on *Persuasion* or *Tom Jones*, say, Crane's kind of question
about formal relations and relative excellence of construction is to
violate those texts in obvious ways; neither work demands that we
compose elaborately argued, solemn essays demonstrating excellence, relating either parts to wholes or whole works to other novels.
They ask us to experience them as fictions, not to analyze and rank
them.

My elaborate argument about the various versions of Auden's
"They Are and Suffer" can be seen, now, not simply as a violation of
Auden's final intentions—my choice of his earlier version over his
mature judgment—but as a violation of *both* versions, neither of
which can be said to request (to continue the personification) a comparison with any other work. Curiously enough, we see here a sharp
contrast between questions that *authors* might consider impertinent
and questions that in fact violate their *texts*; Auden would presumably not consider my questions about the comparative value of two
versions impertinent; he raised them himself with his revision. But
each of his *texts*, considered on its own terms, insists only on our
respecting it as it is. Similarly, though we can conjecture that Jane
Austen might view Crane's formal questions as less impertinent to
her own concerns than, say, the criticism of a Freudian, *Persuasion*
itself will want to say, as it were, "All of that formal analysis has been
determined by your mode, not by me."

From this point of view, we are not much helped when critics
openly confess, unlike Crane, that they are violating intentions.

As we saw, Roland Barthes, in one phase, could happily talk of liberating three authors, Sade, Fourier, and Loyola, from the limitations imposed by their respective interests in sadism, utopia, and religion:

> Reading texts and not books, turning upon them a clairvoyance not aimed at discovering their secret, their "contents," their philosophy, but merely their happiness of writing, I can hope to release Sade, Fourier, and Loyola from their bonds (religion, utopia, sadism); I attempt to dissipate or elude the moral discourse that has been held on each of them; working, as they themselves worked, only on languages, I unglue the text from its purpose as a guarantee: socialism, faith, evil.[7]

In contrast, Serge Doubrovsky (and Barthes himself in one phase) would insist that the text's intentions must in some sense be honored,[8] yet it is clear that in practice the "text" is being defined in a very broad sense by a critical mode and that, in our terms, violations are being openly encouraged, not, as with Crane, condemned.

Thus the question of whether this or that critical practice is more alien to the *text's* intentions is immensely complex; assertions like Crane's (and mine) that we respect intentions will always be vulnerable to the simple question: "Why is it that only critics of one school ever *think* of discussing such questions?" The only answer must be, not that the questions are foolish or destructive, but that they have been generated by a mode.

2. It follows inevitably (and should thus need little discussion) that modes and the danda they uncover will vary greatly in the amount of diversity or uniformity they seek and yield. Some modes openly seek what amounts to the same conclusion in all inquiries, the only variety being not in the goal but in the road traveled. Thus the explicit aim of Barthes in the work just cited is to show that three authors whom we have always thought of as radically different really produce "the same writing," since they have "the same sensual pleasure in classification, the same mania for cutting up..., the same enumerative obsession..., the same image practice..., the same erotic, fantasmatic fashioning of the social system" (p. 3).

Fortunately, when Barthes gets down to work, he often seems to forget this monotonous program and "lapses" into a sensitive respect for the differences among his chosen writers. He is also saved from monotony by being blessed with an inventive mind; in our earlier terms, his idiosyncrasies are often at least as interesting as those of the authors he is talking about, although he was perhaps generous with himself in choosing three "monotonous" dogmatists like Sade, Fourier, and Loyola—writers who in a sense cry to the reader: "Liberate me!" He competes less well with Balzac in *S/Z*, and least well with Racine.[9]

In contrast, some modes, like Abrams', protect the critic (and the reader) from knowing in advance where they will come out.

3. It also follows—since the world is full of an actual wild diversity of texts—that, regardless of our choice of mode, we will find some texts yielding more readily than others to any chosen form of violation. A well-made play may seem obviously suited to elaborate formal analysis. Robbe-Grillet's novels and movies seem equally well suited to those who wish to show that texts are infinitely deconstructible. Somewhat less obviously, *Mein Kampf* yields readily to Burke's pursuit of moral and political motives that Hitler would prefer to conceal. At the opposite extreme, a "self-destructing" work of modern art may seem totally resistant to formal analysis, and a couplet by Pope may seem firmly "undeconstructible." But we can now see why such degrees of resistance to modal violations neither can nor should be allowed to determine the questions a critic asks.

As I have said earlier, some have argued that the goal of pluralism should be to discover a proper match between text and mode.[10] The pursuit of such true marriages can yield one good kind of criticism. But it is often more profitable to pursue violations. Apply Crane or the Russian formalists to the well-made play or to a detective story and you may get dull results, a simple restatement of what every reader half-knows already. Apply them to *Tristram Shandy*[11] or Ionesco's *Rhinoceros*, and you may learn something.

Thus modal data—that is, danda—can range, just like idiosyncratic inventions, from shocking to dull, from fruitful to repetitive, depending on the quality of the source and the tact of its application. The mode itself may be inherently dull, or it may have been too thoroughly exploited. Fashions in modes are partly caused by overmining. Suddenly we all look up from our tracing of historical sources, or, twenty years later, from our *Explicators*, and say to each other, "You know, I just don't want to read another study like that for a long time." But modal pursuits are far less likely to peter out than merely personal minings. Since modes are larger and richer than their practitioners, they can—or at least the better ones can—educate even the "average" sensibility. Just as subjecting myself to Shakespeare, allowing his work to dominate what I say about him, can to some degree raise my imagination to the point of learning something to teach other readers, so subjection to a mode can to some degree improve my powers of observation and my capacity to relate data to generalization.

We talk so much about the harm done by systematizers that we tend to forget this value. We romanticize the contributions of the free spirits who simply respond and report their responses, and we forget both the immense dullness of most unschooled responses (because they can give us no more than we already have in our public data bank or what, though "original," is dull or useless) and the invaluable gifts we have all received from whatever modes we have learned to use (usually identical with whatever "school" we were trained in).

In any case, it should be clear by now that modal pluralism leads to an expanded repertory of modes that are capable of liberating us in precisely this way. Not any old mode will do, because many of them are incapable of leading their practitioners to better observations and generalizations than they could have made on their own. By "better" we of course imply, by now, a fairly long list of criteria. The better modes do no *unintentional* violence to common knowledge (they either respect the demands of the text or give good reasons for whatever violence is done). They uncover valued danda concealed, or not easily revealed, by other modes. They can be taught to others in ways that serve critical vitality; that is, they represent a genuine body of communicable knowledge about how to do a kind of work. And so on.

Using such tests, loose and unwieldy as they are, we can see now how it is that some modes put a heavier burden of proof on their would-be detractors than others do. Any mode that has won the enthusiastic adherence of large numbers of intelligent critics has already passed one of the tests, and when I approach that mode, whether for the first or hundredth time, *I* am being tested more than the mode. One reads everywhere these days the sound epigram, "I do not read Shakespeare; he reads me," but the same can be said of any great critical mode. My limitations are tested—and, if I am fortunate, reduced—by encountering any great mode as practiced by even an average critic.

But where, then, does this leave me with the deconstructive modes that I have questioned? In the first place, it leaves me aware that I have so far done little more than violate their own texts. I have simply not yet managed the act of full re-creative sympathy toward any one of them that I attempted with my three pluralists. Thus I must go on inquiring about them rather than rest satisfied that I have shown them up. At the same time, I now have a right to be radically skeptical about their own dogmatic statements of universal competence or "totalization." The exclusivities and necessities that sprinkle their pages I can now translate into hypotheticals; and when (as I now find, for example, in rereading Paul de Man) repeated experience yields increasing insight, I can add his danda to the potential riches of my world.

Violation as Respect, Respect for Violation

Taught first by Burke and then by the new overstanders, I can now reconsider other critics who seem, at first encounter, to be violating the text in outrageous ways. Since we no longer see violation of the text's demands as necessarily based on misunderstanding it, since in fact the very act of understanding many a text is what will lead to asking "improper" questions and finally rejecting its demands, we can now not only tolerate but insist on modes that remind us how stultifying routine respect for texts can be. And we can now see why various "reader-criticisms" should inevitably have arisen as a reaction against the heavy and uncritical emphasis on the autonomous text placed by some versions of academic scholarship and some versions of New Criticism.[12] We will still find good reason to repudiate many examples of reader-criticism and in doing so will violate, as it were, their authors' intentions; but we will not do so because of their intentional violations of intentions.

When we look beneath the surface of many of the new liberation movements, we find, as I showed in chapter 5, that fear of stasis is supreme. You who argue for a single reading would silence *me*, would make my reading illegitimate, would close down the enterprise. It is not just that you would make it pointless for me to *publish* my own active and distinctive responses; you would make it impossible for me to *have* them. Thus it is that Norman Holland expresses a passionate desire to preserve for all readers the legitimacy of their own active engagement and feels that, to do so, he must reject René Wellek's placement of the poem as a system of norms. Wellek's theory that the poem is "a structure of norms, realized only partially in the actual experience of its many readers," stems, Holland suspects,

> as much from a desire to honor literature and to abase oneself before its beauty or power as from a need for explanation. That is, we surround the aesthetic transaction with an almost religious aura when we call ourselves the imperfect, incomplete experiencers of something that goes beyond what any one human

could experience or when we say that we are "always" the inadequate performers of a superhuman duty the literary work im-
poses. Such a view, moreover, blurs reason and observation with
obscurity; it subordinates the lively and human appreciation of
human achievement to something transhuman. It puts literature
on a pedestal.

Such a view, he goes on, instead of hailing the variety of readers'
responses as a rich critical resource, will reduce all difference to
"some aberration, some failure on the readers' part."[13]

My own notion of a just community of readers trying—among
other things—to understand each other would lead to a similar insistence that readers' differences be not just respected but cultivated; but
it would multiply richness even further, for the reader we seek to
propagate is one who is so active, so broadly experienced, so thoroughly "possessed" by texts previously understood that his very
individuality, no longer idiosyncrasy, will teach us not only something about himself but something about the text and the world. We
defend active reading both as an end in itself and as a means to the
propagation of active readers, and both ends require readers committed to justice rather than indiscriminate killing. Understanding
is a first step toward whatever overstanding is to be added to our
joint exchange.

Texts and modes for dealing with them will die unless each generation of readers can learn both the arts of recovering what texts
demand and the arts of seeing through, judging, repudiating, trans-
forming, and re-creating texts—in short, of appropriating them in
"inappropriate" ways.

Thus the meaning-multipliers that I rejected (insofar as they repudiated the desirability of understanding) now reenter the scene,
offering to give direction to our inquiry. If we ignore their polemic
against the effort to understand (since it is either directed at straw
men or assumes what we cannot surrender, the desirability and possibility of understanding), we can follow them into whatever
labyrinth they enter, hoping to discover new illumination at the end.

Whatever we discover, we shall still find plenty to quarrel about:
what criticism is *for*, how traditions should be honored or violated,
whether Western culture is really a unitary bourgeois monster that
has us in its maw, whether a given cultural scene requires more overstanding than understanding. But at least we shall have freed ourselves from pointless monistic disputes about *the* proper method for
pursuing such differences.

Once the Author is removed, the claim to decipher a text becomes quite futile.... The birth of the reader must be at the cost of the death of the Author.—Roland Barthes

A man is necessarily talking error unless his words can claim membership in a collective body of thought.—Kenneth Burke

The significance of the Mass. As biological organisms, we must all, irrespective of sex, age, intelligence, character, creed, assimilate other lives in order to live. As conscious beings, the same holds true on the intellectual level: all learning is assimilation. As children of God, made in His image, we are required in turn voluntarily to surrender ourselves to being assimilated by our neighbors according to their needs.

The slogan of Hell: Eat *or* be eaten.
The slogan of Heaven: Eat *and* be eaten.—W. H. Auden

For Books are not absolutely dead things, but doe contain a potencie of life in them to be as active as that soule was whose progeny they are: nay they do preserve as in a violl the purest efficacy and extraction of that living intellect that bred them.... As good almost kill a Man as kill a good Book; who kills a Man kills a reasonable creature, Gods Image; but hee who destroyes a good Booke, kills reason it selfe, kills the Image of God, as it were in the eye.... A good Booke is the pretious lifeblood of a master spirit, imbalm'd and treasur'd up on purpose to a life beyond life.... We should be wary therefore ... how we spill that season'd life of man preserv'd and stor'd up in Books.—John Milton

Our Many
Different Businesses
with Art

In defending violations of the text's demands, we have at the same time been steadily redefining justice and understanding. The reciprocity of the two terms becomes clearer as we go: just "violations" will be those that are based on a prior act of understanding, and understanding will lead to deliberate violation when justice requires it. To understand all is *not* to excuse all.

The danger of arrogance in such a position can be averted only through the most careful attention to what we mean by understanding. Most attempts at critical refutation are no doubt conducted by critics who think they understand the refuted position. Yet we know from personal experience that many refutations, like many "friendly" reconstructions, have little or no relevance to the victim's real position. Thus critics are often like those conversational boors who "understand" everything one says according to some preconceived method of reduction: "I know why you defend Shakespeare with so much heat: you have never worked through your dependence on your father" or "Your attack on pornography obviously springs from your own sexual hangups." Even when such "violations of the text" connect with some genuine motive in the accused person, they bring the conversation to a dead stop (unless the conversation is *about* motives). They reduce debate about reasons (*Why* is [or isn't] Shakespeare preeminent? *Why* is pornography a social evil [or social good]?) to the speaker's motives. Similarly, claims to understand a critic can halt critical dialogue if the "understanding" is in fact a reduction to explanatory terms totally foreign to the views being explained.

That is indeed one kind of critical killing. When I reduce your effort to discuss reasons to a mere expression of irrational forces (your id, your class, your upbringing, your inherited language), I make it impossible for you to reply—except, of course, with similar charges. Criticism stops and reductive vilification begins.

The only kind of "killing" that will finally nurture our enterprise will be based on a different kind of understanding altogether, and it is in pursuing what that might be that we come to our clearest conception of how the life of criticism is best served by a limited pluralism.

Understanding, Once Again

On close examination, my unshaken reliance on understanding, even when understanding fails, seems to depend on rejecting the distinction between my "self" and my critical community. The critical vitality I desire and the critical justice I demand can be enjoyed only to the degree that I live among other critics whose vitality I respect and who have learned to deal justly with each other. Thus even if I think strictly in terms of self-interest, I am driven to pursue critical survival for as many of my fellow critics as possible. And that pursuit will be best served by cultivating the arts of surrendering to other minds— that is, by understanding.

To say this is obviously nonsensical according to some definitions of understanding. What kind of understanding could possibly justify it?

Because the word is almost hopelessly vague, I have sought unsuccessfully for some more precise term for what I have in mind. The *Oxford English Dictionary* lists fourteen distinct meanings for "understand," with many additional subvariants: to understand oneself or a person, an idea, art, statement, fact, or process; and so on. And, as a noun, "understanding" ranges, as indeed one would expect, over the whole of man's effort to apprehend the world and human society. For some, it refers to the total rational faculty that distinguishes us essentially from beasts, a synonym for Aristotle's "reason" or for Burke's "symbol-making and using." Others reduce it to a particular part of the mind or soul, rated from high ("the principall part of the soule," for Sir Thomas Elyot) to low ("the meanest faculty in the human mind, and the most to be distrusted," for De Quincey). And it can of course refer to a simple bargain: "They came to an understanding."

Thus for something or someone to be understood can mean everything from the self-evident ("I take it as understood from the beginning that ... ") to the highly dubious ("What I understood him to mean was ... ").

The understanding we seek is compatible with most of these definitions but not quite with all. It can include both the clear bargain among thieves and the full trust among friends. It is easy in its kinship with everyday expressions about success in comprehension: "They see eye to eye"; "I dig you"; "Oh, I get it"; "I see what you mean"; "I've finally got her figured out"; "They're on the same wavelength." Every language must have scores of such terms, most of them combining claims to intellectual activity and some degree of emotional engagement. Indeed, a surprising number provide for *emphatic* union: "Of course!"; "Obviously!"; "I'll drink to that!"; "Jawohl!"; "Bien sur!"; "Evidamente!" A large proportion imply strong emotional engagement: "Right on!"; "Welcome home!" (as used in argument); "That really grabs me!" On the other hand, when they imply reduction of the person understood to less than a person or when the understanding is solely for the understander's benefit, they take on unpleasant airs: "Stop analyzing me"; "I had him there"; "I see through you"; "Now I know what you're up to"; "He sure took me in"; "She has him eating out of her hand."

The capacity to share such expressions is what makes daily life possible. Everything we say or write, and almost everything we do, depends on our assumption that understanding is possible. Every expression for *mis*understanding logically entails the possibility of success: "You lost me there," "I don't get it," "Come again, please." In developed societies even the elementary functions of eating and defecating depend on understanding and trusting the intentions of other minds: cooks and waiters, designers of toilets and sewage systems. And in all societies, no matter how primitive, the number of actions that are not baptized with human understanding are very few: perhaps certain brute acts—killing when you are hungry, some forms of rape. Even the lone frontiersman, planting crops or setting traps, lives in a medium of inherited understandings; he is rightly confident that he can understand some of the intentions of other human beings.

Warmed by the successes of my empire-building term, still undefined, I might take a last, unnecessary step, without expecting that many will take it with me: the kind of understanding I am now stalking is finally what defines us as human beings. Our ability to understand is presupposed in every definition of man I can think of: man the rational animal; the playing animal; the language-using animal; the economic animal; the laughing animal; the symbol-making and symbol-exchanging animal and thus "inventor of the negative";[1] the animal that makes cultures with meanings;[2] the tool-making animal (though we will now emphasize the capacity to *explain* an invented tool and thus pass it along and improve it); the creature of God who found "his/her" natural state by disobeying a command that presupposed and indeed insisted on understanding.

Drawing back from such unnecessary aggrandizement, and without aspiring to an impossible formal rigor, I must now hazard a stricter definition of the understanding that deserves, for me, such high honors.

Understanding is the goal, process, and result whenever one mind succeeds in entering another mind or, what is the same thing, whenever one mind succeeds in incorporating any part of another mind. *

What is most clearly ruled out by this definition is the identification of understanding with a separate, single faculty of the mind: *"the* understanding." Understanding in my sense must include, true enough, some such coordinating intellective faculty as *the* understanding. We can't engage in a process without having a faculty suited to the process. But it is a communal, not a private, property, and it is not confined to so-called intellectual matters; it includes, for example, much of what some phenomenologists and psychologists mean by *empathy*. Kant argued that the understanding is universal in the sense of being shared by all human beings. The understanding we seek is also enjoyed to some degree by everyone, and it is never isolable in any one mind. No person can have it except in conjunction with at least one other person, living or dead. And it is not so much something people have, a possessed faculty, as it is something people perform or achieve, mind with mind. We cannot quite say, at least in standard English, "I performed understanding with my partner." We do sometimes say, "We achieved (or came to) understanding," as if it were a static state. But obviously we must have *done* it before we could claim to have achieved it.

Though it cannot occur without at least two participants, such understanding need not be strictly mutual: you can understand me even when I am misunderstanding you. But when it becomes mutual, additional wonders come in its wake. Trust, love, productive joint labor, all "rule-bound" playing (whether of a game, a symphony, or a drama), and indeed the day-by-day functioning of any culture—all these depend on making understanding reciprocal.

One modern tradition of individual efforts to understand the world implies an ordering quite different. The lone scientist is pictured in his sterile white coat, a rude, misunderstood Arrowsmith who discovers, by what we call independent thought, a truth which he can communicate only with the greatest difficulty, if at all; or we imagine the lonely artist in his garret, a mad, misunderstood Van Gogh who creates, out of his effort to understand a private vision, new forms

---

*As we all know, materialists have long since proved, and behaviorists have recently proved again, that mind does not exist as something distinguishable from brain. But just for convenience I shall go on using the term, meaning by it whatever the materialists and behaviorists were trying to change when they offered their proof.

that are often incommunicable. It is not difficult to multiply examples of lonely achievement, but romantic accounts neglect to mention that the isolated, suffering hero (these days often a heroine) had necessarily entered a human community of understanding long before the lonely peak was scaled or the blank pages were written in blood. Not autonomy but autism is the fate of any infant who does not learn to perform understanding with at least one other person.

The notions of "entering" another mind, or of incorporating "part" of a mind, are not meant quite so metaphorically here as might at first appear. I cannot remove the metaphorical overtones, since for most moderns to enter a mind literally must somehow require a physical process. In that view the "parts" of a mind are either physical sections of the brain or, at best, functions distinguished in would-be scientific inquiry: the id, ego, and superego, or what not. But I mean a different sort of entering and a different sort of part, intangible but at least as literal as the intangible parts of an atom. If we think of the mind as what is made by symbols* as well as what makes and shares them (most notably in verbal form but also in the "languages" of mathematics, music, painting, etc.), then any symbolic construct I "take in" or "give out" is a part of my mind: $5+7=12$; the sentence I have just written; the joke my friend told me yesterday.[3]

Understanding thus occurs first, and perhaps most undeniably, whenever information is exchanged successfully. I say, "The telephone book is lying on the lowest of the three green tables," and the five-year-old child, unlike any computer we might devise, runs no risk of being sidetracked by the thought that the telephone book "lies" in the sense of "telling untruths," nor will he search-and-scan for some book of statistical "tables." The physics professor puts an equation on the board, an equation that represents a "part" of his mind, and the minds of some students fully incorporate its meaning.

Second, the sharing of information shades imperceptibly into, and

*Also "signs," but that's another and slightly simpler story, of a gift shared, more obviously, with the higher mammals. It should be noted that for our purposes here the quarrel about whether mind and brain are identical is unimportant, though of course my way of raising questions has already determined, by definition, that the mind, as the total coordinating faculty that makes human sharing possible, must be talked about in different terms from those we use for talking about the brain. Forced into brain-talk, we would have to discover, as some have done, that the brain cannot be confined to the cranium. Mind-brain controversies are perennial because (I put it dogmatically but with little confidence) controversialists insist on reducing all languages to one. But it is not at all self-evident that a single language can accommodate all that is worth knowing about the mind/brain. Perhaps human functioning, what used to be discussed with words like psyche or soul, is a bit like the critical universe underlying my pluralistic search: it is quite possibly in some sense "one," but it is so complex that it is available only partially to any one perspective; in short, it is an essentially contested concept.

in fact depends on, an understanding of intentions and motives: "Get me the telephone book." "Did you hear the one about . . . ?" Here the "part" shared is sometimes hard to distinguish from the total person: the mother smiles at the child, and the child, inferring with absolute accuracy the love behind the smile, smiles back with his whole body.[4] Or the part shared can be a fairly impersonal design: I read the instructions for assembling the Christmas toy, and, if I am lucky, I understand; if I am more mechanically gifted, I take in the designer's plan simply by looking at the parts, without recourse to words. Or the part shared can consist of extremely elaborate patterns of inference about the motives and actions of persons real and imaginary: the impassioned reactionary newspaper columnist spends three paragraphs praising the liberal congressman from California, and most of his readers recognize his irony for what it is; Shakespeare writes Othello's recognition scene, and I experience tragedy.

Our capacity to infer intentions is most remarkable when it succeeds in what we might call seeing behind a text or reading between the lines: someone says what he does *not* mean and someone else understands what he *does* mean. It is true that much of our daily talk goes completely astray, because the garbling of channels is carried too far. But if we consider all the outlandish tasks we attempt, our successes surely are among the most mysterious and remarkable events in the universe, and they are completely inexplicable according to most models of communication. Here is a sign from a grocer's wall:

Due to paper shortage
We are to discontinue use
  Doubling bags
  Only when
    it is
        necessary

It takes no very precise grammarian to recognize that the statement "doesn't make sense," but customers have no difficulty with it at all. Though the text is garbled, the intention is simple and clear and utterly accessible. Thus we complete each other's sentences, correct each other's malapropisms and double negatives; we teachers even manage sometimes to tell a student, "What you really mean is so-and-so, though you *say* such-and-such." Though we miss such targets often, each day is filled with many bull's-eyes.

PROFESSOR: As you can see, this whole theory is like the modification of Plato's theory of ideal forms effected by Pistorius . . .

BOLD STUDENT: Plotinus.
PROFESSOR: What?
BOLD STUDENT: You mean Plotinus!
PROFESSOR: I said Plotinus, didn't I?
BOLD STUDENT: No, you said Pistorius.
PROFESSOR: Well, anyway, I meant Plotinus.

We all detect lies, reject advertising hyperbole, figure out what toddlers and babblers want. Most of us can employ and decipher deliberate metaphors and ironies that would throw the cleverest computers into frantic and hopeless searchings and scannings. Yet even the simplest of typos, like the most elaborate of ironies, could not be corrected without our capacity to understand precisely what another person means in contrast to what he has "said."[5]

Without pretending to work through the problems that philosophers of language have encountered in the notions of meaning and reference, it is clear that understanding in our sense provides a referent that is both in some sense independent of the particular text and a final test of our readings. The text I produce does not intend something "out there"—a preexistent reality that you, as reader, must infer behind my words; rather it intends its own understanding, and that, of course, presupposes an understanding of the meaning I was trying to embody in the first place. My intentions-as-inferable-from-the-text (not to be confused with motives that fail to get themselves realized) are only rarely a "meaning" about some reality "signified" by my words as "signifier." Regardless of how closely what I say corresponds to what we take to be independent reality—ranging from "testable by the methods of hard science" to "unverifiable by any known means"—it *makes* a reality that can then be interpreted and so to some degree understood, even when, as in the grocery sign, my words are scrambled. It also offers itself, as it were, to the less tender acts of overstanding that the interpreter may go on to commit; these in turn offer themselves as invitations to understanding. The realities constructed and reconstructed as this process continues are testable, finally, only by the tests of understanding. They are seldom if ever something external to the process, something solid that is reached for in the fluid language of each text. But they are real, nonetheless; the intentions of the grocery-store sign are hard as nails. It is only when texts are torn free of intentions that they become uninterpretable.

Sharing of intentions usually includes, third, strong value judgments: the famous critic leaves the abominable first-night production after Act 1, I predict a damning review, and when the review is in fact hostile I know that I have understood; the ranting political orator leads his auditors into a chant—"Kill the Pigs!"—and knows that their hatred joins his; the teacher of literature, working through "Sunday Morning" with love and patience, finds after a week or so that some students show undeniable signs of hearing and loving the poem and thus of sharing understanding with the poet and the teacher.

Such diverse examples show that, if understanding is always in itself a good thing, this is certainly not because it always serves other ends we would all consider good. Whatever claim to universal value it has must be of another kind.

The word "incorporation" in my definition implies a metaphor of organic growth, a growth that depends on nourishment "taken in" from other minds. In that metaphor we see at least three reasons why "to understand," viewed in this way, is a value for all human beings, and especially for literary critics. (In calling my definition metaphoric I do not in any sense intend to diminish its claim as a true picture of how minds grow together. Mind is not body, but somehow mind is incorporated, and minds thus incorporate each other. Where literalness ends and metaphor begins is impossible to determine, but the borderline is not a line between truth and falsehood.)[6]

First, all minds depend for their life, from birth to death, on other minds. The infant enters the human condition by imbibing it from those around him. The adult survives only by continuing to understand. This is true both literally, or "bodily" (if you misunderstand everyone, you will end quickly in disaster; at the very least you may be put away or, quite possibly, you may die), and figuratively (the mind that stops taking adequate nourishment wastes away). I must pursue understanding lest I perish.[7]

Second, though many do not realize how important understanding is, everyone sees its value for *some* purposes, and no one willingly embraces misunderstanding *for himself* and as an end in itself. We do say, "He deliberately misunderstands," but that always means that, "Pursuing other ends, for which understanding X is unimportant, he is willing to sacrifice an understanding of X—he is willing to violate X's 'text.'" But everyone experiences many moments each day when, whatever his purposes, understanding will be important.

In fact, I can think of no human exchange in which *neither* party has a strong motive to seek understanding. At least one person has reason to regret failure whenever failure comes. It is true, of course, that much of our life is organized to subvert the understanding of others: our society provides astonishing rewards for skillful liars and con men. But to say this says something against our society, not against understanding. It will lead none of us to argue that "liar" and "con man" are neutral, value-free terms. What is more, no con man ever seeks, as he perfects his sting, to misunderstand his mark.

There are two obvious objections to this claim to universal value. First, many theorists deny it. But my way of defining understanding entails, as I argued in chapter 5, that no one can deny it without violating the denial in two ways: by claiming to understand what I am affirming, and by asking me to understand the denial. Second, it is not hard to imagine cases of accidental profit from misunderstanding (in contrast to the deliberate profiteering of many advertisers and politicians). You tell me to meet you in time to catch the nine o'clock plane, I mishear this as "one o'clock," the first plane crashes, and I survive, thanks to misunderstanding; you sell me worthless stock that turns valuable, and I share my winnings with you in mistaken gratitude. But the profit in such cases is never, as it is in understanding, from and in the act of communication itself. What is more, we all experience far more bad consequences of misunderstanding than of understanding.

It is apparent, then, that, even to describe the way we come to have mental activity at all, we must rely on understanding as a universal norm. The universe of discourse issues a supreme command, a moral command about our whole mental life: Thou shalt work to improve the chances of understanding—which is to say: Thou shalt work to further the meeting of minds and thus the making of minds.[8] In one sense it is a command that we cannot disobey; for even those who deny the possibility of understanding cannot choose whether to engage in the making of minds through attempted meetings: they can choose only whether to do it badly or well.

We now can see more clearly why the connections I drew earlier between vitality, justice, and pluralism were at each stage dependent on understanding. I could not possibly consider my pursuit of understanding as even more important than any formulation of truth along my way unless I believed in the existence of a plurality of fully vital critical selves on which I depend for my critical nourishment.

We can also see that it does not matter whether I can incorporate another person's complex meanings totally, so long as the meanings that I can incorporate are in fact nourishing. I need not produce a confident duplication of everything an author says in order to know whether I am fed. It is not even true that my growth depends solely on success in the pursuit of understanding; for I can be stung into thought by gross misunderstanding, and, so long as my *effort* is to understand, I will not remain as I am, satisfied with my present size and shape.

Understanding Five Different "Authors"

To talk in this way presupposes that each reader is many potential readers who depend for actualization on the powers of the text and on the reader's own capacity both to move with it and to know when to resist: "So far and no further; at this point I must reject you, even expose you, show you up for what you are." But it also implies that the concept of "the author" is by no means simple.

Thus no general exhortations for or against authors or intentions can be applied regardless of specific differences from encounter to encounter.[9] (Here we simply duplicate what I have said earlier against general defenses of texts or readers.) We cannot always treat the author as an authority. Not only do many authors obviously not understand their own intentions, either as they make their revisions or as they make critical statements after the event of composition, but many have intentions that must finally be repudiated if we are to serve critical justice and vitality. However, the main reason we cannot treat them as authorities is that we have many different conceptions of "the author," each of them potentially harmful for some critical tasks, helpful for others. If we are to avoid the very faults of monistic freezing that I have deplored, we must undertake, as the final act of plurification, a discrimination among authorities.

WRITERS, DRAMATIZED AUTHORS, IMPLIED AUTHORS, CAREER-AUTHORS, AND PUBLIC "CHARACTERS"

We can distinguish five figures to whom the word "author" is sometimes applied.

There is first a postulated *flesh-and-blood person*, a man or woman who writes only sometimes and who otherwise lives a more or less troubled or happy life. I shall call this "real" person *the writer*. In theory, though seldom in practice, we might want further to distinguish the immeasurably variegated and finally unknown man or woman from the *postulated writer*, the figure made by a public with the help of more or less careful biographers. In a sense not ordinarily useful to critics, the real James Joyce escapes even Richard Ellmann, the real George Eliot escapes even Gordon Haight. Nora Joyce and G. H. Lewes knew them in a way that no document can preserve. It is perhaps fortunate that we usually have available only that more public figure, our "collection of postulates" about a given writer. Though such postulates can get in our way, they can sometimes be immensely useful, as I shall try to show. To know the writer in "real life," on the other hand, is often a barrier to the work itself. Poor Nora could never be expected to appreciate what that man Joyce was up to.

There are, second, *dramatized authors*. Only the most inexperienced readers assume that the "I" who purportedly narrates much fiction, the poet who speaks in all lyrics, or the "author" who intrudes even into some modern drama has any simple or easily discovered relationship with the writer. Such dramatized speakers may, of course, be presented as very close to the writer's own life, or they may be so different as to give almost no aid to the critic who would attempt a biography. No one can say in advance of any act of reading whether its dramatized speakers will reveal anything directly about the writer or, again, whether inferences about the writer must be complex or simple.

Neither the writer nor the dramatized author bears any predeterminate relationship to the *implied author*, the creating person who is implied by the totality of a given work when it is offered to the world. Every stroke implies, inescapably, a kind of person who would choose to make that precise stroke. A scene heightened implies an author who values that kind of heightening. A judgment passed, whether explicitly in commentary or tacitly by the structure of events (who wins, who loses, and why), implies a judge.

The distance between writer and implied author can theoretically range from what is in effect unnoticeable to grotesque disparities. The implied author's virtues and weaknesses may be roughly equivalent to what intimates of the writer come to know or to what he or she writes in a private journal. On the other hand, heroic implied authors can be created by cowards, and generous, tender-spirited implied authors can be created by self-centered monsters. Comic playwrights cough blood while writing joyful denouements; tragedians may create their best scenes of misery when their private lives are finally in sufficient order to permit sustained labor. Readers are often shocked when biographies reveal a Robert Frost, say, whose petty egotism seems entirely foreign to the "Robert Frost" of the poems, or a Mark Twain whose mask as benevolent comedian fits less and less well as his misanthropy grows. But we should not need biographies to reveal such conflicts; they must be present in some degree in every sustained literary effort. Many a writer of theodicies must come to the moment when he moans to friends, "I can't go on." And many a nihilist must rise from his desk after a few hours of creative flow about utter meaninglessness, thinking, "By God, it's been a good day."

This is not the place to extend the analysis of various spokesmen for the implied author offered in *The Rhetoric of Fiction*. Here it should suffice to note that some writers choose to dramatize in the text a narrative voice that speaks explicitly for the implied author's norms: the "I" in most poems by Wordsworth cannot be distinguished from the Wordsworth that we are expected to infer as author of the poem. Other writers create surrogates who cannot be trusted. If we infer that a speaker or reflecting consciousness has been made deliberately un-reliable, we say "ironic" and give the implied author credit (as in Browning's "Mr. Sludge, the Medium," and indeed most dramatic monologues). Usually, if we find an accidental conflict between a narrator and what is implied by the rest of the tale, we blame the implied author, and thus the writer, for botching the job (if in *Bleak House* we find Esther Summerson's view of the world sentimental and decide that Dickens sees it as wholly admirable, we condemn Dickens).

From these three "authors" we can distinguish a fourth, the one pursued openly by most biographers, employed as a tacit concept by most critics, but declared irrelevant by many: the sustained creative center implied by a *sequence* of implied authors. Implied authors may remain fairly constant from one work to another by the same author (as in Jane Austen's novels), or they may vary greatly, as in the extreme case of J. I. M. Stewart, a scholar whose detective stories require an "author" with an entirely different name: Michael Innes. The various implied authors invented as a career develops may be different to the point of seeming to be unrelated persons (compare very early and very late Faulkner) or uniform (e.g., "the incompa-rable Max" Beerbohm, a constant self through most of a lifetime).

Criticism has no term for these sustained characters who somehow are the sum of the invented creators implied by all of the writer's particular works. For lack of a good name, I shall call such a sustained character (still quite different, of course, from the writer, with his quotidian concerns, his dandruff, his diverticulosis, her nightmares, her battles with the publisher) the *career-author*. Relations between writers and implied career-authors are even more diverse than those between writers and the implied authors of particular works. Some careers are planned and relatively unified; we might say that Milton's real life was relatively close (though obviously not identical) to the life of Milton the career-author. Some authors, as a forthcoming work by

Lawrence Lipking will show in detail, work as hard at planning the trajectory of their artistic careers as they work at their actual writing.[10]

Finally, we should distinguish the career-author from the fictitious hero created and played with, by author and public, independently of an author's actual works. Our only current word for this is "image," but I resist contributing to the corruption of this good old word; it still has so many other duties to perform. "Character," in the old sense of "reputation," comes close to what I have in mind.

The distinction is at least as old as Aristophanes' public satire against the "character" of Socrates, but it became important only with the invention (was it really only with Sterne's *Tristram Shandy*?) of the best-seller promoted by the public shenanigans of a "character" playing out roles popularized in his own work. Dickens making a fortune reading aloud from his works (that is, dramatizing a carefully selected public character); Mark Twain becoming famous for anecdotes that he never told; Norman Mailer enacting the public's notion of "the writer"—these all to some degree fly free of any actual creation by the author. Some authors have been able to make these communal inventions work for them; public experience can, as in the novels of Saul Bellow, feed back as material into further creation. Other authors report that they feel trapped by their public roles.

This list of five "authors" by no means eliminates all ambiguities in the term. The notion of implied author, for example, could be further divided, depending on the degrees of subtlety in implication employed by writers and on degrees of penetration or ingenuity shown by readers. In post-Freudian times a writer often cannot count on public norms of inference about what a given stroke means *in* the work and thus *about* its author. Perhaps there never was a time when such matters were simple, but it seems safe to say that when Homer openly praised Odysseus' and Telemachus' virtues, condemned the perfidy of Penelope's suitors, and promised vengeance later in the *Odyssey*, he reaped from all readers or auditors the quiet but by no means unimportant benefit of being judged sound in his morality. Today a writer must know that openly to praise virtue or condemn vice may lead to trouble with many readers: "You are rationalizing, or covering up your true intent, which is ironic, or . . . ." To put it another way: to imply something depends on *someone's* making an inference, and different audiences will infer different implied authors from identical words. Some critics will specialize in outsmarting the writer and inferring a real nature regardless of subtleties in the invented signs. And so on. But we can save such complexities for critical moments when they are required, turning for now to a demonstration, necessarily somewhat extended, of how the effort to understand this or that "author" can be useful or harmful in different critical enterprises.

THE AUTHORITY OF THE WRITER: THE LAW OF DISPARATE GIFTEDNESS

Once we have freed ourselves from misleading simplicities about the author, we must ask whether it is possible to recover a respect for authors without losing an important element of our freedom as readers. We seem to be faced with two truths pulling in opposite directions. Understanding is a supreme value, yet we know that the texts offered by many authors will enslave us if we succumb to their wishes. Can we, in short, learn how and when to respect the richness of our inheritance of texts without repudiating the important need for violation? It is obvious that I am in many senses, for good and ill, master of every text that falls into my hands; I can maim or destroy it, remake it, even find an access of bliss as I make it obey my will. Can we find a useful language for describing the dangers in such mastery, the losses I incur when I refuse to let the text master me?

One answer is that it all depends on which text. Give me a genuine classic and I shall treat it respectfully; give me a work of Mickey Spillane and I shall feel free to use it for my purposes, which are more valuable than his. Milton is my master, but I shall treat many another author with the contempt he deserves.

Such an answer is obviously too easy. How do I distinguish in advance the authors who will feed me from those who need my kindly or cruel offices of correction? Besides, every critic who defends the reader's right to impose on or freely re-create a text believes that his freedom is as important when dealing with Milton as with *Mad Magazine*.

Indeed, the mistake in much traditional talk about "the classics" was precisely in its assumption that one could know in advance which authors would best feed which readers and that works considered canonic must be granted a special reverential touch. Canons either liberate or kill, depending on the attitudes or habits of mind of the readers who construct and honor them. But what habits should those be? The habits of the slave? The apprentice? The friend (that ideal reader Coleridge pleads for)? The crony or conspirator? The schoolmaster? The rival? The killer? Surely we must say much more about such choices than that "it all depends."

It is here that a law of rhetoric, first formulated, so far as I know, by Dionysius of Halicarnassus, can come to our rescue. Dionysius called it, somewhat pretentiously, the Law of Nonisorropic Psychopoetic Powers, but I think we can make do with a simpler name, "the law of disparate giftedness." It goes like this. In any act of interpretation, there is a strong probability that the speaker has more gifts to offer in the exchange than the listener. That's why the listener is listening. The speaker is speaking and the listener listens because they both know in their bones that more is likely to happen in the rhetorical transaction that way than the other way round.

On the whole, speakers know more about what they mean, care more about it and take more pains with it, than listeners, and profit in the exchange will depend on a listener's acknowledging this probability before he offers to become an authority. A corollary of the law goes like this: "Most interpretations will be, as human achievements, relatively inferior to the texts they interpret. Interpretations of those interpretations will on average be one step further down the line of human quality, and so on ad infinitum." (I refuse to ask what this corollary says about this book of criticism of criticism of criticism.)

On another occasion I would want to argue that Dionysius' law applies to all human interchange. Tacit acknowledgment of its power is in fact what makes good conversation, as distinct from verbal contest, possible; for in good conversation each participant knows how to judge when to treat "equals" as superiors and when, in turn, to take the floor and exercise an earned authority. But for now we are interested in an even stronger version of the law, one found demonstrated only in the preserved documents with which critics deal. The law is obviously strengthened whenever we are dealing with anything "tested by time," even if only the time required to get a book past a publisher's reader and into print.

There is so much good argument available about the validity of the test of time (e.g., by Samuel Johnson in the opening of his *Preface to Shakespeare*), that I would be embarrassed even to mention it were there not so much current talk that ignores the test and the reasons for its effectiveness. It is the simplest matter in the world: winnowing. Time winnows. Even six months can winnow. We have had so much talk about how time errs, and so much effort has been devoted (with little actual success) to unearthing rich kernels, buried by generations of chaff, that we forget the obvious: the writers who come to our attention do so because they have been found, by many other listeners or readers, to be of the kind that command our admiration; they carry authority because they *are* unusually gifted.

Each reader has every temptation to doubt that this is so. I am not likely to *feel* inferior as I pick up a given text. After all, is the text not absolutely dependent on me? And what if the reader is William Shakespeare reading Holinshed's *Chronicles*? Where is the law then? When Jane Austen reads Fanny Burney, or Marshall McLuhan and Roland Barthes read advertisements, should they be humbled before the law?

Obviously, our modes of winnowing are imperfect, and each of us is surrounded by millions of texts whose writers may be less gifted than the reader. But there is no sure way to know in advance, and the fact is that even the average text that "falls" under our scrutiny has been subjected to a winnowing far more rigorous than we ourselves have undergone. In the end, the chances of *my* being able to offer a Charles Dickens or Virginia Woolf as much as they can offer me, *in this exchange*, are infinitesimal.

What we are in great danger of losing, in a time of democratic education (which I favor) and egalitarian critical theories (which I mistrust), is that sense of respect for the text without which no reader will ever work beyond first impressions. It is of course true that there are destructive ways of cringing before a classic. But most important reading experiences come from works which for many readers will not be engaging on a first encounter. It may be (though I doubt it) that readers raised on the classics are never forced to rely on a kind of reading known to us who made our way more or less blindly from comic strip to Corneille: I mean the experience of slogging on, through a long book, for no other reason than trust in authority, trust in the tradition that has conferred authority on this text, to discover finally that the initial boredom was entirely our own, not the classic's. In a revulsion against such trust, I at one time decided that much of my youthful and deferential slogging had been hypocritical: I even urged my students not to "worry about what anybody else thinks of the book; attend only to your own honest responses." Well, of course we should attend to our honest responses, but a great deal depends on how we think of ourselves as we respond. The students I exhorted were by no means isolated, culture-free, private egos. Their spontaneous responses were already not in any simple sense free of the effects of cultural authority. To listen to "my own" responses without attending to what sensitive readers in my culture have said about a work is in fact to confer a spurious authority on whatever authority happens to have reached me in my past. When the members of any culture lose their sense of the difference in weight among responses, when they forget what is added when responses are shared and tested over decades and centuries, they will soon find themselves producing and consuming works that possess little more than a capacity to "grab you."

We all know how this works, because we have all had the experience of overlooking qualities on a first reading that subsequent readings reveal. Where was I, I ask, when I dismissed Herodotus as a boring primitive? What was wrong with me when, as a college student, I tossed *Nostromo* aside as unintelligible? Well, where I was was where I was; and if I had believed then what I am told now, that whatever I claimed to find was as important as what the authors actually offered, I might have stopped there.

THE AUTHORITY OF THE IMPLIED AUTHOR

It remains true that no preliminary respect for the *writer's* authority can finally survive unless it is earned by the writer's creation of a work that is in fact superior—which in our present terms means the creation of an implied author who carries authority from beginning to end. Here we see at work a second corollary of Dionysius' law: not only does time winnow writers, but writers winnow their own diverse "selves." Authors are thus more gifted, as it were, than people. Most writers we want to interpret, even those whose natural gifts are only average, have spent more time and creative energy on what they choose to publish than any interpreter is able or willing to spend. The writer thus makes himself an authority on the material in hand. Mark Twain has lived with Huck Finn for years; Henry James has lived with Isabel Archer through many drafts, written and unwritten; George Eliot knows Middlemarch, both the town and the novel, better than any reader ever will. Thus each of them has more to offer on *this* subject, on how *this* text should be read, on what I must become to read it, than I do.

One major act in the creation of any great text is the writer's successful effort to slough off mediocrity. Authors often report their surprise in discovering a new, superior self. Some writers in fact attempt to elevate their lives to live up to their invented second selves (and I think we have underestimated the immense ethical effect of such self-emulation), but the gap inevitably remains large. No human being was ever as witty and mature and generous-spirited as the imagined geniuses who give us the works of Shakespeare or Jane Austen or Flaubert or Henry James. Witty and mature and generous-spirited some great writers no doubt really were, even when they shopped for groceries. Regardless of how drab their words were as they chose their cabbage or brussels sprouts, it seems unlikely that they were as drab as mine manage to be at such moments. But to say so much is simply to repeat the first reason: there *are* imaginative geniuses in our world, geniuses who devote their energies to making concentrated versions of an already unusually rich imaginative life—to distilling an essence of wit or maturity or imaginative sympathy. Nobody was ever as marvelous as the implied author of *Emma*; Jane Austen collected her moments of marvelousness from many hours and many days. Flaubert shows us in his letters that he could not regularly make himself into that miraculous second self he creates when choosing the hundreds of thousands of signs of authority he offers in the finished *Madame Bovary*.[11]

In other words, the successful author earns his authority by coming to know his work with great intimacy as he writes it, to know its demands upon him, to know how much of himself has had to be purged if he is to serve the work and thus his readers. The critic who chooses to remake the work can earn his authority only in the same way: by respecting the author's inherent superiority, at least until the author proves that he does not deserve it. Some works are more worth writing and reading than others; some works are better performed than others. To pretend that *my* easy reworkings of the works of genius are justified without my having to earn my way is to produce a criticism that is "democratic" in the worst senses: egalitarian, reductionist, and self-indulgent.

The notion that whatever comes into my head about a text is as important, simply because it is mine, as the author's own conception embodied in the text, is at best a hypothesis; and, unless I happen to be in fact a better artist than the author, it is likely to stunt my growth. It is true that the other hypothesis—that the author's various "readings," embodied in successive revisions and confirmed by the decision to abandon the text to my hands, should regulate mine—will not always be confirmed by a closer look. But if it is not, all I have lost is time and labor; and I have not really lost them, because I will have stretched myself even in discovering the author's limitations. To assume that I am, at the outset, as big and rich and deep and various as the work in hand insures that, regardless of its actual quality, I will come out of the engagement about the same size as when I went in.

Some reader-critics, as we have seen, claim to free us from the enslaving conviction that a poem is capable of being encompassed in a single logical formulation. But does anyone really wear those chains? No one in fact defends the notion that a single set of propositions will serve as the equivalent of any poem. What is more, we are threatened by far more serious forms of enslavement, particularly the conviction now growing among our students that criticism is at best the reduction of the work to my own size and at worst simply the flinging of Greek-fed, polysyllabic bullshit.

In short, the speaker I meet in any carefully prepared speech or written text is likely to be immeasurably more gifted *for this occasion* than I am. The law and its corollaries hold even with respect to writers we think of as quite ordinary or those who write with great speed and seeming lack of revision, like Georges Simenon or Trollope. Even those we consider hacks often expend themselves extravagantly in their works. And it is not uncommon, in fact it is the norm, for writers we find worth discussing to spend anywhere from a year to five years of daily labor on a book, many hours a day, packing in and purging out, reshaping versions of their genius that we then think we can remake between now and the deadline for the next issue of *Diacritics*.

Nothing prevents me from making, in turn, another occasion by making another text on which I shall be a genuine authority—nothing, that is, except the facts, comforting or damning, about how the law applies to me. There is nothing inherently misguided about the explicit effort of some new new critics to rival the works they criticize. I become a bit suspicious, though, when I see the rivalry conducted by tearing down, or simply ignoring, the rival edifice. Only the critic who, first, is as imaginatively gifted as his subject; who, second, spends as much time and creative energy on the work as the author did; and who, finally, is as capable as the author of purging the ordinariness that in all lives threatens to engulf all special gifts—only such an interpreter can survive a public jousting.

All this being so, what greater disservice can a critic do than feed my complacency, flatter my capacity to turn out a hasty "reader-centered" reading (a poor thing but my own), freed of the author's authority, limited only by my own preexisting limits—limits that must unfortunately reveal me as a prisoner of my past experience?

Four Kinds of Reader Misreading

No critical principles can prevent misreading. To say that we will respect the authority of implied authors still leaves critics with the task of deciding what that authority teaches, and it leaves us with the even more difficult tasks described in chapter 6: of what to do with the work once we have received from it what it offers, and of what to do about works that lose more and more authority the longer we look at them.

But if, as I believe, the most serious critical errors are those that lead us to diminish our world, to overlook the riches that are there, whether in "literary" works or in criticism, to cut greatness down to our size, then a respect for implied authors can be the most important single enabling act of criticism. I have perhaps already said enough about the way in which this respect can guard against neglect of the simple preliminary step of *working* to reconstruct what is there. But it is perhaps even more important as a protection—for those whose fault is not any lack of energy or labor—against the ravages of critical dogma. Authors and their works are among the most varied, complex, and wonderful "objects" that our world offers us. Whatever will help us preserve the diversity and richness is surely even more important than the comforts offered by any reduction into system.

It is in the nature of the case I am making that illustrations of it could be as various as the variety of critical reductions and that what one mode will label a reduction will to another mode be a restoration of the true richness of the work. Still, it is important to look in detail at a few representative cases in which plausible abstract concepts about art or artists have led to debased pictures of both.

Preconceptions about the Writer and the "Career-Author": A Lesson by the Master

Here is a sequence of sentences abstracted from a modern author. Can you tell me, first, what they mean; second, who probably wrote them; and third, whether they are brilliant, average, or poor?

"I'll go away—if you wish me to . . ."
"Are you married?"
"No, I'm not married."
" . . . But if you go shan't I see you again?"
"Do you *like* to see me?"

Obviously these extracted sentences can carry an indefinite number of meanings, most of them utterly banal. Which is to say, they are practically meaningless. They could have been written, indeed *have* been written, by hundreds of authors, and spoken by hundreds of thousands. You have no way of knowing who wrote them, and you see that as they stand they carry no brilliance whatever.

Now here's another sentence, and it comes from the section of the same short novel that yielded those banalities:

> They lost themselves, these words [not those I have quoted], rare and exquisite, in the wide bright genial medium and the Sunday stillness, but even while that occurred and he was gaping for it she was herself there, in her battered ladylike truth, to answer for them, to represent them, and, if a further grace than their simple syllabled beauty were conceivable, almost embarrassingly to cause them to materialize.

Ah, now we feel more comfortable—some of us: Henry James! We begin to know something of where we are. We are in the realm of the Jamesian—perhaps even the late Jamesian. Now we can predict, without seeing the text, that those Hemingwedgian banalities we just quoted were probably after all subtleties, not flat words of clichéd romance but words of simple "syllabled beauty," "rare and exquisite." But what, then, is meant here, in this long sentence, by "almost embarrassingly to cause them to materialize"? Reference to notions like Jamesian or late Jamesian will not help us here. The dictionary, *pace* some critics, can do no more than get us started. And reference to no single category of interpretation *in my own mind* will help—except one: follow the guidance provided by the author *in this tale*. Without *that* author, I have no clues. I cannot even guess whether this elaborate sentence is a good one or a poor piece of self-parody by a James too late entirely.

Unless we want to take an absurd refuge in a decision not to care whether a sentence packs a great deal of literary value skillfully or simply gives us a sloppy general invitation to speculate, we are thus forced to look further at the context.

I inform you now that the story we are quoting is not just late James but late late James: "The Bench of Desolation," one of the last stories he wrote. Those simple sentences—"Are you married?" "No, I am not married"—are, just like the fussy long one, late late James. And like the long fussy sentence, the simple ones are used as part of a marvelous, strange, and comic plot, of a shape no other author, before or since, has attempted. To show why this is so would require a leisurely analysis of the whole tale. Here I can give only a hint at the great difference between what the author did and what you or I would probably do with those banalities and fussinesses.

As we might expect, the full delights of this unique story have been largely overlooked in published comment; critics have substituted instead a reduction to whatever dim lights were cast by predetermined categories.

To see how this works, observe how Leon Edel pursues a general criticism imposed by an extra-textual "author": the aging, "disillusioned" James. Edel subdues the story into just one more example of the "sad" final tales, full of "sacred rage," in which James "sets aside . . . his good humor and howls, like Lear."[12] "The Bench of Desolation" is one more late example dealing "with human waste, mistaken lives, wrong decisions, lost opportunities." "Henry James could sail to no Yeatsian Byzantium. For him, in his old age, there seems to have been only the cold bench and the desolation of the metropolitan jungles. There is terror behind the melodrama and the coincidences of these tales" (p. 10).

Now it happens that Edel's thematic summary does apply nicely to some of the last tales—most obviously to the last of all, "A Round of Visits." But it bears only a remote connection to "The Bench of Desolation." The preexisting categories of the reader—in this case an expert on the author's life and art who could certainly not be asked to respect James more—have dictated a reading which the inventive old author quite clearly repudiates. Instead of expressing bitter howls of rage, "The Bench of Desolation" shows . . . .

Ah, but what does it show? It is in fact a most extraordinary story, one of a kind. And the kind, naturally, has no recognized name. It is as different from most of the other late tales as *Titus Andronicus* is from *Cymbeline*.

The only adequate demonstration of such a claim would be, as the commonplace goes, a complete reading of every word. Short of that, suppose we look again at the sentences we have already quoted. Each of them is, in itself, undistinguished, and the overtly "Jamesian" one *could*, as we said, be a piece of sad self-parody. Torn one by one out of the context provided by James's new form, each sentence could mean almost anything, including the reverse of its seeming intent (one can easily invent a context in which "No, I am not married" would mean to the auditor "Yes, I am married, alas!" or would be a lie, an invitation to a seduction, a boast, a confession of love, or a revelation of imaginative failure).

But who except a literary critic with a program would ever dream of wrenching them out of James's context? Read where it belongs, each stroke reveals itself as a brilliant step—not a step in illustration of late late James's anger and bitterness but a step in the wonderfully wry "comedy" of Herbert Dodd and Kate Cookham.

I call it a comedy not because the word is very apt but to dramatize how much the tale resists Edel's terms. Consider the events that precede the long sentence about those "rare and exquisite words." We should first remind ourselves that the words, in their "simple syllabled beauty," are about money, a precise sum to be transferred from Kate Cookham to Herbert Dodd.

> "There are twelve hundred and sixty pounds, to be definite [the middle-aged Kate tells the middle-aged Herbert, once her fiancé], but I have it all down [deposited] for you—and you've only to draw."

Now we know why, after Herbert Dodd has savored those "rare and exquisite words" in the bright, genial medium and the Sunday stillness, the adverb *embarrassingly* is used when the words are almost caused "to materialize." Or at least we know when we read the *next* words:

> Yes, she let her smart and tight little reticule hang as if it bulged, beneath its clasp, with the whole portentous sum, and he felt himself glare again at this vividest of her attested claims. She might have been ready, on the spot, to open the store to the plunge of his hand, or . . . to impose on his pauperized state an acceptance of alms on a scale unprecedented in the annals of street charity. Nothing so much counted for him, however, . . . as the short, rich, rounded word . . . [draw]. . . . "To draw—to draw?" Yes, he gaped it as if it had no sense; the fact being that even while he did so he was reading into her use of the [banking] term more romance than any word in the language had ever had for him.

Here we have, I submit, the materials of what might have been a comic, even farcical, account of a greedy male's encounter with a woman who offers him what he most wants in life—hard cash. You and I could no doubt make much of that. We could ransack our experience in life and literature for similar scenes in which terms of hard cash sound beautiful to a greedy listener. What you and I could not have done is build a story in which such a scene carries as much rich meaning and emotion as James, our authority, actually gives us.

But again, to see that, we must return the scene to *its* larger context. It is now high time to remind ourselves of the outlines of this delicate, unlikely story:

> Vain and pretentious Herbert Dodd, shabby-genteel proprietor of a failing secondhand book and print shop, proposes marriage to Kate Cookham, the first woman entering the shop who "appeals to him . . . by her apparently pronounced intellectual side." Offended

later by the sight of her getting off a train with another man, he writes a letter breaking off the engagement. She threatens to sue, confirming his sense that she is vulgar and thus a fate well escaped. He takes up with another woman, Nan Drury, pretty but stupid. When Kate does sue, he proudly bankrupts himself to pay what he can, then marries Nan, who promptly—it actually takes but a sentence or two to cover ten years—bears and buries two children and then dies herself, killed, in Herbert's view, by the poverty Kate has forced on them.

Living in self-pitying but proud, resentful poverty, spending his leisure sitting in his accustomed place on what he calls his "bench of desolation," he discovers one day that a handsome ladylike woman observing him is Kate Cookham. She is no longer the least bit vulgar. In the ensuing conversations, which constitute three-fifths of the whole novella, Kate reveals that she has come to give him the money she has earned, using his breach-of-promise payments as capital. She has done what she could to save him; moreover, she tells him that if he had fought the suit he would have had to pay nothing.

He wrestles ineffectually with his pride, grasps at the money, but at the same time begins to see her genuine qualities. Finally, arriving at a new level of self-knowledge, he accepts her and her money—that is, *his* money—and the story ends with the two middle-aged characters joining their lives on the bench of desolation.

Now that, I submit, is a *peculiar* human experience, a marvelously unlikely combination of rich comedy and melancholic wisdom. It is a pattern of experience which, even in this raw summary, neither you nor I would have invented, and its completed form surrounds those original words with a seriocomic radiance that only James could have made.

Suppose we look more closely at the final two short sentences I have quoted, now at last in their context. Herbert Dodd has almost accepted the money she has offered him, is in fact playing with the envelope in his hand as they have what looks like their final conversation.

Now watch what James does:

She had gathered herself in; after giving him time to appeal she could take it that he had decided [to accept the money] and that nothing was left for her to do. "Well then," she clearly launched at him across the broad walk—"well then, good-bye."

She had come nearer with it, as if he might rise for some show of express separation; but he only leaned back motionless, his eyes on her now—he kept her a moment before him. "Do you mean that we don't—that we don't—?" But he broke down.

"Do I 'mean'—?" She remained as for questions he might ask, but it was well-nigh as if there played through her dotty veil an irrepressible irony for that particular one. "I've meant, for long years, I think, all I'm capable of meaning. I've meant so much that I can't mean more. So there it is."

"But if you go," he appealed—and with a sense as of final flatness, however he arranged it, for his own attitude—"but if you go shan't I see you again?"

She waited a little and it was strangely for him now as if—though at last so much more gorged with her tribute than she had ever been with his—something still depended on her. "Do you *like* to see me?" she very simply asked.

At this he did get up; that was easier than to say—at least with responsive simplicity; and again for a little he looked hard and in silence at his letter; which, at last, however, raising his eyes to her own for the act, while he masked their conscious ruefulness, to his utmost, in some air of assurance, he slipped into the inner pocket of his coat, letting it settle there securely. "You're too wonderful." But he frowned at her with it as never in his life. "Where does it all come from?"

"The wonder of poor me?" Kate Cookham said. "It comes from *you*."

He shook his head slowly—feeling, with his letter there against his heart, such a new agility, almost such a new range of interest. "I mean so *much* money—so extraordinarily much."

The full concentration of emotion and meaning in that experience is not in any simple sense something that I as reader have made. It is true, of course, that I had to remake it and that what I have written by way of describing it is but a pale reflection of what James did for and to me. It is James, the marvelously subtle author implied in the tale, who has provided the unique synthesis I now value. "Language" could not do it, not even language as perfected into the late style of Henry James. "Writing" did not give those sentences their meaning, as some critics seem to suggest. The English language, the resources of James's style, the enterprise of writing—all these are necessary but not sufficient causes of "The Bench of Desolation." The equally necessary but equally insufficient re-creative work of this reader did not give those words their power. Nor did Edel's ponderous, aging, embittered "James" do it to fulfill his trajectory as career-author. Henry James did it. He made something you and I could not have made, and it is simply self-maiming to pretend that any blissful improvisation on his words, sentences, or themes—even this one of mine—can equal the value of his making.

It is self-evidently true that for everyone except James the story remains inert until it is remade. It is also true that my reading will add or subtract some elements or effects that yours will subtract or add. Finally, having experienced the unique form, I may want to move to some kind of overstanding, judging it by political, moral, psychoanalytical, or metaphysical standards. Pursuing such differences is as essential to the life of criticism as discovering the core of agreements on which they depend, and, if the reader-critics were content to exhort us to a fully active role, there would be only good in them. But that is often not their message.

INDIFFERENCE TO THE WRITER'S TASK: TELLING A GHOST STORY

My confident assertions about "Henry James" appear oversimplified as soon as I face the following questions: "How do you *know* that your picture of the implied author is truer to the actual achievement than Edel's picture of the career-author, derived from his immense knowledge about the writer? Can you prove that the Henry James Edel sees in the story is a reduction and that the inventive James you infer from the story is not simply *your* invention?"

The answer is of course that proof in such matters is never decisive; if I am pushed by rigorous questioning, I can always be forced back to beliefs about human probabilities and ultimately to beliefs about what it is probable that a writer "like James" would do.

The pushing might go like this. First, Edel will, without question, find evidence in "The Bench of Desolation" that seems amply to support his picture of the howling, embittered James. I will naturally reply that this evidence is highly selective—that if we are to make our critical concept *adequate* to the complete tale, we must see it in different terms, since it includes many parts, such as the end itself, that do not "howl" but instead convey a strong tone of comedy. Edel can simply reply that I am misreading those moments, or that I have missed James's true emphasis, or that James has deliberately covered his tracks with misleading clues. And how do I answer that?

Unless I can answer clearly, we shall soon invent the kind of controversy about "The Bench" that has almost buried *The Turn of the*

Screw. With a little ingenuity—and with considerably less respect for evidence than Edel shows—we could invent readings that would make each character into either villain or hero: Kate Cookham destroys the hero; no, she saves him. Nan is the truly destructive force; no, she is the victim of the two self-aggrandizing manipulators. No, the truth is that society or the capitalist system is to blame, as it grinds poor Herbert into poverty and self-abasement. And so on. Such readings may never become quite as numerous as we now have of *The Turn of the Screw*, both because James more nearly effaces "himself" from that tale and because there *may* be—who can tell?—fewer invitations in "The Bench of Desolation" to conjecture about the central figure's pathology. Certainly it would require considerable ingenuity to make the *narrator* of "The Bench" into a psychopath, though no more, perhaps, than has been exercised by many interpreters of *The Turn*.

Because there seemed no good place to begin or end in dealing with critical chaos about *The Turn*, I was long determined never to write another word about it. In *The Rhetoric of Fiction* I had used conflict among its critics (who were already legion by the late 1950s) to illustrate the consequences of James's chosen manner of telling—the manner of the carefully limited, dramatized, partially unreliable "reflector." Making a general case about "the costs of objective narration," I devoted only a few pages to the story itself.

It was easy to predict at the time that neither my own words nor any other critical essay would ever eliminate controversy about how to allocate praise and blame among the ghosts, the governess, and the two children. James's technique and critics' interest in ambiguity would insure irresolution, even if one assumed, as fewer and fewer critics seemed to do, that James had intended some kind of determinate effect. What I did not predict was the continuing multiplication of hypotheses and of resulting controversies about ever more imaginative readings. In fact I felt fairly sure that critics would turn, in simple fatigue and boredom, to other works with similar narrators. Indeed, for seventeen years I could not bear to look either at the story or at the flood of readings that I saw rising in the journal pages and booklists.

Recently, however, I found myself required (by a reading list in "Freshman Humanities") to teach the story once again, this time to entering college students. But of course one does not just teach such a story—not now, not in the 1970s. One teaches it out of an anthology of criticism about it; and though I did my best to keep my charges at the task of reading the story, I myself felt duty-bound to read, along with it, some 180 pages of "background" and "early criticism" and "major criticism."[13]

The contrast in quality was even greater than I had expected: on the one hand, an appalling chaos of critical opinions, most of them poorly supported by argument, some of them plainly absurd; on the other, a fine story that turned out to be a delight to teach. I would still not choose to introduce literature to freshmen with that story, partly because they cannot be expected to deal with its heavy burden of critical inventions; but for that very reason it provides an excellent illustration here, an extreme case of the kind of choking of channels that threatens to occur more and more widely unless we can find better ways of distinguishing among novel interpretations.

There would be no excuse for contributing further pollution to these waters if there were not a curious omission in almost all interpretations: hardly any of them refer, explicitly or even by indirection, to what a human being might conceivably do if he attempted to write a story according to the new hypothesis being offered. Each interpretation springs full-bodied from an assertion of a possible *reading*, not a possible *writing*. There are always many references to the text but no reference to the kind of artist James would have to be to give us this (actual) text *if* he were pursuing this (hypothetical) intention. Many of the readings could well serve as the basis for a good story, provided that a Henry James had decided to tell it. But Henry James wrote a single version (with minor revisions),[14] and, even in the broadest interpretation of its ambiguities, James must have faced, like every writer, the essential problem of moving from page 1 to the final page with some sense of an accomplished task.

To say this does not in any way commit us to any one notion of how conscious or unconscious James may have been about the artistic reasons for his choices, and it does not commit us to believing that what an author says about his intentions is a secure guide to what a story is. We simply bypass the vexed question of the flesh-and-blood author's conscious intentions by concentrating on the choices actually made and referring them to various notions of what might conceivably compel you or me to make similar choices. Our thought thus resembles closely the thought of any anthropologist or historian who infers human purposes from mysterious artifacts: it is at least conceivable that a human being might have made this thing, given such-and-such a purpose—and it is inconceivable that he would have done so given certain other purposes. Such reasoning is obviously highly fallible, but unlike most of the conjectural essays about literary ambiguities, it is subject to a kind of confirmation or refutation: we are not left simply with rival assertions about permanently inaccessible domains, what James (or the story) *means*.*

Critical history teaches, even more clearly about this story than about most, that when the results of a writing task are freed from any conception of what that task might have been, they inevitably convey many different, even contradictory, "meanings." We need not pass any ordinances against those who want to free the story from the author's "conscious intentions," as Edmund Wilson explicitly freed it after other critics convinced him that James must have intended the ghosts in the story to be real.[15] But we have every right to insist that if a critic offers his reading as an interpretation of the art that informed the author's choices, conscious or unconscious, that reading can be properly tested by the hardest of all critical questions: Can you show me how James or you or anyone else could ever have done what James has done here *if* he were trying to write a story along your lines?

Viewed in the light of this practical test, the broad range of interpretations of *The Turn* looks even weirder than before.

It is important to remember that during the first few decades of the story's life the predominant reading was "straight": it was seen as a horrifying tale of corruption by demon-ghosts. An innocent young woman, a parson's daughter, is hired to take sole responsibility for the adopted children of a gentleman who orders that in no circumstances is she to appeal to him once she has taken charge. She discovers that the children have been corrupted by two malign ghosts. She decides to fight the evil to save the children; but though she manages to exorcise the ghosts with her courage, and even saves one child by sending her away, she must witness their triumph in the death of the boy.

Disagreement during this early period centered on two things: whether the story is any good or, more frequently, whether an author is morally blameworthy for portraying such horror and ugliness.[16] Then, in the 1920s, new and startling interpretations began. The history has been summarized so many times that there is no point in

---

*One of the sanest discussions of James's intentions in *The Turn* is by Dorothea Krook, "Intentions and Intentions: The Problem of Intention and Henry James's 'The Turn of the Screw,'" in *The Theory of the Novel: New Essays*, ed. John Halperin (New York: Oxford University Press, 1974),353–72. For an account of much of the best evidence against what can be called the "impugning" critics see her "Edmund Wilson and Others on 'The Turn of the Screw,'" in *The Ordeal of Consciousness in Henry James* (Cambridge: At the University Press, 1967).

retracing it here in detail. It is enough for our purposes to note how rich that history is in the invention of possibilities, how poor in examples of critics' actually meeting each other in understanding.

Every likelihood has been explored. There are no ghosts; the governess has hallucinations because of sexual neurosis, or she invents them to conceal her own vicious conduct. There are indeed ghosts, but the governess deals with them mistakenly, either by going mad, by joining them, by ignoring "what everyone should know" about exorcism, or by failing to go for help from the master. She is not only dreaming of romance with the master, as the text itself clearly states, but she is pathologically attached to him. She either falls in love with ten-year-old Miles, identifying him with the master, or deliberately hugs him to death because she cannot tolerate her picture of his sexuality—which according to one view must be homosexual. No, actually the governess makes up the whole story to appeal to Douglas, her lover, the "second narrator," who owns the manuscript and reads it to the assembled party in the opening episode. No, *Douglas* makes up the whole story and writes the manuscript, passing it off as real to add a turn of the screw. Douglas is Miles; no, Douglas was the master who hired her. The governess is James's portrait of his sister, Alice, who we know had a mental breakdown; James did not dare to treat her case directly. *The Turn* is a religious poem, the governess its pious heroine. You are all wrong: Mrs. Grose, the housekeeper, is the villainess, responsible for all that goes wrong.

No one can hope to make any sense out of such variety if it is taken as a list of hypotheses about the story James wrote rather than the stories he might have written. If art is the making of the misshapen, bumbled objects implied by most of this criticism, then art is not worth bothering about. You and I can turn out dozens of equally ambiguous hypothetical "stories" between breakfast and lunch. But if there is something distinctly admirable about what James accomplished in writing what even he called a potboiler—and indeed there is—some of us will want to pursue a criticism that can respect whatever that quality is.

What happens if we postulate an immensely gifted artist, a flesh-and-blood writer who worked hard to purge everything unnecessary from his works so that they would earn the kind of praise that we in fact give to Henry James? The postulate is not, one would think, implausible; it might well be the first one to occur to us if we had no theories to suggest more startling possibilities. Our "postulated writer" can now be compared with the author implied in any interpretation of the story that occurs to us. Does the implied person who would make these choices in any way resemble the gifted writer, our postulated Henry James?[17]

What proceeding in this way means can be seen most clearly by first considering an obviously absurd reading. Suppose we took seriously Eric Solomon's argument that the governess "and Miles, and, indeed, Miss Jessel and Peter Quint, have all been the victims of that most clever and desperate of Victorian villainesses, the evil Mrs. Grose," the housekeeper, and that we thus have been given a great and subtle detective story.[18] Solomon has worked with some care to use no evidence that does not in some way plausibly support what I take to be his satiric hypothesis (though his interpretation is anthologized as if the *editor* took it straight). In other words, he offers a good deal of "confirming" evidence. What he does not offer is any suggestion of how James, if he has any claims as a serious artist, could ever have provided so much data contradicting the hypothesis—data unmentioned by Solomon. Indeed most of the events and devices are simply ignored in Solomon's account, except, of course, in highly general talk about James's effort to throw us off the scent.

Now the interesting point is that a James who would do that would have to be a highly skillful writer—of a kind. We cannot refute Solomon by arguing simply that, if the story was intended as a detective mystery, James has botched it. Skill would be required in the author implied by such a tale. But here we come to the crux: it is absolutely the wrong kind of skill and thus the wrong kind of author—wrong when tested against everything we know or could possibly postulate about the *writer* Henry James. The implied author we have discovered will not match the postulated real person. We postulate a great, or at least competent, writer who is passionately devoted to the creation of good fiction. We discover an implied author either so diabolically secretive and elitist or so unbelievably irresponsible and inept that only one reader in almost a hundred years has been able to figure out the point of the story, and that point turns out to be realized in considerably weaker form than is managed by, say, A. Conan Doyle in story after story. A story that most or all readers will for nearly a century misread, that waits patiently for the one reader who will dismiss nine-tenths of it as a smokescreen—surely there is no point in teaching such a story to freshmen or to anyone. Indeed, if that is what art is, there is little point to any of our endeavors.

But no one will think James that sort of artist, once the question is put clearly. The chances that James intended Mrs. Grose as the villain of the piece are thus the same as the chances that James was not an artist to be taken seriously, either because he was a bumbler or because he held a contemptible theory of art. Such chances are not, of course, absolutely zero, but anyone who takes them as significant must fold up shop as a critic. In short, we have all the evidence we need for rejecting Solomon's absurdities without detailed refutation —which is to say that we can accept and enjoy his parody of a criticism loosed from its moorings in art.

I dwell on such an easy case only to make the structure of thought clear. When we test more plausible interpretations, our task will of course be more difficult and our conclusions less sure; but the procedure can be the same.

It is important to stress that in what follows I am not offering a definitive reading, whatever that might be. What we seek is both a reading and a way of testing it against a postulated "Henry James"—in short, a procedure that might then be used in debate among critics seriously interested in James's art. To pass our test, the reading—our hypothesis—must account for how any writer as skillful as the James *everyone* postulates would have found it necessary or appropriate, given the hypothesis, to do all or most of what was done. It will not do to show that the proffered reading explains everything as it might have been written by a Robbe-Grillet or an A. Conan Doyle. We are unashamedly exploiting the "extrinsic" here, reading the story as in fact we all read stories: using, where needed, our postulates about how a certain kind of human being might address other human beings.

There is no absolute rule to guide us in our choice of hypothesis. We do not begin innocently with this story, and we might well start with one or another of the more elaborate readings based on the unreality of the ghosts or the neuroses of the governess. But we can see in advance that all such beginnings will require an elaborate explanation of why James chose to begin his story with a frame setting that is, if these hypotheses are correct, deliberately misleading. We thus might reasonably begin with that setting itself and try out a reading that will not on the face of it require a lot of explaining away.

The story had *held us*, round the fire, [*The Turn of the Screw* begins,] sufficiently *breathless*, but except the obvious remark that it was *gruesome*, as on Christmas Eve *in an old house* a *strange tale should essentially be*, I remember no comment uttered till somebody happened to note it as the only case he had met in which such a visitation had fallen on a *child*. The case, I may mention, was that of an *apparition* in just such an old house as had gathered us for the occasion—an appearance, of a *dreadful kind*, to a *little boy* sleeping in the room with his mother and waking her up in the *terror* of it; waking her *not to dissipate his dread and soothe him to sleep again*, but to *encounter also herself*, before she had succeeded in doing so, the same sight that had *shocked him*. [My italics]

And so we go on, about how the ghost's "appearing first to the little boy, at so tender an age, adds a *particular touch*," how adding a second child adds "another *turn of the screw*," how it would be "*too horrible*," and how it is "beyond everything. Nothing at all that I know touches it," for "*dreadful—dreadfulness*," "for *general uncanny ugliness and horror and pain*."

Here we have been offered a possible intention for a story, a plausible task for a writer. Our present enterprise requires us, if we take it seriously, to attempt to think like a storyteller and imagine what the most skillful artist we can imagine would find either necessary or appropriate for realizing such an intention.

Immediately we see a major problem with this intention: it obviously fits too many shoddy performances in the world. Every ghost story, every movie of *The Exorcist* kind, tries to effect that last turn of the screw. It is hard to imagine a Henry James who would write a "mere" ghost story, and this in itself no doubt explains why so many have been unable to see it as a ghost story at all. We do not want, cannot want, simply to horrify readers who are as silly as the silliest of those who are dramatized sitting around that fire. We want to horrify people like the first narrator, who speaks in the opening we have quoted: sophisticates, connoisseurs of refinement in ghost stories. We want, as James put it in his Preface, written much later, to "catch those not easily caught, . . . the jaded, the disillusioned, the fastidious."[19] These words have been cited as evidence that James wanted to trick the jaded into thinking he had written a ghost story when in fact he had written a psychological study. Does that make sense? Perhaps; but surely, for a writer of the kind we have postulated, "catch" more plausibly means "capture," not "deceive."

With the qualification made, let us write a story. We believe, or will pretend to believe, that there are such things as ghosts (there is evidence that James in fact may have believed in them, but this is not important to our exercise; he was troubled because real ghosts did not seem to behave like the demons he needed).[20] But our own beliefs are less significant than our effort to write a ghost story that will surpass everything for "general uncanny ugliness and horror and pain," producing in "the jaded" what ordinary ghost stories produce for the unsophisticated.

Shall we make our ghost, or ghosts, real or imaginary?

We cannot possibly choose to make them *decisively* imaginary. Though there are many other possible stories that might be destroyed by creating a real ghost, we must, if we want the greatest possible "breathless" holding of the reader in dreadful dreadfulness, make our ghost or ghosts convincingly real. And so we offer, as most critics now concede that James did offer, unequivocal evidence that at least one ghost is real. [21]

Shall we make our ghost, or ghosts, benign or malign? Well, of course they must be demons:

> Wonderful and interesting therefore at a given moment, they [ordinary, friendly ghosts] are inconceivable figures in an *action*—and "The Turn of the Screw" was an action, desperately, or it was nothing. I had to decide in fine between having my apparitions correct and having my story "good"—that is producing my impression of the dreadful, my designed horror. Good ghosts, speaking by book, make poor subjects, and it was clear that from the first my hovering prowling blighting presences, my pair of abnormal agents, would have to depart altogether from the rules. They would be agents in fact; there would be laid on them the dire duty of causing the situation to reek with the air of Evil. [Preface] [22]

Clearly such demons require victims if they are to horrify. Who should the victims be? What do we all in fact find most dreadful in the way of victimization? Well, the first answer is obvious: a child. Yes, of course, a beautiful, innocent child, confronting evil, and—dare we face this dreadfulness, in the 1890s?—being corrupted by it. (In the 1970s we know from a dozen books and movies that it adds a turn of the screw to have Rosemary's baby be the devil himself—or herself.)

But this bears thinking about. If it is horrible to see children corrupted by evil, what could make an even more horrifying spectacle, one even more wrenching for "the jaded"?

We've got to show the destruction of a child, or children, by a demon, or demons, but how do we keep intelligent readers engaged "breathlessly" by that kind of horror? What will add a turn of the screw for them?

Well, surely we must add another main character, someone who can observe the events, suffer in them, and raise for even the most sophisticated reader varieties of mystery and horror not essential to your basic ghost story: he or she will to some degree provide new complications. As James says,

I feel myself show them best [moving accidents and strange en-
counters] by showing almost exclusively the way they are felt [by a
sensitive observer], by recognizing as their main interest some
impression strongly made by them and intensely received . . . ; we
get the thickness [that we want] in the human consciousness that
entertains and records, that amplifies and interprets it. [P. 103]

What, then, should be the nature of this consciousness? Shall we
make it a vicious, or a stupid, or a totally insensitive person, or someone who at least starts out the adventure as innocent as a child,
though able to see and reflect as a child cannot? A vicious person
might do, perhaps; though then we would have to face a serious
problem of how to show that monstrous consciousness reflecting this
kind of story. Would such a person not laugh in ghoulish delight at
every turn of the screw? No, better to show the person (at least at the
beginning) as another innocent victim caught in the web of evil and
then—yes, surely this will add—nearly destroyed.

Shall he or she, then, be strong or weak? Certainly vulnerable, at
the very least. A powerful, heroic, confident (male?) hero able to
combat the ghosts not only with courage but with a strong likelihood
of winning—that clearly will not do. If we are to horrify, the ghosts
must in some sense win or nearly win; and if they are to destroy, or
nearly destroy, both the child and the "observer," the observer must
be as vulnerable as possible without losing the force needed to reflect
the events with some intensity and to fight back with some courage.
Besides, we want to turn the screw not just of any kind of horror but
of the horror that includes pity; and the most pitiful victims, next to
children, are of course innocent young women. A young woman,
then, will be best, rather than some mature veteran of life's battles
(compare James's choice of Pemberton for the entirely different effects
of "The Pupil").

Should our observer be merely that—a passive and reluctant witness, a chance visitor to the haunted house—or someone responsible
for the child's welfare? To raise the question is to answer it. Though a
governess is not the only possibility, she will serve well, especially if
we can contrive some way to give her a total and impossible responsibility, one in which she is unable to rely on any other strong authority
in her battle with total Evil.

Shall she be charged with the care of only one threatened child or at
least two? Clearly—as we are told in the opening section—a second
child will add a turn of the screw. A third would probably yield
diminishing returns.

Shall they be two little boys, two little girls, or a boy and girl? To raise the question is again to answer it.

Shall we have one ghost only or at least two? We could never face ourselves if we overlooked the sexual suggestions that can be added, in a tale about horrible nameless evils, by the presence of both a male and a female ghost, a male and a female child. Even without that motive, the appeal of the symmetry would be irresistible.

So far we have been forced to our choices almost as rigorously as Poe claimed to be in discussing how he wrote "The Raven." But we are coming to somewhat more difficult matters.

Shall we make our governess a person who is absolutely lucid and unquestionably reliable in her report of what she sees, so that the reader never has any doubts about her being a pillar of support for the children? To do so sacrifices far too much. We might set out, as indeed James does with many of his narrators, to take "a very sharp line" in portraying the governess, giving her "absolute lucidity," ruling out "subjective complications," making her "particular credible statement" authoritative.[23] But we finally see—perhaps only as we make our last revision—that we must make her extremely vulnerable to alarms, even sufficiently anxious and highstrung to throw the reader into frequent but temporary doubt about whether she is to be relied on. To do so will engage the reader in the most intense way possible; he must then grapple with those ghosts almost as if he were in their presence. Obviously, the worst thing we could do would be to put between him and those presences an omniscient, safe, secure narrator.

Shall we then show her as steady and unshaken in her own conviction that she has seen real demons offering real corruption to her charges, or shall we portray her as often besieged with doubts and indeed, like Hamlet, seeking desperately to test the ghosts' reality and having to face the possibility that she is going mad? We can see possibilities for good—that is, immensely gripping and horrifying— versions in either direction, with different costs to be paid in each. But is there not a more delicious challenge in the second alternative? If we choose it, we must decide, further, to what degree to make the reader share her doubts. Hamlet doubts the ghost for a while, but the spectators never do. Shall we allow our spectators to question her vision because she leaps to inferences that are not obviously sound, succumbs to alarms and exaggerations that may make the reader doubt her soundness? If we go too far in this direction, we shall of course lose our horror or at least exchange it for another kind: the horror of watching a psychopath destroy two innocent children. We must therefore decide whether to tread the delicate path of maintaining the horror of seeing children genuinely corrupted while we at the same time add the potentially conflicting horror of watching an observer disintegrate under the effort to cope with the horror. But is there not a special turn of the screw in seeing children being lost to utter evil partly because their only protectress is incapable of defending them? In short, the kind of horror we seek will be reinforced the more we pity the children, and we will pity them the more they are themselves helplessly "exposed." As James wrote to an acquaintance, "But ah, the exposure indeed, the helpless plasticity of childhood that isn't dear or sacred to *some*body!"[24] We must expose them both to the demons *and* to their hapless protectress. If we show her trying to force the children to acknowledge their communion with the demons, seeking, with less and less attention to their feelings and more and more to her own plight, for corroboration of their corruption, we shall turn the screws of horrible torture for those damned and hapless children.

We shall at the same time be running a risk of misleading certain readers who are easily misled. The more horrifying we make our tale, the more we shall risk the judgment of readers that it is too horrible, too ugly. As we have seen, many of its original readers were in fact shocked to the point of complaining of James's immorality in presenting a story that was so "distinctively repulsive" (*The Outlook*, 1898), so "very cruel and untrue," though clever (*The Bookman*, 1898); it was also remarked that he was "not a safe author to give for a Christmas gift" (John D. Barry, 1898).[25]

Such readers—readers who cannot bear too much ugliness and pain—will naturally be tempted to escape us by deciding that our deliberately flawed "reflector" has made it all up, that the ghosts are not real, that what we have written is a study in pathology. We are aware now, in 1979, as we could not have been, writing our story eighty years ago, of the way in which "jaded" readers prefer to escape horrors by speculating on psychology. We are also aware that if we were making a movie we could take care of this difficulty a bit more easily: one good clear shot of a ghost establishes that ghost's reality, unless the director takes extraordinary measures to raise doubts. As writers, however, we must pursue what turns out to be an extraordinarily elusive line: too much doubt about the governess's lucidity and we undermine the reality of what she sees; too little and we weaken the torture.

Having decided that the last turn of the screw of dreadfulness is provided by showing the children caught between real demons and a

protectress who, even in the best interpretation, does not provide a
safe and inviting alternative—having decided, thus, to make them
"as exposed as we can humanly conceive children to be"—we must
therefore make the governess, herself, and the reader with her, sometimes confident that the ghosts are real—and sometimes not; sometimes confident that they can be combatted—and sometimes not. We
must show her desperately seeking proof, increasingly aware that if
the ghosts are not real she is, as she says, "either cruel or mad." Thus
we increase both the awful intensity of her plight and our own intellectual and emotional involvement as we watch her make her ever
more serious mistakes, her ever more gruesome and quite possibly
mad inferences.

But shall we then, all this having been decided, show that at least a
good share of her "wild" guesses prove to be correct, based on the
ghosts' actual behavior? Of course. Otherwise, at the end the ghosts
will not prove to have been real and thus ugly and dreadful.

No need to ask, then, whether the story should end with the children safe and sound, rescued by the governess. There would be
nothing finally horrifying in that. At least one of them must be destroyed. Whether to rescue the other one, as James in fact rescues the
(by then) foul-speaking Flora (p. 77), is a more difficult question, but
there is at least some economy in clearing the scene for a final confrontation between one ghost, one child, and the governess.

Shall we have the governess entirely alone throughout, as she tries
to cope with the ghosts, or shall we give her a confidante? Sheer
expository difficulties require someone to be talked to, but we can
gain great advantage by making that someone a bluff, kindly, no-
nonsense person whose very lack of imagination will at first confirm
the ghosts' reality, then throw doubts on the governess's interpretations, and then, with a final "I believe," confirm the reader's worst
fears.

Finally—to cut short a chain of inferences that could, if we are on
the right line, be made as long as our finished story itself—shall we at
the very beginning set the tone, so that the reader will have clues
about the world he will inhabit, a warning to expect something other
than the usual ghost story, and some hint that he is not to escape the
tale's power to horrify through some easy hypothesis about the governess's total unreliability? Of course. And so we shall give the
governess a direct badge of human authority:

"She was a most charming person, but she was ten years older
than I. She was my sister's governess," he quietly said. "She was

the most agreeable woman I've ever known in her position; she'd have been worthy of any whatever. It was long ago, and this episode was long before. I was at Trinity, and I found her at home on my coming down the second summer. I was much there that year—it was a beautiful one; and we had, in her off-hours, some strolls and talks in the garden—talks in which she struck me as awfully clever and nice. Oh yes; don't grin: I liked her extremely and am glad to this day to think she liked me too. If she had n't she would n't have told me. She had never told any one. It was n't simply that she said so, but that I knew she had n't. I was sure; I could see. You'll easily judge why when you hear." [P. 2]

Though James often reveals himself in the Notebooks thinking about stories quite explicitly in the kind of if-then form we have been employing, it would be absurd to claim that we have hit the precise calculations that he made. Nor do I want to claim that the reading I have implied with this exercise is firmly established *by* my exercise. I would claim, however, that we have at least begun the kind of testing that any hypothesis about any story by James should be able to withstand: it is not simply conceivable but probable that a writer like James, pursuing the intentions promised in his own frame-setting, would write a story very much like *The Turn of the Screw*. It is inconceivable that anyone remotely like Henry James would write, starting with Solomon's hypothesis, a story anything like this one. Our version implies an extremely subtle author who knows how to get what he wants from competent readers, making every stroke count. The Mrs. Grose reading, like *most* others, implies an author willing to waste immense tracts of inert text in order to conceal his true intent. He sets out to deceive everyone but those few readers clever enough to recognize that almost everything he wrote was pure red herring.

The same sort of test can be applied to the more plausible readings based on the governess's pathology. In one of the most detailed arguments against her sanity, Harold C. Goddard provides clear clues about how our choice of readings implies a choice of "author."[26] His hypothesis is on the face of it not implausible: *"Two children, under circumstances where there is no one to realize the situation, are put, for bringing up, in the care of an insane governess"* (p. 195; Goddard's italics). Goddard is an intelligent and close reader. He admits that his hypothesis may have been suggested to him by the fact that when he was a child he was himself in the care of such a governess. Yet he provides far more extensive argument for his finally simple reading than I should ever want to work up for my uncomfortably complex one;

and, unlike most interpreters, he is utterly serious about trying to meet the objections to his reading raised by the many elements in the text that seem to conflict with it.

If my point were to establish a reading of *The Turn*, I would be forced, by the detail of Goddard's argument, to an extended encounter here. But what is important is not to refute his reading—which in any case one could never do in a head-on encounter—but to bring to the surface what it implies about the *kind of author* James would have to be to write what he did write *if* he had anything like that reading in mind. Goddard does not talk about James so much as about effects. But we can easily infer his conception of James: he is an aesthetic purist who considers horror ugly and who therefore, in the name of beauty, will seek to "redeem the narrative" from the charge of being *too* horrible (as in fact it seemed to those who took seriously the ugly notion that little Miles, and perhaps even little Flora, have actually been captured by Evil). *This* James must work to save his story from "the charge of ugliness" by rendering "even its horror subordinate to its beauty."

To achieve beauty and mitigate horror his Henry James must of course do some of the things that our postulated author found himself having to do. But one of his overriding intentions becomes, unavoidably, the exercise of "consummate skill" in throwing "the reader off the scent" (p. 190). Vast tracts of the story are now designed principally to deceive us: "If on your first reading of *The Turn of the Screw* the hypothesis did not occur to you that the governess is insane, run through the story again and you will hardly know which to admire more, James's daring in introducing the cruder physical as distinguished from the subtler psychological symptoms of insanity or his skill in covering them up and seeming to explain them away" (p. 202).

Goddard's reading thus postulates a James quite different from ours: "With this hypothesis as a clue, we can trace the art with which James hypnotizes us into forgetting that it is the governess' version of the story to which we are listening, and lures us, as the governess unconsciously lured Mrs. Grose, into accepting her coloring of the facts for the facts themselves" (p. 195).

With such a method, it is a foregone conclusion that every objection can in one sense be "met." For example, the major difficulty that confronted Goddard's James is the likelihood that, if the governess were really insane, someone would recognize this and interfere to save the children (p. 194). The problem raised, the answer comes. All the details which in our view were fashioned to make the isolation of

the governess and children more horrible and pathetic are now designed to rule out any intelligent observer who could spot her madness. The qualities in Mrs. Grose that our James invented to keep her
inadequate as an aid but useful for making the exposition dramatic
were invented by Goddard's James to protect us from any corrective
vision.

Similarly, though Goddard by his own testimony is highly selective
in his quotation of James's own statements about *The Turn*, what he
does quote requires him to postulate a James who in all sincerity
simply cannot stoop to telling anyone what he was up to; he must
engage in a "very charming and good-humored, but a nonetheless
very unmistakable, side-stepping" in order not to offend readers who
read *The Turn* as a horror story.

The sly James who emerges from such readings is by no means
lacking in skill, but he is quite remote, I would argue, from any figure
we will ever infer from the story as written *if* we think of it as a
creation designed by a serious artist to realize its inherent possibilities
to the highest degree. It is simply inconceivable to me that "my"
Henry James, had he decided to write a story designed to realize
Goddard's version to the full, would have written *The Turn of the
Screw*.

Everything we have said about the implied James goes even more
strongly for the self-portrayed governess who writes most of *The
Turn*. To think of a mad governess who could and would write her
own story in this way entails the absurdity of thinking that Henry
James could commit such an absurdity. Think of the thousands of details that such a narrator would suppress—given the skills at suppres-
sion and distortion that she must have. Think of the fact that she
herself tells us, again and again, that the ghosts do not appear to
Mrs. Grose (she and Mrs. Grose quite explicitly share the beliefs of all
believers in ghosts—for example, the audience of *Macbeth*—including
the belief that ghosts have the power to appear selectively). Why
would either a mad person or a formerly mad person trouble, in telling her story, to talk about her own "dreadful liability to impressions
of the order so vividly exemplified" by the appearance of Quint and
about Mrs. Grose's "exemption" from "my more than questionable
privilege"? And imagine any Henry James you can dream of giving
such a narrator the following words, and then ask yourself whether
he should expunge them from the story or keep them in:

> She [Mrs. Grose] had seen nothing, not the shadow of a shadow,
> and nobody in the house but the governess was in the governess's

[my] plight; yet she accepted without directly impugning my sanity the truth as I gave it to her, and ended by showing me on this ground an awestricken tenderness, a deference to my more than questionable privilege, of which the very breath has remained with me as that of the sweetest of human charities. [P. 25]

Or, for one last example: why, if James had decided to write simply a beautiful study of madness, would he include, as all writers of true *horror* stories do include, an obligatory lyrical interlude, the "weeks" of glorious summer after the governess has been charmed by the actual appearance of Miles? Here is a passage that I believe has not been mentioned by any of the "impugning" critics:

> She gave with her apron a great wipe to her mouth. "Then I'll stand by you. We'll see it out."
>
> "We'll see it out!" I ardently echoed, giving her my hand to make it a vow.
>
> She held me there a moment, then whisked up her apron again with her detached hand. "Would you mind, Miss, if I used the freedom—"
>
> "To kiss me? No!" I took the good creature in my arms and after we had embraced like sisters felt still more fortified and indignant.
>
> This at all events was for the time: a time so full that as I recall the way it went it reminds me of all the art I now need to make it a little distinct. What I look back at with amazement is the situation I accepted. I had undertaken, with my companion, to see it out, and I was under a charm apparently that could smooth away the extent and the far and difficult connections of such an effort. I was lifted aloft on a great wave of infatuation and pity. I found it simple, in my ignorance, my confusion and perhaps my conceit, to assume that I could deal with a boy whose education for the world was all on the point of beginning. I am unable even to remember at this day what proposal I framed for the end of his holidays and the resumption of his studies. Lessons with me indeed, *that charming summer*, we all had a theory that he was to have; but I now feel that *for weeks* the lessons must have been rather my own. I learnt something—at first certainly—that had not been one of the teachings of my small smothered life; *learnt to be amused, and even amusing, and not to think for the morrow*. It was the first time, in a manner, that I had known *space and air and freedom, all the music of summer and all the mystery of nature*. And then there was consideration— and consideration was sweet. Oh it was a trap—not designed but deep—to my imagination, to my delicacy, perhaps to my vanity; to whatever in me was most excitable. The best way to picture it all is to say that I was off my guard. They gave me so little trouble—they

were of a gentleness so extraordinary. I used to speculate—but even this with a dim disconnectedness—as to how the rough future (for all futures are rough!) would handle them and might bruise them. They had the bloom of health and happiness; and yet, as if I had been in charge of a pair of little grandees, of princes of the blood, for whom everything, to be right, would have to be fenced about and ordered and arranged, the only form that in my fancy the after-years could take for them was that of a romantic, a really royal extension of the garden and the park. It may be of course above all that what suddenly broke into this gives the previous time a charm of stillness—that hush in which something gathers or crouches. The change was actually like the spring of a beast. [P. 14; my italics]

Would you not, oh gifted reader, would you not have the sense to change that passage drastically if your game was to make a case for her insanity? Well, of course you would not, *if* it was your intent to deceive as many readers as possible. But if you wanted to move skillfully from doubt to illusory calm to the gruesome reality of the beast leaping in this jungle of evil, would you not perhaps try to write just such a lovely picture of what, for such a governess, happy "governing" at Bly for some weeks was—and might have continued to be but for the sudden appearance of Peter Quint?

PRECONCEPTIONS ABOUT A PROPER STRUCTURE: *The Citizen of the World*

I turn now to an entirely different pattern of teaching by a different version of "the author": what Oliver Goldsmith taught me about critical method as he tried, at first unsuccessfully, to get me to read his *The Citizen of the World*. I assume that his book will not be well known to many of my readers, even those who know *The Vicar of Wakefield* and *She Stoops to Conquer*. Could that be because our criticism has no good way of talking about the greatness of a collection of miscellaneous "letters"?

Though I was at one time "an eighteenth-century man," I never was tempted to read *The Citizen*. But then, two years ago, for reasons unimportant here, I was obliged to write about it. At first I found it dull, and soon I was skipping, thumbing ahead to guess at what possible kinds of organization I might discover in this miscellany of 123 periodical essays.

I could find none. But, unity or no unity, I had to dig in. The question was, into what?

No one who read the "Chinese letters" of Goldsmith as they first appeared in 1760–61 could have overlooked their great range in subject and effect. Commissioned as "papers of amusing character,"[27] they exhibited what every reader would expect in periodical letters: a variety of instruction and delight confessedly miscellaneous. And they were uniformly judged, as far as we can tell, by such traditional rhetorical standards as pleasure and utility (for the reader) and variety, good sense, and genius (in the author):

> Were we to examine these reflections of *our Citizen of the World* by the standard of originality, our pleasure would be greatly diminished; but let us view them with regard to utility, and we must confess their merit. What seems cloying to an hundred persons of fastidious appetites, may prove wholesome delicious nourishment to thousands. These letters, if we mistake not, made their first appearance in a daily news-paper, and were necessarily calculated to the meridian of the multitude.... It is rather extraordinary, that the philosophic *Lien Chi Altangi* could handle so many topics agreeably, and sustain the fatigue of so long a course without weariness, than that he has sometimes stumbled. All his observations are marked with good sense, genius frequently breaks the fetters of restraint, and humour is sometimes successfully employed to enforce the dictates of reason.[28]

Such commodious rhetorical standards were almost automatic in criticism of the time, especially when it dealt with commodious forms like the periodical essay; and for nearly two centuries critics took them for granted in judging *The Citizen*, just as anyone not committed to a theory might today take them for granted in giving a common-sense explanation of why "The Talk of the Town," say, is superior to the personal essays in this week's student newspaper. It would never have occurred to John Forster, for example, writing in 1848, to worry about whether the collected letters made a unified, coherent, or organic whole. For him, the test was still rhetorical: *The Citizen* "amused the hour, was wise for the interval beyond it, is still diverting and instructing us, and will delight generations yet unborn."[29]

To modern critics it has seemed evident that when the series of "Chinese letters" was edited into a book, *The Citizen of the World*, the author invited a different, more "organic" standard. Thus, most recent critics who have taken *The Citizen* seriously have assumed that, if one is to prove artistic success, one must prove some kind of unity.[30] Echoing thousands of studies of the unity of poems, novels, and plays, critics have pressed all the available buttons: it is organized by a "frame tale"; no, it is organized as a "pattern of ironies"; no, it is consistent as a satire. Each account seems plausible, read by itself; all of the evidence cited does indeed support the hypothesis offered. It is only when one returns to the collection itself that the implausibility of such efforts becomes clear: one hundred and twenty three letters to the folks back home, written by the Chinese visitor to London, Lien Chi Altangi—letters immensely diverse in subject, form, and effect, published every three or four days for nearly twenty months.

One can dramatize the problem by asking each critic, "How many letters did you totally ignore as you accumulated your evidence?" The answer would be tedious if traced in detail, but it would show something of the thinness that can result when critics allow standards about texts to preclude talk about authors.

Can we hope, by taking thought about the author and his achievement, to do less injustice to a work of this kind? To do so, must I give up my distinction between the flesh-and-blood writer and the implied author? I know from experience that the distinction can be immensely useful in dealing with many literary works, as it was with "The Bench of Desolation" and with *The Turn of the Screw*. I have long known that it can hamper me in dealing with certain kinds of lyric. What happens if we relax into older habits of thought about the genius of the real man, Goldsmith?

Suppose we begin our work on this miscellany by seeking simply for *signs of skill*—skill shown, of course, by "the implied author"; somehow the distinction between the implied author and the "real" Goldsmith immediately grows blurred. We are at once relieved of all anxiety about whether the work "as a whole" is unified. We are still interested in form because we could never discern any skill that was not in some sense an exhibition of form. But in turning to Goldsmith's skill we can at least for a time attend *to whatever binds his readers to him*, without worrying about how the various bonds relate to each other. We can also gladly forget about whether any particular skill is unique to Goldsmith or is shared with others who were caught, as some would tell us, in the prison house of the *écriture* of his time. Skills we admire can be taught or inherited or shared by several in a school; while we will admire most the author who most perfects them, they can still carry their binding power when they are not uniquely Goldsmith's.

I begin with the more obviously "formal" or "intrinsic" skills and move toward the more obviously rhetorical or "extrinsic," although—as even my first example will show—these cannot in Goldsmith be finally distinguished.

His most obvious gift is the one that made *Citizen* a basic school text

until quite recently: his unfailing knack in casting sentences that capture us on a first reading and then improve under analysis. "The
ignorant critic and dull remarker can readily spy blemishes in eloquence or morals, whose sentiments are not sufficiently elevated to
observe a beauty; but such are judges neither of books nor of life" (p.
425). The delicate parallelism of

critic	eloquence	books
remarker	morals	life

is easy to note, difficult indeed to explain, and impossible to rival. I
cannot pretend to say what a full analysis of style, in the hands of
someone trained in linguistics and stylistics, would reveal in *The Citizen*. But one needs no such analysis to experience the appeal of an
astonishing virtuosity, creating a multiplicity of forms, each qualifying as art in anyone's definition. Like Goldsmith's paragraphs, and
indeed his individual essays viewed separately, these brief forms are
in themselves complete, self-fulfilling, autonomous, inviting to pure
contemplation even as they amuse or edify. The Beginnings "require"
their Middles and Ends at least as surely as the parts of any poem or
play. And the structures can be said to complete themselves internally; expunge or transpose any part and you destroy the whole. In
short, Goldsmith, like all great periodical essayists, builds thousands
of masterful short verbal forms. But modern criticism has for the most
part, even in its encomiums, given us no way to distinguish his kind
of skill from dabbling.

Second, our criticism of his skills must pursue the great variety of
thematic and dramatic sequences that Goldsmith plays with along his
way. The most obvious of these is the relatively prolonged story of
the adventures of the Chinese visitor's son, culminating in his marriage to the beautiful slave, revealed, in what is clearly a parody of
romantic endings, as the daughter of "the Man in Black." It is this
sequence that Hopkins stresses as the source of narrative continuity
(see note 30). But it is a curious kind of continuity indeed if it is not
mentioned—as Hopkins fails to note—in 108 of the 123 letters! To
talk of this narrative in Hopkins' way, seeking a unity that is not
there, can lead only to the rejoinder that *The Citizen* is at best an ironic
novel manqué. But there are many little sequences, some as short as
the two-letter adventure of Altangi with the London prostitute. In
letter 8 he describes her as "one of those generous creatures," full of
virtue, sincerity, and truth, symbolizing a "land of innocence, and a
people of humanity." In letter 9, published three days later, he has
discovered the formal completion of this adventure: as the reader has

known all along, enjoying a clear bit of dramatic irony, she proves to be one of the "infamous disciples of Han"—a whore. The two letters thus make a unit, in one sense, but they also build connections with other moments, before and after, when Altangi will make a fool of himself.

Though there are literally thousands of completed forms of these and other kinds, the further one pushes for such "intrinsic" sequences, the more obvious it is that Goldsmith's own achievement is being touched only at a tangent. It seems likely that even the most penetrating search for either linear or organic forms will leave us asking: But what of the *rest* of "the book"? Great patches of almost every letter, and a great number of letters, will not even be mentioned if we persist in talking of intrinsic interrelations. What, for example, about the many letters that are dictated by current events, discussed once or twice, and then forgotten (the war with France, the publication of *Tristram Shandy*, the death of the king, and so on)?

A pursuer of intrinsic form might answer that, once Altangi has commented on any two such events, formal connections will have been established between them as a kind, and thus among all possible occasions. But it feels artificial indeed to describe them in any language of intrinsic form. We need, instead, rhetorical words like appetite (of the audience) and genius, wisdom, or shrewdness (of the author). The most obvious appeal of such occasional pieces is to those readers who have been preheated by their knowledge of the piece itself. Intrinsic terms cannot do justice either to the *desire* of readers to see what, this week, the Citizen will have to say about Public Event X; or the gossipy pleasure they will take in the account; or the *appetite* they will then feel for some unspecified commentary on some as yet unknown future public event; or their *admiration* for the skillful author who promises more of the same. Goldsmith clearly had his attention as much on the "human interests" of his audience as on their interests as connoisseurs of beautifully articulated structures. Insofar as we wish to appreciate his skill, we must somehow reconstruct ourselves as his kind of audience. For this reconstruction, we shall require some assistance from historical inquiry, and so the text, *in this view of its excellence*, is *not* autonomous.

We might, of course, deplore such moments as lapses, as excrescences on the body of his art; we might choose to ignore them or to recognize them only as non-art, just because rhetorical considerations have led to a neglect of coherence. The temptation to do so will be greater if we accept the modern commonplace that correlates excellence strictly with universality or permanence of appeal. Insofar as

Goldsmith deliberately caters to a temporary interest in his audience, so the doctrine runs, he repudiates *art*—and of course risks losing the interest of any serious critic of a later time. We have no immediate interest in whether the nobility of 1760 were "degenerate" or whether the French were less disinterested in their philanthropy than the English, or whether funeral elegies written on the "great" were ridiculous. Only insofar as Goldsmith relates such parochial interests to some universal concern will we take the results as art.

The issues of evaluation raised by a doctrine like this are immensely complex, but many of the most interesting questions about Goldsmith's art, including the question that concerns us most—What *is* his art?—will be ruled out or obscured if we take the doctrine at face value.

The conflict between such modern doctrines and the rhetorical criticism that *The Citizen* is leading us toward is in some ways similar to the conflict in the eighteenth century itself between rule-critics and those who insisted that rules bow to artistic success—that is, successful effects produced in an audience. But the "rules"—most notably the infamous insistence on abiding by the three unities—were themselves always placed within a criticism that was far more concerned with effects on audiences than has been true of modern organicist views, with their theory-spawned rules about organic unity, coherent point of view, and objectivity. Even the most rule-bound of neoclassical critics argued for their claims in terms of what breaking the rules would do to the spectator of a play.

One could thus argue that the distance between a Thomas Rymer, say, and the famous declarations of independence by critics like Pope and Johnson was much less difficult to traverse than the chasm between the modern search for intrinsic form and the search I am conducting here for a criticism adequate to Goldsmith's art. It was as natural as breathing for critics who questioned the rules to do so by reference to effects the rules had set out to serve. In Pope's famous words from "An Essay on Criticism,"

> If, where the rules not far enough extend,
> (Since rules were made but to promote their end)
> Some lucky licence answer to the full
> Th' intent propos'd, that licence is a rule (ll. 146–49).

It was equally natural for Johnson to move freely in the "Preface to Shakespeare," for example, back and forth along the line of force joining the author and the audience, at one moment talking against the rules as destructive of dramatic effect and in the next breath appraising qualities of the author's genius, self-evidently the source of all powerful effects.

Such critics, schooled in a classical theory that was hospitable to talk about authors' gifts, trained by the most admired works of the time to accept and praise "variety," along with other relatively miscellaneous gifts, would have been baffled, I suspect, by rules that outlawed Goldsmith's free "extrinsic" references or demanded an "objective" unity without reference to any audience. But perhaps precisely because they found Goldsmith's practice so fully in harmony with their critical presuppositions, they did not develop (indeed, no one to my knowledge has ever developed) a fully articulated rhetorical criticism adequate to the "structures of appeal" in works like *The Citizen*. I am not at all clear what such a study of rhetorical bondings might yield, but I am sure that it would include what I turn to now, the many signs of skill in the implied author (who in our thought becomes indistinguishable from the writer, Goldsmith) as found in 123 moments of glorious writing just over two centuries ago.

One might attempt to list these structures of appeal in the order in which they are experienced, *if* they were in fact met as discrete appeals. But it is in the nature of "variety" that a given stroke will carry more than one appeal. Still, if we are to see just how much was being said when traditional critics praised Goldsmith's "variety," we must risk a brief analysis.

First, consider his *appeals to the reader's self-esteem (what must be called flattery if and when Goldsmith does not believe that the ascription of virtue is justified)*. As a citizen of London, I pick up the *Public Ledger* and find myself congratulated for being (*a*) an Englishman—that is, a citizen of a nation that on the whole is the most generous, enlightened, advanced, and best-governed—in a word, the most "polite" of all (see, for example, letter 4); (*b*) a cosmopolitan—that is, like the author, I am a citizen of the world; though patriotic, I am too sophisticated to talk without irony of my patriotism, and I really take all mankind into my tolerant, amused vision; (*c*) a penetrating critic of the folly and greed that surround me, *even* here in England; I am the kind of person who can savor both the comic misreadings committed by the visitor Altangi and the comedy of British idiosyncrasy viewed in a universal light (see letter 45).

Second, Goldsmith offers *appeals to pleasure in satire*. To list Goldsmith's satiric objects (most of which reinforce the first appeal) would fill pages; they include many different kinds and manifestations of pride, luxury, license, hypocrisy, superstition, ambition, pedantry, and fraudulence; varieties of ignorance and folly in politics, marriage customs, scholarship and the arts, travel, medicine, and religion; many specific "humours," like the spleen and other kinds of hypochondria; social climbing, pretensions to wisdom; and a variety of "classes" (attacked in whole or in part), such as women who aspire to masculine achievement or noblemen who dabble in the arts.

However, the mere list only hints at what any one satiric letter shows clearly: that the satire is for the most part amiable, since the reader is for the most part cheerfully exempted from its charges. He can read safely as attacks are made on people of other nations, classes, and professions. Even if he happens to be a doctor, say, the caricature of a quack will probably not cut too close to the bone; still, it comes close enough to give the reader the *illusion* that he is broad-minded in tolerating it. Rarely does Goldsmith allow a depth that might seriously disturb an attentive reader, and even then, as in "City Night-Piece" (letter 117), the literary mode in which potentially shattering questions are raised is so conventional that the reader can easily maintain his distance. For it is Altangi, the foreign visitor, who cries, "Why, why was I born a man, and yet see the sufferings of wretches I cannot relieve!" (p. 454). The threat to wealth implied in an attack on the evils of poverty is finally deflected to another question entirely: "Why was this heart of mine formed with so much sensibility! or why was not my fortune adapted to its impulse! Tenderness, without a capacity of relieving, only makes the man who feels it more wretched than the object which sues for assistance." Which leaves *us* with an easy escape hatch.

One might, with a little intellectual stretching and considerable cynicism, incorporate all of the remaining appeals under these first two. But we infer a Goldsmith who quite obviously did not believe that every human motive falls either under the enhancement of self or the degradation of others. When we talk of *The Citizen*, it is important not to attempt abstract classifications along logically coherent lines. The pleasure of learning something, for example, or the pleasure of detecting an irony have both been reduced, by some philosophers, to the pleasure of being flattered. Goldsmith warms our growing friendship by assuming what we readers assume in playing our roles as genial philosophers: that there are many kinds of human motivation and that degrees of authenticity, disinterestedness, egoism, and fraudulence are discernible in each kind.

Goldsmith offers, third, pleasure in *the recollection of commonplace wisdom*. As early reviewers noted, the level of instruction here is never threateningly high. Whether the instruction is half-hidden beneath an ironic surface, as in the story of the three lovers of British liberty (letter 4), or is offered directly, as in the "cautions on life, taken from a modern philosopher of China" (letter 83), we never go very deep, and we seldom are asked to think in unfamiliar ways. Readers who desire depth can go read Hume, but those who want to be instructed delightfully, even comfortably, can read sound moral thought like this:

> Avoid such performances where vice assumes the face of virtue, seek wisdom and knowledge without ever thinking you have found them. A man is wise, while he continues in the pursuit of wisdom; but when he once fancies that he has found the object of his enquiry, he then becomes a fool. Learn to pursue virtue from the man that is blind, who never makes a step without first examining the ground with his staff.

Anyone who is tempted to scoff at this kind of truism should think first of the modern examples he has himself enjoyed. Popular rhetoric in serial form, whether it gets collected or not, almost always includes a large element of such reiteration of established wisdom. In our own time, most of the serialists who have succeeded have, it is true, dressed their received truths in the guise of daring, lonely originality; one thinks of the *unpopular* and *skeptical* essays and radio addresses of Bertrand Russell, the many "slashing," "daring," "revolutionary," and "shocking" columnists whose collected pieces earn a following: the Jimmy Breslins, Murray Kemptons, Mike Roykos, and Hunter Thompsons, all claiming to forge new and unpopular truths. But we also have had many Westbrook Peglers, Max Raffertys, and William Buckleys, "daring" to revive old and equally conventional ones. All deal in commonplaces, necessarily, just as our closest rival to Goldsmith, E. B. White, is exceptional not in originality of ideas but in his "self-portraiture" as a crotchety but kindly, shrewd, infinitely perceptive, and "various" genius of our time.

Fourth, we find the appeal of *new truth*. In Goldsmith, as in most popular essayists, we do find a smattering of what to many readers will seem daring novelty. He thus presents a curious mixture of "neoclassical" and "romantic" elements (at least he will do so to anyone who divides the world into two parts, the classical and the romantic). Anyone reading through *The Citizen* in search of romantic tags will find them everywhere, and from its sales figures it would be easy to demonstrate that Goldsmith, as a preromantic, did not really come into his own until the romantic period; for there was but one London edition of *The Citizen* in his lifetime and only five London editions before 1790, yet there were *seven* editions between 1790 and 1800! Do we not see here the triumph of Goldsmith's claim to individuality and originality; of his questioning of universal standards of truth and beauty (he can sometimes sound almost like a modern anthropologist); of his radical skepticism about miracles and wonders; of his insistence on the value of novelty and change?[31]

A fifth appeal is to *the pleasure of ironic deciphering*. Though it is wrong to say that the whole of *The Citizen* is ironic, every commentator has been aware that much of it is. Most critics have recognized that part of our sense of Goldsmith's "variety" derives precisely from the almost impossibly quick shifts of tone he expects of us. Goldsmith knew many satires in which an exotic traveler observes local vices and foibles, but he capitalized more fully than any I have read on the possibilities this device offers for variety of effect. Earlier "visitors" tend to stress one of three possibilities: (1) steady satire on ridiculous local customs, as in the many versions of "The Devil on Crutches" (it is true that such satire is "steady" only in effect, not in tone, for the narrator is seldom a "consistent" character; instead he is shifted at will from reliable to ironic statement and back again, while the steady attack is maintained);[32] (2) steady exploitation of interest in the exotic (the traveler reveals how strange is the world he comes from); and (3) steady exploitation of the comic ignorance of the visitor, with irony in every line.

Goldsmith's choice was to create an extraordinarily rich mixture of all three, and we should not be surprised that his diversity has produced confusion and controversy, not just in our own time, when ironologists abound and invite angry denunciations for overinterpretation, but from the very beginning. Readers early were troubled because Lien Chi Altangi was not consistently the exotic visitor, wise in Chinese matters, ignorant of English ways. In his wonderfully complex "Editor's Preface" Goldsmith says that many readers at first "were angry not to find him [the Citizen] as ignorant as a Tripoline ambassador, or an Envoy from Mujac" (p. 13). But instead of a straightforward defense of his Citizen, Goldsmith provides a shifting, playful mixture of bona fides and undercuttings:

> The distinctions of polite nations are few; but such as are peculiar to the Chinese, appear in every page of the following correspondence. The metaphors and allusions are all drawn from the East. Their formality our author carefully preserves. Many of their favourite tenets in morals are illustrated. The Chinese are always concise, so is he. Simple, so is he. The Chinese are grave and sententious, so is he. But in one particular, the resemblance is

peculiarly striking: the Chinese are often dull; and so is he. Nor has my assistance been wanting.... In the intimacy between my author and me, he has usually given me a lift of his Eastern sublimity, and I have sometimes given him a return of my colloquial ease.

And then, in a manner close to the self-conscious narration of the *Tristram Shandy* that the Citizen is to attack in letter 53, the editor interrupts a fit of moralizing about the taste of the times: "during this fit of morality, lest my reader should sleep, I'll take a nap myself, and when I awake tell him my dream." The dream suggests the variety that is to come: it mocks those who have offered "the furniture, frippery and fireworks of China" and portrays Goldsmith as offering "a small cargoe of Chinese morality." But then it mocks that decision, sending his "wheelbarrow" full of offerings to the bottom of the Thames. Waking in a fright, the editor turns to discuss himself. Neither a poet nor a philosopher,

> at present I belong to no particular class. I resemble one of those solitary animals, that has been forced from its forest to gratify human curiosity. My earliest wish was to escape unheeded through life; but I have been set up for half-pence, to fret and scamper at the end of my chain. Tho' none are injured by my rage, I am naturally too savage to court any friends by fawning. Too obstinate to be taught new tricks; and too improvident to mind what may happen, I am appeased, though not contented. Too indolent for intrigue, and too timid to push for favour, I am—— But what signifies what am I.

Now this is a curious piling-up of ironies indeed, and that final question must surely be answered: "What you are matters a great deal. Your *book* signifies precisely what you are: Goldsmith, a writer alive in your time and coping with it essay by essay. What you are can thus never be precisely identified with any *part* of your book. Even to say that you are 'ironic' or 'cosmopolitan' will oversimplify."

The word "irony" can obscure more than it illuminates. Even if we confine our interest to intended, stable, covert ironies, considering only statements that Goldsmith requires us to reconstruct into meanings that he foreordains, we find at least three kinds, all of them more precise than the ironic view that Quintana and others have seen as the unifying principle of the book.

a) Goldsmith and the reader stand securely together as Altangi commits an error either of fact or judgment or both, as in his misreading of the signs over pubs: "The houses borrow very few ornaments from architecture; their chief decoration seems to be a paltry

piece of painting, hung out at their doors or windows, at once a proof
of their indigence and vanity" (p. 19).

b) Goldsmith, the reader, and Altangi stand securely together
against some other victim:

> You are not insensible, most reverend Fum Hoam, what number-
> less trades, even among the Chinese, subsist by the harmless pride
> of each other. Your nose-borers, feet-swathers, tooth-stainers,
> eyebrow pluckers, would all want bread, should their neighbours
> want vanity. These vanities, however, employ much fewer hands
> in China than in England; and a fine gentleman, or a fine lady,
> here dressed up to the fashion, seems scarcely to have a single limb
> that does not suffer some distortions from art. [P. 23]

The effect is like the first one, except that here the narrative voice is
not repudiated. What is complex beyond the reach of final explanation is the ordinary reader's successful operation in determining
when Altangi's words must be reconstructed and when they must not
be.

c) Goldsmith, Altangi, and the reader attend to some third narrative voice, whose words they all understand to be either self-betrayals
or unreliable commentary. The structure of the bond here is just like
the others, but the surface effect is of further variety. The introduction
of Beau Tibbs, for example, in letters 54 and 55, provides innumerable
instances of shifts of tone, ranging from Tibbs's giving himself away
without anyone's noting it except the reader, to the overt judgment
by Altangi that the "company of fools may at first make us smile, but
at last never fails of rendering us melancholy" (p. 232). If I ask
whether Goldsmith stands by that final generalization, or whether, as
with many of Altangi's judgments, he silently repudiates it, I discover
just how remarkably controlled the tone is. No one, not even Hopkins, has suggested that Altangi's condemnation is too harsh or that
Goldsmith is really attacking *him* on behalf of the misjudged Beau.
We are here so little concerned with Altangi himself that his generalizations do not serve to characterize him further; they are Goldsmith's
generalizations. Yet they are tonally quite unlike the many nonironic
essays.

A sixth appeal is to *pleasure in the exotic*. Though this appeal over-
laps the pleasure of learning, it includes a kind of titillation that has
little to do with satisfying curiosity or feeding an appetite for wisdom.
The Citizen ridicules those who succumb to fads and fashions. But at
the same time the book profits, as Goldsmith knew it would, from its
exotic aura. Chinese names, manners, maxims, and anecdotes

sprinkle almost every letter, and when Goldsmith cannot find what he needs in his sources, he freely turns Western legends and anecdotes into "ancient Chinese lore." We can be sure that even his most sophisticated readers, perforce moved by their reading into "the meridian" of pleased response, would enjoy the genuine exotica while at the same time playing two other games he invites them to: recognizing and admiring some of his Western transformations and guessing about doubtful cases.

Seventh, there is the *pleasure in parody, particularly parody of the exotic*. Related both to satire and to the other kinds of ironic invitation to reconstruct meanings, this appeal depends on the reader's ability to recognize the clichés of exotic romance and to enjoy seeing them mocked. Like all forms of invitation that make use of information not given on the surface of a text, parody both flatters the reader (appeal 1), satirizes (appeal 2), and gives at least the illusion of conveying truth (appeals 3 and 4). It also requires the deciphering energy of irony (appeal 5). Thus parody cannot be grasped without producing some degree of identification with the author, since he has as much as asserted that the reader shares his knowledge and his evaluation of the original. And the "author" here cannot be distinguished from the "writer."

Finally, there is the *pleasure of comic drama*. Every critic, at least until recently, has mentioned that *The Citizen* contains a collection of notable characters, all comic or humorous. Some have seen these characters not only as "humorous" but as "humours"—as highly caricatured two-dimensional folk who go through the same paces each time they come on stage. The London characters, like those who engage in the Oriental adventure and then come together in the final parodic wedding, are never offered as developed persons. It is in the nature of this genre that it will not permit a developed drama any more than it will permit a really serious development of philosophy, a sustained and challenging comment or satire, a deep analysis of the psychology of Londoners or of their social structure, a developed literary criticism, or, indeed, any other kind of discourse that requires scope for its perfecting.

Altangi himself, one might object, is given sustained and elaborate portrayal. Hopkins argues that he is consistently undermined by irony and is thus a sustained center of dramatic interest. But the fact is that we seldom see him as a character in his own right, for our attention is almost always on Goldsmith, for whose consistent rich maneuvers the inconsistent Altangi serves, sometimes as mask and sometimes as direct spokesman.

These eight structures of appeal do not exhaust the skills of this author and the pleasure and instruction they yield: Goldsmith's rich metaphoric gift, his ability to describe the London setting with great vividness, his mastery of the vocabulary of praise (letter 43), and so on.

The only explicit portrait of the Goldsmith implied in these appeals is in the Preface. When interpreted through its intricate ironies, the identification with the captive bear or monkey is perhaps our best clue to the *kind* of thing Goldsmith knows himself to be attempting. He belongs "to no particular class"—*except* of course the class of those solitary entertainers who fret and scamper to satisfy human curiosity. We find in his description, as we find in the book, an author who is determined to entertain but who will do so with metaphors that bite, and instruct through biting; a man determined to be more honest than most commentators; a man savage, obstinate, improvident, not contented; a shrewd, disillusioned man, but still benevolent; a cosmopolitan, sometimes indeed almost cynical about his spectators. Yet he *will* entertain.

It follows that to list the implied virtues of intellect, morality, and imagination exhibited by the author does as little justice to him as any summary of any book does to the whole; paraphrase can violate the "structure" of our relation to an authorial character just as it can the life of a plot. The portrait is made up of *all* the appeals we have mentioned, themselves still an abstraction from the cumulative delight and instruction found in every line of every page.

Each virtue binds us further to Goldsmith every time it is exemplified. And each new exemplification reinforces our conviction about the chief virtue of all: imaginative richness. Thus we read on, or around and about, not to discover *what will happen* but to discover *what our hero's genius will reveal* when he turns to the next subject and the next after that. There will of course be specific kinds of "suspense," yielding a sequential appeal, especially for contemporary readers; once Altangi has enlivened any current event with his wry, eccentric vision, readers will expect and desire more of the same whenever another major public event occurs. A letter on "a noble death" predicts a letter on the coronation; on such occasions, readers must have awaited Altangi's words with an engagement as intense, of its kind, as they would feel between acts 4 and 5 of a well-plotted play. But the nature of the engagement, though certainly *formed* in one sense, is largely obscured when one attempts to use formal language to describe it.

Usually the "suspense" will be even more generalized. Even after weeks and months of variety, even when readers might have begun to suspect that all subjects suitable to the genre have been exhausted, they will hunger for more. But more of what? Why, of "Goldsmith," regardless of his subject. The appetite has become so generalized, in a work like *The Citizen*, that it applies beyond the boundaries of the work and indeed the boundaries of what we have learned to call art. Having consumed these 123 banquets, I shall of course go on to those offered in *The Bee*. Nor will it matter very much if some of them fall short of perfection. Once Goldsmith has established himself in my soul, even his way of being dull is interesting, since it adds to my engagement with his total character. It is of course especially unimportant if, reading in the 1970s, I find passages that are dull unless viewed as historically revealing—unless, that is, they are violated with my improper questions about what two centuries have done to the work. It is true that this genre is especially vulnerable to time, especially dependent on later readers' learning. The fact will be troublesome, however, only to a criticism that worries about self-subsistent qualities of the work. As signs of Goldsmith's skill, the details that depend on immediate historical reference are permanently accessible to reconstruction; they need not be universal as *topical appeals* so long as they demonstrate a permanently appealing gift.

What is important is to recognize that our experience of this special kind of "career-author," possessing, as he does, every admirable quality except those inimical to his genre (such as philosophical profundity, psychological depth, sustained *poetic* invention), is as "tightly organized" as is our experience of sequential forms. If we try to add or subtract virtues from the particolored portrait, we begin to encounter criteria as rigorous as those we find in linear works when we try to expunge or transpose events, episodes, or characters. Suppose we try to erase this "Goldsmith's" benevolence, or his awareness of how awful and ridiculous men and women tend to be, or his wit, or his capacity for irony, or his determination to see British manners in a cosmopolitan light, or his anger about injustice and the cruelty of some British institutions, or his amused tolerance of harmless vices, or his beautifully sustained stylistic grace and "correctness." Any of these virtues lost would weaken our engagement. What is more, it is hard to think of others that could be added. To imagine other virtues and ways of realizing them in serial essays would require of me a comparable "genius," comparable gifts of controlled variety. When a personality has been perfected in this way, the critic cannot meddle. He can only describe and perhaps—though I shall not attempt it here—find ways of appraising the merit of rival characters: Montaigne or Lamb. say, or E. B. White or E. M. Forster.

I have tried to suggest that there is in *The Citizen* as much artistic skill in the maker, and thus artistic pleasure for the receiver, as in all but the very best novels, satires, plays, and poems of its period. I see it as Goldsmith's most important work, clearly outranking *The Vicar*, say, or *She Stoops to Conquer*—works far more often discussed. Surely exemplars of this kind from other periods deserve more critical attention than we have given them. It is a curious literary kind, admittedly, not high-, low-, or middle-brow. In every period it is enjoyed by a very broad range of readers, from those committed to high art to those who read little more than the daily papers and magazines where the periodical essays appear; the "meridian" is thus often broad enough to include almost all readers for a given period. It can thus be even more interesting to cultural historians and sociologists than to critics. Perhaps no one will ever claim that its exemplars, even at their best, rival the greatest novels and plays and epic poems, but a good share of the world's imaginative genius has gone into their creation, and they surely deserve a critic who will postpone all "improper" questions—which in this case include questions about "artistic" unity and structure—until he has fully savored the self-portraiture of a genius.

The Uselessness of Rules

I have so far recommended respect for what we call the author in three quite different ways.

In "The Bench of Desolation" we discover James's full achievement only if we surrender to the implied author, rejecting Edel's initially plausible notions of what the *writer* would have been most likely to write at a given time of life. In doing so, we are of course making tacit use of certain other notions about the writer—his genius, his irrepressible inventiveness, his mastery. Without the deep commitment to a writer who is likely to be worth attending to, we would have no grounds for digging into one more tale, after the scores of other tales by James we have read. What finally controls our discoveries, however, is not such expectations but what James made. Since what we discover is even more inventive than we have any right to expect of the old man, we must now consciously or unconsciously revise our picture not only of the flesh-and-blood writer but also of the "career-author." Embittered or not, the "real" James was able to add to his career the imposing novelty of "The Bench of Desolation."

In seeking the art of *The Turn of the Screw* the task is entirely different because of the immense barrier of existing criticism. It was not biographical preconceptions but a failure to test critical inventiveness against biographical likelihoods that allowed critics to rewrite the story with such wild abandon. It may appear that in appealing, against such interesting witnesses, to what "an author like James" would probably do, I commit the very fault that I questioned in Leon Edel. But the author I appealed to is quite different: not a plotted life that at a given point in its trajectory *must* write a given kind of work, but a kind of gift that I have seen at work in novel after novel and find, here again, at work. My picture of this "author" cannot tell me in advance what James will do, and it therefore cannot lead me to *certain* decisions among the few plausible interpretations of what James in fact did. But it can rule out all readings that make of the story something that no serious writer of any skill could possibly have perpetrated, and I think in this case it yields a reading that honors James's choices and thus puts the burden of proof on those whose readings must explain away many of those choices. It is of course true that many fine artists create failed works; but their failures are of a kind that artists commit, and we rest satisfied with the judgment of failure only after we have made plausible guesses about what might have led a gifted human being to abandon to us this report on his creative endeavors. In short, *The Turn* is too fine an achievement to be reduced to what any one of us might have written about these materials, relying on whatever is suggested to us by our childhood experience of governesses, ghosts, or ghost stories.

In dealing with Goldsmith's *The Citizen of the World* we are forced, by the nature of the achievement, to work even more aggressively in collapsing the distinctions that are to some degree useful in reading "The Bench." Beginning with tacit inherited notions of what sorts of object a great writer will create, searching for the kind of formal excellence that the Henry Jameses give us, I stand helpless before a person whose gifts are of an entirely different kind. This time, attention to the text and its career-author force me, reluctantly, to a substantial revision of my notions of what it takes to be a great writer. The author implied by the diverse implied authors of 123 essays lacks all of James's grand architectonic genius. In the end what we have re-created is not a great formed text but a greatly gifted man who has given us many texts and promises to give us many more. It is he whom we understand, admire, and even love; his writing comes to seem a kind of conduct, a way of being in the world that sets us a model of what it might mean to cope with the world's various opportunities,

problems, and woes. Flesh-and-blood author and career-author become indistinguishable, because we can here make direct and certain
inferences about the writer himself. Whatever sustained gifts of inventiveness Goldsmith attributes to "Goldsmith" must in fact be real;
whatever genius we find exhibited by the one is irresistibly granted to
the flesh-and-blood writer. Thus one of my own critical credos bites
the dust. I had always said that one can never make secure inferences
from implied author to real writer, and I could cite innumerable errors
made by biographers who thought they could. Now I am forced to see
that my examples of the sharp distinction were always of moral qualities. A skillful writer can fake generosity, kindness, universal sympathy, patience, courage—any moral virtue whatever. But nobody
could fake the intellectual and aesthetic virtues we found in *The Citizen:* they must be exercised before our eyes. So again: critical
preconceptions—this time my own—have had to bow to the author;
quite literally, I have been forced to surrender to Oliver Goldsmith.
My abstractions—coherence, organic wholes, even the implied
author—kneel to his powers.

THE ECLIPSE OF THE IMPLIED AUTHOR BY THE "MASTER"

As long as a writer's gifts are more or less in harmony with general
opinion about them, readers may be aided by their preconceptions
about the career-author. If, that is to say, the career-author and the
public "character" are not inharmonious, readers are likely, in approaching a new work, to find their previous experience an aid to
understanding. We have seen, for example, that when Goldsmith
nods, the character of "Goldsmith" does not suffer much; and that
can only be because the reader imports into a given "installment" the
qualities built by the series. This is not, simply, the same as my
forgiving Shakespeare for not blotting his thousand bad lines because
I know him to be a great writer; for the "bad lines" are themselves
"Shakespearian," and so, too, the later works of Faulkner, the
juvenilia of Jane Austen, the weaker essays of Goldsmith, are still
Faulknerian and Austenian and Goldsmithian; and I can love the
authors even in their relatively weak attempts, partly because knowledge of the general intent helps me infer what success in them would
have been.

Counterexamples are easily found. Early in T. S. Eliot's career,
before the first unmistakably religious poems had appeared, readers
whose picture of him was based on the wastedness of *The Waste Land*
had immense difficulty comprehending, let alone accepting, what

seemed an unaccountable shift in the career. Similarly, many admiring readers of Faulkner, having built a public character of "America's greatest novelist," the southerner who employed regional grotesques and an incredibly rich, freewheeling style to show the comedy and tragedy of the past dying into the present (or some such commonplace), were suddenly thrown off balance when *A Fable* appeared in 1954. It wasn't "southern" enough, it was too overtly concerned with religion, it was "turgid and apocalyptic," leaving its readers "uncertain of what the author is trying to say," as Malcolm Cowley states in his *Encyclopaedia Britannica* article. The actual career-author was off in new directions, leaving the "character" behind as an obstacle to understanding. *A Fable* would perhaps have been difficult to take in even if written by an unknown; read by those looking for "Faulkner," it was infuriating.

Thus, in our criticism of any author who creates a career-author (that is, anyone who writes more than one work) or whose public creates for him an independent "character," there comes a time when received opinions about these two can blur our vision of any one of his actual achievements; for the critic may either praise the work for virtues that are really in earlier works or overlook valuable qualities because the "image" has turned ugly. Both misreadings result from dependence on unexamined ideas about "the author." For our final example of the importance of respecting authors' actual achievements, we should look at a work that has been misread in both of these ways.

Thaïs

> "What's all this [about] irony and pity?"
> "What? Don't you know about Irony and Pity?"
> "No. Who got it up?"
> "Everybody. They're mad about it in New York."

Mad about it they still were, in 1926, when Hemingway's splendid spoofing appeared in *The Sun Also Rises*. But it was not everybody who had been responsible. It was mainly Anatole France, abetted by his almost unanimously enthusiastic critics. And of all his works, the one that must have seemed to fit the formula best was *Thaïs*, already a quarter of a century old when Jake Barnes learned of irony and pity.

"Irony and pity" is not a bad formula for the effect of *Thaïs*, as formulas go. It is at least as useful—and at least as misleading—as "pity and fear" for tragedy. There is, however, a surprising difference. If I tell you the story of any classical tragedy, even in very brief form, you will know at once why someone might talk about that story using the terms "pity" and "fear." But if I tell you of the priest who lost his soul converting the prostitute, you will not be able to predict any determinate reaction—except, perhaps, that the story will produce in everyone a slight bit of ironic wonder at the grand reversal. In other words, a teller will be able to turn such material in almost any direction he chooses, making it into a tragedy, a comedy, a farce, a celebration of God's wonder and mystery—or a tale playing with pity and irony.

It is true that the story of even a tragedy like *Oedipus Rex* can be retold, with a little effort, as other than tragic—as farce, say, or as a satire against the unjust gods. But there is, in the *Oedipus* material, something more resistant to such deflections than one finds in the *Thaïs* material. Even the malleable stuff that went into *The Turn* was inherently more resistant than this. The fact is that the story of Thaïs and the Man of God had been told in hundreds of different versions before *Thaïs*, with many different effects, while the story of Oedipus, at least until this century, was always told as a tragedy, and the story of children haunted by devils is always, in its twentieth-century retellings, horrifying or pathetic, never comic or even tragic. (Farcical parody is, of course, another matter entirely.)

Let us begin with three possible stories of Thaïs and Paphnutius. The first, which I shall call "The Hourglass," was intended by E. M. Forster as a summary of "the pattern" of *Thaïs*.[33]

> *Thais*, by Anatole France, is the shape of an hour-glass.
>
> There are two chief characters, Paphnuce the ascetic, Thais the courtesan. Paphnuce lives in the desert, he is saved and happy when the book starts. Thais leads a life of sin in Alexandria, and it is his duty to save her. In the central scene of the book they approach, he succeeds; she goes into a monastery and gains salvation, because she has met him, but he, because he has met her, is damned. The two characters converge, cross, and recede with mathematical precision, and part of the pleasure we get from the book is due to this. Such is the pattern of *Thais*.... It is the same as the story of *Thais*, when events unroll in their time-sequence, and the same as the plot of *Thais*, when we see the two characters bound by their previous actions and taking fatal steps whose consequence they do not see. But whereas the story appeals to our curiosity and the plot to our intelligence, the pattern appeals to our aesthetic sense, it causes us to see the book as a whole. We do not see it as an hour-glass—that is the hard jargon of the lecture room which must never be taken literally.... We just have a pleasure without knowing why.... If it was not for this hour-glass the

story, the plot, and the characters of Thais and Paphnuce would none of them exert their full force . . . .

Plenty of irony here, all right. But what kind? There's no hint of pity, only "curiosity," "intelligence," and "aesthetic sense." The "pattern" is aesthetically pleasing, and presumably part of our pleasure comes from our ironic awareness of the crossing lines.

The neat formula for a neat story is indeed in itself pleasing—so pleasing conceptually that it has been borrowed by other critics, when they needed an illustration of neat fictional form. There are only two things wrong with it: it bears hardly any relation at all to what we find in France's version, and, if taken seriously, it will surely discourage anyone from wanting to read the book. All of the pleasure is in the summary. Why bother to read nearly two hundred pages when the form can be experienced in three sentences?

What is worse, by using the hourglass figure, Forster makes his *summary* sound more interesting, "aesthetically," than it is. What he *describes* is really no more interesting than an X. One can only assume that he chose the hourglass because it suggests a more beautiful symmetry than one finds in two crossed straight lines. "The Hourglass" might become interesting, of course, given a bit of appropriate expansion, if told to an audience of devout Christians. An uncritical Christian faith would presumably make even a short version of the X seem a powerful ironic illustration of the mysterious ways of the Lord God. Even for such a telling, however, an abstract figure is a sorry reduction, as we see in my second tale—the story as it might have existed long before *Thaïs*—a version I shall call "The Salvation of Thaïs."

There was once a priest famous for his goodness and piety. Devoting himself quietly to good works, asking nothing of the world and offering his whole life to those who suffer in it, he seemed destined to end his days as he had begun them, in blessed obscurity. But God called him to a great sacrifice, without letting him know at first just how great the sacrifice would be. "In the city of Alexandria," God said to him in a dream, "there is a famous courtesan named Thaïs. Go and save her soul by converting her to belief in Christ the Lord." And Paphnutius, for that was his name, did as God had commanded him. Sacrificing the quiet life that he loved, suppressing his loathing for the wicked ways of the city, he went unto Thaïs and preached the gospel to her. At first she merely mocked him, but then she grew angry as he plagued her with his sermons. She determined to seduce him, to show the hypocrisy that she knew must be in his heart. And, using all the wiles of which she was consummate mistress, she succeeded: Paphnutius succumbed and, in succumbing, fell in love with Thaïs and forgot his God.

But Thaïs was strangely remorseful for what she had done. Slowly the truth dawned upon her: she had committed a great sin, because the words of Paphnutius had been true. And so she cast off her sinful life, betook herself to a convent, and lived such a saintly life that, when she died, all knew she had gained eternal life. But Paphnutius was driven by his aroused lust into sin after sin, and when *he* died, alone like a wretched, vicious beast, his soul was delivered to eternal torment. And all who knew of this story wondered at the ways of God, who had sacrificed one of his lambs to save another.

If the hourglass, or X, pattern fits any version, it ought to fit this. But as I have reconstructed the skeleton of a tale that might have been meaningful to an audience of believers, I have obviously left the X far behind.

For a third version we could tell a sentimental story about the lovely Thaïs. But for that you must go to Massenet's opera (and I'm afraid I cannot recommend it) or seek out the movie (1918) "based on the novel of Anatole France" and starring Mary Garden.[34] Or we might tell one of those satirical *fabliaux* in which the central scene, Paphnutius' seduction, would use comic devices to heighten our picture of the hypocritical priesthood. Instead, let us move somewhat closer to *Thaïs* and tell the story of "The Secular Damnation of Paphnutius: or [as the subtitle of the first American translation of *Thaïs* read] The Vengeance of Venus."

An ignorant, dull-witted, arrogant, and fanatical priest, Paphnutius, lives in the Egyptian desert in the time of Saint Anthony. Dwelling in self-imposed filth, surrounded by ugliness, persecuting his senses with foolish ascetic practices which he believes will win his sanctification, denying himself all of the pleasures which alone make life endurable, he tortures his already scarred mind with a scheme for a really spectacular and glorious work: saving a courtesan whom he once had lusted after in the days before his conversion. He seeks her out, unaware that his main motive is lust, rationalizing his quest with hollow religious clichés, ignoring all of the rich beauties of the world he passes through, and dogmatically rejecting all that can be said against his own superstitions.

He finds her in her glory, the most beautiful woman in the world, loved by all, the living avatar of Venus. Generous, tender, lovely in spirit as in body, surrounded by the exquisite gifts of her lovers, she is the unconscious priestess of the only religion that no skepticism can fully undermine. But she is vulnerable: she was once converted, when a child, to Christianity. Paphnutius, playing upon her sense of guilt and her desire for a life of perfect purity, reconverts her, burns her beautiful possessions as idols, subjects her to painful debasement (including some degree of physical torture), and shuts her up in a convent.

Her natural beauty and purity of spirit survive even this treatment, and she remains almost as glorious in her new sanctity as she had been in her days of love. But his encounter with her has only further deranged Paphnutius. Moving through ever crazier schemes for self-aggrandizement in the name of self-abasement, he finally begins to see the hollowness of his religion. God has deceived him; he will *not* be among the blessed. No, what is worse, God is dead. Doubt, despair, fear overwhelm him. Returning to embrace Thaïs, whose beautiful memory now seems his only reality, he finds her dying. He clasps her corpse to him and knows at last that he has denied himself the one genuine moment of happiness he might have had, that in fact he has been an accursed fool all along. He has desecrated *this* life in a world that offers no other.

As you have guessed, this is a rough summary of the events of *Thaïs*.

Now there are two obvious points to be made about "The Secular Damnation of Paphnutius." The first is that his story has about as much similarity to an hourglass as *King Lear* has to a Christmas tree. Such a priest encountering such a courtesan and moving to such a doom does not produce symmetrical images. There is no clear crossing from salvation to doom, for Paphnutius is damned from the beginning. And there is no crossing from damnation to salvation, for Thaïs is blessed throughout. There is, in fact, very little movement at all.

The second point follows: as the story stands, it is not a very good one. Although it will be, for all but devout Christians, a more interesting story than "The Salvation of Thaïs," it is still terribly flat, scarcely a story at all. The protagonist is now unequivocally Paphnutius, but he is already morally hideous and spiritually empty at the beginning, and at the end he is only slightly more hideous— and to some degree aware of his emptiness. Little has happened to change him, and not much more has happened to Thaïs. What is worse, almost everything that *has* happened has been predictable from the beginning; in other words, not much can have happened to the reader. I should think that if I were to work up a 200-page expansion of this version, *in its present tone*, most readers would say at the end, if they could finish it at all, "So what?"

I can think of only one kind of reader for whom "The Secular Damnation" would be exciting if told "straight" by a good novelist: the reader for whom all of the ideas implicit in this version would appear either original or daring. The religion of love is celebrated, sensual indulgence is taken for granted as superior to asceticism (even prostitution is not in itself an evil); self-denial *is* evil; pursuit of ugliness is a sin, and ugliness itself is a more serious punishment than "loss of fortune" or death might be; and, finally, the universe is empty: belief in God is at best an illusion for the genuinely pious, at worst a trap for an egotist like Paphnutius. No doubt many readers in France in 1890, when *Thaïs* appeared, would have found even "The Secular Damnation" an exciting inversion of the traditional tale and of its Christian norms. Probably many Americans during the next few decades found similar pleasures in something like my imagined version. But for us, now, whether we think of ourselves as religious or not, there can be little excitement in Anatole France's intellectual daring. My version, however skillfully it was expanded, would find no readers today. But what, then, of *Thaïs*?

The truth is that *Thaïs*, once one of the world's best-selling "masterpieces," finds few readers now. When Anatole France died in 1924, he was almost certainly the most admired author in the Western world. He had received the Nobel Prize—almost as a matter of course—three years before. In his own country, he had long since been considered what the young intellectuals of Paris declared him in a poll taken that year: "the greatest living author." In America he had for decades been praised as the French "man of letters" par excellence, the highest embodiment of "the totality of French culture"— and that of course meant for many Americans the highest embodiment of Culture itself. He had even been acclaimed a "real master" by Henry James—the master himself.

In the criticism of the time, one finds many signs that his admirers thought of themselves as a select few and that those who questioned his importance—and there were an increasing number of these as the decades passed—did so, like the envious Arnold Bennett, in the belief that most readers would never appreciate France, "and would only buy him under the threat of being disdained by the minority, whose sole weapon is scorn."[35]

What would have surprised Bennett, and what surprises me a half-century later, is that France was headed for one of those great popular successes that few "elitist" authors ever attain. We never know, of course, how many books that are bought are actually read, and I strongly suspect that many who bought France's works, in the flood of inexpensive editions that suddenly began to appear, must have been puzzled and finally defeated by what they found. Having bought *The Crime of Sylvestre Bonnard* or *The Revolt of the Angels* or *Penguin Island* or *The Gods Are Athirst* or *Thaïs* (the most popular of all), having bought them, in fact, because they had appeared on someone's list of the world's great novels, readers must often have found themselves grappling with ideas and technical maneuvers that were either puzzling or repugnant or both. Still, the fact remains: after 1924, all of France's major works went through edition after edition in America, as in the rest of the world. *Thaïs*, which had appeared in three American editions in its first twenty years, appeared in ten editions in the next eighteen, and among them was that badge of classical status, the Modern Library edition, in 1925.

Today the eclipse of Anatole France is by no means complete, but it would be hard to think of many authors of his quality who have fallen so far so fast. It is true that French editions of all his works are still in print, and there is still an expensive American edition of the complete works. Twenty of his titles are available separately to readers of English, and school editions of many of his works are still widely used in teaching French. But he just does not figure any longer on any literary scene that I know, on either side of the Atlantic. Serious readers do not read him; critics not only do not read him, they do not even lecture on him. Recently I have been asking acquaintances whether they have read any France. The younger ones have almost all said no; the older ones have almost all said yes, but only one of them had read anything in the last twenty years. *Thaïs*, once an international best-seller translated into eighteen languages, the book that Apollinaire could call "one of the most delicately wrought works of the nineteenth century," and its author, whom Edmund Wilson in the twenties thought immeasurably greater than Paul Valéry (France's successor in the French Academy), have almost disappeared.*

Readers who look for a good story, a "good read," and, after sampling a few pages in this book, find only what I reported in "The

---

*As is perhaps too easily inferred from my tone, these words originally served as an introduction to a new English translation of *Thaïs* published by the University of Chicago Press in 1976.

Secular Damnation," will no doubt decide that the disappearance is all to the good. Perhaps no one can now read *Thaïs* without wondering at first how it ever could have been *widely* popular. And aside from that historical question, what is one to *do* with all this freight of ideas that seem so thoroughly dated: this self-congratulatory cosmopolitanism, this easy skepticism about moral and—much worse—about political commitment, the heavy anticlericalism, the precious celebrations of Eros, the dilettantish taking-up of this or that commitment, always softened with expressions of worldly-wise detachment—such seeming ideas are in fact only slogans that serve to confirm one generation of readers and to turn off the next. When one reads, for example, the young James Branch Cabell's adulatory words about France in his introduction to the translation of *The Queen Pédauque* (1923), one can see that Cabell's praise for what he takes to be a literary quality—France's peculiar kind of irony—is really a celebration of the one right attitude toward life: the stance of the ironic man. When everyone who was anyone took up "irony and pity," the phrase summarized a complex of "ideas" and "feelings" about life that was exciting while it lasted but that inevitably passed with the coming of the thirties and then of World War II. By 1939, none of Anatole France's classics could any longer be found on the Modern Library list. When the ideas of "the master," Anatole France, passed out of fashion—so one might argue—*Thaïs* lost its appeal.

Contemporary evidence shows that readers identified with France in ways that went beyond the effects of any one work or even all of them together. He stood for his readers in the battle of life, representing one possible way of coping with the terrors of a universe recently unmasked as cold and impersonal. Everybody who was anybody had learned that if you scratch beneath the surface of things, as all great thinkers for more than two centuries had been doing, you find a heart of darkness, a terrifying emptiness where men had once seen God. And here was a man who had probed as far into that abyss as anyone and yet could *do* things with it—he could *write* about how to live with it; and, what was perhaps even more important, he could live intensely, celebrating life and its sensual pleasures even while scoffing at those who took those pleasures too seriously. Thus such a figure comes to *represent* me, in my time. His appeal in many respects resembles that of Goldsmith to his contemporaries (one finds in France's works themselves, as well as in his public stance, most of the appeals exhibited in *The Citizen*). But there are two obvious differences: "Anatole France" depends much more than Goldsmith on appearing as leader of the avant-garde (the fourth appeal, pp. 309 ff.), and his fame is thus much more immediately dependent on actions other than his publications: the signing of manifestos, the spreading of rumors about his mode of life—his reading, his dining, his love-making.

Later generations inevitably seek more up-to-date representatives: France is replaced by Gide and Proust, Gide and Proust by Camus and Sartre, Camus and Sartre by—whoever happens to be your present hero or heroine.* And once the public character has lost all magical powers, the works must make their way on their own, sadly hampered by everyone's conviction that nobody would be caught dead reading that old poseur.

The question now becomes: Does the present rejection of "the master" obscure a work of art worth preserving?

The great public figure, even more famous for being a writer than for his actual writings, was also famous for his sayings, among them one that went like this: "I have only two enemies: Christ and chastity." But what of readers who have decided not to hate but to be indifferent to Christ, who no longer have before them any models of chastity that might be hated or feared? Must not such readers inevitably find *Thaïs* boring, because it seems to depend on an outmoded image of the battler with Christ and chastity? Only, I would suggest, if they insist on taking its ideas as the early idolators did: as final truths about the world and clues about how to live.

Many readers recognized from France's earliest publication that he was "not a novelist" but, rather, a "man of ideas." Some few found him merely a "mental dilettante," as Paul West later put it, with "nothing coherent to say," a man who tried "to reconcile high intellectual ambitions with his impossibly cluttered mind," but who redeemed the clutter by creating "a prose of immaculate concision ...which only Camus and Colette have equalled."[36] Far more, as I have suggested, found his appeal, particularly in the earliest years, in the ideas themselves, though it was always difficult to make a case for any great originality or profundity. What was not generally recognized (and has now been forgotten) was that France's "delicate style" and "exquisite form"—the features of his work most often praised—were inseparable from his "ideas"; the form is made out of the ideas in ways that make freshness and profundity and even

---

*It is surprising how consistently modern Americans have relied on French culture to provide these representatives. I can remember how devastated I felt when the news came in 1960 that Camus had been killed in an automobile accident: *my* representative was gone. Now, only eighteen years later, even if he were still living, he could not serve in the same way for me. Others have supplanted him; and though his works survive for me, they must do so, as it were, on their own.

soundness fairly unimportant. It is in rediscovering the delicate interplay of idea and character that one discovers how France made the
hideous dry bones of "The Secular Damnation of Paphnutius" live.

Turning to the real thing at last, I ask you to read these first four
paragraphs slowly, pupils, and then comment on the words "falsely"
and "odor" in the final two sentences.

The desert, in those days, was settled by anchorites. From mud
and straw, these hermits built countless huts along the banks of
the Nile, far enough apart that their inhabitants could live in isolation, yet near enough that they could aid one another when necessary. Above the huts, churches raised their crosses here and there,
and the monks gathered in them on holy days to attend the celebration of the mysteries and participate in the sacraments. There
were also houses right at the water's edge, where the cenobites,
each enclosed in his narrow cell, met together only to better appreciate their solitude.

Anchorites and cenobites lived in abstinence, taking no food
before sunset and then eating only bread with a dash of salt and
wild marjoram. Some of them, burying themselves in the sand,
made homes of caves or tombs and lived lives that were still more
singular.

They observed vows of continence, wore cowled hair shirts,
slept naked on the ground after long vigils, prayed, sang psalms,
and, in a word, performed masterpieces of penitence every day.
Mindful of original sin, they refused to give to their bodies not
only pleasure and satisfaction but even the care that is considered
necessary by those who live in the world. They believed that
physical affliction purified the soul and that the flesh could receive
no more glorious adornment than ulcers and open sores. Thus was
the word of the prophets observed: "The desert shall be covered
with flowers."

Some of the inhabitants of that holy Thebaid spent their days in
asceticism and contemplation, while others earned their living
braiding palm fibers, or working for neighboring farmers at harvest
time. The pagans falsely suspected some of living by robbery or of
joining the wandering Arabs who pillaged caravans, but in truth
the monks despised wealth, and the odor of their virtues rose up to
heaven. [Les gentils en soupçonnaient faussement quelques-uns
de vivre de brigandage et de se joindre aux Arabes nomades qui
pillaient les caravanes. Mais à la vérité ces moines méprisaient les
richesses et l'odeur de leurs vertus montait jusqu'au ciel.]

One has no trouble with that kind of irony, of course, except
perhaps to wonder why everyone talked of France's *delicacy*: the stink

is strong, the satire direct. Whether we think that the irony is heavy or not, it is clear that we have here something entirely different from "The Secular Damnation." Here is a stylistic vitality that even in translation makes an entirely new thing of the materials. What begins as a sympathetic narrative voice, describing the hermits' life in language that they might themselves have used, suddenly reveals itself, in the third paragraph, to be utterly naive: "They believed that physical affliction purified the soul and that the flesh could receive no more glorious adornment than ulcers and open sores. Thus was the word of the prophets observed: 'The desert shall be covered with flowers.'"

This sly fulfillment of prophecy introduces a "novel" in which almost every word and phrase has to be retranslated into the unspoken words of Anatole France, "the ironic man." It is thus not exactly the story of Paphnutius that we read, as in "The Secular Damnation of Paphnutius," but something that almost might be called "The Elevation of Anatole France." To read the work at all, we must engage in a kind of playful philosophical conversation with its implied author, a conversation in which we never receive his words directly. In a moment we will read, "The ancients of the desert extended their power to include sinners and godless men. Their benevolence was sometimes terrible." The delight here, for the reader who sees himself and France together among the godless (even if the identification is only for the duration of the book), comes from the seemingly slight but powerful difference between the word "terrible" as spoken by the pious and naive narrator and the word "terrible" as spoken by the insinuating author.

"Paphnutius had a profound knowledge of the ways of faith. He knew hearts well enough to recognize that Timocles was not in God's grace, and the day of salvation had not yet come to this hell-bent soul." "Profound" may be again a bit heavy and a bit easy, but coming as a response to the long account by Timocles (the skeptic), Paphnutius' judgment is wonderfully silly.

"Crobyle [the slave girl] called him [Paphnutius] her sweet satrap and held up the mirror for him to see himself, and Myrtale tweaked his beard. Paphnutius, however, was praying and did not notice them." At such moments we hear the overt account in a voice that could be Paphnutius' own conscience-bound rationalizations. We are, in fact, so often inside his mind that we come to think of the whole story as if told by him, though of course there is much told that he could never tell. But the covert voice of the author is even stronger. Thus the effect here is almost as absurd as if it read: "Myrtale tweaked my beard, but I was praying and did not notice her."

"Since God, whose ways are inscrutable, did not deem it appropriate to enlighten his servant, Paphnutius, plunged into doubt, decided
to think about Thaïs no longer." In some works that sentence might
be taken at face value; except, perhaps, for the word "appropriate,"
which seems odd, it could all be written in a spirit of total piety. But
we who encounter it as we move into the last part of *Thaïs* have long
since known that every word carries both the meaning it might have
for the self-deluded Paphnutius and the meaning it has for the enlightened, skeptical reader: God's ways *are* inscrutable for the
would-be saint, and they are inscrutable in an entirely different way
for the reader, who is asked to be fairly certain that no God exists.

All the delight of such writing comes in the precise texture of each
line. We need not accept every claim to sophistication made by the
implied author. To the degree that we finally reject his claims, we
shall no doubt lose some of the titillation that certain "ideal readers"
of his own time must have known. But we can easily make ourselves,
with his help, into the kind of (temporary) sophisticate who can distinguish what is sound from what is blind in the narrator's point of
view. We are not even disturbed greatly when we find many passages
in which the ironies are too complex for deciphering: we know that
we are in good hands and that no doubt we could, with just a bit more
effort, make it all out clearly. Indeed, it increases our pleasure if we
can feel that France is always just a bit ahead of us: there is more here
than meets even *our* discerning eyes.

Besides, our assumed position, understanding "France," entails
the belief that the world cannot, after all, be "made out." Paphnutius
and the narrator think the world is simple even when God is inscrutable; but *we* know that it is ultimately baffling to the core. Pursued by
a vision of Thaïs, her bare breast "filmed over with the blood oozing
from her open heart," Paphnutius becomes more anxious. "His suffering was a cruel affliction. But, as his body and soul remained pure
in the midst of these temptations, he trusted in God and gently re-
proached him." On the one hand, we have no doubts about the gross
impurity of his body and soul; we know that the phrase "trusted in
God" and the word "gently" must be translated into Frankish, as it
were. But was it a "cruel" affliction or not? Yes and no. Perhaps. The
words are what Paphnutius thinks, but are they not also, in another
sense, what we can believe? Often, very often, we cannot tell; and not
being able to tell becomes part of our pleasure. Indeed, the mixtures
become more and more complex as the work proceeds. The narrative
voice itself occasionally takes on some of France's sophistication, yet

we have little trouble with this inconsistency of point of view. The implied author as ironic man never changes.

Philosophical irony of this kind is certainly not coherent thought, yet no one who lacks an interest in philosophical ideas can ever enjoy it very much. It feels somehow misleading to call *Thaïs* a "novel of ideas," though that's the only term we have for works (actually of many different sorts) in which our attention is more on thoughts than on the fate of characters. Though the author pretends that the ideas matter very much, they matter to him and to us very little as ideas, since they are (even, I suspect, for most of the more alert original readers) subordinated to the intellectual pleasure of hearing at least two voices talking at once, one of them betraying itself to the other.*

We have no name, I think, for the kind of work in which the central interest is a speculative, wryly amusing conversation with the implied author, conducted behind the main character's back, with the author presenting himself as "the ironic man." It might be described as a subvariety of that large class of works that Sheldon Sacks calls the "apologue"—works in which the invention and disposition of characters and episodes are determined more by a pattern of ideas than by the development of characters and their fate.[37] But the trouble is that here we have no real *pattern* of ideas. A schematic statement of how the author's various truths interrelate would betray the work as much as E. M. Forster's hourglass does. France was never a systematic philosopher. He changed his mind often. Though he was always "a skeptic," he embraced throughout his life a succession of dogmas. If it was true that Henry James's mind was never violated by an idea, it was true of France that his mind was raped almost daily. There *were* times in his later life, particularly after he committed himself in the Dreyfus Affair, when he stood for a relatively clear position as a pro-socialist critic; Georg Lukács was later to make of him almost a proto-Marxist hero, far more penetrating in his criticism of bourgeois culture than Hugo and the equal of Zola.[38] But no reader can emerge from *Thaïs* with a clear sense of what the novelist believes. It is essential to the

*It would be interesting to study France's influence on all those modern novelists in whose words we find similar sustained ironies achieved through "point of view." After all, 1890 was "very early" modern. It is likely that *all* the great modern novelists, from Joyce to James to Faulkner, had read France. Some of them—"novelists of ideas" like Aldous Huxley and James Branch Cabell—would have learned far more from him than from novelists who are today prominent in criticism and literary histories. And—for one last bit of speculation about influence—is it accidental that the formula from Hemingway with which we began, *irony and pity*, should be so clearly applicable to Hemingway's own works? What better summary is there of the intellectual and emotional effect of the final sentence of *The Sun Also Rises* than those two shopworn words?

special mocking tone of *Thaïs* that no firm assertions can be attributed to the author; our only clear picture at the end is of what he is against: all passionate ideological commitments are absurd, even though some are more absurd than others. After skepticism has done its work, what abides—and that on very shaky ground—is simply Venus and all that she stands for: beauty, tenderness, a tolerant generosity (but with limits: Thaïs is proud that she has not sold herself to those who do not love her), and a simplicity shared by Thaïs and by some—strangely, not all—of the beasts and birds.

To fuss as I have been doing about the *kind* of work we have here may seem less like mere pedantry when we remember what other critics have made of it. It was inevitable, for example, once E. M. Forster had settled on "The Hourglass" as his view of *Thaïs*, that he should judge the "talkative Alexandrians at Nicias' banquet" to be "just decorative." The scene that is by far the longest in the work, the scene that is longer than the entire history of Thaïs' past before Paphnutius meets her, the scene that is longer than Paphnutius' imitation of Saint Simeon Stylites, is for Forster "just decorative." But in the nameless kind of work we are trying to understand, a scene like this is not simply appropriate; a broad display of philosophical voices in open and sustained conflict is required.

In fictions that portray a sympathetic quest for salvation, the hero can himself survey the field and make his choices. Hesse's Siddhartha, for example, can try out each ideology he encounters, appraise its deficiencies, and change himself accordingly. But Paphnutius cannot lose his fanaticism, except at the end, without ceasing to be Paphnutius. Consequently, we must be presented with a succession of other spokesmen, each one treated with more or less gentle mockery. But how are we to allow them a full expression of their views if the protagonist is himself so fanatical that he cannot engage in a real discussion with anyone?

We see the problem in the impoverishment of the encounters with various voices that take place before the banquet. Only by throwing a group of "philosophers" together, each standing for a way of life, with the tongue-tied protagonist watching in uncomprehending horror, can France achieve to the full what James Branch Cabell called "his amorous toying with ideas."

Textual scholars have found that France worked harder on revising the banquet scene than on any other part of *Thaïs*. Names and positions were shifted about, added, dropped. The result is not, nor should it be, a coherent tableau, with the kind of dialectical progression that is shown, say, in Plato's *Symposium*. Though a few of the participants in France's symposium can be roughly "placed"—Cotta is the (slightly stupid) Ciceronian man of civic responsibility, Nicias is The Skeptic, Eucritus is The Stoic, and so on—it is clear that what France worked for is a lively impression that *all* of man's major ideologies here reveal their absurdity, or at least their irrelevance, when displayed before the living beauty of Thaïs. Even those who worship her as Venus, even Nicias who loves her (but with such skeptical reserve!) are absurd.

If every position is undercut with irony, if even Thaïs is gently mocked for almost every opinion she expresses, it remains true that most of the characters are clearly pitied in their error. Since all of their desires are equally illusory and beyond fulfillment, all are equally pitiable.

The pity for Paphnutius is especially complex. It would have been easy to make him simply hateful or simply farcical, but to do so would be to blame him; and what the author wants to blame are his atrocious *ideas*. It was not clear to me on first reading, and even now it is not entirely clear, how France manages to make me pity the dreadful creature. Most of what he says or thinks or does is abominable, like his treatment of Thaïs on the road to the convent:

> She followed him obediently along rough roads, under a burning sun. Fatigue wrenched her knees, and thirst inflamed her breath. But, far from feeling any of that false pity which softens the hearts of the profane, Paphnutius rejoiced at the expiatory sufferings of this flesh which had sinned. In the transport of holy zeal, he wanted to beat this body whose beauty bore striking witness to its infamy. His meditations supported his pious fervor, and, recalling that Thaïs had received Nicias into her bed, he formed such an abominable image of this sin that all his blood flowed back to his heart, and his breast was ready to burst. His curses, stifled in his throat, gave way to the grinding of his teeth. He sprang up and stood before her, pale, terrible, full of God, looked straight into her soul, and spat in her face.

Can we pity such a man? In many a fictional world we could not. If *Thaïs* were a "novel," "The Pitiful Tale of Paphnutius' Awakening," its author would be required to work much harder than France works here to attenuate our disgust and build our sympathy. He does, of course, what he can—what is required. We are persuaded that Paphnutius cannot really choose what to believe or how to act. Since we can discover no feasible alternative for him, he too is a victim. Given his admirably passionate desire for something more lasting than the idea-games and orgiastic horrors of the banquet, he is clearly more sinned against than sinning. And of course he can benefit throughout from that curious paralogism, the almost irresistible process that makes us sympathize with the character who is given the most prolonged "inside view": (1) In life, what I know directly in this way is only myself. (2) Here is a slice of the same stuff. (3) Therefore....

Paphnutius is, in short, a grotesque innocent, and, though we can deplore him without pity through much of the work, when he finally acknowledges to himself his love for Thaïs, recognizes the emptiness of his pieties, and grasps the enormity of the deception that has been perpetrated upon him, one feels that in this world (whatever one thinks about the real world) the statement attributed to France in another context can apply: "I pity us all."

But we cannot go very far in this direction without deflecting our attention from the wry intellectual ironies that we care about. The pity we feel is necessarily attenuated, as any thinly spread and thought-dominated pity must be. Nobody will ever weep, we can be sure, over the "tragedy" of Paphnutius. In *Thaïs*, however—where all effects are subordinated to the intellectual delights of recovering the ironies—that is not a fault but a virtue.

But another, perhaps subtler, kind of pity pervades the work. It is hard to describe and harder to illustrate, a pity that perhaps will be felt only by readers who, like France himself, began life with a belief in what might be called simple Christianity. Put baldly, it is a pity, throughout *Thaïs*, not just that "Christianity" is too often the grotesque parody embraced by Paphnutius but that the purer Christianity of Ahmes and Thaïs and Palemon is, after all, totally illusory. Ahmes' tender energy, Thaïs' longing for purity, the Franciscan joy and simplicity of some few of the monks—what a pity that only an illusory system of beliefs could produce such beauty of soul. Nicias wishes he could, for one day, live Paphnutius' ascetic life, and we do not see in this a wish to be the brutish Paphnutius. It is a lament that Nicias and Anatole France can no longer experience the joys of any full belief.

Thus we return to the "irony and pity" that earlier readers felt were the mark of this author. As a phrase marking a pose, it early became outmoded. France himself could never maintain for very long the skeptical detachment on which the pairing depended. But there is more than a skeptical pose here. The irony is masterful: no one has ever sustained the voice of naive piety with more deliciously intricate skills than France shows here. And though pity may not be the highest emotion we hope to attain, the pity for what is revealed through the irony seems to me both genuine and important.

In short, as a work that drives us into a kind of intense mental activity quite unlike sustained philosophical inquiry, using the whips of irony to cause enough pain and threat to arouse our pity for the victims but not enough to make us risk our souls, *Thaïs* is revealed as indeed the work of a master.

OVERSTANDING, ONCE AGAIN

To understand *Thaïs* has required us to overthrow not only our preconceptions about the public character, Anatole France, but all standard categories about novels, about novels of ideas, and about the possible shapes of fiction. I can think of no work sufficiently like *Thaïs* to be of much help in our effort to understand it—which is to say, to come to an understanding with the author it implies. It is true, of course, that at every moment we are in some sense using all of our past experience with literature, and we cannot hope to escape the categories of perception we have derived from that experience. But only the authority who embodies himself in the tale can finally give us the guidance we need in deciding what riches are to be garnered in *this* field.

Just how long we shall choose to remain engaged in the act of respectful understanding will depend, as we saw in discussing critical justice, on what the text has to say about its own value. But as we turn again to explicit acts of *over*standing, it is important to underline how thoroughly value judgments have been implicated in our acts of understanding all the while. We have by no means been engaged in a kind of interpretation that, as some would have it, precedes the act of critical judgment. When interpretation is the pursuit of a just understanding, reappraisals of worth occur as the pursuit goes on: each of the four texts I have tried to understand has increased in stature under my prolonged gaze, just as my three pluralists earlier appeared to grow larger and larger, the closer I looked at them.

The fact remains that such critical understanding is never the only proper goal of the critical path. Even at its best—when the works understood are preeminently great and the critic is preeminently sensitive to their qualities—the effort to understand will never foreclose the seemingly limitless paths of overstanding. Neither the nature of art works nor our own legitimate interests will allow us to reject whatever improper questions promise to lead us to new territory.

When I qualify my conclusion about *Thaïs*, for example, with the

phrase "but not enough to make us risk our souls," I immediately
invite a flood of questions about whether we can finally admire such a
work as much as we admire those that risk and demand much more.
Most of France's important successors until recently could no longer
"amorously toy" with the abyss,* and some of them, like Samuel
Beckett, have even tried to find ways of saying that in all honesty
nothing can be said. Many others have attempted new affirmations,
quite different from the languorous, gentle Eros-worship that seems
so dated in France. Such differences call for a philosophical, moral, or
religious criticism that would inevitably, for most of us, place *Thaïs*
somewhat lower than the greatest achievements of all time or even of
the last hundred years. Even the reader who agrees with me that its
datedness has done most of the damage it can ever do, that the
"elitist" ideas were, after all, not *that* bad, and that in fact the implied
author of *Thaïs* is at least as mature or profound as we encounter in
the more aggressively nihilistic works written in our own time—even
this reader will no doubt finally conclude that, in one perspective or
another, *Thaïs* falls short. But surely the more important thing to be
said about it is that, as we have reconstructed it, it can bear the
crosslights of many perspectives; it becomes interesting again because
it not only allows but invites many perspectives.

We arrive here at a possible principle for evaluation, but it cannot
be put so simply as one might like. I cannot quite say, much as I might
like to at this point, that the more perspectives or critical languages a
work invites the better it is. We can perhaps suggest a more useful
formulation—though this book is not the place to pursue it in
detail—by comparing our notion of responsiveness-to-languages
with the philosophical notion, held by most philosophers until at
least the seventeenth century, of a hierarchy of degrees of reality in
created things. According to that view, popularized among modern
academics by A. O. Lovejoy's *The Great Chain of Being* (1936), stones
are not simply less interesting than vegetables, and vegetables less
interesting than kangaroos, and kangaroos less interesting than
people; they in fact possess less reality, less actualization of the potentialities of being. In the language I have been developing for *Thaïs*,
one could translate that ancient picture into something like this: A
stone insists on fewer perspectives for its "criticism" than does a
vegetable, and so on up the hierarchical scale. Though we may sur-

---

*Yet some more recent critics and novelists could be described in these same words.
One critic's amorous toying is another's *errance joyeuse*. Fashions in abysses come and
go, and they seem to require in their historian as much training and analytical skill as
once went into constructing a *Summa Theologica*.

prise each other by discovering how many different things can be said about the stone, we soon exhaust what it *insists* that we say, and shortly thereafter we exhaust even the sources of what we *can* say. Not so with human beings and their works—and this is now seen as not simply a point about our interests or the capacities of our languages. It has to do with the superior degree of reality of the things themselves. No matter how much you say about human beings and their works, they will "obviously" demand further languages, further perspectives.

Unfortunately for the sake of critical simplicity, we cannot simply continue the hierarchical scheme in terms of quantity and say: "Among the works of man, those are best that either allow for or insist on the greatest number of critical languages." Every human work, even the simplest, will *allow* an indefinite number of perspectives for its description and judgment; even the simplest detective story, for example, will in some sense respond to every mode I have mentioned in this book, even though it may in effect deplore the questions asked as somehow alien. And it is not at all clear that the best detective stories are inferior as art to the sloppiest 800-page historical sagas just because the latter *insist* on more kinds of questions.

Before we can hope to find a plausible standard, we must, therefore, add to our quantitative measure precisely the qualitative judgments that have caused our confusion of tongues in the first place. It is not simply the capacity to *respond* to many questions that makes a great text; all human works will do so. And it is not simply the fact of *insisting* on a variety of questions that will establish a work's preeminence. It is always, alas, the capacity to respond *well* that wins our justified admiration, and the task of establishing whether or not that capacity is present is not describable in the terms of a single mode. It will always be in fact many tasks; and even when they are performed by excellent critics, they will yield results that are not easily intertranslated.

It may still be true, however, that somewhere within this notion of "responding well" to a multiplicity of languages a rough criterion is to be found. The works that endure seem to be those that both insist on a variety of questions and then respond superlatively to many. *Thaïs*, I have said, insists on a great variety of critical modes; no sooner have I done my formal analysis than it seems to shout: "Yes, but you have not asked me about the truth of my philosophizing, or about the delicacy of my sexual insights, or the accuracy of my historical reconstructions...." As a rich and powerful culmination of many forces—not just the author's rising genius but the history of modern literature, of French culture, of Western philosophy, of romantic conceptions of the ironic man, of popular awareness of the death of God—*Thaïs* is inherently inexhaustible. But to say this is not to say that it will look preeminently good in all perspectives. I have argued that both the perspective provided by Forster's search for a pattern (the hourglass) and that provided by a public attending to "the master" debased the work from what it really is. I have also suggested that in the perspective of any sophisticated philosophy *Thaïs* will shrink somewhat (though I can conceive of a defense against my implicit charges, one that would argue that I have reduced France's ideas to simplicities that he would reject; I have given elsewhere a somewhat fuller treatment of France's ideas as dramatized in the long, interesting, almost infinitely ironic banquet scene). The point is that, in each mode, the chosen perspective will reveal standards of coherence, correspondence, or comprehensiveness sufficiently rigorous to prevent those who respect them from babbling. At the same time, we should expect that most works will, like *Thaïs*, invite conflicting judgments springing from alternative perspectives. Only the greatest of classics seem capable of insisting on and *responding well* to almost every conceivable perspective; and even they all seem to suffer in *some* views (as Homer is turned, in Plato's perspective, into a writer dangerous for the souls of the young).

The same rich invitations to understanding and overstanding are offered by the other texts considered in this chapter. Though our reconstruction has given them an authority that will rule out certain kinds of contemptuous questions, it has in each case revealed radically novel human achievements that will both respond to an unlimited variety of interesting questions and prevent our answers from falling into single, monotonous patterns. I may, for example, want to follow current fashions and ask what each has to say about the institution of writing or about the inescapable incoherence found at the heart of every work; but if I do, I shall hardly be able to reduce them all, as they stand living before me, to a single predictable message: "Repudiate clear messages!" Or I may, following the interests I attributed to Crane in chapter 2, decide to ask where, in the scale of human achievement, they should finally be placed, and I may conclude that James after all wrote greater fictions than "The Bench" or *The Turn of the Screw*; that *Tom Jones* and *Tristram Shandy* are more important than *The Citizen of the World*; and that Samuel Johnson performs the "self-portraiture of genius" even better than does Oliver Goldsmith; but if I do, I shall hardly be able, as the works stand living before me, to take such comparisons either as *the* end of criticism or as saying, in themselves, much of what I care to say about these marvelous works.

In short, we seem to have found a way of pursuing critical vitality by honoring the necessity of both understanding and overstanding. An absurd impoverishment will result from exclusive emphasis on either. But we see in conclusion what we glimpsed at the beginning: we cannot simply pass a universal toleration act that says, "You go your ways of understanding and I'll pursue the many paths of overstanding." The final quality of whatever we do will be vitiated whenever we bypass justice, attempt premature overstanding, and so destroy fine works because they don't fit our favorite templates.

Conclusion: Modes and Pluralisms as Shared Tenancies

Many readers will have recognized that to move from topic to topic as I have done, defending the legitimacy of contrasting reconstructions within each topic, is to treat critical modes not as positions to be defended but as locations or openings to be explored—in the traditional rhetorical teminology, as *topoi* or *loci*. To work with (or in, or within) a topic, one need not (indeed, in critical controversy one *can* not) establish it as proved, as a permanent and unique truth. One need only show that the choice of topic makes sense to fellow inquirers; that is, it must be a place where at least two inquirers can dwell together in understanding. It is not a position on which one stands, not a pedestal from which one looks out upon a world of error. Rather, it is an inhabited place in which a valued activity can occur among all those who know how to find their way in.

The characteristic form of conflict among those who see critical topics in this way will be quite different from conflict among those who seek to establish a final monism. A monist, even of the most generous-minded kind, says to his opponents something like this: "I will listen to you as best I can, in order to discover whether there is anything in what you say that might help me improve my monism. Now, having listened, I can show you just what is wrong in your position—though I may borrow some of your insights." The topical pluralist, in contrast, will characteristically engage with opponents like this: "Presumably, what you have said can lead us further. Let's begin by being sure I have understood you, and then let's see where it leads, what it enables *us* to do, and what, if anything, it prevents our doing."

It is probably true that no one can maintain that kind of disinterested inquiry for long. It is also true that trying to hear too many voices at once can silence me. All critical vitality depends on accepting limitations, and it is as impossible to speak for all voices as it is to reduce them all to one. Thus the pluralist, unlike the monist, must live with no hope whatever of getting everything clear at last; he believes, in principle, and he always discovers, in practice, that truth is forever richer than its formulations. It is thus writ in heaven that any critic who has not given up will remain to some degree confused. But there is a great difference between the exhausted swimmer who is convinced that the patternless waves he struggles through extend in all directions without limit, and the one who says to himself, "There *are* islands. Swim a bit further, and you will certainly find another one, perhaps even more hospitable than the last one you rested on."

The monist avoids confusion by simply refusing to enter the roaring waters at all. Secure on his one island, he need never feel anxious, except perhaps about how to do better missionary work. And his security can serve to keep some part of the life of criticism going. A student is lucky if, somewhere along the line, he finds a really able monist, one who knows what he knows and why, who is not afraid to teach what he knows, and who knows how to show its radical difference from the benighted ideas of all other critics. That student, however dogmatic he may become, will at least be able to perform critical inquiry (assuming that his monism is, like most of those we bother about at all, an *enabling* one, one that shows its devotees how to *do* something in and for the world). Moreover, he will not suffer from a despairing relativism—at least for a while; for though his inquiry may entail some skewering of straw men (and thus the inducing of despair in some other *live* opponents), his results will be something more than a blind drifting in the winds of fashion.

But an entirely different level of self-education begins at the moment one's first monism encounters a second one and both are seen as equally vital. That moment cannot occur except on pluralist assumptions. Given the other attitudes, it is by definition impossible. The closest thing to it occurs in the encounters sought by the intelligent monist who recognizes that the doctrine he and his students espouse will be all the stronger if it is championed against living arguments. Nobody in this interesting century of ours wants to be caught dead praising a cloistered intellectual virtue. But only the pluralist believes, not only in confronting arguments with other real arguments, but also in confronting entire modes with other viable modes.

Such a confrontation can never be brought to an end, because even pluralists will necessarily engage each other from different locations. When I enter the place where you dwell and have your being, I bring with me ways to some degree alien, and the results of our meeting will always provide what looks like evidence for those who want to claim total indeterminacy of meaning or the permanent impossibility of understanding.

Thus I have no doubt whatever that if each of my three pluralists attempted to incorporate this book into his pluralistic world, he could easily do so; yet the digestive process of each mode would change me from what I set out to be. Hard as I have tried for understanding, my total account is an act of overstanding that is at best compatible *only for the most part* with each of their pluralisms. In the same way, each of them could describe a number of other pluralisms in order to validate pluralism as an attitude or enterprise, but the total view would, for each, still be recognizably distorted by the pluralist's terministic screen.

Booth Craned, Burked, and Abramsed

I work, for example, in harmony with Crane, but not in a form that could ever duplicate what he would say. I have exemplified again and again his claim that if one wants knowledge, and especially knowledge about quality, one must distinguish problems and discriminate products. That is, whenever I have pushed myself "down" the scale of generality to the point of discovering something made ("Surgical Ward," Abrams' *Natural Supernaturalism*, James's stories, specific essays by Goldsmith, *Thaïs*), I have arrived at statements corrigible or falsifiable in discourse. Crane and I could in consequence talk together about them, without destructive misunderstanding. Further, insofar as I have discussed the three pluralisms as self-contained modes, as specific "concrete" syntheses of method, definition of subject, and assumptions pursuing specified ends, I have again entered Crane's domain of knowledge, in the sense that we could pursue a reasoned exchange about my assertions.

But it is evident that where I am is not in any simple sense "on his chart"; I am not one of those who loves knowledge for its own sake, in Crane's way and to his degree, for I have "rhetoricized" the whole pluralistic enterprise. In the first place, my goal is practical: how to improve the practice of controversy by increasing the chances of understanding. I have, in fact, made understanding into a supreme goal, running the risk of implying that it is better for two human minds to share erroneous views than for one to have the truth and the other to misunderstand him. Thus my pluralism is uncomfortably close to what Crane would consider a mere eclecticism, a critical stance that serves not truth but human community.

He could, of course, accommodate me, in the sense that he could describe me in these terms; but in doing so, he would inevitably reduce me: I did not write this book in order to be fitted into a place on *his* chart. On the other hand, I can say of him, as I can say of few critics I have read, that he would not place me without having labored to understand me, and his pluralism gives him the equipment to make that labor profitable. Since he would want knowledge about me more than victory over me, he would be ashamed to engage in easy misplacement. Thus we could talk together—as of course we did, for over two decades.

I need not predict what Burke would do, for he has already said that my effort to free myself into his way left him dancing with tears in his eyes. His reply makes it quite clear that he has no real difficulty in accommodating me, fitting me into his vital progress: I am one of the fixers, one of those who engage in "administrative rhetoric," trying to subdue others to their own domain. If left to my own devices, I would thus freeze the dialogue, "perfecting" it into some supreme well-defined (however complex) System that would leave him and everybody else but myself far below, unaware of what a *truly* comprehensive vision would reveal. Perhaps if he attempted to deal with me rather than simply defend himself against me, he would finally discern a repressed metaphysical motive in all that I have attempted:

> It is as if Booth were trying to find the ultimate Word-of-Words. His Logology, flexible as it appears, is finally an attempt to find a replacement for the benign and all-salvaging God of his childhood. Fearing, as we all do, that the world will fall apart without his aid, he in fact has decided to play God, and to show that he can construct an intellectual world in which all can be saved if they will only come half way: all men understand each other, they are *made* in understanding. The making of minds is achieved in the meeting of minds, and since all human beings are made in this process, all are finally children of God. Some, however, persist in heresy, and it is the job of us missionaries to go out into the world to save them—that is, just get them to listen to each other and to us. What Booth is doing is thus benign in itself, and it can even play a part in the great dramatistic enterprise that is bigger than any of us. But you will have noted, surely, that when the chips are down Booth falls right back into Chicago-style ways. Note the disproportion

between the small number of pages devoted to approving what he calls "inappropriate" criticism and the number given to reconstruction of forms according to intentions. He's really a formalist critic who has very little to say about that great subject of *my* career: the grammar and rhetoric and symbolic of motives.

My practice is, then, uncomfortably close to what Burke would consider a formalism that manufactures entities and paints itself into a corner.

In some such way, Burke can easily accommodate me and, in doing so, will inevitably reduce me: I did not write this book in order to become one more voice in his drama. On the other hand, I can say of Burke, as I can say of few critics, that he would not place me without having energetically engaged with me as a problem; and though I can be sure that he would not have worked as hard as Crane to understand me, I can know in advance that his response would teach me about myself and make me eager to talk with him about it. Since he would want an energetic exploration of further consequences and complexities more than victory over me, he would be ashamed if I caught him "winning" with easy put-downs. Thus we could (and did) talk together.

It is even clearer that Abrams could accommodate me within his historical pluralism. Putting aside our many similarities—our respect for authors' intentions, our commitment to a plurality of voices— Abrams would want to see me *in history*. Anyone reading his book, my response, and then his response to that response will recognize that I have again and again attempted to *fix* upon him views that for him are in historical flux (see, especially, pp. 182–83, above). What is more, if need arose, Abrams could easily show that my pluralistic inquiry is a product of its own time—that I could never have written a book like mine a hundred years ago, or even fifty, and that its pattern is one that I inherit from traditions he has analyzed: the apocalyptic threat of doom; a call for prophets (with three of them responding); and the promise of a new heaven and a new earth if only people would try to understand each other. "Indeed," I hear him saying,

> if you look closely at Booth's language you will find many hints that his confidence in mankind's possibilities, and his faith in the efficacy of argument, spring from an ultimate commitment much more static than he pretends. He believes in God, in some sense, and he does not really believe in the reality of history except as a play of innumerable flickering shadows dimly perceived in the particolored lights and distorted perspectives of human life. His

prophetic voice is muted, because he is ashamed to say out loud what he really believes: it's just another version of the old belief in salvation—not salvation found at the end of time but salvation found in any moment of understanding, which is timeless. In short, his beliefs can be traced.

What is worse, each pluralist is treated almost as if he existed sub specie aeternitatis. Why did Booth not develop the *history* of pluralistic efforts that is left so truncated in his account? In such a history Booth would appear as . . . .

Thus Abrams could easily accommodate me and, in doing so, would inevitably reduce me: I did not write this book in order to become a moment in someone else's historical account. On the other hand, I can say of Abrams, as I can say of few critics, that he would not historicize me without having labored to understand me and my problem. I can know in advance that he would both discover problems that I have overlooked, and must then recognize, and that he would teach me truths about my origins that I never dreamed of. He would thus insure my eagerness to learn from him and to argue with him. Since he would care more for our learning together than for easy victory, he would be ashamed if I caught him in an easy historicism—one that reduced me to a tottering figure where I have attempted to stride. Thus we could (and did) talk together.

At the same time, I can reply to each of them that my rhetorical or heuristic or topical pluralism has shown immense respect for what each of them cares for. Though I have in effect "placed" each of them and have thus reduced each to a part of my total enterprise, the position each occupies has been allowed to be so large, and so free of labels, that I have proved to myself that I cannot fully "contain" any one of them: they thus insist on a *continuing* usefulness. To attempt a summary of that usefulness here would be to violate what I believe about it: that it is not reducible to labels about "approaches." The very length of my reconstructions offers demonstration, to the extent that I can give one, of a sympathetic breaking-and-entering into complex enterprises, not simple fixed positions.

What I embrace, then, and what I try to understand, are three *ways*, three permanently useful accommodations of critical variety. I have come to know the value of a pluralism of pluralisms not by resolving the umbrella paradox (which in any case arises only from my own entitizing extension of one of the three ways, Crane's) but by discovering (1) that each mode has yielded results important to me; (2) that each mode promises to yield similar results whenever I give it a chance; (3) that I cannot extend any one of them fully to incorporate the others—that is, I am unwilling to give up the very peculiarities and "exaggerations" that cause me trouble; yet (4) that my "total" assent to any one of them does not, finally, inhibit—though it complicates—my assent to the others.

Pluralism will not guarantee either that the next mind I meet will have much to teach me or that, if it does, I will rise to meet it. Inequalities of readiness are built into this view, but so is equality of needs and rights and opportunities in the exchange. Without the possibility of that equality, not a meeting of minds but an imposition of wills (or a skewering of straw men) must occur; and what we will see will be a reinforcement of maimed selves, malformed, unlicked critters, able at best to engage in a losing struggle for survival or power, locked in a zero-sum game quite unlike the miraculous multiplication tables of understanding: the more *you* get, the more there is for me.

Limits Again

The question remains: Once I have started adding modes rather than subtracting them, how far should I go? Life is too short, and our power of sympathetic thought too limited, to allow for many attempts at full justice. How many acts of understanding should a good pluralist strive for?

To insist on a general answer to that question would in fact be to persist in the search for a single truth, one that could tell me what I now lack or would warn me when I have had enough. But we should by now be permanently wary of any abstract criterion of richness or polytopicalism. Our goal is rather what it has always been: the reduction of meaningless controversy, of unjustified critical killing—which is to say an *increase* in the kind of debate that yields critical understanding. Whether I decide, finally, to allow my mind to be fully colonized by Frye, by Barthes, by Derrida (all of whom have so far established only broad beachheads, but who knows what is to come?), I can at least resist public pretensions to full understanding until I have attempted a fuller justice than I have as yet done. In that attempt I will discover, if and when I am driven to it by my critical need, how far I am to go.

And so, here at the end, I find that, depending on the point of view, I can be called either a skeptic, a monist, an eclectic, or a pluralist. I am skeptical, radically skeptical, about the possibility or desirability of finding an ultimate resolution of our debates about poems and modes. Both the concept of "the poem" and the concept of "the right way of criticism of the poem" are *essentially* contested. Yet I am quite unskeptical, indeed I am dogmatically monist, about such questions as whether critical discussion can have meaning or whether people can often understand each other if they try.

At the same time, I have clearly been eclectic all the while in the dictionary sense of "rejecting a single, unitary, and exclusive interpretation, doctrine, or method," being "on a constant search for varied experience," and engaged in "the selection of doctrines or elements from various and diverse sources according to their presumed utility or validity." It is not entirely clear that I have avoided encapsulation in the final clause in Webster's *Unabridged*: "usually for the purpose of combining them into a satisfying or acceptable style, system of ideas, or set of practices." Though skeptical about final systems, have I not been constructing my own synthesis, however loose-jointed, out of what are at best mere fragments from Crane, Burke, Abrams, and a half-dozen others even less fully represented?

It is scarcely surprising, then, that what I have called pluralism Stephen C. Pepper calls eclecticism.[39] Others would call it relativism. The important point is not what we call it but rather *where*, in our process of recovering a critic's offerings, we stop our sympathetic act of asking only "proper" questions and begin our improprieties. The eclecticism I repudiate murders in order to dissect, and murders hastily, seeking parts for the all-important new synthesis. The "eclecticism"—that is, pluralism—I embrace will, in the end, still be guilty of reducing other critics' work and placing it in contexts undreamed of in the originals. It is committed, however, to remaining inside a mode to the last possible moment, as it were, before lapsing into heresy. It will thus at given moments appear dogmatically monistic, dogmatically committed to preserving those exemplars in criticism that can, in their integrity, best help any critic to serve the enterprise of artistic creation. And by "clinging to the last possible moment" it will sometimes produce those lasting "conversions" to pluralism of the kind that Crane's and Burke's conflicting triumphs produced in me.

Such pragmatic concerns carry a strong moral freight, but the morality is not an obligation that somehow contrasts with intellectual responsibility, dragged in at the end from some other domain. No critic can separate inquiry from responsibility: "Pursue truth, but let the moral chips fall where they may"; or "Seek critical truth—and, incidentally, while you are at it, try to be fair, try not to kill off critics unnecessarily, try to understand them." If critical truth is inherently plural, inherently dependent on a vital, just, and understanding interchange among many critics with many modes, *critical* truth *is* critical understanding, and it cannot be found—or better, enacted —except by those who hold these commitments to be inextricable from it.

At the same time, it is in the nature of things that I cannot offer any one simple code to further the cause of critical understanding. Codes will themselves be plural, and none will reduce the morality of literary scholarship to a few graces they hold in common: "Don't plagiarize," "Don't misquote," and "Don't cook your evidence." It is true that one of the goals of pluralism is to discover what standards we in fact share behind the seeming conflicts among our diverse Hippocratic oaths (my own little oath for pluralists I here—with a due sense of its comic inadequacy—tuck into the Appendix). But every vital mode, however pluralistic it strives to become, will finally entail versions or orderings of vitality, justice, and understanding that, though binding, will be to some degree in conflict with other modes.

CRITICAL UNDERSTANDING AS AN END IN ITSELF

Critical understanding is both a fact of our present lives (we all manage it to some degree daily) and an ever-receding ideal to work for (none of us takes in more than a fragment of what could feed us). But whenever it occurs, it requires no further payoff. Just how highly we should value its pursuit will depend, of course, on answers to religious, metaphysical, or anthropological questions that I cannot pursue here. Most threateningly, thinking about pluralism has led us again and again to problems of the one and the many, and any pluralist who believes that understanding is real (read: "God exists"?) can easily be tempted to seek final harmonies in Supreme Vitality, Justice, and Love, that Great Multiplier Who asks no more than that I grow out of my solipsism and learn to live in Him/Her as well as I can.*

*I must dodge here the immensely interesting and complicated question of whether, in my sense, I can ever hope to "understand God." Mine is a secular inquiry which ought to stand on its own feet, whether God as a Person exists or not, and whether, as Person, God is fully or only partially "incomprehensible," as medieval theologians debated. But it should be obvious to all who know anything about theological speculation that my whole effort to grapple with pluralistic understanding could easily be translated into theological terms. I have carefully avoided the word "faith" for my persistence in the face of negative evidence, because the word carries such heavy connotations of irrationality for modern readers. But some theologians would say that faith in an inexhaustible truth that transcends and validates any particular and neces-

Fortunately, the case for pluralism in pursuit of understanding in no way requires that we all embrace, as I do, the goings-on of the Logos. Nor does it depend on whether we are monists or pluralists about the ultimate stuff of things, that question that so exercised William James. I have tried to argue not from abstractions about the universe but from the facts of our lives as critics, facts which turn out to be values we share with, and derive from, a human critical life that predates and nourishes the life of literature and criticism. Vitality, justice, and understanding, accepted as goods-in-themselves in all human life, lead us into pluralism as critics, just as they led each of us, not so long ago, out of our initial infantile ideocentrism into the recognition of a world built of many centers, irreducible to any one.

We need feel no crisis of confidence in criticism today unless, accepting the notion that plurality itself is threatening, we attempt to defend or discover one supreme truth. When we make counterstatements, when we deconstruct and demystify the "subject" and "the object," when we deontologize, when we attack interpretation, seek converts to the art of misreading, and profess our confidence in the universal power of anxiety, to *what* are we all the while assenting? Well, for one thing we are all demanding justice for our programs, respect for our own vitality, an effort on the part of others to understand what we have to say. But in all logic we cannot demand these good things without according them to others. In doing so, we discover that at least some of those "others" deserve not only tolerance, kindness, or mercy but approval at least as strong as the approval we accorded to our own previous views.

The life of critical modes is always somewhat chancey. Whole schools die overnight. Most new criticisms do not survive their infancy. It is entirely possible that the apocalyptic dissolutions now

---

sarily fragmentary portion of it—that is, any one mode—not only is analogous to religious faith: it is identical with belief in God.

I find it interesting that Matthew Arnold hints at the same identification in his defense of Saint Paul as less narrow than the Puritans who made him their chief source of doctrine about "the one thing needful": "Now all writings ... must inevitably, from the very nature of things, be but contributions to human thought and human development, which extend wider than they do. Indeed, St. Paul...shows, when he asks, 'Who hath known the mind of the Lord?'—who hath known, *that is*, the true and divine order of things in its entirety,—that he himself acknowledges this fully. And we have already pointed out in another Epistle of St. Paul a great and vital idea of the human spirit,—the idea of immortality,—transcending and overlapping, so to speak, the expositor's power to give it adequate definition and expression" (*Culture and Anarchy*, chap. 5, par. 7; my italics).

proclaimed to be not just the latest but the last word will prove to be justified. Nothing guarantees the survival of this most curious of all human inventions: the production of written works of the mind that are essentially about *other* works of the mind.

We cannot even say that the death of all written criticism would be the worst tragedy that could befall our culture, provided other forms of critical understanding endured. What we can say, even those of us who do not think that all meaningful life depends on what professional critics do, is this: Wherever understanding is maimed, our life is threatened; wherever it is achieved, our life is enhanced.

The world of critical and artistic achievements lies before us in all its dappled grandeur. Must we forever try to map it in a single color, in a single projection, and then use our inevitable failures as proof for what Plato considered the worst of all human conditions: misology, the mistrust of critical understanding?

Appendix

A Hippocratic Oath for the Pluralist

I. I will publish nothing, favorable or unfavorable, about books or articles I have not read through at least once. (By "publish" I mean any writing or speaking that "makes public," including term papers, theses, course lectures, and conference papers.)

The world is not at the moment in need of more words from me simply because they are mine, regardless of the subject and regardless of how little I know about it. To publish my opinion on Foucault—a rather strong one, as it happens—will help no one, not even myself, since I have not yet read more than about two dozen pages by Foucault.

[With one stroke, this self-denying ordinance wipes out at least a fourth of all published criticism. Perhaps a half. In any case, the worst part, however large or small. I can think of a score of comments on my own work that are here flushed down and out; those of you who have been publicly discussed, whether in seminars or in print, can think of others.]

II. I will *try* to publish nothing about any book or article until I have *understood* it, which is to say, until I have reason to think that I can give an account of it that the author himself will recognize as just. Any attempt at overstanding will follow this initial act of attempted respect.

Many of us have learned, from various earlier new criticisms, to treat each poem with something like the attention its author hoped for. The arts of interpreting critical works, good and bad, are as difficult, manifold, and rewarding as the arts of what we call literary interpretation. Just as I must earn my right to criticize a poem by dwelling with it until I can find my dwelling *in* it, I earn my right to criticize criticism in the same way. Paraphrasing Coleridge: Before I damn a critic's errors, I will try to reconstruct his enterprise as if it were my own. (Compare Abrams on Coleridge, Mill, and Bentham, p. 193, above.)

[With this ordinance, we wipe out, at a low guess, another fourth of what is published.]

III. I will take no critic's word, when he discusses other critics, unless he can convince me that he has abided by the first two ordinances. I will assume, until a critic proves otherwise, that what he says *against* the playing style of other critics is useful, at best, as a clue to his own game. I will be almost as suspicious when he presents a "neutral" summary and even when he praises.

"If we take in our hand any discussion by one critic of another, let us ask, *does it reveal any concrete reconstruction of the rival's enterprise? No. Does it reveal any proof that the rival's defeat (whether with open attack or 'friendly' reduction) is necessary to establish the new enterprise? No.* Commit it then to the flames: for it can contain nothing but sophistry and illusion." (See p. 177, above.)

IV. I will not undertake any project that by its very nature requires me to violate Ordinances I–III.

CORROLARIES:

a) I will not write any history of criticism, or analysis of *the* types of criticism, unless driven to it by thirteen demons and unless I decide to spend the lifetime required to do the job decently.

b) I will not write any history or analysis of general terms, like romanticism, pastoral, comedy, irony, rhetoric, understanding, or pluralism, unless driven by the same demons and unless I am willing to spend the years required. I will remember that if it took M. H. Abrams twenty years to write *Natural Supernaturalism*, a history of one poem by Wordsworth, it *ought* to take *me* at least as long to perform tasks no less complex.

[With this stroke, we eliminate at least half of the works remaining. It is in fact only by the most marvelous stroke of Providence that we do not wipe out *Critical Understanding*.]

V. I will not judge my own inevitable violations of the first four ordinances more leniently than those I find in other critics.

Using these five simple ordinances, we could quickly reconstruct our experience of criticism: we would write and read only about one-fourth as many critical words; we would experience a renewed sense that our critical sanity does not depend on "covering" as many works as possible; and we would find leisure to enter full-heartedly into those that met or expanded our interest and heightened pleasure and profit from what we did read.

We could achieve all this, as a profession. But I will not allow my own practice to depend on the remote hope that we will.

Notes

Preface

1. Many anthropologists and sociologists claim that human culture is made in the sharing of symbolic meanings; much, perhaps most, of our reality is created precisely in such sharing. We have a culture to the degree that we have together created a common understanding of symbolic meanings. The point may seem obvious to many humanists, until they encounter controversy about whether cultures are created by meaning or by practical needs and functions. A subtle and persuasive argument for the primacy of meaning over pragmatic function in the formation of all cultures, including our own uniquely pragmatic culture, is advanced by Marshall Sahlins in his *Culture and Practical Reason* (Chicago: University of Chicago Press, 1976):

> Ricoeur observes that in the strongest case of the word as praxis, the "imperative word," the "effect" requires the presence of symbolizing beings in a symbolized context, as the "understanding" includes at once a project and a system of valuations which differentiate the world and men's actions in it. One may make the same point in another way. It is easy to see in Malinowski's understanding of language as *work* and of meaning as the response *produced* in the hearer, the same reduction of human subject to manipulated object that informs his ethnographic technique. The Alter in this conception is merely a means to an end, a raw material to be worked upon like any other. But again... the sequel to a remark in the behavior of another is not the same kind of relation as the effect of a tool on the shape of an object; it is not "produced" as a material good is produced. Not merely because the Other is an intentional being like myself. More decisively because the communication implies a community, and therefore the bringing to bear on the "effect" of all those common conceptions of men and things which, ordering their interrelations, determine the specific "influence" of the word. [Pp. 82–83]

Chapter One

1. A critic can even be so confident as to feel no need of argument except irony: "*The Times Literary Supplement*... makes a point of testifying that Mr Amis is modern literature and the late W. H. Auden a major poet and a mind of world importance. There is [thus] no need here for a full account of our cultural plight" (F. R. Leavis, *The Living Principle: 'English' as a Discipline of Thought* [London: Chatto & Windus, 1975], p. 12).

2. See, for example, Roland Barthes's quest for the *paradoxa* that will free us from our *doxa*, our received opinions, in *Roland Barthes par Roland Barthes* (Paris: Editions du Seuil, 1975). For an extended use of the metaphor of criticism-as-warfare, see Serge Doubrovsky, *The New Criticism in France* (Chicago: University of Chicago Press, 1973; originally published in 1966 as *Pourquoi la nouvelle critique: Critique et objectivité*). See especially "A Postface by Way of Preface."

3. *Critical Inquiry* 4 (Winter 1977): 231–52. Some years ago I developed my own complaint, along with a brief argument for pluralism, in *"The Rhetoric of Fiction* and the Poetics of Fictions," *Novel* (Winter 1968); reprinted in *Now Don't Try to Reason with Me* (Chicago and London: University of Chicago Press, 1970), pp. 151–69. See also "Pluralism and Its Rivals" in the same volume; "Straw Men and the Life of Criticism," *Western Humanities Review* 12 (Winter 1958): 81–86; and "Three Functions of Reviewing at the Present Time," *MMLA* 2 (Spring 1978): 2–12. A good illustration of how monistic assumptions will make hash out of a pluralist's position is John Ross Baker's "From Imitation to Rhetoric: The Chicago Critics, Wayne C. Booth, and *Tom Jones,*" *Novel* (Spring 1973): "Is it possible to enter Booth's 'camp' in order to understand his work without at the same time becoming a member of his army? The location of the camp is Chicago, and the governing principles are Neo-Aristotelian. . . . If we must become Chicago critics in order to arrive at a 'true interpretation' or a 'true refutation' of *The Rhetoric of Fiction*, then communication among critics becomes indeed impossible—a strange situation arising from the arguments of self-professed pluralists who recognize in theory the legitimacy of alternative approaches" (pp. 197–98). Obviously. How stupid of us all not to have thought of that. It all makes sense *if* critical enterprises are frozen into "positions" or if we must "become" one kind of critic as against all others. It makes no sense at all if we think, instead, of engaging in *various* enterprises.

4. David Hume, *An Enquiry Concerning Human Understanding*, Section VIII: "Of Liberty and Necessity," Part I. With characteristic force and clarity, Hume asserts that the very fact of prolonged controversy on any subject proves "that there is some ambiguity in the expression, and that the disputants affix different ideas to the terms employed in the controversy. For as the faculties of the mind are supposed to be naturally alike in every individual; otherwise nothing could be more fruitless than to reason or dispute together; it were impossible, if men affix the same ideas to their terms, that they could so long form different opinions of the same subject." We shall come, in chapter 5, to W. B. Gallie's claim that there are certain "essentially contested concepts," concepts that can never, by their nature, be resolved by semantic clarification. Placing these two views in opposition, we can now ask whether semantic clarification will ever resolve the seeming dispute (in which case, we would say that Hume clearly rules out Gallie's concepts when he excludes questions that lie entirely beyond the reach of human capacity), or whether we must adopt one or another of the remaining "attitudes" I describe.

5. Every good critic engages both in semantic clarification of how his terms have been used previously and in what might be called semantic assistance to his own readers. An excellent example of how terms that have been used in contradictory senses can be rehabilitated with a little care can be found in Theodore Ziolkowski's Introduction to his *Disenchanted Images: A Literary Iconology* (Princeton, N.J.: Princeton University Press, 1977), pp. 3–17. The terms clarified are image, theme, motif, and symbol.

6. Gottfried Wilhelm Leibniz, *Nouveaux Essais*, bk. 1, chap. 2, § 21. Quoted by Robert

Latta, ed., in pt. 4 of his introduction to Leibniz's *"The Monadology" and Other Philosophical Writings* (Oxford: Oxford University Press, 1898), pp. 154–55.

7. From Sir James Mackintosh, "Dissertation on the Progress of Ethical Philosophy Chiefly During the Seventeenth and Eighteenth Centuries," *The Miscellaneous Works of the Right Honourable Sir James Mackintosh* (London, 1854), vol. 1, p. 240, n. Quoted by Richard McKeon in "Propositions and Perceptions in the World of G. E. Moore," in *The Philosophy of G. E. Moore*, vol. 4, in the Library of Living Philosophers, ed. Paul Arthur Schilpp (Evanston: Northwestern University Press, 1942), p. 474 n.

8. True intellectual differences are obscured by radical differences of tone. Tonal differences are not unimportant, as I shall show later on, because extremes in either direction—the air of certainty and the air of universal toleration—can destroy critical exchange. But it is important not to allow such differences to obscure the deeper differences that can subsist among those who, read superficially, may sound like blood brothers, and the deeper similarities that can often be found among those who seem engaged in war to the death.

Here are two critics who call themselves pluralists (the italics are mostly mine):

> The *only* proof there can be of a hypothesis about any particular thing lies in its power of completeness and coherence of explanation within the limits of the data it makes significant—and this *always* relatively to the other hypotheses pertinent to the same data with which it has been compared. We *must* be guided, however, in choosing among alternative hypotheses, by a further criterion—the classic criterion of economy: that that hypothesis is *the best*, other things being equal, which *requires* the fewest supplementary hypotheses to make it work or which entails the least amount of explaining away.... And we *must* be careful, further, not to construe our "data" in too narrow a sense and so be satisfied with hypotheses that *clearly conflict* with facts external to the works we are considering.... [R. S. Crane, *The Languages of Criticism and the Structure of Poetry* (Toronto: University of Toronto Press, 1953), p. 179]

> Since these different ideological principles can coexist *simultaneously* (and for my part, I can, in a certain sense, accept both *simultaneously*), we *have to* conclude that the ideological choice is not the essence of criticism nor "truth" its ultimate test. Criticism *is something other* than making correct statements in the light of "true" principles. *It follows* that *the major sin* in criticism is not to have an ideology but to keep quiet about it. There is a name for this kind of *guilty silence*; it is self-deception or bad faith. *How can anyone believe* that a given work is an *object* independent of the psyche and personal history of the critic studying it.... *It is inconceivable* that the creative laws governing the writer should not also be valid for the critic. All criticism *must* include...an implicit comment on itself; *all* criticism *is* criticism both of the work under consideration and of the critic;... it *is essentially* an activity.... *It is pointless* to ask whether or not an activity is "true"; the imperatives governing it are quite different. [Roland Barthes, "Criticism as Language," *Times Literary Supplement*, 27 September 1963, p. 739]

Tonally these critics *sound* dogmatic; they seem, quoted out of context, more sure of their conclusions than anyone ought to be in the shaky domains of criticism. Yet both claim to be pluralists.

Now come two critics who have never, so far as I know, thought of themselves as anything other than advocates of a single correct mode of criticism:

> A poetry *may be* distinguished from a poetry by virtue of subject-matter, and

subject-matter *may be* differentiated with respect to its ontology, or the reality of its being. *An* excellent variety of critical doctrine arises recently out of this differentiation, and thus *perhaps* criticism leans again upon ontological analysis as it was meant to do by Kant. . . . The distinction in the hands of critics is a *fruitful* one. There is *apt to go along with it* a principle of valuation. . . . [John Crowe Ransom, "Poetry: A Note in Ontology," *The World's Body* (New York: Charles Scribner's Sons, 1938), p. 111]

Now there is, of course, some semantic difficulty in using the words "liberal" and "progressive" to refer to certain kinds of contemporary thought and also to the thought of Melville and his time. Since Melville's day, these words have undergone various changes in connotation. As for the word "liberal," I use it literally and generally. It means a kind of thought which cherishes freedom and is free, free of dogma and absolutism; a kind of thought which is bounteous, in the sense that it is open-minded, skeptical, and humanist. [Richard Chase, Preface to *Herman Melville, A Critical Study* (New York: Macmillan Co., 1949), p. viii]

The first pair—the pluralists—are aggressively sure of themselves; the monists are tentative, even gentle. I would not want, however, to suggest that there is no correlation whatever between tone and substance. For one thing, the reader to some degree experiences tone *as* substance: the author's *ethos* is always part of his case. And for another, the tone an author adopts is likely to contaminate his views. If he writes with a series of *musts* and *necessarilies*, he is likely to persuade himself that all other views are inferior.

9. *Theory of Literature*, by René Wellek and Austin Warren (New York: Harcourt, Brace & Co., 1949), p. 141.

10. Paul de Man, *Blindness & Insight: Essays in the Rhetoric of Contemporary Criticism* (New York: Oxford University Press, 1971), p. 8.

11. William Empson, "The Intentional Fallacy, Again" *Essays in Criticism* 23 (October 1973): 435.

12. Gregory L. Ulmer, "Sociocriticism," *Novel* 11 (Fall 1977): 71.

13. Stephen C. Pepper, *World Hypotheses: A Study in Evidence* (Berkeley and Los Angeles: University of California Press, 1942), p. 9.

14. "Interpreting 'Interpreting the *Variorum*,'" *Critical Inquiry* 3 (Autumn 1976): 195–96. In a later article, Fish explains how this rejection of objectivity need not lead to utter skepticism; though "there are no inherent constraints on the meanings a sentence may have," the rhetorical "situations" in which sentences are uttered offer rigorous constraints that make agreement among readers "not only possible, but commonplace" ("Normal Circumstances, Literal Language, Direct Speech Acts, the Ordinary, the Everyday, the Obvious, What Goes without Saying, and Other Special Cases," *Critical Inquiry* 4 [Summer 1978]: 625–44). Presumably for those operating within a given "situation," the constraints of soundness will operate much more strongly than Fish seems to suggest in the long passage I have quoted in my text.

15. P. M. Wetherill, *The Literary Text: An Examination of Critical Methods* (Oxford: Basil Blackwell, 1974). Two ambitious efforts to reconcile all the virtues of the major modern critics, while extruding the weaknesses, are Lee T. Lemon's *The Partial Critics* (New York: Oxford University Press, 1965), and Stanley Edgar Hyman's *The Armed Vision: A Study in the Methods of Modern Literary Criticism* (New York: A. A. Knopf, 1948).

16. David Daiches, *A Third World* (Sussex: Sussex University Press, 1971), pp. 44–45.

17. See David Tracy, *Blessed Rage for Order: The New Pluralism in Theology* (New York: Seabury Press, 1975), and Hans Urs von Balthasar, *Die Wahrheit ist symphonisch: Aspekte des christlichen Pluralismus* (Einsiedeln: Johannes Verlag, 1972). See also William E. Connolly, ed., *The Bias of Pluralism* (New York: Atherton Press, 1969): "Pluralism has long provided the dominant description and ideal of American politics . . . ; it is said to promote, more effectively than any other known alternative, a plurality of laudable private and public ends" (p. 3).

18. Similarly, the pluralism that Ernest Gellner says dominates contemporary thinkers seems to be not really a methodological pluralism. "There is a remarkable consensus on one point amongst recent thinkers and schools, even when they are otherwise . . . opposed to each other: they all reject monism, and warmly espouse pluralism. The world is (or our aims are) many and not one" ("The Pluralist Chorus," *Legitimation of Belief* [London: Cambridge University Press, 1974], p. 1). True enough: who would deny that our aims in dealing with the world are many and not one? Yet each thinker is likely to see his way of dealing with those many aims as uniquely valid.

19. B. F. Skinner, *Beyond Freedom and Dignity* (New York: Alfred A. Knopf, 1971), esp. chap. 5, "Alternatives to Punishment."

20. In *Albert Einstein: Philosopher-Scientist*, vol. 7 in the Library of Living Philosophers, ed. Paul Arthur Schilpp (1949; La Salle, Ill.: Open Court, 1970), pp. 4–7.

21. The full passage illuminates our problem:

> The total, three-dimensional shape of the cone is not represented by either of the two actual percepts. Moreover, the total shape cannot be actual, or subject to perception, because any actual percept would exclude, or be incompatible with, the shape of a circle or a triangle. We seem to have no other choice but to admit that the cone, as contrasted with its alternative actual aspects such as a circle or a triangle, exists in the state of disposition or potentiality. This is to say that the cone is the disposition, or power, to show an actual aspect of a triangle within one perspective and some alternative aspect, for example, a circle, within another. The alternative aspects exclude each other as actual observations—no observer can have two of them at the same time—but as observable, i.e., in the capacity to appear in different perspectives, they are connected and co-exist. [P. 640]

22. Claudio Guillén traces the main lines in the history of "perspective," from visual to intellectual metaphor, in "On the Concept and Metaphor of Perspective," *Comparatists at Work: Studies in Comparative Literature*, ed. Stephen G. Nichols, Jr., and Richard B. Vowles (Waltham, Mass.: Blaisdell Publishing Co., 1968), pp. 29–90. See also chapter 3, "Faulty Perspectives," in E. D. Hirsch's *The Aims of Interpretation* (Chicago: University of Chicago Press, 1976), pp. 36–49.

CHAPTER TWO

1. See, for example, Locke's optimistic program as he begins the *Essay Concerning Human Understanding* (2 vols., ed. Alexander Campbell Fraser [Oxford: Clarendon Press, 1894], 1:26).

2. Serge Doubrovsky, *Pourquoi la nouvelle critique: Critique et objectivité* (Paris: Mercure de France, 1966), translated as *The New Criticism in France* by Derek Coltman, with an introduction by Edward Wasiolek (Chicago and London: University of Chicago Press, 1973), p. 51.

3. *The Languages of Criticism and the Structure of Poetry* (Toronto: University of Toronto Press, 1953), p. 23. Hereafter referred to as *Languages*.

4. Crane believed that these four elements were derived from Aristotle's four causes: purpose = final cause; subject matter = material; method = efficient; and principles = formal. But he would emphasize that what is form and what is matter are relative to the human activity being discussed; for example, the structure of a poem can be the matter of a critical discourse while being the form of the poem's making. Once we have begun such adjustments, what had seemed like static labeling becomes highly fluid, and it is scarcely surprising that interpreters do not even agree—as of course they should—that the object, manner, means, and end of the *Poetics* derive from formal, efficient, material, and final causes, in *that* order.

5. "Referentiality of literary meaning is thus so basic an assumption that it involves the whole frame of interpretation and the very nature of descriptive poetry. I shall try to show that this postulate is a fallacy, and that the representation of reality is a verbal construct in which meaning is achieved by reference from words to words, not to things" (Michael Riffaterre, "Interpretation and Descriptive Poetry: A Reading of Wordsworth's 'Yew-Trees,'" *New Literary History* 4 [Winter 1973]: 230).

6. "On Value Judgments in the Arts," *Critical Inquiry* 1 (September 1974); reprinted in Elder Olson, *"On Value Judgments in the Arts" and Other Essays* (Chicago: University of Chicago Press, 1976), p. 311.

7. M. H. Abrams, *The Mirror and the Lamp: Romantic Theory and the Critical Tradition* (New York: Oxford University Press, 1953), p. 6.

8. See Crane's "The Concept of Plot and the Plot of *Tom Jones*," *Critics and Criticism: Ancient and Modern* (Chicago: University of Chicago Press, 1952). For the essays on *Persuasion* and Hemingway's story, see his *The Idea of the Humanities and Other Essays* (Chicago: University of Chicago Press, 1967), vol. 2.

9. Auden, *Collected Shorter Poems, 1927–1957* (New York: Random House, 1966), p. 16. For the original sonnet, see W. H. Auden and Christopher Isherwood, *Journey to a War* (London: Faber & Faber, 1939), p. 275. For the revision, see *CSP*, p. 134. The most extensive analysis and complaint about Auden's silent revisions are made by Joseph Warren Beach, *The Making of the Auden Canon* (New York: Russell & Russell, 1957).

10. Roland Barthes, "Triomphe et rupture de l'écriture bourgeoise," *Le Degré zéro de l'écriture* (Paris: Editions du Seuil, 1953), p. 79. The point is slightly obscured in the translation given, in *Writing Degree Zero*, by Annette Lavers and Colin Smith (Boston: Beacon Press, 1968), pp. 55–57.

11. *Roland Barthes par Roland Barthes*, p. 48. See also Barthes's "Réquichot et son corps," *L'Oeuvre de Bernard Réquichot* (Brussels 1973), p. 23.

12. The many changes Barthes exhibits from work to work have often been discussed, but the most careful tracing I have seen is Elizabeth Neild's, in her unpublished Ph.D. dissertation, "Toward a New Contextualism: The Complementary Theories of Kenneth Burke and Roland Barthes," University of Chicago, 1977.

13. *Barthes par Barthes*, p. 50.

14. *Languages*, pp. 23–25.

15. Kenneth Burke, "The Problem of the Intrinsic (As Reflected in the Neo-Aristotelian School)," *A Grammar of Motives* (New York: Prentice-Hall, 1945; reprinted, New York: George Braziller, 1955; and Berkeley: University of California Press, 1969), pp. 465–84.

16. Crane, "I. A. Richards on the Art of Interpretation," *Ethics* (January 1949); reprinted in *Critics and Criticism*, p. 36.

17. William James, *A Pluralistic Universe*, Hibbert Lectures at Manchester College on "The Present Situation in Philosophy" (New York: Longmans, Green & Co., 1909); see especially the lectures on "Monistic Idealism" and "Hegel and His Method."

18. *Critics and Criticism*, p. 42.

19. Crane made this point in many different ways, perhaps most impressively in the long essay "Shifting Definitions and Evaluations of the Humanities from the Renaissance to the Present," *The Idea of the Humanities*, 1:16–170.

20. Roman Jakobson, "Closing Statement: Linguistics and Poetics," *Style in Language*, ed. Thomas A. Sebeok (Cambridge, Mass.: M.I.T. Press, 1960), p. 350

21. Jan Mukařovský, "Standard Language and Poetic Language," in *A Prague School Reader on Esthetics, Literary Structure, and Style*, ed. and trans. Paul L. Garvin (Washington, D.C.: Georgetown University Press, 1964), pp. 17–30, quotation on p. 18. See also Paul Ricoeur's definition in *Interpretation Theory: Discourse and the Surplus of Meaning* (Fort Worth: Texas Christian University Press, 1976): "Here by literary work I mean a work of discourse distinguished from every other work of discourse, especially scientific discourse, in that it brings an explicit and an implicit meaning into relation. . . . We can then say that what a poem states is related to what it suggests just as its primary signification is related to its secondary signification where both significations fall within the semantic field. And literature is that use of discourse where several things are specified at the same time and where the reader is not required to choose among them. It is the positive and productive use of ambiguity" (pp. 46–47).

22. *Languages*, pp. 115–39. See also his long series of short, brilliant, and often slashing reviews written for *Philological Quarterly*, republished in *English Literature, 1680–1800: A Bibliography of Modern Studies* (Princeton: Princeton University Press, 1950———).

23. See, especially, "On Hypotheses in 'Historical Criticism': Apropos of Certain Contemporary Medievalists," *The Idea of the Humanities*, 2:236–60.

24. John R. Searle, *Speech Acts: An Essay in the Philosophy of Language* (Cambridge, Eng.: At the University Press, 1970), p. 56. For a sustained attempt to show that Searle places too much confidence in the constraints on ambiguity imposed by "normal" circumstances, see Stanley Fish, "Normal Circumstances . . . And Other Special Cases," *Critical Inquiry* 4 (Summer 1978): 625–44. Fish sees his opponents as "all those who think that it is necessary to anchor language in some set of independent and formal constraints, whether those constraints are given the name of literal meaning, or straightforward discourse, or direct speech acts, or the letter of the law, or normal circumstances, or the everyday world," and who assume "that the constraints must be specifiable once and for all, and that if they are not so specifiable at *some* level, we live in a world of chaos where communication is entirely a matter of chance" (p. 644). Whatever the validity of Fish's strictures about speech-act theory, it does not seem to me that he has grappled with the more powerful "constraints" that are imposed on interpretation by our common-sense responses to skillful literary works. If it is true, as he says, that a *sentence* cannot just mean "anything at all," because it will always be in a determining "situation" (p. 643), it is more obviously true that most literary works are in a sense *designed to* a situation, and that most situations—let us say Molière attempting to make a highly

sophisticated audience laugh at a hypocrite—show astonishing durability through time. Fish's critique of Searle would have to be modified considerably if he took that durability seriously. But to be durable is not the same as being fixed "once and for all," and Fish is quite right in insisting that when sentences—or plays—are extracted from a human setting they can mean everything and anything.

25. See Norman Malcolm, "The Groundlessness of Belief," chap. 9 of his *Thought and Knowledge* (Ithaca, N.Y.: Cornell University Press, 1977), pp. 199–216, for a good summary of how Wittgenstein and his followers deal with the impossibility of proving every proposition within a system of beliefs. "Wittgenstein remarks that 'a language-game is only possible if one trusts something.' Not *can*, but *does* trust something. I think he means by this trust or acceptance what he calls belief 'in the sense of religious belief.' What does he mean by belief 'in the sense of religious belief'? He explicitly distinguishes it from *conjecture (Vermutung)*. I think this means that there is nothing tentative about it; it is not adopted as an hypothesis that might later be withdrawn in the light of new evidence.... It does not rise or fall on the basis of evidence or grounds: it is 'groundless.'" Such talk can usefully be compared with what I say in chapter 5 about the invulnerability of pluralism, as an "attitude," to factual refutation. I do object, however, to the connotations of "groundless," since they suggest what Malcolm surely does not mean: that there are no good reasons to be given for the belief.

26. Crane, "The Critical Monism of Cleanth Brooks," *Modern Philology* (May 1948); reprinted with minor alterations in *Critics and Criticism*, pp. 83–107.

27. *Languages*, p. 192.

28. Of the innumerable profound and condensed essays in pluralistic semantics by Richard McKeon, perhaps the closest to our purposes here is "The Philosophic Bases of Art and Criticism," *Modern Philology* (November 1943 and February 1944), reprinted in *Critics and Criticism*, pp. 463–545. A rigorous philosophical defense of pluralism is given in Elder Olson's "The Dialectical Foundations of Critical Pluralism," *"On Value Judgments in the Arts" and Other Essays*, pp. 327–59. Robert Marsh's original work on pluralism, much of it yet unpublished, is only partially represented by the work cited below (chap. 4, n. 15). See also Walter A. Davis's two works, "Theories of Form in Modern Criticism: An Examination of the Theories of Kenneth Burke and R. S. Crane" (Ph.D. diss., University of Chicago, 1960), and *The Act of Interpretation: A Critique of Literary Reason* (Chicago and London: University of Chicago Press, 1978).

29. This is the route that has been followed cautiously—one might almost say surreptitiously—by Richard McKeon. He has never yet published his sixteen-fold charting (itself in theory indefinitely multipliable) of the permutations possible among intellectual variables. The passionate drive for a neutrality yielded by "empty topics," the intense opposition to "entitizing," exhibited in McKeon's construction of such aids to a "philosophical semantics," were quite foreign to Crane's temperament. He profited from but never attempted the kind of conspectus on the whole intellectual world offered by McKeon in works like *Thought, Action, and Passion* (Chicago: University of Chicago Press, 1954) and "Philosophy and Method," *Journal of Philosophy* 48 (1951): 653–82.

30. Crane, *The Idea of the Humanities*, 1:122.

CHAPTER THREE

1. For example, in the Impresario's introduction of God and Satan for the splendid dialogue, "Epilogue: Prologue in Heaven," that concludes *The Rhetoric of Religion: Studies in Logology* (Boston: Beacon Press, 1961), pp. 273–74.

2. Crane, *Languages,* p. 109.

3. Burke seems to suggest, in his reply (p. 128, above), that I need to become acquainted with his words on the Chicago critics. But he is surely being sly: of all his sweet and troubling words, surely he could expect those to be most deeply inscribed upon my heart. See, especially, "The Problem of the Intrinsic" (n. 15, chap. 2, above).

4. See, for example, *The Philosophy of Literary Form: Studies in Symbolic Action,* 3d ed. (Berkeley: University of California Press, 1973), pp. 344, 347–48. (First published, 1941.) Also *A Rhetoric of Motives* (New York: George Braziller, 1955), pp. 189 ff. (First published, 1950.) The point about logical as opposed to temporal beginnings occurs again and again.

5. René Wellek, "Kenneth Burke and Literary Criticism," *Sewanee Review* 79 (Spring 1971): 171–88. (Quotation on p. 187.)

6. "As I Was Saying," *Michigan Quarterly Review* 11 (Winter 1972): 9–27; quotation on p. 22.

7. *Attitudes toward History* (1937; 2d rev. ed., Los Altos, Calif.: Hermes Publications, 1959), p. 260.

8. *A Grammar of Motives,* p. 25.

9. *Counter-Statement,* 2d ed. (Los Altos, Calif.: Hermes Publications, 1953; reprinted Berkeley: University of California Press, 1968), p. 138. (First published, 1931.) I refer here to article 11, "The Individuation of Forms," of "Lexicon Rhetoricae." Here, as elsewhere when Burke "identifies" something with something else, one can find in his immediate context clues about how the equation should be qualified: "Form, having to do with the creation and gratification of needs, is 'correct' in so far as it gratifies the needs which it creates. The appeal of the form *in this sense* [my italics] is obvious: form *is* [Burke's italics] the appeal."

10. The sequence can be found in many places, e.g., in the first of the "Five Summarizing Essays" in *Language As Symbolic Action: Essays on Life, Literature, and Method* (Berkeley and Los Angeles: University of California Press, 1966), "Definition of Man," p. 18. (I shall from now on use the abbreviation *LSA*). Seeing inquiry as probing processes rather than proving results, Burke has naturally heard threatening prophetic voices on his left flank, considerably more willing than he to give up traditional standards of evidence. In the late sixties he tried to show that Marshall McLuhan's "probes" were both less responsible and less adequate to the world than Burke's own ("Medium as 'Message,'" *LSA*, pp. 410–18). A fair number of new "rivals" have come on the critical scene a bit too late for full confrontation: the continental deontologizers and deconstructionists and their American cousins. I would not want to claim that Burke foreknew *everything* that Barthes, Derrida, de Man *et cie* have shocked the academic world with, but I am sure that, if they ever get around to reading him, they will be tempted to moderate their claims to originality. (See note 12 to chapter 2, above.)

11. Burke puts his own motives in many different ways, but his statement at the

beginning of *A Grammar of Motives* is representative; see esp. pp. xvii ff. Cf. his reply, p. 131, above.

12. *The Philosophy of Literary Form*, p. 74.

13. Burke's attack on behaviorist reductions has been unrelenting (see, for example, part 1 of *LSA* and chap. 7 of part 3), but it is always made in terms that attempt to incorporate the validities in the partial view. His most recent restatement is in "(Nonsymbolic) Motion/(Symbolic) Action," *Critical Inquiry* 4 (Summer 1978): 809–38, esp. 833 ff.

14. *LSA*, p. 45.

15. *LSA*, p. 20. I am indebted to Tom Tollefson for his unpublished tracing of Burke's "comic" alternative to the two unacceptable or impossible routes.

16. *The Rhetoric of Religion*, p. 184.

17. Burke often uses this suggestive verbal formula for his unpacking of the implications of any position. One might say that his life-work is to study such prophecy, using past symbolic actions, in order to speak prophetically about the consequences of present symbolic actions. If I can prophesy after the event about how (let us say) Hobbes's reduction of world to body led to Hobbes's conclusions, I should be able to show where Skinner's choice of motives will lead.

18. Perhaps Burke's best summary of how languages work as screens, without leaving us helpless to deal with the screens, is in *LSA*, part 1, chapter 3. The contrast between his kind of pluralism and relativism is fundamental to his program, but it is not easily stated in short form. To me, his own summary, "Our Attempt to Avoid Mere Relativism" (in *LSA*, pp. 52–54), is cogent. But I find that everyone who reads it without knowing much of Burke finds it cryptic. See also *The Philosophy of Literary Form*, pp. 73–74.

19. The goals of comprehensiveness, scope, and representativeness are implicit throughout, but see especially *Grammar*, chap. 3 of part 1: "Scope and Reduction."

20. *Philosophy of Literary Form*, p. 108.

Chapter Four

1. "What's the Use of Theorizing about the Arts?" in *In Search of Literary Theory*, ed. Morton W. Bloomfield (Ithaca, N.Y., and London: Cornell University Press, 1972), pp. 3–54.

2. "A Note on Wittgenstein and Literary Criticism," *English Literary History* 41 (Winter 1974): 541–54. Hereafter cited as "Wittgenstein."

3. *The Mirror and the Lamp*, esp. chap. 1. Hereafter cited as *ML*.

4. Morse Peckham, *Studies in Romanticism* 13 (1974): 360.

5. The two discussions of narrative truth and narrative method by historians that have impressed me most are J. H. Hexter's *Doing History* (Bloomington: Indiana University Press, 1971) and W. B. Gallie's *Philosophy and the Historical Understanding* (1964; 2d ed., New York: Schocken Books, 1968).

6. The word "demonstration" has a curious range of meanings. I am of course not thinking of its kinship with unquestionable proof but rather with one of the three kinds of rhetoric that are discussed by Aristotle and most later rhetoricians. But I am deliberately extending the word beyond the kind of rhetoric that "praises or

blames, in the present" to include any establishment of values, past, present, or future. See n. 12, below.

7. *Natural Supernaturalism: Tradition and Revolution in Romantic Literature* (New York: W. W. Norton, 1971). All citations in the text will, unless otherwise noted, be to this book, cited as *NS*.

8. Peckham, pp. 360–61.

9. J. Hillis Miller, "Tradition and Difference," *Diacritics* 2 (Winter 1972): 7 (my italics).

10. See Abrams' prefaces to *ML* and *NS*.

11. Harold Bloom, *A Map of Misreading* (New York: Oxford University Press, 1975), pp. 29–30.

12. Probably the most influential and cogent recent argument for the probative force of *ethos* is that of Chaim Perelman and L. Olbrechts-Tyteca in *The New Rhetoric: A Treatise on Argumentation*, trans. John Wilkinson and Purcell Weaver (Notre Dame, Ind.: University of Notre Dame Press, 1969). A briefer statement of their views can be found in "Act and Person in Argument," *Ethics* 61 (1951): 251–69. Theirs is also the fullest statement in modern times of the workings of epideictic (or demonstrative) rhetoric in general.

13. E. D. Hirsch, *Wordsworth Circle* 3 (1972): 19.

14. This variety has been objected to as revealing Abrams' confusion about causation: a reader knows not where to have him. See P. H. Butter's review, *Modern Language Review* 68 (January 1973): 157–59. I attempt to deal with this objection below, pp. 164–65.

15. See, for example, R. S. Crane, *Critical and Historical Principles of Literary History*, ed. Sheldon Sacks (Chicago: University of Chicago Press, 1971), reprinted from *The Idea of the Humanities*; Arthur Lovejoy, *The Great Chain of Being* (Cambridge, Mass.: Harvard University Press, 1936); Robert Marsh, "Historical Interpretation and the History of Criticism," in *Literary Criticism and Historical Understanding*, Selected Papers from the English Institute, ed. Phillip Damon (New York and London: Columbia University Press, 1967), pp. 1–24; see esp. p. 21.

16. One seeming exception, Croce, is no true exception, because of his radical particularism. Collingwood can be read as yielding some of what I am saying, but the unfortunate truth is that very few critics these days read Collingwood, let alone actually use him.

17. See Edward Wasiolek, "Wanted: A New Contextualism," *Critical Inquiry* 1 (March 1975): 623–39; Edgar Lohner, "The Intrinsic Method: Some Reconsiderations," in *The Disciplines of Criticism: Essays in Literary Theory, Interpretation and History*, ed. Peter Demetz, Thomas Greene, and Lowry Nelson, Jr. (New Haven, Conn., and London: Yale University Press, 1968), pp. 147–72.

18. In the last decade or so, philosophers in great numbers have rediscovered what almost all philosophers until the nineteenth century believed: that there is no implacable barrier between fact statements and value statements, or between what "is" and what "ought to be." For "Two-Score and More of Witnesses against the Fact-Value Split," see Appendix B of my *Modern Dogma and the Rhetoric of Assent* (Notre Dame, Ind.: University of Notre Dame Press, 1974; paperback ed., Chicago: University of Chicago Press, 1974). Intellectual history on its fashionable side moves in fits and starts, and it is amusing to find proponents of the last word lagging on one flank: Doubrovsky, in *Pourquoi la nouvelle critique: critique et objectivité* (Paris, 1966; trans. by Derek Coltman, *The New Criticism in France* [Chicago:

University of Chicago Press, 1973]), still relies on the split as a self-evidently sound base for his refutation of Lucien Goldmann's Marxist criticism (pp. 192 ff.).

An unusually cogent argument, which I had not read when I compiled my list, is given in the last chapter of John R. Searle's *Speech Acts: An Essay in the Philosophy of Language* (Cambridge, Eng.: At the University Press, 1969). To use Searle's terms, I am arguing here that a poem's "embodying" a great tradition is a kind of "institutional fact." The social "institution" of writing and reading and criticizing poetry determines, before any particular act of criticism, what words like "great" and "good" will mean. "Institutional facts exist within systems of constitutive rules" (p. 186). The institution's constitutive rules, in this case about what greatness is and how poems "embody" it or "inherit" it, entail evaluations that readers "ought" to arrive at if they understand or see the facts—because that is what the "facts" mean. In Searle's terms: "Some systems of constitutive rules involve obligations, commitments, and responsibilities." Translated: This kind of literary history, when it succeeds, works within a system of constitutive rules that involve critical standards.

The most likely objection to the move I have made here is that many inferior poems also embody or inherit great traditions. Many a poor Romantic poem will show many of the features that Abrams finds in fragments of *The Recluse:* the lone seeker or seer attempting to redeem mankind by fusing his mind with nature in a new kind of marriage; the circuitous journey of the soul on its daring secular pilgrimage; the transmutation of Christian themes into secular terms; and so on. The answer to such a charge must surely be: show me your poem, and show me that it really does "embody" and "inherit" the great themes and motives in their full reality and not merely in pale propositions or sloganized reductions; if you can find in any poem what Abrams has shown that he can find in Wordsworth's poems, then surely you must decide that what you thought was a bad poem is a good one. In short, one test of your poem will be what the test of Wordsworth's has been: its ability to sustain the historian's effort to tell its full story.

A more important objection is raised by my former student Don Bialostosky, who writes: "Doesn't Abrams really demonstrate the greatness of Wordsworth's achievement by an exploitation of all the topics of extrinsic criticism . . . rather than by some new topic which you call the incarnation of greatness? After all, he shows what Wordsworth has meant to his readers, among them some important men. He shows what Wordsworth's enterprise meant in the course of the poet's own life history as well as in the history of his age (there is an expressive criticism which dwells on the expression of that larger spirit through the personal expression—this is important in *Natural Supernaturalism*). Finally, he presents to us the poet's view of the world and man's place in it and shows that view to have originality and dignity. What other topics does he need to show greatness?"

It is true that Abrams moves flexibly among those three extrinsic modes, but to me all three are here subsumed under the historical and in a curious way are strengthened by it. That Bialostosky does not feel persuaded by my argument for the importance of the story itself, for the *telling of the story* as itself the chief act of criticism, is scarcely surprising, but it offers further discouraging evidence of how impossible it is, in my analytical account, to express the narrative force of Abrams'.

19. Abrams has returned to this question in an unpublished lecture, "Art-as-Such: The Sociology of an Aesthetic Theory" (delivered to the International Congress for the Enlightenment at Yale University, July 1975).

20. Thomas McFarland, "Complex Acts of Invention," *Yale Review* 61 (1972): esp. 279–88.

21. J. Hillis Miller, "Tradition and Difference," p. 11.

22. Perhaps most notably Paul de Man. But the lament about inherited and inescapable substances can be found from Nietzsche on.

23. Jerome J. McGann, "Romanticism and the Embarrassments of Critical Tradition," *Modern Philology* 70 (1973): 252. McGann makes almost all of the objections I have mentioned, finding that the book excludes far too much, that it is irrelevant to the study of poets after the Romantic period, that it is far too "rationalistic" and "unitary," and finally that Wordsworth is not, after all, central to Romanticism.

24. Peckham, p. 364.

25. Miller, "Tradition and Difference," p. 13.

26. Charles Rosen, *New York Review of Books*, 14 June 1973, pp. 12–18.

27. For a brief account of the early use of history as a base for *Geisteswissenschaft*, see René Wellek's "The Revolt against Positivism in Recent European Literary Scholarship," in his *Concepts of Criticism*, ed. Steven G. Nichols, Jr. (New Haven, Conn., and London: Yale University Press, 1963), esp. pp. 259–60. For the new discoveries of history, the successive issues of *New Literary History* provide perhaps the best single source.

Chapter Five

1. For a whole collection of such voices, see Alwin Diemer, ed., *Der Methoden- und Theorienpluralismus in den Wissenschaften* (Meisenheim am Glan: A. Hain, 1971).

2. See chap. 2, n. 28.

3. See chap. 4, n. 15.

4. Both appear in Crane's *The Idea of the Humanities*, the first in vol. 1, pp. 16–170, the second in vol. 2, pp. 45–156, reissued in paperback, with a foreword by Sheldon Sacks (Chicago and London: University of Chicago Press, 1971).

5. "Fiction d'un individu (quelque M. Teste à l'envers) qui abolirait en lui les barrières, les classes, les exclusions, non par syncrétisme, mais par simple débarras de-ce vieux spectre: *la contradiction logique*; qui mélangerait tous les langages, fussent-ils réputés incompatibles; qui supporterait, muet, toutes les accusations d'illogisme, d'infidélité ... Cet homme serait l'abjection de notre société: ... qui supporte sans honte la contradiction? Or ce contre-héros existe: c'est le lecteur de texte, dans le moment où il prend son plaisir" (Roland Barthes, *Le Plaisir du texte* [Paris: Editions du Seuil, 1973], pp. 9–10).

6. Burke, *Language as Symbolic Action*, pp. 37–38.

7. Burke, *Philosophy of Literary Form*, pp. 329–43.

8. E.g., "On Methodology," in *Philosophy of Literary Form*, pp. 66–88, and "Poetics in Particular, Language in General," in *Language as Symbolic Action*, pp. 25–43.

9. What follows is derived both from Crane's *The Languages of Criticism and the Structure of Poetry* (esp. pp. 6–8, 9–10, 169–73, and 178–79) and from personal discussion. See my early and rather clumsily imitative "Macbeth as Tragic Hero," *Journal of General Education* 6 (October 1951): 17–25; revised and reprinted as "Shakespeare's Tragic Villain" in *Shakespeare's Tragedies*, ed. Laurence Lerner (Harmondsworth, Middlesex: Penguin Books, 1963), pp. 180–90.

10. Peter Medawar, "A Geometric Model of Reduction and Emergence," *Studies in the*

Philosophy of Biology: Reduction and Related Problems, ed. Francisco Ayala and Theodosius Dobzhansky (Berkeley: University of California Press, 1974). See also Dobzhansky's "Introductory Remarks" and Bernhard Rensch's "Polynomistic Determination of Biological Processes."

11. The quotation and the formulation of the criteria are from Ernest Nagel, *The Structure of Science* (New York, 1961), as quoted by Ayala (p. x).

12. W. B. Gallie, *Philosophy and the Historical Understanding* (New York: Schocken Books, 1968), pp. 157–91. The first edition was published in 1964. The most rigorous proof for the existence of essentially contested concepts is constructed in a powerful work that I did not see until *Critical Understanding* was almost out of my hands, Morris Weitz's *The Opening Mind: A Philosophical Study of Humanistic Concepts* (Chicago: University of Chicago Press, 1977), especially chapter 1–3 and 8. Weitz's book could be called an argument for a limited pluralism, though he does not talk of the word "pluralism." He extends the notion of the essentially contested concept to include some that do not meet Gallie's first criterion ("the concept must be appraisive"). Wittgenstein's concept of "game," for example, is essentially "open," Weitz argues, even though not "appraisive" of a human achievement. After such deliberate broadening, the essentially contested concept (one foresees a time when we shall all be talking of ecc's) "is one whose criteria of use must be flexible, hence nondefinitive, in order to be applicable to new cases, with their new properties, or to extant cases with possible new interpretations of their present properties" (pp. 42–43).

13. See Stephen Toulmin, *Human Understanding*, 3 vols., pt. 1, *The Collective Use and Evolution of Concepts* (Princeton, N.J.: Princeton University Press, 1972——).

14. "Lisez lentement, lisez *tout*, d'un roman de Zola, le livre vous tombera des mains" (Barthes, *Le Plaisir du texte* p. 23). See also Barthes's short section explicitly on "ennui" (p. 43), and the discussion of boredom in Jonathan Culler's *Structuralist Poetics: Structuralism, Linguistics and the Study of Literature* (London: Routledge & Kegan Paul, 1975), pp. 262–64.

15. J. Hillis Miller, "Stevens' Rock and Criticism as Cure," *Georgia Review* 30 (Spring and Summer 1976): "The *mise en abyme* of uncanny criticism . . . is not the abyss itself in the sense of some direct representation of the truth of things. . . . There is no 'truth of things,' as such, to be represented. The *mise en abyme* of uncanny criticism is rather the ordering of the abyss . . . its formulation in one or another terminology or figure. Any such formulation, whether it is called 'the Dionysian,' 'the uncanny,' 'allegory,' *'la dissémination,'* 'the aporia,' *'la différance,'* 'decentering,' 'deconstruction,' . . . 'cure' . . . or whatever, can quickly become, like any other critical word, a dead terminology able to be coldly manipulated by epigones, mere leaves covering the ground rather than a means of insight into it." Though everything Miller says could be described as in the service of a higher truth, the emphasis is always on actional terms revealing "the inner drama or warfare of current literary criticism" (pp. 347–48).

16. Preface to the 1970 edition of *Mythologies*, trans. Annette Lavers (New York 1972). (*Mythologies* was first published in 1957.)

17. Stanley Fish, "Interpreting 'Interpreting the *Variorum*,'" *Critical Inquiry* 3 (Autumn 1976): 195. See p. 19, above.

18. In Derrida, as in many other liberators, it is often not easy to tell whether we are being liberated from dead feelings or from past intellectual error. But it is always

clear that we must plunge into this wave of the future or be damned as reactionary defenders of ethnocentrism, logocentrism, and recuperation. See, for example, the "Exergue" to *Of Grammatology* (*De la Grammatologie* [Paris: Editions de Minuit, 1967]), translated by Gayatri Chakravorty Spivak (Baltimore: Johns Hopkins University Press, 1976):

> By alluding to a science of writing *reined in* by metaphor, metaphysics, and theology, this exergue must not only announce that the science of writing— *grammatology*—shows signs of *liberation* all over the world. . . . I would like to suggest above all that, however *fecund* and *necessary* the undertaking might be, and even if, given the most favorable hypothesis, it did *overcome* all technical and epistemological *obstacles* as well as all the theological and metaphysical *impediments* that have limited it hitherto, such a science of writing runs the risk of never being established. . . .
>
> Perhaps patient meditation and painstaking investigation on and around what is still provisionally called writing, far from falling short of a science of writing or of hastily dismissing it by some *obscurantist reaction*, letting it rather develop its positivity as far as possible, are the wanderings of a way of thinking that is faithful and attentive to the *ineluctable world of the future* which proclaims itself at present. . . . *The future* can only be anticipated in the form of an absolute danger. It is that which *breaks absolutely with constituted normality* and can only be *proclaimed, presented*, as a sort of monstrosity. *For that future* world and for that within it which will have *put into question* the values of sign, word, and writing, for that which guides our future anterior, there is as yet no exergue. [Pp. 4–5; italics mine except on "grammatology" and "presented."]

Needless to say, everything I write about Derrida is, like everything he writes, *sous rature*, "under erasure": cross out this footnote. See Geoffrey Hartman's interpretation of Derrida's *Glas* in "Monsieur Texte II: Epiphany in Echoland," *Georgia Review* 30 (Spring 1976): 169–97. Like Miller, Mr. Hartman sees the new disseminations as a direct threat to traditional cognitive purposes, and he worries the conflict perceptively and with appropriate multiplication of paradox: "Can this disseminative kind of reading still be called a reading? . . . Derrida's engine . . . reproduces itself merely, giving us doubles that make us see more doubles still. The result for our time may be a factional split between simplifying types of reading that call themselves humanistic and indefinitizing kinds that call themselves scientific. The fate of reading is in the balance. In a classroom darkly" (p. 183).

19. If an attack on a position for being illogical could do the trick, M. H. Abrams' "The Deconstructive Angel," *Critical Inquiry* 3 (Spring 1977), would have led all deconstructionists to the altar to confess their sins. For reasons that we are grappling with throughout this book, the "enemy" is somehow untouched by such attacks.

20. In *Modern Dogma and the Rhetoric of Assent*.

21. Doubrovsky (see chap. 2, n. 2).

22. Tzvetan Todorov, "Poétique," in *Qu'est-ce que le structuralisme?* ed. François Wahl et al. (Paris: Editions du Seuil, 1968), p. 101. Todorov softens the murderous in his later revision (Paris: Editions du Seuil, 1973), p. 17. See also Nietzsche's dictum, "If a temple is to be erected *a temple must be destroyed*: that is the law—let anyone who can, show me a case in which it is not fulfilled!" (*On the Genealogy of Morals*, second essay, sec. 24, trans. Walter Kaufmann and R. J. Hollingdale [New York: Random House, 1967], p. 95). The similarities between this metaphoric view of critical warfare and Harold Bloom's oedipal metaphors for how poets relate to earlier poets are obvious. See Bloom's *The Anxiety of Influence: A Theory of Poetry*

(New York: Oxford University Press, 1973) and *The Map of Misreading* (New York: Oxford University Press, 1975).

23. Nietzsche, "Mixed Opinions and Maxims" (1879), no. 137 (in the Kaufmann trans. of *On the Genealogy of Morals*, p. 175).

24. Morse Peckham, "The Infinitude of Pluralism," *Critical Inquiry* 3 (Summer 1977): 810.

25. See the forum on "The Limits of Pluralism" in *Critical Inquiry* 3 (Spring 1977): 407–47. Miller, "The Critic as Host," is quoted from p. 447; Abrams is quoted from p. 438.

26. Barthes, "Dominici, or the Triumph of Literature," in *Mythologies*, trans. Lavers, p. 43.

27. *Unended Quest: An Intellectual Autobiography*. First published as "Autobiography of Karl Popper," in *The Philosophy of Karl Popper*, vol. 14 in the Library of Living Philosophers, ed. Paul Arthur Schilpp (La Salle, Ill.: Open Court, 1974; reissued in paperback, La Salle and London: Open Court 1976).

28. Barthes, *Sade/ Fourier/ Loyola* (Paris: Editions du Seuil, 1971), trans. Richard Miller (New York: Farrar, Straus & Giroux, 1976), pp. 8–9.

29. Barthes, *S/Z* (Paris: Editions du Seuil 1970), p. 212: "Comment un code peut-il avoir barre sur un autre sans fermer abusivement le pluriel des codes?"

30. Kant, *Critique of Pure Reason*, trans. Norman Kemp Smith (London, 1950), p. 47.

CHAPTER SIX

1. F. W. Boreham, *A Faggot of Torches* (New York and Cincinnati: Abingdon Press, 1926), p. 154.

2. Harold Bloom, *A Map of Misreading* (New York: Oxford University Press, 1975), p. 4 and passim. Bloom himself provides good "strong" criticism of some deconstructionists' violations.

3. See *Roland Barthes par Roland Barthes* (Paris: Editions du Seuil, 1975), p. 86.

4. Stephen C. Pepper, *World Hypotheses*, pp. 48–50.

5. See Kenneth Burke, "*Coriolanus*—and the Delights of Faction," *Language as Symbolic Action*, pp. 81–97, esp. p. 90.

Since the distinction between data and danda enables me to accept the validity of many kinds of meaning not provably intended by the author, it is obviously quite different from E. D. Hirsch's distinction between meaning and significance. For Hirsch, *meaning* is strictly what the author intended in a given historical act of writing; *significance* is whatever later interpreters add to a meaning which can alone yield validity in interpretation (see Hirsch's *Validity in Interpretation* [New Haven: Yale University Press, 1976] and *The Aims of Interpretation* [Chicago: University of Chicago Press, 1976]). In *A Rhetoric of Irony* I found Hirsch's distinction useful in working with stable irony, but it has led to a good deal of pointless polemic about the status of unintended readings. The data/dandum distinction might help shift the discussion to how different kinds of validity relate; claims about danda discovered in diverse acts of overstanding can be validated or invalidated by anyone willing to enter what we might call the proof-world of a given mode. The ethical weight that Hirsch wants to give to the author's meaning can thus be lifted, and debate about both the validity and the morality of interpretation can be relocated among various kinds of overstanding for various social or moral purposes. The best critique I know of Hirsch's grant of ethical force to "author's meaning" is Jack W. Meiland's "Interpretation as a Cognitive Discipline," *Philosophy and Literature* 2 (1977–78): 23–45.

6. A. G. W. Cameron, "The Origin and Evolution of the Solar System," *Scientific American* 233 no. 3 (September 1975): 33.

7. Barthes, *Sade/Fourier/Loyola*, trans. Richard Miller (New York: Hill & Wang, 1976), p. 9. (The original French edition was published by Seuil in 1971.)

8. Doubrovsky, *The New Criticism in France*, p. 67.

9. Barthes, *Sur Racine* (Paris: Editions du Seuil, 1963); the first essay, "L'Homme Racinien," appeared in an edition of Racine's plays (Paris: Club Français du Livre, 1960). The book appeared in English as *On Racine*, trans. Richard Howard (New York: Farrar, Straus & Giroux, 1964). The "violations" committed by this book were of course the first blow in the famous "quarrel" of the late sixties. See Raymond Picard, *Nouvelle Critique ou Nouvelle Imposture?* (Paris: J.-J. Pauvert, 1965–69), trans. Frank Towne as *New Criticism or New Fraud?* (Pullman: Washington State University Press, 1969); and Doubrovsky, *The New Criticism in France*, especially chapters 1 and 2.

10. Most notably, Robert Marsh (see chap. 4, n. 15) and Walter Davis. In *The Act of Interpretation: A Critique of Literary Reason* (Chicago: University of Chicago Press, 1978) Davis provides the most elaborate effort I know of showing a necessary matching of mode to work. For Davis, there are three, and only three, major theories of literary form: the "emotive" form of the Aristotelian tradition, as represented by Ronald Crane; rhetorical form of the kind pursued by Kenneth Burke; and dialectical or cognitive form. Some literary works clearly require by their nature the application of one or the other of these modes: there are emotive, rhetorical, and dialectical forms, and the pluralist will strive to match the work to the proper method. Some other works, like Faulkner's "The Bear," *seem* to be amenable to all three formal inquiries, but with effort the pluralist can discover even in such seemingly mixed works that either emotive or rhetorical or cognitive intentions subsume all others, and he will then choose finally the critical mode most appropriate to the work.

Despite many similarities between Davis's work and mine—including the choice of Crane and Burke as two of three main possibilities—our differences are finally crucial, though *perhaps* resolvable. He does not, except indirectly, face my main problem here: how to deal with a plurality of pluralisms. And I do not, even indirectly, attempt to establish a limited list of critical modes; even if I did, I would be unwilling to attempt any kind of proper matching of mode to type of work. Implicit in my account is always the assumption—one that from his dialectical point of view would seem deplorably rhetorical—that every critical mode that is of interest to intelligent readers is capable of being applied to every work, regardless either of the announced intentions of the author or the intentions of the work (that is, the author's choices as finally embodied). Though every mode can presumably be strengthened (and some are feeble indeed), none, except perhaps for the most trivial, is inherently limited to literature of a certain kind.

Where my inquiry would meet his, in the great rambling structure of innumerable expanding and contracting critical modes, would be in that one very neat corner of one rather constricted room where debate is held about intended forms. It was in that room that *A Rhetoric of Irony* was mainly written, and it is toward disputes within that room, as I see it, that Davis's important and wide-ranging pluralistic theory is directed. He and I naturally agree that that room is the most important of the whole house of criticism—that if it were removed, the building would crumble into unrelated fragments. But the pluralism he develops, however useful it may be for disputes within that room, becomes for my inquiry here one more monism, attempting to take over the world. See his note 72, p. 168.

11. As a graduate student, I decided to put Crane's mode to the test by discovering the unity of *Tristram Shandy*, perhaps of all great English novels the one most often called disunified and thus the least likely candidate for a formal mode seeking unities. I never did discover "the" unity of *Tristram Shandy*, but the search for it, in seeming violation of its demands, uncovered unities that other critical modes had overlooked. See my unpublished dissertation, "The Self-Conscious Narrator in Comic Fiction before *Tristram Shandy*," and "Did Sterne Complete *Tristram Shandy?*" *Modern Philology* 48 (February 1951): 172–83.

12. Paul de Man sees the failure of New Criticism as tied to its anti-intentionalism: analysis of texts torn from notions of intentionalism led to conclusions about ambiguity and irony that were in disharmony with their quest for unity ("Form and Intent in the American New Criticism," *Blindness and Insight*, pp. 20–35). From my point of view the New Critics never rejected the quest for the *text's* intentions, but they tended to reduce the variety of actual intentions to a few basic qualities—unity, coherence, complexity, irony—and thus seemed to a later generation to impose a straitjacket on the reader. For an excellent reappraisal of the new critics, see Gerald Graff's forthcoming *Literature against Itself: Literary Ideas in Modern Society* (Chicago: University of Chicago Press, 1979).

13. Norman N. Holland, *5 Readers Reading* (New Haven and London: Yale University Press, 1975), pp. 246–47.

Chapter Seven

1. Burke's complete definition, discussed clause by clause in chapter 1 of *Language as Symbolic Action*, goes like this:

> Man is
> the symbol-using (symbol-making, symbol-misusing) animal
> inventor of the negative (or moralized by the negative)
> separated from his natural condition by instruments of his own
>   making
> goaded by the spirit of hierarchy (or moved by the sense of order)
> and rotten with perfection. [P. 16]

Of the slogan-definitions I cite, Burke's is obviously closest to the one I have implied here: man the inventor of the weighed affirmative. I am not entirely clear about the consequences of shifting from Burke's accent on the negative (which always *implies* a weighed positive) to my emphasis on our capacity to say "Yes, I understand" (which always implies that I could have said no). Clearly, every synonym for "I understand you" implies the possibility both that I might have misunderstood and that I might reject what I have understood. "Yes" and "no" depend on each other, and we define human beings when we say that they alone among creatures discuss the reasons for their yeses and nos. We can be sheep, we can be mules, but we are sheep and mules who insist on *explaining*. Thus for both

Burke and me, what is most important is not the primacy of either yes or no but the possibility of symbolic exchange about both: that is, understanding. See *Modern Dogma and the Rhetoric of Assent*, esp. chap. 3, pp. 101 ff.

2. Even those who carefully avoid talking about essences usually find that the human condition is made of and defined by the understanding of symbols. Marshall Sahlins, for example, in his argument against those who subordinate meanings to practical function, puts his emphasis on how meanings make cultures, and his own language might seem, to some, not essentialist but "relativistic": "So far as the concept or meaning is concerned, a word is referable not simply to the external world but first of all to its place in the language—that is, to other related words. By its difference from these words is constructed its own valuation of the object, and in the system of such differences is a cultural construction of reality." It takes no great amount of translation to see that Sahlins is in fact defining what makes the human condition distinctive: "But the arbitrariness of the symbol is the indicative condition of human culture" (*Culture and Practical Reason* [Chicago: University of Chicago Press, 1976], pp. 63, 62).

A staggering range of "understandings" is revealed even in a glance at the book titles that include the word. In the University of Chicago library, the 400–500 titles range neatly from *Understanding Adolescence* to *Understanding Youth* (no *Understanding Zest*, no *Understanding Zeal*). Most of them seem to reveal the same essential ambiguity that is shown in these two: what authors claim to understand are the abstractions—adolescence, youth, nationalism, IQ; but what they must first understand, before the abstractions make sense, are people—adolescents, young folks, nationalists, persons who think (or fail to). The efforts at understanding that come closest to our interest here are of course those that explicitly set out to understand understanding itself. No reader should be surprised by now if I say that even the ones that have proved most helpful to me cannot, so far as I can see, be harmonized into a monistic view either of a single subject, "understanding," or of a single method for understanding it. Yet surely the following are not talking about totally disparate subjects, whether any one of us can demonstrate a common ground or not: Paul Ziff, *Understanding Understanding* (Ithaca: Cornell University Press, 1972); David Hume, *An Enquiry Concerning Human Understanding* (1748); Stephen Toulmin, *Human Understanding* (Princeton: Princeton University Press, 1972); Kant, with his three *Critiques* (1781–90); Coleridge, with his many shifting efforts to relate "understanding" and "reason," the latter usually coming out as winner (e.g., in *The Friend*, ed. Barbara E. Rooke, 2 vols. [Princeton: Princeton University Press, 1969], esp. 1:154–61; 2:503–4); to say nothing of innumerable inquiries into understanding found in modern treatises traveling under other names (interpretation, hermeneutics, the art of reading, translation, and so on).

3. Sahlins points out that in American usage, which is what I follow here, "sign" and "symbol" mean precisely the opposite of what they mean in continental usage, which derives from Saussure's *Course in General Linguistics* (see *Culture and Practical Reason*, p. 59, n.). If we take signs as expressions that are motivated—that bear some natural relationship to the thing indicated—then the sharing of their meanings must be added to our more specifically symbolic "understanding." Since human beings share with other animals the meaning of many *signs*, in this definition, we must grant that we have a kinship in understanding with all living creatures, since all read and share signs. As Burke would say, all living things are critics. It is obvious that the higher animals also share with us *some* gift for understanding *symbols*—expressions that are "unmotivated," "arbitrary." To the degree

that they do, we can simply follow Burke, one more time, and say, "Welcome, brothers and sisters."

In one version of the ontological proof for the existence of God, the fact that our minds *all* share understanding of *some* symbolic relations (e.g., mathematical relations) and thus cannot be said to have made such truths (but are, rather, made *by* them) is taken as proof that God exists. See Augustine's "On the Free Will," Book II, esp. chapters 8–15. As Richard McKeon summarizes the argument in the introduction to his translation (*Selections from Medieval Philosophers* [New York: Charles Scribner's Sons, 1929], p. 7): "The fact of thought [that is shared by more than one thinker] is indication of the existence of God."

4. Research seems to have proved that the child's first smiles are entirely programmed; even a blind child will smile at a given stage, that is, his or her first smiles will occur at about the same time as with normal children (see Selma Fraiberg, *Insights from the Blind: Comparative Studies of Blind and Sighted Infants* [New York: Basic Books, 1977], pp. 116–18). Presumably such smiles do not express human understanding, whatever we take them to say about God's management. But once a loving response has been recognized and in turn responded to, the child has clearly entered the world of human understanding. Of course only the most seriously lost children have failed to enter that world long before the first meaningful smile, through elementary exchanges via all the senses: I shout my hunger to the amorphous world, and the mind that, unbeknownst to me, informs a part of that world responds with delicious warm milk: ah, they understand me!

5. Donald Davidson provides some lovely examples of such routine but miraculous reconstructions in an unpublished paper, "A Nice Derangement of Epitaphs" (delivered at the annual convention of the American Philosophical Association, 1977).

6. See *Critical Inquiry* 5 (Autumn 1978) for discussions by Paul Ricoeur, Donald Davidson, Karsten Harries, and others of the cognitive claims of metaphor.

7. To develop what such a statement means about the pronoun "I" would require a book in itself. Taking hints from the psychologies of the social self developed by George Herbert Mead and John Dewey and from Michael Polanyi's argument that all mental life is "convivial" (to say nothing of many other recent critiques of the autonomous self), I have developed notes toward such a book in *Modern Dogma and the Rhetoric of Assent* (see esp. pp. 126–36). A similar critique (though one that is to me threateningly obscure) appears to be developed by Jacques Lacan in a work that I have only begun to read (*The Language of the Self: The Function of Language in Psychoanalysis,* trans. Anthony Wilden [Baltimore: Johns Hopkins University Press, 1968]).

8. For a self-indulgent and profane elaboration of the decalogue that this command implies, see my "The Meeting of Minds," *College Composition and Communication* 23 (October 1972): 242–50.

9. An interesting study in the confusions that inevitably result when critical debate is posited as opposition between defenders of author, reader, text, or society can be seen in the issue of *Novel* devoted to the conference, "Towards a Poetics of Fiction" (*Novel* 11 [Fall 1977]). One of the most aggressive and potentially misleading attacks on the author is found in Roland Barthes's "The Death of the Author" ("La mort de l'auteur," *Manteia* 5 [1968], translated in *Image/Music/Text* by Stephen Heath [New York: Hill & Wang, 1977]):

Once the Author is removed, the claim to decipher a text becomes quite futile. To give a text an Author is to impose a limit on that text, to furnish it with a final signified, to close the writing. Such a conception suits criticism very well, the latter then allotting itself the important task of discovering the Author (or its hypostases: society, history, psyché, liberty) beneath the work: when the Author has been found, the text is "explained"—victory to the critic. Hence there is no surprise in the fact that, historically, the reign of the Author has also been that of the Critic, nor again in the fact that criticism (be it new) is today undermined along with the Author. In the multiplicity of writing [as distinct from "works" by Authors] everything is to be *disentangled,* nothing *deciphered;* the structure can be followed, "run" (like the thread of a stocking) at every point and at every level, but there is nothing beneath: the space of writing is to be ranged over, not pierced; writing ceaselessly posits meaning ceaselessly to evaporate it, carrying out a systematic exemption of meaning. In precisely this way literature (it would be better from now on to say *writing*), by refusing to assign a "secret," an ultimate meaning, to the text (and to the world as text), liberates what may be called an anti-theological activity, an activity that is truly revolutionary since to refuse to fix meaning is, in the end, to refuse God and his hypostases—reason, science, law. [P. 147]

There is more at stake, then, in the battle with that Author, capital A, than might at first appear.

10. Lipking's work is tentatively called "The Life of the Poet." I am indebted to his unpublished lecture, "Famous Last Words: The Poetic Endings of Virgil, Goethe, Whitman, and Eliot."

11. Testimony to this distilling process can be found in many forms throughout the history of literature. Hazlitt, for example, arguing that "no really great man ever thought himself so," uses as one argument the fact that every genius knows too much about himself to think himself great. "Besides, every one must be sensible of a thousand weaknesses and deficiencies in himself; whereas Genius only leaves behind it the monuments of its strength. A great name is an abstraction of some one excellence; but whoever fancies himself an abstraction of excellence, so far from being great, may be sure that he is a blockhead, equally ignorant of excellence or defect, of himself or others. Mr. Burke, besides being the author of the *Reflections,* and the *Letter to a Noble Lord,* had a wife and son; and had to think as much about them as we do about him" ("Whether Genius Is Conscious of Its Powers?").

To me, the best brief explanation of why implied authors outshine their makers is Samuel Johnson's in *The Rambler,* Number 14: "Among the many inconsistencies which folly produces, or infirmity suffers in the human mind, there has often been observed a manifest and striking contrariety between the life of an author and his writings. . . . For many reasons a man writes much better than he lives" (Saturday, 5 May 1750; in *Essays from the* Rambler, Adventurer, *and* Idler, edited by W. J. Bate [New Haven and London: Yale University Press, 1968], pp. 38–44).

Some current celebrations of irony, discontinuity, and "unreadability" might seem to deny my point about an achieved authority based on successful purgations and distillations. But it is important to recognize that the claim about authority can hold quite independently of the kind of achievement an author is hailed for. Jonathan Culler, for example, argues that Flaubert's irony "is less a technique for producing meanings than a way of undoing them or producing uncertainty" ("The Uses of Uncertainty Re-viewed," *MMLA* 11 [Spring 1978]: 14–15). But Culler reveals, not only in his curiously confident readings of Flaubert's uncertainties and his admiration for Flaubert's achievement but also in his contempt for those who read Flaubert in the wrong way, that for him Flaubert *has* made a work of art that carries its own authority. The very title of his book, *Flaubert: The Uses of Uncertainty,* alerts us to expect that the "inconsistencies" we discover will be somehow *achieved* inconsistencies. This point should be kept quite distinct from any quarrels critics may have about what kinds of achievement are worth making.

I cannot be sure, but I think that it is a confusion of these distinct issues that has led Culler and Fredric Jameson into a misreading of my own work as "denouncing" such " 'irresponsible ironies' as are legion in Flaubert" and as trying to "tame irony, to make it nothing but a tool which authors use to produce intended, determinable meanings" ("The Uses of Uncertainty Re-viewed," p. 15). Before Culler concludes that my sense of my own intentions is irrelevant to what I actually meant, I hope that he will take another look at how much of what I have written contradicts what he sees in me. There is, perhaps, the possibility that I am deliberately cultivating uncertainties in order to prevent his reading me properly. But then, again, perhaps there is not.

12. Leon Edel, ed., *The Complete Tales of Henry James,* vol. 12: *1903–1910* (New York and Philadelphia: J. B. Lippincott, 1964), pp. 7, 10–11.

13. Henry James, *The Turn of the Screw: An Authoritative Text, Backgrounds and Sources, Essays in Criticism,* ed. Robert Kimbrough (New York: W. W. Norton, 1966). Unless otherwise noted, all of my references will be to this anthology, cited as "Kimbrough."

14. Kimbrough, pp. 91–94.

15. See Wilson's postscript to the 1948 edition of *The Triple Thinkers,* reprinted in *The Story: A Critical Anthology,* ed. Mark Schorer (Englewood Cliffs, N.J.: Prentice-Hall, 1950), pp. 583–85.

16. Kimbrough, quotations from "The Independent" (p. 175); from Walter de la Mare (p. 177); and references to Gilbert Chesterton's opinion that it should not have been published at all (pp. 184–85).

17. Those who remember what Crane had to say about testing our hypotheses against negative evidence (pp. 90–92, above) will recognize that I am here following his advice, but I am making the postulates about the writer, on which the advice depends, much more explicit than he was inclined to.

18. Eric Solomon, "The Return of the Screw," Kimbrough, pp. 237–45.

19. Kimbrough, p. 120.

20. See the Preface (Kimbrough, p. 121).

21. In chapter 5 (Kimbrough, pp. 23–24).

22. Preface (Kimbrough, p. 121).

23. For a brief summary of the statements by James to this effect, see *The Rhetoric of Fiction,* p. 312.

24. Letter to Dr. Waldstein (Kimbrough, p. 110). See also letter to F. W. H. Myers (Kimbrough, p. 112).

25. Kimbrough, pp. 172, 173.

26. Harold C. Goddard, "A Pre-Freudian Reading of *The Turn of the Screw*" (written "about 1920 or before" but first published in *Nineteenth-Century Fiction* 12 [June 1957]: 1–36 [Kimbrough, pp. 181–209]).

27. *Collected Works of Oliver Goldsmith*, ed. Arthur Friedman, 5 vols. (Oxford: Oxford University Press, 1966), 2:ix. Except where otherwise noted, my quotations are all from this work. What follows is a reduced version of my article "The Self-

Portraiture of Genius: *The Citizen of the World* and Critical Method," *Modern Philology* 73 (May 1976): 85–96.

28. *Critical Review* 13 (1762): 397–400, as quoted in Friedman, pp. xii–xiii.

29. John Forster, *The Life and Adventures of Oliver Goldsmith* (London: Bradbury & Evans, 1848), pp. 222–24.

30. Robert H. Hopkins, for example, in *The True Genius of Oliver Goldsmith* (Baltimore: Johns Hopkins University Press, 1969), defending Goldsmith as a "master of comic satire and refined irony" (p. vii), and *The Citizen* as a unified masterpiece of "irony and satire . . . from beginning to end" (p. 230), argues that "narrative continuity . . . is provided . . . by a frame tale" (p. 102). The case may seem plausible until one notices that in his long argument about ironic coherence and narrative continuity he does not even mention about 100 of the 123 letters, thus totally ignoring about five-sixths of the text! Ricardo Quintana shows himself much more aware of the variety in the work in his *Oliver Goldsmith: A Georgian Study* (New York: Macmillan, 1967), chap. 4. But in making his argument that *Citizen* is "in a manner unified," he cites or alludes to less than a dozen letters (pp. 75–81)—even fewer than Hopkins. Since the kind of unity he seeks is quite different, the letters cited are different; only one of Quintana's (no. 116) is mentioned in Hopkins' argument. Any reader of *Citizen* can easily find at least thirty letters whose subject matter and effect cannot, in the most generous view, fit either conception of unity; and of course those letters are mentioned by neither critic. The only serious rival to organic unity that I discover in recent criticism is thematic unity or "harmony." Something of the power and range of Goldsmith's art can emerge from such accounts (see, for example, Michael D. Patrick's "Oliver Goldsmith's *Citizen of the World*: A Rational Accommodation of Human Existence," *Enlightenment Essays* 2 [1971]: 82–90). But to me the critics invariably understate the lively variety of the essays by describing variations *on a theme* rather than *in an unpredictable person*.

31. Almost a century later, Forster could see Goldsmith's radical ideas as a chief mark of his greatness. He offers several pages listing the occasions when "the Chinese citizen so lifted his voice that only in a later generation could he find his audience" (*Life*, p. 226).

32. As Sheldon Sacks argues in *Fiction and the Shape of Belief* (Berkeley and Los Angeles: University of California Press, 1964), inconsistency of narrative tone is indeed the normal condition of fictional satire (see esp. pp. 31–49). Our recognition that we are engaged with satire enables us to move securely through what otherwise might seem wildly extravagant shifts in the narrator from ignorance and folly to wisdom. No doubt our recognition, from the introduction on, that Goldsmith will often use Altangi for satirical attacks enables us to make the shifts from moments when Altangi attacks the British to moments when his own position is attacked. But *The Citizen* is considerably more "miscellaneous" than the satires considered by Sacks; only some such notion as "the rich varieties provided by imaginative genius" can account for our being able to comprehend the tonal shifts I am considering.

33. E. M. Forster, *Aspects of the Novel* (New York: Harcourt, Brace & Co. 1927), chap. 8.

34. I don't *know* that it was a dreadful exploitation of the virtuous-whore theme. But the reviewer in *The Motion Picture Classic* talked mainly of the heroine, a woman of "sensuous charm" and "wide violet eyes," dwelling in Alexandria, that "golden city," which was "so noble in art and beauty, so ignoble in pleasure and excess."

For this tidbit, as for most of my information about France's reputation, I am indebted to Marjorie R. McEwen's *Anatole France in the United States* (Northfield, Minn.: Edwards Brothers, 1945).

35. Arnold Bennett, *Books and Persons, Being Comments on a Past Epoch, 1908–1911* (New York: George H. Doran, 1917), p. 60. The comment first appeared in Bennett's column on 29 October 1908, and it served to introduce some slight reservations that Bennett felt, after reading *Penguin Island*, about France's preeminence. Still, even two years later, France was for him "the greatest man in the Académie Française" (p. 232).

36. Paul West, *The Modern Novel* (London: Hutchinson, 1963), pp. 154–55.

37. Sheldon Sacks, *Fiction and the Shape of Belief*, esp. chaps. 1 and 6.

38. Georg Lukács, *The Historical Novel* (London: Merlin Press, 1962), chap. 4, esp. pp. 257–58. (The book was first published in Russian in 1937.) "France's enlightenment is less the abstract and closed outlook that it is with his followers . . . and more a defensive, superior skepticism towards both the openly reactionary tendencies of his time and (which is his distinctive note) the limits and questionableness of bourgeois democracy."

39. Having rejected "dogmatism" and "utter skepticism," and finding himself with four irreducible "world theories," based on four "root metaphors"—formism, mechanism, contextualism, and organicism—Pepper must decide whether he sees these four as ultimate rivals or collaborators in our search for the truth about the world. His solution is to adopt tentatively, while waiting for further inquiry, two quite different standards. In judging any particular world theory, he will be "rational," applying rigorously the standards of a particular view. The trouble is, of course, that according to those standards all other views will be rejected. That's where the whole problem arose in the first place: according to the standards of "rational clarity," each of the four survivors in his inquiry would cancel the others out.

> That an eclecticism should be excluded from within world theories is obvious in the interests of clarity; otherwise, how can one see just where the maximum of structural corroboration [what I have called coherence] lies? If a world theory partly developed in one set of categories is broken in upon by a foreign set of categories, the structure of corroboration is broken up and we cannot clearly see how the evidence lies. For intellectual clarity, therefore, we want our world theories pure and not eclectic. [*World Hypotheses*, p. 330]

And so Pepper is forced to turn, "in practice," to a looser standard, that of "reasonable eclecticism":

> We wish in matters of serious discussion to have the benefit of all the available evidence and modes of corroboration. In practice, therefore, we shall want to be not rational but reasonable, and to seek, on the matter in question, the judgment supplied from each of these relatively adequate world theories. If there is some difference of judgment, we shall wish to make our decision with all these modes of evidence in mind, just as we should make any other decision where the evidence is conflicting. In this way we should be judging in the most reasonable way possible—not dogmatically following only one line of evidence, not perversely ignoring evidence, but sensibly acting on all the evidence available.
> . . . Having done all that we can do rationally to organize the evidence on the topic in question [his examples are truth, value, time, universals, relations, causality, self, and society, but his argument will apply to any effort at a general view of any subject] in terms of structural corroboration, and finding as a rule

that there are four equally justifiable hypotheses explaining the nature of the subject, we shall have the wisdom not to conclude that we know nothing about the topic, but, on the contrary, that we have four alternative theories about it, which supply us with a great deal more information on the subject than any one of them alone could have done. [Pp. 330–31]

He then adds a brief hope that his four theories are gradually "closing in upon the world," that the collaboration will finally prove to be cooperation "in a single enterprise. . . . We know a lot about our world, both in its detail and in its general structure, and we have good reason to believe that we shall know a lot more" (p. 332). But he is quite clear that no one can hope that his four "relatively adequate" world theories can "be harmonized or amalgamated into one interpretation that will do justice to them all" (pp. 344–47).

Although Pepper's picture of a relatively adequate world view is in many ways radically different from my view of a relatively adequate (and accurate, and coherent) critical mode, I find what he calls "reasonable eclecticism" remarkably similar to the critical pluralism I must settle for.

Index of Concepts

The more ambitious the index, the greater the temptation to substitute index-dipping for reading the book. Yet even the simplest index, taken by itself, distorts every concept it contains; by providing a new context for each term, it ceases to be a mere report and becomes an invitation to misreading. The dangers are compounded whenever an index must, like this one, list many concepts that are not the author's own and many others for which definitions shift as the book progresses.

I offer the following unusually risky elaborateness because I hope that some few re-readers will find in its inevitable "distortions" some hints about subjects, organizations, and problems that will carry them far beyond the book itself. Indeed, I must confess that in constructing it I discovered unsuspected problems that the book might well have pursued further. Such invitations to further thought, along with temptations to misreading, are uncovered most pressingly in the more ambitious entries, such as those under Criteria, Locations, Modes, Methods, Pluralisms, Poem, and Principles. All of these should be read as cowering between the implicit quotation marks provided by the entry "Skepticism about total views."

irreducibility of, as evidence for pluralism, 214; as larger than their practitioners, 40–41, 253–54; as limiting observation, 42, 167–68 (*see also* Terministic screens); as necessarily distorting other modes, 33, 106–7, 128, 168 (*see also* Refutation); new, invention of, 40; as not entities, 91; not summarizable in propositions, 28–29; as permanent resources, 40–41, 193–94, 222; as pragmatic choices (*see* Pragmatic criteria, for evaluating modes); as ratios within Burke's pentad, 112–13; related to kind of poem, 132; schema of, 54–57; seepage from, into pluralism, 25, 80, 89–90, 91–92, 93–94, 102, 125; as shared tenancies, 45, 339–45 (*see also* Pluralism, topical); as sources of improper questions, 250–55; study of, as cure for misunderstanding, 38 (*see also* Semantics); as term, itself evaluative, 212; and texts, reciprocity between, 77, 77n, 132, 253; as transpersonal, 28–29, 40–41, 253–54; as universally applicable, 250–51, 369n.10; variably inclined to violation, 253; varieties of interrelation among, with respect to pluralisms, 93–94, 125; as voices, 40; as ways of limiting infinite interpretation, 125 (*see also* Pluralism, limits of). *See also:*
—*For analyses of variables among: see* Consequences (*see also* Pragmatic criteria); Criticism, ends of; Method; Methods; Principles; Subject matters (*see also* Locations, *all entries*)
—*For author-centered modes:* Author; Author, as authority; Dramatism; Expressive criticism; Writer *(all entries)*
—*For form-centered modes:* Composition; Formal modes; Patterns; Poetic *(all entries)*; Poetics
—*For history-centered modes:* Historical modes; History
—*For reader-centered modes:* Dramatism; Ethical modes; Reader-criticism; Rhetorical criticism
—*For "world"-centered modes:* Ethical modes; Philosophical modes; Political

criticism; Psychoanalytical criticism; Religious modes; Sociological criticism
Monism, 1–2, 24, 25, 39, 56–57, 96, 213, 221; analogies to, 14–15; as attitude toward conflict, 12–17; based on scientific models, 177; defined, 12, 42–43; disguised as pluralism, 5; as dogma, 39, 62, 166, 278, 354n.3; as dogmatic assertion of latest novelty, 16; epistemological (*see* Thoughts); extent of, 15, 17; linguistic (*see* Language, as principle); metaphors for (*see* Conflict, metaphors for); metaphysical, 73; in natural science, 248–49; not identical with dogmatic tone, 12, 355n.8; ontological (*see* Ontological principles; Things); as panacea, 39; of physical matter, 112; in political science, 210; in practice, 249; as practiced by pluralist, illustrated, 80; processive (*see* Action, as principle); as proscription of kinds of talk, 221–22; reduction of many causes to single, 154–55; and relativism, reciprocally related, 91–92; as source of induction by exclusion, 13–14; as stunting psyches, 345; topical pluralism's resemblance to, 345–46; as universal "temptation," 73; universality of, in all practical criticism, 43; uses of, 226, 340
Monotony, 5, 222, 241; of questions, 252–53
Moral improvement, as means of improving debate, 10–11
Morality, as criterion for evaluating poem, 295
Motion, physical, as essential to account for man's drama, 122–23. *See also* Causes
Motives: of critic, 17 (*see also* Aggression; Ego; Malice); in history, 157; for pluralistic search, 7 (*see also* Pluralism, reasons for adopting); for reduction, 17, 20, 24, 28 (*see also* Misunderstanding, causes of); rhetoric, grammar, and symbolic of, 109. *See also* Intentions
Movies, 295
Multiplication of meanings, 4–7, 69–70, 169–70. *See also* Ambiguity

Music, 238

Musical variety, as criterion for evaluating poems, 50

Narrative: amenability of modes to production of, as criterion for evaluating modes, 159–63; chronological, limits of, 158, 181; as criticism, illustrated, 159–63; as demonstration, 138, 143–44, 150–63, 171, 178–79 (*see also* Narrative, as knowledge); historical, as fusion of idea, structure, shape, and value, 178; historical, as necessarily an abstraction, 181; as "iconic" of event, 178; interest, as demand of one kind of text, 238–39, 241; irreducible to proposition, 143–44, 149; as knowledge, 143–49, 159, 174–75, 179–80 (*see also* Narrative, as demonstration); limits to ambiguity in, 187–88; line, as sign of skill, 304

Narratives, historical, 138, 190–92; as necessarily plural, 181

Narrator, as a suffering consciousness, 292–93

Narrators, as themselves creating implied authors, 299–301

Nature of life, as source of criteria, 49

Naturwissenschaft, 174

Necessities: artistic, illustrated, 284–301, 332 (*see also* Composition); changed to hypotheticals, 22, 44

Negative, definition by, 107

Neoclassicism, 309–10

Neoplatonism, 145, 183

New Criticism, 9, 38, 49, 78. *See also* New Critics *in Index of Persons and Titles*

Nihilism, 171–72, 324, 326; as commonplace, 330; integrity in facing, as criterion, 336; as one source of critical skepticism, 18; as source of general pity, 334

Nineteenth century, as period of "controversy," 96

Nominalism, 146, 179–80

Noncontradiction, law of, questioned, 110, 365n.5, 366–67n.19

Nonverbal art, xi

Norms, agreement about moral, as source of authority, 272

Novel of ideas, as ambiguous concept, 330–32

Novella, 278–301

Novelty of ideas, as criterion for evaluating poems, 309–10, 324

Objective criticism, 57

Objective/Subjective, 219

Objectivity, 187; as criterion, questioned, 306; rejections of, 19, 151; search for, as dangerous, 115. *See also* Proof

Omission, as inevitable consequence of working in any mode, 168, 342–44. *See also* Reduction

One and many, dialectic of, 131, 133; as problem, 93, 347

Ontological principles. *See* Modes, as entities; Paradox, umbrella; Poem, as made object

Ontological proof, 372n.3

"Ontological situs of work of art," 12. *See also* Locations of poem

Options, opening of, as end of criticism, 110–11

Order, temporal, related to logical order, 104

Ordinary-language philosophy, as cure for misunderstanding, 38

Organic wholeness, as criterion for evaluating poems, 302–15

Overstanding, 41, 235–57, 284, 335–39; examples of, 233–34, 240; performed best after understanding, 243; uses of, chap. 6 passim, 370n.11. *See also* Improper questions; Violations

Paradox: as heuristic (Barthes), 354n.2; of one and many 28, 131, 133; patterns of, 90; of substance, 107, 110, 130–31

Paradox, umbrella, 28, 33–34, 70, 92–94, 200–203, 344–45; embrace of, 95–96

Paradoxes of controversy, 11

Paralogism, artistic inference as, 334

Paraphrase, 60 (*see also* Reduction); as destructive of life of historical narrative, 150; literal, uses of, 61, 322–23

Parasitical readings. *See* Understanding, logical priority of

Psychoanalysis, 38
Psychoanalytic criticism, 26, 54, 129, 135,
   159, 239, 243; caricatures of, 259
Pure poetry, 4, 57, 108
"Purification of war," as end of criticism,
   122
Purity, as stylistic value, 150–51
Purpose. *See* Criticism, ends of

Qualities, general, as critical constants,
   limitations of, 49–53, 67, 278–301
Quotation, as data, 184–85

Racism, as criterion for evaluating
   poems, 2, 243
Rationality, plurality of kinds of, 169. *See
   also* Proof, kinds of
Reader: as center of exchange among
   texts and cultures, 237–38, chap. 6 passim (*see also* Reader-criticism); level of,
   in periodical essays, 316; possible roles
   of, 272
—education of, as end of criticism: by
   developing ingenuities, 132; by encouraging reading, 321; by keeping options open, 110–11; by offering
   "equipment for living," 114–15. *See also*
   Liberation; Vitality
—experience of: as less various than
   critical variety implies, 54; skepticism
   about, 18; as true poem, 55, 57. *See also*
   Reader-criticism
Reader-criticism, 2, 17, 19–20, 48, 57, 60,
   93, 120, 160, 216, chap. 6 passim,
   255–56, 283–84, 359–60n.24, 367n.19;
   Crane's notion of "common sense"
   related to, 86; limits of, 41, 272–75,
   chap. 7 passim; as norm, 169–70. *See
   also* History, deconstructionist
Reading: as conversation with implied
   author, 329; encouragement of, as end
   of criticism, 321
Realism: conflict of, with emotional effect, 292; Platonic, 179–80
Reality: assumptions about, 93 (*see also*
   Metaphysics; Ontological principles;
   Things); as known, 165; as made in
   discourse, 265; nature of, as source of
   criteria for evaluating modes, 49; reflection of, as criterion for evaluating

poems, 93. *See also* Correspondence;
   Truth
Reasons: as distinct from motives, 259; as
   distinct from causes (*see* Causes)
Recovery, arts of. *See* Understanding
"Recuperation," 367n.18. *See also* Understanding
Reduction: of artistry to causes, 259;
   charges of, 91, 130–31; of critical
   reasons to physical causes, 26–27; of
   differences to unities, 72–73; examples
   of, 13–14, 82, 99–100, 105; harmful,
   40–41, 75; inevitability of, 30–31, 105–6,
   280, 284, 307, 342, 344, 346; from language to language, 208–9; as tested by
   comprehensiveness, 90
Reductive dichotomies, 81
Reference, problem of, 9–10, 44–45,
   47–48, 265, 358n.5
Referents. *See* Things
Reflexive method. *See* Locations of discourse; Pluralism, topical; Rhetorical
   criticism
Reflexive principles. *See* Circularity
Reflexivity of critical understanding, 38.
   See also Circularity
Refutation: as easy and inevitable from
   alien perspective, 8, 76, 180–81;
   meaningless, 12, 36, 98, 221, 227. *See
   also* Killing; Misunderstanding;
   Monism
Refutations, multiple, as evidence for
   skepticism, 161
Relativism, 340, 356n.14; charges of,
   against pluralists, 80, 83–84, 362n.18;
   charges of, answered, 104, 106–7, 121,
   125, 139–42, 168–69, 189; complete (*see*
   Skepticism, "utter"); of conclusions to
   modes, equivalent to pluralism, 27–28;
   cultural, 210; cultural, as hinted at in
   Goldsmith, 309–10; as employing double standard, 112; as motive for building straw men, 27; as reduction to
   physical motion, 112; related to
   pluralism, 33, 139, 164; as skepticism,
   17–18; types of, distinguished, 17–18,
   26
Religion, 347; as poet's motive, 119. *See
   also* God
Religious: conversion, as unlikely cure

response to fashions in criticism, 16; about single ultimate "language," 38, 39, 113–14, 134, 209, 213, 254–55; topical pluralism's resemblance to, 343–44; about total views, 20, 32, 84, 96, 140–41, 210, 254–55, 340, 345, 348 —"utter," 24, 26–27, 84, 245; essential incoherence of, 336; impracticality of, 18

Skill(s): of author, as object of criticism, 302–18; kinds of, in postulated writer, 288–301; signs of (*see* Appeals, to reader)

Slips-of-the-tongue, understanding of, 264–65

Smiling, responsive, as first sign of "understanding," 372n.4

Sociological criticism, 26, 212, 243, 316

Solipsism, dogmatic monism as, 347

Sonnet form, as source of criterion, 46–47

Sounds, similarities of, as clues to hidden meanings, 129

Speaker, authority of, in conversation, 97. *See also* Author, as authority; Ethos

Speech-act theory, 359n.24, 363n.18

Splitting. *See* Method, differentiating

Stalemate, uses of, 105

Story, 362n.5 (*see also* Narrative); as context for judgments, 282

Story line, inadequacy of, as summary of poem's power, 323–24

Structuralism, 38, 76, 174, 215–16; reductive refutation of, 22

Structuralist parallels, as "mere" analogy, 82

Structure of poem. *See* Composition; Form; Forms

Style, 303–4; and ethos, 151; as personal expression, 151–52; as proof, 150–52

Stylistics, 78, 304

Subjective/Objective, 219

Subjectivism. *See* Reader-criticism; Relativism; Skepticism

Subject matter of criticism. *See* Locations of poem; Overstanding

Substance. *See* Entities; Things

Substances, attacks on, 216

Sufficient cause, author's skill as, 283–84

Superficiality, as useful quality, 308–9, 313

Suspense, interest in implied author as

kind of, 314

Symbolic action, 47–48, 57, 100, chap. 4 passim; as comedy, 108

Symbolicity/Animality, 101, 115–16, 122–23, 129, 362n.13; in practical criticism, 120, 135–36

Symbols, 263; contrasted with and related to sign, 371n.3

Symmetry, as formal appeal, 294

Synonymy, 68, 151–52

Synthesis, 69; as end, 123–24; supreme, as final goal of criticism, 215–16. *See also* Analogies; Skepticism, about total views

System, 142, 155. *See also* Paradox, umbrella; Schemata; Skepticism, about total views

Tact and taste as tests of method, 140, 176–77, 254. *See also* Idiosyncrasy

Teachability, 249; as criterion for evaluating modes, 254; of pluralism, 222; as test of vitality, 222. *See also* Education

Temperament, as affecting operation of modes, 59, 88–89, 140. *See also* Idiosyncrasy

Temporal: connections, as literal causes, 145; sequence, transitions as evidence for, 154–55

Tenancies. *See* Locations of discourse

Terministic screens, 113, 133, 362n.18 *See also* Modes

Terminology, problem of, 26n, 237n

Text: as actualization of reader's potential, 268–77 (*see also* Reader-criticism); contrasted with *work* (by Barthes), 241–42, 272n.9; demands of, 238–41; found in rhetorical relation, 238; intentions of, 251; locations of (*see* Locations of poem); skepticism about, 18; as source of limits, 238–42

Textual variants, problem of dealing with, 63–65

Textuality, insistence on, as criterion for evaluating poems, 50

Thematic: judgments, as related to formal success, 67 (*see also* Modes, "world"-centered); readings, as inevitably "fitting the facts," 60

Index of Persons and Titles